Gapped sentences – each question is made up of three discrete sentences. Each sentence contains one gap which has to be completed with only one word which is common to all three sentences.

Preparing for Part 5 – a two-page section preparing students for the comprehension questions and summary writing task required for Part 5 of the revised Cambridge Proficiency Examination.

Practice Test

This section consists of complete Use of English practice tests in the same form as the revised Cambridge Proficiency Examination Paper 3.

Appendices

The appendices on phrasal verbs, idioms/fixed phrases, words often confused, word formation, prepositions and verbal constructions at the end of the book aim to help students in their studies as well as teachers in checking the students' competence in these difficult areas of the English language.

How to use the book

The book is designed for use in class or self-study. The teacher is encouraged to adapt the book to the needs of the students and according to individual preference. The material in the book is structurally graded and is intended to be practised over the duration of the Proficiency course.

Components

Student's Book
Teacher's Book

UNIT 1a Grammar: Tenses

PRESENT

Present Simple	Present Continuous	Present Perfect	Present Perfect Cont.
habitual actions or permanent states He **goes** swimming every day. She **works** in a bank.	repeated actions with **always, forever, constantly** (often to show annoyance) You're **always leaving** the cap off the toothpaste.	recently completed actions She **has just painted** her room.	past actions producing visible results in the present She **has been painting** her room. (It smells of paint.)
arranged future actions (timetables, programmes, etc) The match **begins** at 8:30 next Monday evening.	actions in progress/ temporary actions He's **sleeping** at the moment. They're **hunting** for a flat.	actions beginning in the past and continuing up to the present, focusing on the result He **has written** three books.	an action beginning in the past and continuing up to the present, focusing on the action especially with *for* or *since* She **has been waiting** for two hours but there's still no sign of him.
laws of nature/scientific facts and instructions Ice **melts** when heated. First you **chop** the meat, then you **fry** it.	fixed arrangements for the near future They **are going** on an excursion tomorrow.	indefinite past actions or experiences She **has seen** this film. (We do not know when.) I've **been** to Berlin twice.	action showing annoyance, irritation or surprise What **have you been doing** to my computer?
dramatic narration The lights **go** out and a figure **tears** out of the villa.	current trends and developments Oil prices **are rising** at present.	repeated actions still continuing He **has worked** as a teacher for four years. (He is still a teacher.)	
Time Expressions: usually, often, always, every day, in the morning, on Mondays etc	**Time Expressions:** now, at present, at the moment, these days, still, today, tonight, nowadays etc	**Time Expressions:** since, yet, for, already, just, ever, so far, recently, lately, still, how long etc	**Time Expressions:** for, since, how long, lately, recently etc

Stative verbs describe a state and do not have continuous forms. These include verbs related to:

senses	see, hear, smell, feel, taste
thinking	think, agree, believe, consider, doubt, expect, feel (=think)
emotion & feeling	feel, forgive, hate, loathe, like, dislike, love, mind, wish, etc
other	appear/seem, be, belong, have (=possess), keep (=continue), matter, owe, possess/own etc

Notes

- Verbs of the senses can have continuous forms, but then there's a change in meaning.
  I'm seeing my dentist tomorrow. (= a prior arrangement) **but:** *Do you see those birds? (ability to see)*

- The verbs **think, consider** and **expect** can have continuous forms when they refer to an activity.
  Be quiet, please! I'm thinking. **but:** *I think you are wrong. (= I believe)*

- **Have** can have continuous forms in certain expressions such as: **have a bath, have a nap, have fun, have a good time,** etc.
  We were having a good time at the party when the fire broke out. **but:** *Since you have his phone number, you can call him. (= possess)*

6

Contents

Introduction

The *CPE Use of English 1 for the revised Cambridge Proficiency Examination* is a practice book intended for advanced students of English who wish to sit the revised CPE examination as well as other examinations at the same level of difficulty. It can also be used by advanced students, who wish to polish up their skills in the difficult grammatical area of structures and usage.

The Teacher's Book for the Student's Book contains the answers overprinted on the relevant pages of the Student's Book.

How the book is organised

Each unit consists of three main sections: Grammar, English in Use and a Practice Test.

Grammar

In this section there is a condensed presentation of grammar structures followed by graded exercises which practise the various phenomena, including conversational grammar four-option multiple choice sentences. There is also a Verbal Construction Appendix (Appendix 6) which students can use as a reference guide for specific structures.

English in Use

This section consists of:

Open cloze texts – modified cloze texts containing fifteen gaps.

Phrasal verbs – presentation of phrasal verbs clearly set out in coloured tables and with relevant exercises. (To be used with reference to Appendix 1)

Idioms/Fixed phrases – presentation of idioms/fixed phrases in coloured tables with relevant exercises. (To be used with reference to Appendix 2)

Prepositions – verbs, nouns and adjectives followed by prepositions written in alphabetical groups and tested in sentence form. (To be used with reference to Appendix 5)

Key word transformations – discrete items with a lead-in sentence and a gapped response to complete using a given word.

Fixed phrases – presentation of fixed phrases in coloured tables with relevant gap filling and four-option multiple choice sentences.

Note expansion exercises – notes to be expanded into complete sentences.

Register transfer exercises – one text including certain information followed by a gapped text providing the same information in a different register.

Mistake identification exercises – sentences with deliberate mistakes to be identified and corrected by students.

Proverbs – commonly used proverbs with explanations through exercises.

Word usage – word formation texts containing ten gaps (to be used with reference to Appendix 4), four-option multiple choice cloze texts and sentences to be completed using the most appropriate choice from groups of words often confused. (To be used with reference to Appendix 3)

Collocations – exercises designed to familiarise students with word-combination.

1 Put the verbs in brackets into the appropriate present tense.

0 Our firm *is launching* (launch) two new products next week.
1 "Why .... (he/leave)?" "Because he .... (play) football at 6:30 this evening."
2 Dancers at the ballet school .... (train) for the performance since last November.
3 You .... (not/really/expect) me to eat this stew! It .... (smell) awful!
4 I .... (try) to complete that jigsaw for over three months now!
5 "Why .... (you/feel) Annie's forehead?" "I .... (think) she's got a temperature."

6 The place looks like a bombsite! What .... (do) all day?
7 Come on John! You .... (know) me since high school! You .... (not/really/believe) I would do such a terrible thing.
8 The opposition party .... (appear) to be making ground in the opinion polls.
9 Randall .... (kick) the ball into the net and it .... (be) a goal!
10 He .... (study) most of the year, but now it's summer, he .... (work) in a shop.
11 You .... (always/leave) the bathroom tap running.

HAS BEEN TO / HAS BEEN IN / HAS GONE TO

He **has been to** Berlin. (=He has gone and come back.)

He **has been in** Buenos Aires for a year. (=He lives there.)

He **has gone** to Toledo. (=He hasn't come back yet.)

2 Fill in the blanks with **have been to, have been in** or **have gone to** in their correct form.

0 I *have never been to* (never) Cambodia, but I might include it on my itinerary next year.
1 Mrs Bates .... Cologne. She won't be back for at least three weeks.
2 Nick .... Wales for three years now, studying for his degree.
3 Why don't you ask Clare about the tropics? She .... Thailand.
4 He .... visit his father. I'm afraid you've just missed him.

3 Put the verbs in brackets into the **Simple Present** or **Present Continuous**.

Terry Poole (0) *is* (be) an engineer who (1) .... (work) for an international aid organisation. Although he normally (2) .... (work) in Indonesia, at present he (3) .... (supervise) a project in Rwanda which (4) .... (involve) the co-ordination of local people, aid workers and engineers like himself. Although he (5) .... (enjoy) the experience, he (6) .... (doubt) the project will be finished soon.

4 Put the verbs in brackets into the **Present Perfect** or **Present Perfect Continuous**.

Stonehenge (0) *has been* (be) the subject of archaeological debate for many years. No one (1) .... (yet/explain) satisfactorily why or how it was built, although teams of experts (2) .... (excavate) the site for years and a team of American scientists (3) .... (recently/start) working in the area with sophisticated new equipment. Popular theories (4) .... (suggest) that Stonehenge was built as a temple, but no one (5) .... (manage) to work out how the stones were transported here. A group of students from Bangor University (6) .... (discuss) the possibility of re-enacting the journey from Wales, where such stones are to be found, overland to Stonehenge and sponsors (7) .... (come) forward with offers of financial assistance. The British Museum (8) .... (also/announce) a forthcoming exhibition of artefacts from the Stonehenge period which they (9) .... (gather) over the last five years from all over Northern Europe.

7

FUTURE FORMS

will/shall	be going to	Future Continuous	Future Perfect
predictions, offers, promises, requests, suggestions *Will you help me with the dishes?/Shall I get you some coffee?*	intentions *I know my clothes are dirty. I'm going to wash them tomorrow.*	actions in progress at a certain time in the future *I'll be flying to Paris this time tomorrow.*	actions finished before a certain future time, usually with *before, by, by then, by the time, until/till* *By the end of July he will have been in Athens for two months.*
on-the-spot decisions *"Your clothes are dirty." "Are they? I'll wash them."*	planned actions *She's going to take her driving test next month.*	logical assumptions about sb's actions in the present *He will be sleeping now. (It's midnight.)*	logical assumptions about sb's actions *He will have gone to sleep by now.*
opinions, hopes, fears, especially with think, expect, suppose, imagine, fear, etc *I think he'll pass the test.*	possible action seen in the future as a result of sth else *He doesn't know how to light a fire. He's going to burn himself.*	previously planned actions (instead of Present Continuous) *I'll be seeing Sam tonight. Would you like me to tell him the news?*	**Future Perfect Cont.**
when it is not certain whether sth will happen (prediction) *Perhaps it'll rain tomorrow.*	when there is evidence that sth will definitely happen *She's going to have a baby.*		an action up to a certain time in the future, emphasising the continuity, usually with *by... for* *By next Sunday, they will have been living here for two weeks.*

Time Expressions
tomorrow, the day after tomorrow, tonight, soon, next week, month/year, in a week/month/year etc.

Note
by/before are used with Future Perfect in positive sentences; *until* is used in negative sentences
She will have cleaned the house by 6 o'clock.
She won't have cleaned the house until 6 o'clock.

OTHER WAYS OF EXPRESSING THE FUTURE

be + to - infinitive (future plans, instructions)
The meeting is to take place on Wednesday.   *You are not to leave the premises until 17:00.*

be about + to - infinitive/be on the point of + gerund (immediate future)
They are about to leave.   *They are on the point of leaving.*

CONVERSATIONAL GRAMMAR

5 *Choose the correct item.*

0 "Any news from Tess?"
"Yes. She .... tomorrow on the 9:15 train."
  A will have been arriving **C** arriving
  B will have arrived   **D** arrives

1 "I suppose your report isn't ready yet."
"Don't worry. I .... it by tomorrow."
  A will have been finishing **C** am finishing
  B will be finishing   **D** will have finished

2 "So, are you coming along, after all?"
"Well, I don't know. What time .... ?"
A you're leaving   C will you leave
B will you be leaving   D do you leave

3 "I've called Eddie a hundred times but he won't answer the phone."
"Try once more. He ...."
A will sleep   C will be sleeping
B sleeps   D is to be sleeping

4 "Well, I first came here last June."
"So by the end of May you .... with us for almost a year."
A will have been working   C will have working
B are going to have worked   D will work

5 "Shall I call Eddie at home?"
"I think he .... now."
A will be working   C is to work
B is going to work   D will work

6 "Is Nigel still here?"
"Yes, but hurry up, he is just ...."
A about to leave   C to be leaving
B about leaving   D to leave

7 "Do you know it's Maggie's birthday today?"
"Yes, she .... a party tonight."
A has   C is to have
B is having   D will have

8 "Doesn't she feel nervous about having to teach that class?"
"I shouldn't think so as she's such an experienced teacher. By October she .... teaching for fifteen years."
A is going to be   C will have been
B has been   D is to be

9 "Why don't we go to the cinema?"
"It's too late; the film .... started by now."
A will be   C shall have
B is going to be   D will have

10 "You look gorgeous in that dress."
"Really? I .... it then."
A will be buying   C will buy
B buy   D am to buy

11 "So, when is your maths exam?"
"Well, this time tomorrow I .... for it."
A will be sitting   C will have been sitting
B will sit   D sit

6 *Put the verbs in brackets into an appropriate* **present** *or* **future** *form.*

"If I **(0)** *am* **(be)** re-elected, I **(1)** .... **(give)** you my word that the first issues I **(2)** .... **(tackle)** are those of the environment and education. As of next month, I **(3)** .... **(serve)** my country in a public capacity for 6 years; I **(4)** .... **(hope)** to continue for at least as many more. While the general attitude **(5)** .... **(seem)** to be that things in this country **(6)** .... **(go)** from bad to worse, I believe that by the end of my next term of office we **(7)** .... **(be/able)** to look back and count the improvements that have been made. In fact, I am so confident that if it **(8)** .... **(not/be)** the case, I **(9)** .... **(never/make)** another promise in my life. But I firmly believe that these **(10)** .... **(be)** years of positive change and dramatic improvements."

7 *Fill in* **will** *or* **be going to**.

0 A: I'm going to start learning Chinese.
B: Are you? *Will* you let me know what it's like as I'd like to have a go too?

1 A: Sheila .... have an operation next Tuesday.
B: If you tell me which hospital she'll be in, I'll go and visit her.

2 A: I have to be at work by 8:30.
B: But it's nearly 8:00. You .... be late.

3 A: So I'll book your dental appointment for 4:30, shall I?
B: No later than that, as I .... (not) be at the office before 5 today.

4 A: I'm sure I .... pass the course this time.
B: I hope you do. You've worked really hard this term.

5 A: Look at those clouds. It's definitely going to rain.
B: Is it? I .... bring the chairs in from the garden, then.

6 A: So, are you ready to go?
B: I've told you a thousand times! I .... come.

7 A: If you buy the flowers, I'll get some chocolates.
B: OK, but get a move on or we .... be late.

PAST

Past Simple	Past Continuous	Past Perfect	Past Perfect Cont.
actions completed in the past when there is direct or indirect time reference *He **left** an hour **ago**.* *(direct time reference)* *She **phoned before the boss came**.* *(indirect time reference)*	past actions in progress/ at a given point in time *She **was** still **working** at eight o'clock yesterday evening.*	past action which happened before another past action *She **had** already **typed** all the letters before her boss **arrived**.*	a longer past action which continued up to another past action *She **had been cooking** all day long when Tom **came** home with some fish and chips.*
past habitual actions *He **travelled/used to travel** a lot when he was young.*	past action in progress interrupted by another action *She **was leaving** when the phone **rang**.*	as the past equivalent of the Present Perfect Compare: *Bob **had** always **dreamed** of being in a musical, but he never got the chance.* *Tom **has** always **dreamed** of being in a musical; he might make it one day.*	actions producing visible results in the past *She was covered in paint because she **had been painting** her room.*
past actions happening one after the other *He **stood** up, **picked** up his briefcase and **left** the office.*	simultaneous past actions *While Jane **was getting** dressed, Tom **was enjoying** his drink.*		
past actions which won't be repeated *Marilyn Monroe **starred** in "The Seven Year Itch".*	polite inquiries *I **was wondering** if you could help me.*	**Time Expressions:** *before, after, already, just, for, since, till/until, by the time, never etc*	**Time Expressions:** *for, since, how long, before, until etc*
Time Expressions: *yesterday, then, when, ago, How long ago...?, last night/week/year etc*	**Time Expressions:** *while, when, as, all morning/evening, day, night etc*		

USED TO / GET USED TO / WOULD

used to + infinitive (past habitual action/state)	*This theatre **used to be** a hospital.* *He **used to work** till late at night. (He doesn't anymore.)*
be/get used to + gerund/noun (habitual action)	*She **isn't used to driving** on the left.* *I **haven't got used to living** abroad yet.*
would (repeated past action and routine)	*When I was at my grandparents' cottage, I **would** wake up early and go for a ride.*

8 Put the verbs in brackets into an appropriate past tense.

0 He *walked* (walk) to the front of the stage, *took* (take) a bow and *waved* (wave) to the audience.

1 Her clothes were soaked because she ....
.... (walk) in the rain.

2 We .... (not/enjoy) the play so we .... (leave) early.

3 While you .... (sleep) Joan ....
.... (try) hard to finish her dissertation.

4 Susan and Tom .... (meet) when they .... (study) in Edinburgh 20 years ago.

5 In June 1979 they ....
(still/build) this shopping centre.

6 They .... (walk) to the water's edge, ... (wade) in and ....
(swim) to the other side.

7 While the soldiers ....
(advance) they did not realise that the enemy .... (plan) a surprise attack.

8 The politician ....
(already/finish) his speech by the time the TV reporter .... (arrive).

9 By the time Monica .... (get) to the library, Elena .... (already/do) all the research.

CONVERSATIONAL GRAMMAR

9 Choose the correct item.

0 "Where's Christine?"
"I don't know; she .... the office fifteen minutes ago."
(A) left   C has left
B had left   D had been leaving

1 "Why didn't Madeline show up at the party last night?"
"When I called her at 11:00 she ...."
A was still studying   C would still study
B had still been studying D still studied

2 Did you know that Oscar Wilde .... in Paris during his final years?
A has been living   C had been living
B had lived   D lived

3 "You're looking miserable."
"I .... on my thesis when my computer suddenly crashed."
A was working   C would work
B used to work   D have been working

4 "Did you hear the rain last night?"
"Yes, it .... all night."
A had been pouring   C has poured
B was pouring   D was poured

5 "Can't we just order a nice bit of cod?"
"Don't be ridiculous! We .... all this way to eat fish and chips."
A haven't been coming C aren't coming
B haven't come   D hadn't come

6 "I love your car."
"This old thing? We .... it for fifteen years."
A had had   C have had
B have been having   D used to have

7 "What's wrong with Robert?"
"I don't know. He .... up, slammed the door and stormed out of the building."
A got   C was getting
B has got   D had got

8 "Mary has difficulty fitting in."
"Well, I guess she .... to this type of work."
A didn't use   C doesn't get used
B isn't used   D hasn't been used

9 "I loved Christmas as a child."
"So did I. Every Christmas Eve all the family .... the tree together."
A would have decorated C had been decorating
B would decorate   D used to decorating

10 When I lived downtown I .... to the cinema almost every night.
A was going   C have been going
B went   D had been going

11 Sue .... from a severe bout of flu at the time.
A recovered   C would recover
B used to recover   D was recovering

12 "How's Peter doing?"
"I don't know. I .... from him for months."
A have to hear   C haven't heard
B didn't hear   D don't hear

13 "Ted is so inconsiderate."
"What .... you say that, George?"
A is making   C makes
B was making   D had made

10 *Put the verbs in brackets into the appropriate past tense.*

If it (0) *hadn't been* (not/be) for Louis, Joan (1) ....
.... (never/survive) her trip to Paris last month. She (2) .... (not/meet) him before, but she (3) .... (be) certainly glad that she had by the end of her stay. The first thing that (4) .... (happen) was that the hotel where she (5) .... (plan) to stay (6) ....
.... (not/receive) her booking, so they had no room for her. Then, as she (7) .... (try) to get a taxi to take her to another hotel, someone on a motorbike (8) .... (snatch) her bag with all her tickets and credit cards in it. As her French (9) .... (be) quite rusty, she (10) .... (not/know) how to explain what (11) .... (happen). It was then that Louis (12) .... (approach) her and (13) .... (introduce) himself.

CONVERSATIONAL GRAMMAR

11 *Choose the correct item.*

0 "Tina is still looking for a decent flat."
"How long .... ?"
A was she looking   C had she looked
B is she looking   (D) has she been looking

1 "Has Paul come to terms with his examination results?"
"Yes. He .... the fact that he'll have to resit."
A had accepted   C accepted
B has accepted   D has been accepting

2 "Did you have a good time at the Jordans?"
"Not really. I .... I'll ever visit them again."
A don't think   C won't be thinking
B am not thinking   D think not

3 Gerald just can't .... working shifts.
A used to   C get used to
B be used   D used to be

4 Alison feels more sympathy and less anger than she ....
A had   C was
B would   D used to

5 "Will you .... with the audio-video equipment by 12:30 pm?"
"Possibly, but I'll let you know beforehand."
A finish   C be finishing
B finished   D have finished

6 "George is in hospital."
"Yes, I've heard he .... good progress."
A makes   C will make
B is making   D would make

7 "I'm getting my work permit next week."
"It's about time. You .... here for two months by then."
A are   C will have been
B will be   D have been

8 "How do you like your sushi?"
"Well, it's really different. It's the first time I .... Japanese food."
A have eaten   C am eating
B eat   D have been eating

9 "Wasn't sacking Mary rather harsh on his part?"
"Not really; he .... her several times in the past."
A had warned   C warns
B was warning   D will warn

10 "Where's Jonathan?"
"He .... to the travel agent's."
A has been   C has been going
B has gone   D had gone

STRUCTURAL CONVERSION

1 I've **never** been given such a nice present before.
   It's the nicest present I've **ever** been given.
2 He's **never** flown by Concorde before.
   It's the first time he's (ever) flown by Concorde.
3 It's a long time since he visited us.
   He hasn't visited us **for** a long time.
4 **When** did you leave school?
   How long ago did you leave school?
   How long is it since you left school?
5 **The last time** I saw her was a month **ago**.
   I **haven't seen** her for a month.
6 **He joined** the golf club ten months **ago**.
   He **has been** a member of the golf club **for** ten months.
7 It's a month since she moved to Austria.
   She moved to Austria a month ago.
8 **She started** English lessons a year ago.
   She **has been taking/having** English lessons for a year.
   It's a year since she started taking/having English lessons.
9 **Having had** dinner, I went to bed.
   After having dinner, I went to bed.
   After I had had dinner, I went to bed.
10 **I think** there will be a war soon.
   In my opinion, there is going to be a war soon.
   If you ask me, there's bound to be a war soon.
   In my estimation, war is imminent.
11 **I don't believe** that he'll agree.
   It's my belief that he won't agree.
   I have a feeling that he won't agree.
   There's no reason to believe that he'll agree.

12 **While I was walking** down the street, I saw Mary.
   While walking down the street, I saw Mary.
   When I was walking down the street, I saw Mary.
   It was while I was walking down the street that I saw Mary.
13 **Was there** any response to his appeal?
   Did anyone respond to his appeal?
14 **The race takes** place tomorrow.
   The race will/is going to be held/take place tomorrow.
   The race is scheduled to take place/for tomorrow.
15 **She started** doing her homework **as soon as** her brother **had left** for school.
   She started doing her homework **when her** brother **had left** for school.
   She didn't start (doing) her homework **until her** brother **had left** for school.
   She waited until her brother had left for school **before she started** (doing) her homework/or **before starting** to do....
   Not until her brother had left for school **did she start** (doing) her homework.
16 **When did you last have** a haircut?
   When was the last time you had a haircut?
17 **She wrote the book while** she was on holiday.
   She wrote the book during her holiday.
18 **I only slept** for an hour last night.
   I only had an hour's sleep last night.
19 **It is certain that** he'll pass his exams.
   There is no doubt that he'll pass his exams.
   He is bound to pass his exams.

---

12 Complete the second sentence so that it has a similar meaning to the first sentence, using the word given. Do not change the word given. You must use between three and eight words, including the word given.

1 It's been months since I last spoke with Paul.
   contact
   I haven't ....
   .... months.
2 He has never felt so embarrassed before.
   ever
   It's ....
   .... embarrassed.
3 She was going to hand in her notice when the boss decided to promote her.
   point
   She ....
   ..... notice when the boss decided to promote her.
4 He has tried to lose weight before.
   first
   It's ....
   .... a diet.

5 France hasn't won a gold medal in this sport for ages.
   time
   It's ....
   .... medal in this sport.
6 It is certain that he will compensate you for the damage he has done.
   bound
   He ....
   .... to you for the damage he has done.
7 Stephen realised something terrible had happened as soon as he saw May crying.
   aware
   Stephen ....
   .... as soon as he saw May crying.

1a Grammar: Tenses

CONVERSATIONAL GRAMMAR

13 Choose the correct item.

1 "John really ought to lose some weight."
"You're right; he .... very heavily during the walk yesterday."
A was breathing   C has been breathing
B had breathing   D had been breathing

2 "I heard Roy and Alice had an argument."
"Do you know what .... it this time?"
A has started   C had been starting
B started   D had started

3 "I wonder how Jeff is doing."
"I haven't got a clue. It's been a long time since I .... to him."
A have spoken   C had spoken
B spoke   D speaking

4 "It's a pity she had to pull out of the competition."
"Yes, especially since she .... such excellent progress."
A is making   C had been making
B made   D has been making

5 "Who's going to collect your mail while you're on holiday?"
"I have .... asked my cousin."
A ever   C yet
B still   D already

6 "Did you get to see Frances in the end?"
"No. She .... for the airport when I arrived at her home."
A would leave   C had left
B was leaving   D left

7 "Helen moved to London last week."
"Well, I suppose she'll find it difficult to .... on the left."
A be used to driving   C get used to driving
B use to drive   D be used to drive

8 "How long have you been with Sears S.A.?"
"By next month I .... there for a year."
A will be working   C am going to work
B have worked   D will have been working

9 "Did you stay up late yesterday?"
"Not really. I went to bed after Monica ...."
A was leaving   C leaving
B had left   D has left

14 Complete the second sentence so that it has a similar meaning to the first sentence, using the word given. Do not change the word given. You must use between three and eight words, including the word given.

1 I believe the man you're looking for is standing right next to us.
feeling
I ....
.... to us is the one you're looking for.

2 Jeremy joined the cricket club a year ago.
member
Jeremy's ....
.... a year.

3 It was proposed that a new orphanage should be built.
forward
They ....
.... to build a new orphanage.

4 The elections take place next Sunday.
scheduled
The ....
.... next Sunday.

5 I believe there will be an economic crisis soon.
estimation
In ....
.... imminent.

6 The final question in part 6 wasn't answered correctly by anyone.
answer
Nobody ....
.... the final question in part 6.

7 Mozart started composing music during his early childhood.
young
Mozart ....
.... child.

8 According to Dr Donovan, Rosie is bound to be offered the position.
doubt
According to Dr Donovan, ...
.... the position.

9 He's been writing the novel for nearly two years.
started
It is ....
.... the novel.

15 *Read the text below and think of the word which best fits each space.*

POST IN HISTORY

Although it may come as a surprise **(0)** *to* many people, postal services have existed in some parts of the world for thousands of years. **(1)** .... is ample evidence that a postal service existed among the Assyrians and Babylonians. In China a regular postal service **(2)** .... established in the seventh century BC, and **(3)** .... the centuries attained **(4)** .... a high level of efficiency that some 2,000 years after its institution it won the admiration of travellers **(5)** .... Marco Polo. Efficient and highly developed postal services were also established in the Persian and Roman empires. In ancient times, **(6)** .... services were mainly confined **(7)** .... the use of representatives of the state; private citizens **(8)** .... use of slaves, merchants and the like to send their messages and documents. In Medieval Europe, postal services **(9)** .... organised by emperors and by the papacy, **(10)** .... private citizens continued to entrust their correspondence to various travellers. Later, around the 13th century, universities and towns came **(11)** .... have their own messengers. However, it was not **(12)** .... the 14th century that merchants, the private citizens **(13)** .... had the greatest need for a speedy and regular exchange of correspondence, began to **(14)** .... up regular courier services. The needs of business led to the development of the postal service as we know **(15)** .... today.

PHRASAL VERBS 1

16 *Look at Appendix 1 and fill in one of the prepositions or adverbs below, then give a synonym for each phrasal verb.*

- beneath • off • up to • in for • ~~in with~~
- down on • out • on • down with • into

0 Susan gets all the perks because she's *in with* the administration.

1 She feels it is .... her to socialise with uneducated people.

2 As a vegetarian, Paul is .... people who eat meat.

3 He'll be .... it when his parents discover he took the money.

4 Half the staff are .... the flu this week.

5 She doesn't eat crisps or chocolate; she's .... health food.

6 Our dog has been .... its food for days now.

7 Do you know what's .... at the cinema tonight?

8 I don't know what he's been ...., but he looks very embarrassed.

9 The roses have been .... for a few days now.

PHRASAL VERBS 2

act on:	do whatever is advised/ suggested
act up (inf):	behave awkwardly or badly/not work properly
answer (sb) back (inf):	respond rudely to sb
answer for:	be responsible for sth/pay for/vouch for
answer to:	be under the command of sb/have the characteristics described
back down:	cease to oppose or demand
back out (of):	withdraw (from)
back up:	support/confirm
bear on (f):	be relevant to/affect
bear with:	be patient

17 *Fill in the correct preposition(s) or adverb.*

0 The Minister's statement has no bearing *on* this case.

1 The Prime Minister said that he would speak to his advisors and then act .... their advice.

2 You can't change your mind now. It's too late to back .... the deal.

3 The plant manager answers directly .... the head of the company.

4 I was prepared to back .... her story because I knew it was the truth.

5 The baby has been acting .... all day. I think she must be teething.

6 The accused will answer .... his actions in the highest court in the land.

7 Faced with such formidable opposition to his proposal, he had no choice but to back ....

8 I was always in trouble for answering .... when I was at school.

9 If you can bear .... me a little longer, I'll try to explain the reasons behind our actions.

IDIOMS/FIXED PHRASES 1

all but:	nearly, almost/except
all in (inf):	exhausted
all told:	altogether
for all:	in spite of
of all people:	used to express annoyance/ surprise because a certain person was thought to be unsuitable
all along:	from the beginning
all the same:	yet, however
all in all:	when everything is considered
for all I know:	as far as I know
for all I care:	I don't care

IDIOMS/FIXED PHRASES 2

take sth into account:	consider sth
on account of:	because of
on no account:	under no circumstances
on this/that account:	for this/that reason
on the air:	broadcasting (opp.: off the air)
in the air:	uncertain
up in the air:	it exists, but not talked about
clear the air:	remove suspicion or bad feeling
be up in arms:	be very angry
on the alert:	on the look-out; expecting sth

18 *Fill in the blanks with one of the idioms/fixed phrases.*

0 I've *all but* finished; just give me a few minutes.

1 ...., it seemed to be quite a good suggestion.

2 He promised to come to the party on Friday; ...., I don't think we should count on him.

3 .... his hard work, he didn't get a promotion.

4 I don't know how they found out, but they've known about it ....

5 I've been following the election campaign and .... I think the government will win the election.

6 She told me her name was Joan but .... she could be lying.

7 I don't think I'll go out tonight. I'm ....

8 I never expected you .... to say such a thing!

9 You can take the whole lot ....

19 *Fill in the blanks with one of the idioms/fixed phrases.*

0 Instead of bottling up your feelings, let's talk about it and *clear the air*

1 The fire fighters are always .... for forest fires, particularly in the summer.

2 There's a feeling of anticipation .... at the moment.

3 The villagers are .... about the proposed motorway.

4 I haven't been able to travel much lately .... my car having broken down.

5 His future is still ....; he can't decide whether to become a surgeon or a psychiatrist.

6 You must .... his educational background .... when deciding what work to give him.

7 The meeting tomorrow is very important; .... should you be late.

8 There's been a hurricane in Manila, and all flights have been cancelled ....

9 You can't go into the studio just yet as the programme is still ....

PREPOSITIONS

20 *Look at Appendix 5 and fill in the blanks with the correct preposition.*

0 The cinema which was adjacent *to* the bank was badly damaged in the earthquake.

1 The child showed no animosity .... her new stepbrother.

2 What you're saying amounts .... blackmail.

3 Mr Parker was arrested .... exceeding the speed limit.

4 She is finding it difficult to adjust .... the climate.

5 Your calculations do not accord .... mine.

6 She was very appreciative .... all the support she got from her friends.

7 I was totally abashed .... his rude manner.

8 His abstinence .... caffeine lasted only two months.

9 I have an aversion .... spiders.

21 *Look at Appendix 5 and fill in the blanks with the correct preposition.*

1 The recommendations are based .... a recent Home Office report.

2 My little sister still believes .... Father Christmas.

3 Beware .... the strong currents when swimming in this area.

4 I bumped .... an old school friend in town last week.

5 The tourists bartered .... the souvenirs at the local market.

6 When the children arrived at the fair, they made a beeline .... the ghost train.

7 There's a ban .... using hosepipes during the drought.

8 The cat basked .... the warm sunshine.

9 He continually boasts .... his fantastic job .

10 The man begged his wife .... forgiveness.

22 *Complete the second sentence so that it has a similar meaning to the first sentence, using the word given. Do not change the word given. You must use between three and eight words, including the word given.*

1 The suspect could not explain why he had sand in his boots.
   account
   The suspect ....
   .... in his boots.

2 What he told me made me very curious to hear the rest of the story.
   appetite
   What he told me ....
   .... the story.

3 I don't mind staying in on a Saturday night if I have good company.
   averse
   I'm ....
   .... night if I have good company.

4 Miss Hayes will explain the day-to-day running of the office to you.
   acquaint
   Miss Hayes ....
   .... running of the office.

5 I don't know how I can make it up to you for spoiling your plans.
   amends
   I don't know ....
   .... your plans.

6 It is a foregone conclusion that Mark will get the job.
   saying
   It ....
   .... the job.

7 Our teacher doesn't like it when we leave the classroom without asking first.
   approve
   Our teacher ....
   .... without asking first.

8 Those official files cannot be seen by the public until the end of the decade.
   access
   The ....
   .... files until the end of the decade.

9 Being her only niece, Ann is very precious to her.
   apple
   Being her only niece, ...
   .... eye.

17

10 You need to consider the fact that he hasn't spoken French for years.
allowances
You need to ....
.... he hasn't spoken French for years.

11 Sheila was the only one who succeeded in finding the solution to the problem.
up
Only Sheila ....
.... to the problem.

12 I was surprised not to see Meg at the party but I later heard she was ill.
apparently
I was surprised that Meg ....
.... she was ill.

13 I know this route looks dangerous but I can't think of a better option.
alternative
However dangerous this route looks, ...
.... think of.

14 Because of the lack of co-operation he decided to leave the project unfinished.
abandon
He chose ....
.... to lack of co-operation.

15 Helen won't be happy till she gets a full refund.
than
Nothing ....
.... Helen.

16 I always think about transport costs when job hunting.
consideration
I always ....
.... when job hunting.

17 Becky didn't tell you because she assumed you already knew.
granted
Becky didn't tell you ....
.... you already knew.

18 How would you deal with such a challenge?
presented
What ....
.... such a challenge?

19 In my opinion, Simon was a fool not to accept their job offer.
down
I think ....
.... their job offer.

20 The neighbours will look after our house while we are away.
eye
The neighbours ....
.... while we are away.

FIXED PHRASES

in abeyance (f):	halted temporarily
be of/have no fixed abode (f):	be homeless
out and about:	1) outdoors 2) travelling from one place to another
in the abstract:	in a general way
of its own accord:	automatically
agree to differ/disagree:	stop arguing because there is no chance of agreement
in arrears:	have not paid the money they owe
cast aspersions (f):	criticise
cost an arm and a leg (inf):	be very expensive
be thrown off balance:	be surprised/confused
on the ball:	alert
below the belt:	cruel and unfair
be beside oneself with anger/excitement:	to be extremely angry/excited
bide one's time:	wait for a good opportunity
in the black:	not owing anybody any money (**opp.**: in the red)
blaze a trail:	discover/explore sth new
on the blink (inf):	stop working properly (of electrical equipment)
go by the board:	be rejected/ignored/ no longer possible
cut to the bone:	reduced to the/a minimum
out of bounds:	prohibited, forbidden (place)
pick someone's brains (inf):	ask sb to help with a problem/extract information from an expert

23 *Complete the sentences using one of the fixed phrases in an appropriate form.*

1 If you .... until the market improves, you'll get a better return on your investment.
2 Doctors in World War II .... in plastic surgery techniques.
3 Ben's dreams of a university education .... when his father died and he was forced to earn a living.
4 The swimming pool is .... to all pupils unless accompanied by a teacher.
5 A holiday in the UK .... these days.
6 My TV has been .... all week. I'll have to call a repairman.
7 Households that are more than six months .... with their mortgage repayments will face repossession of their homes.
8 You don't need to worry. This kind of rash will usually clear up ....
9 Costs must be .... if the company is to survive the current economic downturn.
10 It's nice to see him .... again after his illness.

24 *Choose the correct item.*

1 During winter the shelters are full of people of no fixed ....
   A residence   C home
   B abode   D domicile

2 Until your finances are in the ...., it's not a good idea to take out a loan.
   A credit   C profit
   B funds   D black

3 The matter has been left in .... until the legal ramifications have been explored.
   A recess   C abeyance
   B suspension   D waiting

4 It was an extremely hostile article which cast .... on the conduct of the entire cabinet.
   A criticism   C disapproval
   B aspersions   D abuse

5 Could I pick your .... on the subject before the meeting?
   A brains   C head
   B mind   D intellect

6 I'm not sure I can answer that. I've only thought about it in the .... before.
   A general   C indefinite
   B hypothetical   D abstract

7 You'll never convince me! We'll just have to .... to disagree.
   A agree   C admit
   B consider   D consent

8 The entire staff was thrown off .... when the news of the takeover was announced.
   A composure   C stable
   B disarray   D balance

25 *Read the following article and using the information given, complete the following letter by writing the missing words in the correct spaces. The words you need do not occur in the article. The first one has been done for you. Do not use more than two words for each blank.*

The French government is planning to introduce new measures to monitor and limit the use of live animals in scientific research. Their aim is to establish new standards for all of Europe. The new measures aim to ensure that the public will be informed as to the conditions in which animals are kept, and scientists will be made to justify their use of live animals in cases where substitutes can be found. A council will also be formed, consisting of scientists, animal rights activists and other qualified members. It is hoped that France's actions will be an example to other European countries which now have few controls regarding the treatment of animals.

Dear John,

   I just wanted to write and tell you about the new (0) *law/bill* that is being (1) .... in here in (2) .... to (3) .... of the way live animals are used in experiments and even to (4) .... their use! It makes all our hard work worthwhile. What they (5) .... to do is (6) .... new guidelines for (7) .... of Europe. It will mean that (8) .... will know about (9) .... the animals are kept. Best of all, it means that scientists will have to explain (10) .... they experiment on live animals at all! Apparently, some kind of committee of (11) .... will also be (12) .... Hopefully, this will (13) .... other countries in Europe change their ways for the better.

   We'll keep you posted. Hopefully the changes here will help with your campaign!

Yours,
Jacques

WORD USAGE

26 *Read the text below. Use the word given in capitals at the end of some of the lines to form a word that fits in the space in the same line.*

A MODERN ITALIAN ARTIST

Amedeo Modigliani (1884 - 1920) was an Italian painter and sculptor whose **(0)** *original*   ORIGIN
paintings, which were characterised by asymmetry of composition, **(1)** .... of   LONG
figure, and simple but **(2)** .... use of line, are among the most important   MONUMENT
of the 20th century. They have also gained **(3)** .... for the entirely personal   POPULAR
atmosphere with which they are invested: a kind of mute **(4)** .... between   RELATION
the artist and sitter that implicates the spectator in a truly **(5)** .... way.   REMARK

After suffering from serious illnesses as a child, he was forced to give up **(6)** ....   CONVENTION
education, and it was then that he began to study painting. After his studies ˙ Italy, Modigliani
left for Paris. There, he was overwhelmed by the painting of Paul Cezanne, which exerted an
(7) .... influence on the earliest phase of his work. Furthermore, his   QUESTION
(8) .... study of African sculpture made a profound impression on his painting style.   EXTEND

Modigliani was not a professional portraitist in the strict sense of the word. His paintings are
almost always portraits of relatives, **(9)** .... of the Parisian literary   PERSON
scene of his times and the contemporary artistic world, along with many portraits of
(10) .... persons.   IDENTIFY

27 *Fill in the blanks with one of the words from the box below in the correct form.*

> • laugh • smile • giggle • ~~chuckle~~ • sneer
> • grin • snigger • smirk • beam • titter • guffaw

0 Mr Jones *chuckled* to himself as he read a funny story in the newspaper.
1 The audience started .... nervously when the cameras pointed their way.
2 The students .... when they saw that their teacher had sat on some chewing gum.
3 I hardly ever .... at jokes. I just don't find them funny.
4 The woman .... with pleasure when she saw her daughter get off the plane.
5 Fiona .... pleasantly at her neighbour when she saw her walking through the park.
6 When he .... loudly at the joke, everyone in the theatre turned to look at him.
7 The boy could do nothing but .... nervously when he was asked to stand up in front of the class.
8 It's disgusting the way she .... at everyone who doesn't dress as well as she does.
9 Mr Smith always .... when he sees me; I get the feeling he knows something I don't.
10 Those teenage girls do nothing but .... when they see boys they like.

28 *Choose the correct item.*

1 A small dog went for my ankles but I adroitly managed to .... it.
A dodge   C shirk
B evade   D duck

2 He's so lazy! We all have to work harder because he's always .... his duties.
A evading   C ducking
B shirking   D dodging

3 The Prime Minister managed to .... any tricky questions asked by the interviewer.
A shirk   C dodge
B duck   D evade

4 The damp has .... his health; he's got rheumatism.
A affected   C swayed
B influenced   D impressed

5 I'm sure that living with a vegetarian has .... me to eat less meat.
A swayed   C influenced
B affected   D impressed

6 Before I pay for the painting, I need proof that it is a(n) .... Picasso, not a copy.
A real   C valid
B authentic   D natural

7 He may appear to be .... but in fact he's a compulsive liar.

A authentic   C natural
B genuine   D real

8 If you have stomach problems it is best to avoid .... food.

A rich   C wealthy
B affluent   D lavish

9 I was rather embarrassed when John gave me such a(n) .... gift.

A well-off   C extravagant
B rich   D affluent

10 Brazil derives the majority of its revenue from one ...., coffee.

A stock   C ware
B merchandise   D commodity

COLLOCATIONS

29 Fill in **artificial, false.**

0	*false* teeth	6	.... light
1	.... passport	7	.... flowers
2	.... alarm	8	.... tears
3	.... hair	9	.... pearls
4	.... note	10	.... impression
5	.... limbs	11	.... additives

30 Think of one word which can be used appropriately in all three sentences.

0 • One doesn't need to be an expert to *appreciate* the beauty of classical music.
  • He seems confident that houses in this area will *appreciate* in value in the next few years.
  • I'll always *appreciate* your help and support.

1 • Her hands were swollen and .... from the unaccustomed hard work.
  • Dieticians consider .... vegetables to be the healthiest option.
  • I think you got a .... deal when you joined that firm.

2 • A .... of dirt and oil lay over the surface of the pond.
  • Lorna Rook has been all over the world promoting her latest ....
  • If you wrap the cheese tightly in plastic .... and put it in the fridge it will last longer.

3 • The original .... of the restaurant included an open kitchen by the front entrance.
  • My heart is set on a couch with an embossed floral ....
  • I have to admit that I met him by ....; I waited in the lobby until he arrived.

4 • Game wardens .... traps to catch poachers and hunters.
  • If you pay on our installment plan, we will .... your carpets free of charge.
  • You can't simply .... the blame on the government whenever things go wrong!

5 • She .... the pillow angrily and started crying, wishing she hadn't told him anything.
  • Danny .... holes in the reports and filed them.
  • The accountant quickly .... the amounts into the calculator.

6 • The school staff needs new .... in order to bring in novel ideas.
  • Having met his parents, I can see that generosity is in his ....
  • The doctors said they would have to carry out a .... test prior to the operation.

7 • After the whole ordeal, we wondered if it was worth the ....
  • The .... at the football match arose when fans of the losing team didn't agree with the referee's call.
  • His chronic back .... was caused by his sleeping on a soft mattress.

8 • Peter's .... and sense of humour made him a welcome guest on anyone's list.
  • Although he claimed not to be superstitious, he put a .... in his back pocket before heading for the exam.
  • The plan was a great success. It worked like a ....

9 • Ever since John broke the window, he's been in the teacher's .... books.
  • Rumour has it that he quit the country leaving nothing but .... debts behind.
  • Poor Mark! I feel really .... about his being laid off on his birthday.

PREPARING FOR PART 5

SUMMARY WRITING I Locating and Paraphrasing Relevant Information

31 a) *Read the passages, then read the following summary question, and decide which four of the eight bold parts should be included in the answer. One has been done for you.*

In a paragraph of between 50 and 70 words, summarise how each child reacted to the storytelling.

Relevant parts: B   ....

Kenneth Grahame was a large, self-effacing Scotsman (at 39, the youngest ever Secretary of the Bank of England) whose shyness and aloofness meant that he had few friends. **(A) To his son Alastair, however, he gave his heart and the wonderful literary gift of *The Wind in the Willows*.**

The creation of this timeless classic started in young Alastair's bedroom, as his father would tell him bedtime stories about the magical world of Toad, Mole, Badger and Otter. **(B) The irresistible combination of fantasy and realism kept the boy spellbound night after night. (C) Soon, he would refuse to go to bed without his father furnishing him with another episode.**

Underlying this wonderful story is a caring father's attempt to quietly instruct his son in the ways of the world. Wisdom, folly, firm action and tolerance are all discreetly displayed in such a way that a young child could understand and appreciate. **(D) 'The Wind in the Willows' has all of the characteristics of didactic children's literature, in that it primarily aims to teach.** However, the ingenuity of its content means that it stands out from other didactic children's literature, making it a novel that can be read simply for the pleasure one finds in the hilarious exploits of Toad and his friends; on a didactic level, it acts as a gentle, benevolent guide.

My husband and I write books for a living. Specifically, we write books for eight to twelve year-olds and teens. As co-writers, we've put together all sorts of stories featuring all sorts of heroes, from princesses and trolls to singing horse riders and animated green slime. **(E) A few years ago we decided to try a new genre and added goblins and various other monsters to our cast of characters.**

Both our children have had the occasional nightmare, but it is our younger one, Susan, who is the more sensitive and more prone to fears of monsters lurking under her bed. **(F) When she was four and her brother Kevin was seven, my spouse and I were asked to write a scary book.** As the level of the books was appropriate to my children's age, I thought I'd "test" the book on them. **(G) I hadn't even finished reading them the first chapter when my daughter sat up and yelled "That's horrible! How could you write something like that?"**

Needless to say, I didn't finish the story. **(H) My seven-year-old hadn't said anything, but it was obvious from his expression that he wasn't exactly enjoying it.** We've gone back to writing non-scary books now, as the experience made us aware that children are extremely impressionable when it comes to ghosts and other things that go bump in the night.

b) *Paraphrase the relevant parts so that you use as few of the words appearing in the passage as possible. The total wordcount for all four parts should not exceed 50 words. Item (B) has been done for you.*

B   *Alastair loved his father's bedtime stories, which were both realistic and imaginative.*

....
....
....

c) *Complete the summary below.*

Alastair loved his father's stories, **(1)** .... After a while, he wouldn't **(2)** .... The experience of the writer of the second passage was very different. Her younger child **(3)** .... Although her **(4)** ....

32 a) *Read the passages, then read the following summary question, and underline the parts which should be included in the answer. One part in the second passage has been underlined for you.*

In a paragraph of between 50 and 70 words, summarise the different accounts of how the Giant's Causeway was formed.

Witness the result of nature's ancient fury. Burning lava pours out of the earth's interior and comes in contact with the freezing air, rapidly cooling into 40,000 black, hexagonal columns. The tops of these columns (the tallest of which is 12 metres high) are relatively flat, and act as stepping stones which lead from the top of a perilous cliff gradually out into the rough Irish sea. Welcome to the world's most spectacular volcanic site: the Giant's Causeway, in Northern Ireland.

'Caledonian Holidays' now offers you the opportunity to visit this awesome site. Near the coast of County Antrim in Northern Ireland, the Giant's Causeway will astonish you with its alien appearance. Let our guides tell you all about its creation, its history, and how it has inspired numerous Irish myths and legends. 'Caledonian Holidays' offers package weekend trips to the Giant's Causeway from Glasgow, Liverpool, Dublin and Belfast. Normally priced at £190 per person, this magnificent journey to the Earth's most spectacular beach is now on special offer, costing only £145 per person. Offer ends on June 30th, so book now by using our free phone number or our web-page.

A According to Irish tradition, the Giant's Causeway has two possible origins, both involving legendary hero, Finn McCool. The first legend says that the Causeway was McCool's labour of love. He had fallen for the charms of a girl from Staffa, an island in the Hebrides, and, in an attempt to see her more often, McCool built the Causeway so that she could cross to Ulster.

The second story presents the Causeway's construction in a less romantic light. The Scottish giant, Benandonner, challenged Finn McCool to a duel to the death. Finn, thinking he would win the duel easily and rid Britain of the giant forever, hastily hurled large stones into the Irish Sea to form a passageway for his enemy to walk across.

Finn's wife, on seeing the giant, feared that her husband would be defeated, and so set out to fool Benandonner. She dressed her husband up as a baby and made him lie in an enormous cradle. She then invited the giant for a cup of tea, pleading for him to be quiet as her "baby" was sleeping. When Benandonner saw the huge "infant", he began to wonder about the size of the father, and ended up beating a hasty retreat back to Scotland. As he ran off, he ripped up parts of the Causeway, which explains why only parts of it remain.

b) *Paraphrase the relevant parts so that you use as few of the words appearing in the passage as possible. One item has been done for you.*

A   *One legend has it that Finn McCool built the Causeway to help his love cross from the Hebrides.*

....

....

....

c) *Write the summary.*

....

....

....

....

....

....

....

....

1c Practice Test One

Paper 3 Use of English

Time: 1 hour 30 minutes

PART 1

Read the text below and think of the word which best fits each space. Use only one word in each space.

TO SLEEP OR NOT TO SLEEP

Are you one of those people **(0)** *who* toss and turn all night, unable to **(1)** .... to sleep? Although many people who have sleeping problems, **(2)** .... chronic or occasional, automatically reach for the sleeping tablets when they see a difficult night **(3)** .... of them, there are a number of so-called "folk" remedies which are not only cheaper but also much safer in the long run. Most people have tried having a hot drink such as milk or **(4)** .... of a number of commercially available herbal infusions before going to bed, but there are other, **(5)** .... well-known remedies, which can help you on your way to a restful night's sleep. One unusual **(6)** .... effective technique involves not warmth, **(7)** .... you might think, but cold. Before going to bed, run very cold water for several minutes over your forearms and legs from the knee **(8)** ...., then dry yourself quickly and hop into bed. You will find yourself feeling totally relaxed and drowsy. Another unusual approach has to do with eating or, to **(9)** .... more precise, chewing. Take a large apple, wash it and eat it slowly, **(10)** .... particular care to chew the peel thoroughly. Chewing is not only relaxing in **(11)** ...., but the peel of the apple contains a natural substance **(12)** .... induces relaxation. Meditation, stretching, walking and **(13)** .... reading are also effective for many people. Clearly, there are many ways to avoid the pillpopping route and **(14)** .... enjoy a good night's sleep. Then again, if all **(15)** .... fails, you could always try counting sheep!

PART 2

Read the text below. Use the word given in capitals at the end of some of the lines to form a word that fits in the space in the same line.

THE PRESENTATION OF HISTORY

When dealing with **(0)** *sensitive* issues such as the atrocities of war
and man's **(16)** .... to man, interpreters of history
may try in vain to give an even-handed **(17)** ....
of the subject. This creates the danger of "softening" the image to
make it a little less **(18)** ...., a little less
(19) .... and a little more acceptable to the
general audience. This is an injustice to history, with too much emphasis
put on the bland and not enough on the harsh reality of the past.
Interpreting our heritage is not a soft option where all that is required
is a nice, **(20)** .... view of the past. It requires
a full working **(21)** .... of the issues and the
evidence, together with a **(22)** .... to
be open about the strengths and weaknesses of our ability to interpret
in a way that **(23)** .... understanding.
If **(24)** .... is required to do that, then it should not
be avoided for fear of presenting something **(25)** ....

SENSE
HUMAN
TREAT

HORROR
SHAME

SENTIMENT
PERCEIVE
WILL

DEEP
PROVOKE
AGREE

PART 3

Think of one word only which can be used appropriately in all three sentences.

0 • One doesn't need to be an expert to *appreciate* the beauty of classical music.
  • He seems confident that houses in this area will *appreciate* in value in the next few years.
  • I'll always *appreciate* your help and support.

26 • Ray married a woman ten years his ....
  • I'll always remember Mrs White, my teacher in .... school.
  • Ripton was at that time a .... official at the Treasury.

27 • Before signing the contract, make sure you read the small ....
  • Pat wore a dress with a pretty floral .... on it.
  • The wild cat hadn't left a single .... for us to follow.

28 • They built a cottage on their little .... of land.
  • The play had too many characters and a confused ....
  • Guy Fawkes Night commemorates a .... to blow up Parliament.

29 • You needn't take the pot out of its .... in order to water it.
  • The government is taking a firm ..,.................... on the issue.
  • The witness was asked to take the witness .... and testify under oath.

30 • They put a stronger .... on the gate to stop their dog from getting out.
  • A .... on a canal regulates the flow of water.
  • Helen blew back a stray .... of hair.

31 • Carmen had always .... hypnotherapy until she found it actually worked.
  • She was .... sideways when she heard she had won the lottery.
  • After negotiation, the price was .... down on condition we paid cash.

PART 4

Complete the second sentence so that it has a similar meaning to the first sentence, using the word given. Do not change the word given. You must use between three and eight words, including the word given.

0 Nobody spoke when the teacher asked who the culprit was.
  remained
  Everyone *remained silent when the teacher asked* who the culprit was.

32 My boss says I can use his car whenever I want to, so long as I'm careful.
  disposal
  My boss ....
  ...., so long as I'm careful.

33 The news was a shock to us.
  aback
  We ....
  .... news.

34 James realised that he could never be an architect.
  cut
  James realised ....
  .... an architect.

35 They chose not to drive because they thought there would be too much snow.
  fear
  They chose ....
  .... too much snow.

36 I'm sick of that programme; I've watched it too often.
  off
  I've ....
  ....; I've watched it too often.

37 I never have enough time these days.
  short
  I ....
  .... these days.

38 They tried very hard to finish by midnight.
  best
  They ....
  .... by midnight.

39 The trapped fireman finally got away through the back window.
  escape
  The trapped fireman ....
  .... window.

PART 5

*For questions **40-44** read the following texts. For questions **40 - 43** answer with a word or short phrase. You do not need to write complete sentences. For question **44**, write a summary according to the instructions given.*

line 1 ———

The chemical senses are the gatekeepers of the body. They provide information about the substances we come into contact with, and thus influence our decisions about what to eat and drink. Although our responses to many flavours may appear to be hard-wired, they can actually be modified by experience. Much of what we like and dislike about flavours is learned.

Scientists are exploring factors related to food choice and intake across the human lifespan. One research programme with human infants examines the role of early experience on development of flavour preferences later in life. The late-term foetus has functional chemosensory systems that can detect tastes and odours, and research has shown that flavours associated with the mother's diet are passed into the amniotic fluid. Such transmission of flavour may provide the foetus with an early introduction to elements of the mother's cuisine.

At the other end of the lifespan, research has shown that loss of sensitivity of taste in the elderly affects the way food is perceived by these individuals. For example, olfactory loss can diminish food cravings and also aversions, leading to lack of preference and subsequently to lack of appetite.

40 Explain the use of the phrase "gatekeepers of the body" as it is used in line 1.

....

....

41 How does loss of olfactory sensitivity affect older people's perception of foods?

....

....

Is your four-year-old reluctant to eat vegetables? Do you have to disguise foods like broccoli and carrots in pies and pasta bakes? Do you have difficulty
line 3 —— convincing him or her to drink milk? Believe it or not, this may all be of your doing.

line 5 —— This is not another one of those guilt trips magazines tend to put women through, like claiming that the reason your child is not doing well at school is that you didn't listen to enough Mozart when you were pregnant. Researchers are looking into the possibility of the mother's nutritional habits during her pregnancy affecting a child's response to certain flavours after the age of three. Unborn children have the ability to smell and taste, and elements which keep some of the flavour of what the mother eats and drinks do end up in the amniotic fluid. Following birth, flavours from foods and drinks consumed by the mother pass into breast milk, and can influence what a breast-fed infant likes or doesn't like in its later life. Apart from food preferences, what nutritional elements reach the unborn child may affect its body's physiological needs well into early adulthood. For instance, if a foetus receives an overloading of calcium through the mother's consumption of milk, cheese, pulses etc, the less likely it is that he or she will be keen on dairy products in later life.

So what is a lady-in-waiting to do? Follow your doctor's advice and make sure you get enough of all nutrients. At the same time don't overdo it. As with most things about being a mum, striking the right balance is essential.

42 What does the writer mean by the phrase "it may all be of your doing" (line 3)?

....

....

43 What does the word "This" refer to in line 3?

....

....

44 In a paragraph of between 50 and 70 words, summarise how a woman's nutritional habits can affect her child before and after its birth.

....

....

....

....

....

....

....

....

UNIT 2a Grammar: Modals

The modals are:	can – could – may – might – must – ought to – will – would – shall – should – have to – need – dare

FUNCTIONS OF MODALS

Ability/Inability

I **can** see smoke in the distance.
She **can't** speak German.
When I was at school, I **could** play the piano. (repeated action)
He **was able to** escape through a window. (single action)
She **wasn't able to/couldn't** finish the report on time. (Both types can be used in the negative for either a repeated or a single action.)

Possibility/Impossibility

Reckless driving **can** result in road accidents.
You **could** be right.
He **may** be lucky this time.
She **might** come with us. (but I don't think so)
You **can't** be serious!
It's almost midnight. She **should** be here any moment now.

Permission/Concession

Can I ask you a question?
Could you give me some advice?
Might I borrow your newspaper? (formal)
May I join you?
You **can** sit here if you want.
You **may** take the last sweet, if you wish.

Obligation/Duty

She **must** pay the rent by Friday. (strong obligation or duty)
I **have to** meet the boss at noon. (obligation)
He **had to** have an X-ray before going to the consultation.

Necessity

I **need to** improve my French.
The house **needs** cleaning.
He **has to see** a dentist soon.
Must I go with you?
Do I **have to/need to** finish this now?
Need he sign the form?

Prohibition

You **mustn't** eat in this room.
You **may not** make personal phone calls during working hours.
You **are not to** eat in this room. (= it's against the rules)
You **can't** park here. (= you aren't allowed to park here)

Absence of Obligation or Necessity

You **needn't** worry – everything's under control.
I **don't have to** leave until 3pm.
You **needn't have waited** for me. (but you did)
They **didn't need to** make any more food. (so they didn't)

Logical Assumption (affirmative)

He **must be** nervous about the test.
You **must be feeling** very sad after the loss of your father.
It's already 6:00. She **must have left** by now.
He **must have been lying** all along.

Logical Assumption (negative)

It **can't be** yours – Isn't yours blue?
She **can't be enjoying** herself; she hates classical music!
He **can't have broken** the kitchen window. He wasn't even there!
You **can't have been listening** properly. Mary would never be so rude to anyone.

Advice

You don't look well. You **should** take a holiday.
You **ought to** try harder. That's what I would do.
You **ought not to** complain so much.

Criticism

We **should have made** sure that the tickets were valid. (but we didn't)
He **ought to have cooked** dinner. (but he didn't)
You **could** have helped me (but you didn't)

Requests, Offers, Suggestions

Can you hurry up, please?
Would/Will you pass me the salt?
I'll give you a lift.
Shall I make the tea?
She **should** go to the dentist's.

CHARACTERISTICS OF MODALS

- They take no -s in the third person singular except for *have to, need* and *dare*.
- They have **no infinitive** or **present participle** forms except for *need, have to* and *dare*.
- They are followed by the **bare infinitive** except for *ought to* and *have to*.
- They form their negative and interrogative forms in the same way as the auxiliaries (e.g. **may not, may I** ...?) except for *need, have to* and *dare*.

Notes

- **Need** and **dare** are usually followed by a **bare infinitive** if they are used as **modals**; otherwise they are followed by a **full infinitive**.
  You **needn't come.**   or   You **don't need to come.**

- **Be able to, be allowed to** and **have to** are used to replace the missing tenses of **can, may** (when expressing permission) and **must** respectively.
  *When you pass your test, you **will be able to** drive.*
  *They **were allowed to** leave as soon as they finished the exam.*
  *He **had to** have an operation.*

- **Could/was able to** are used to talk about a general ability whereas **was able to** is used to talk about an action in a particular situation. Both can be used in negatives and questions.
  *Although he was tired, he **was able to swim** to safety.*
  *He **couldn't/wasn't able to** admit he was wrong.*
  ***Were** you **able to/Could** you find your way?*

- **Have to** expresses external obligation whereas **must** expresses obligation imposed by the speaker.
  *According to the law, all motorcyclists **have to wear** a helmet when riding their motorcycles.*
  *I **must visit** my grandparents more often. (I feel obliged.)*

- **May** and **might** both express possibility, although **may** is slightly stronger.
  *He **may** come if you ask him to.*
  *She **might** come if she has time. (slight possibility)*

1 *Fill in the blanks with the correct form of **can, be able to, must** or **have to**.*

0 Students *have to* pass an entrance examination in order to be accepted by this college.
1 Our father told us that we .... be home by 10 pm.
2 Despite his lack of experience he .... get the job.
3 You .... get a visa to travel to the USA.
4 You .... be careful with electricity.
5 Brian .... buy his new car as he'd been given a bonus at work.
6 If you want to be a member of the club, you .... register with the secretary.
7 I gave up French as I .... get down to studying.
8 She was so short she .... reach the door handle.
9 We .... go yet. It's not that late.

2 *Rewrite the following sentences using the words in capitals as in the example.*

0 It's possible that Eve forgot about the meeting. **MAY**
Eve may have forgotten about the meeting.

1 Would you like me to help you? **CAN**

....

....

2 Give this message to Mrs Bates, please! **WILL**

....

3 I don't believe the President made such a contradictory statement. **CAN'T**

....

4 Is it possible to pay in installments? **COULD**

....

....

5 Do you want to have a look at my article before I hand it in? **WOULD**

....

....

6 Aunt May cooked chicken soup for us, even though we told her we were eating out. **NEED**

....

7 He didn't make sure he had a spare tyre and he got a puncture miles from anywhere. **SHOULD**

....

....

8 It is extremely dangerous to strike a match at a petrol station. **MUST**

....

....

9 It's a good idea to get a dental check-up every six months. **OUGHT**

....

....

10 Is there any possibility of the flight being cancelled? **LIKELY**

....

....

11 Is it possible to pay by credit card? **MAY**

....

....

12 There's a possibility Paul will come to the party this evening. **MIGHT**

....

....

13 It is necessary for governments to take action against tax evasion. **MUST**

....

....

14 Sue didn't leave home in time and now she is running late for work. **SHOULD**

....

....

15 I believe business is now experiencing a severe recession. **MUST**

....

....

16 I don't believe Harry spent the whole evening studying for his French exam. **CAN'T**

....

....

17 Is it really necessary for me to make the presentation tomorrow? **HAVE**

....

....

18 It is doubtful whether he will be appointed Minister of Health. **MIGHT**

....

....

19 It is not advisable to make personal phone calls at work. **OUGHT**

....

....

20 It was wrong of you to rely on Michael's support. **SHOULD**

....

....

21 Perhaps she was behaving so arrogantly because of her insecurity. **MAY**

....

....

22 Is it a good idea to apply for the junior accountant's post? **SHOULD**

....

....

23 It wasn't very polite of you not to notify them about the change of plans. **COULD**

....

....

MAY - MUST - CAN'T

may (= perhaps)
must (= I think/I suppose, I strongly believe)
can't (= I don't think, I don't suppose)

Simple Present Perhaps he **works** as a teacher.	**Present Infinitive** He may **work** as a teacher.
Present Continuous I suppose he **is working** hard.	**Present Continuous Infinitive** He must **be working** hard.
Simple Future I don't think he **will** win.	**Present Infinitive** He can't **win**.
Future Continuous Perhaps they **will be playing** tennis.	**Present Continuous Infinitive** They may **be playing** tennis.
Simple Past I don't think he **worked** very hard.	**Perfect Infinitive** He can't **have worked** very hard.
Past Continuous I don't believe she **was working** last week.	**Perfect Continuous Infinitive** She can't **have been working** last week.
Present Perfect Simple Perhaps he **has left work**.	**Perfect Infinitive** He may **have left work**.
Present Perfect Continuous I think they **have been living** here for years.	**Perfect Continuous Infinitive** They must **have been living** here for years.
Past Perfect Simple Perhaps he **had forgotten** about the appointment.	**Perfect Infinitive** He may **have forgotten** about the appointment.
Past Perfect Continuous I don't think he **had been studying** hard enough.	**Perfect Continuous Infinitive** He can't **have been studying** hard enough.

3 *Read the following situations and write sentences using the modals in the list above.*

0 I don't think Madonna's new CD has been released yet.
Madonna's new CD can't have been released yet.
....

1 I strongly believe David is not lying this time.
....
....

2 George is thinking of buying a house this year but he's not sure whether he will.
....
....

3 I'm sure Linda is earning a high salary.
....
....

4 I think Mark was living in Spain at the time.
....
....

5 Perhaps you will need to hand in a research paper.
....
....

6 I strongly believe he wasn't just speculating when he said that prices will rise.
....
....

MUSTN'T / NEEDN'T

mustn't (= it's forbidden/not allowed)
You **mustn't** eat in the library. You **are not allowed** to eat in the library. You **may not eat** in the library.

needn't (=it's not necessary)
You **needn't** learn it by heart. It's **not necessary** for you to learn it by heart. You **don't need to** learn it by heart. You **don't have to** learn it by heart.

4 *Read the following situations and write sentences using* **mustn't** *or* **needn't**.

0 You aren't allowed to use a dictionary during the exam.
   You mustn't use a dictionary during the exam. ....
   ....

1 It isn't necessary for Brian to finish the reports quickly.
   ....
   ....

2 It isn't necessary for Mary to go to work tomorrow.
   ....
   ....

3 Eating and drinking is prohibited on the Metro.
   ....
   ....

4 It's not necessary to submit my proposal so early.
   ....
   ....

DIDN'T NEED TO / NEEDN'T HAVE

Didn't need to	shows that it wasn't necessary for something to happen and it **didn't happen**.
Needn't have	shows that it wasn't necessary for something to happen but it **did happen**.

He **didn't need to** go to work on Sunday.	It wasn't necessary for him to go to work on Sunday, so he didn't.
She **needn't have bought** so many eggs.	It wasn't necessary for her to buy as many eggs as she did.

5 *Read the following situations and write sentences using* **didn't need to** *or* **needn't have**.

0 It wasn't necessary for Andrew to take so much money for his holiday because everything was less expensive than he expected.
   Andrew needn't have taken so much money on holiday with him.

1 It wasn't necessary for Mr Smith to cook an evening meal for her family last night as her husband took her out to dinner.
   ....
   ....

2 It wasn't necessary for Mr Jones to collect his wife from the airport yesterday as his son volunteered to pick her up.
   ....
   ....

3 It wasn't necessary for Paul to stay up all night. The exam he was studying for was cancelled.
   ....
   ....

STRUCTURAL CONVERSION

1 *Perhaps* she is abroad.
   She *may be* abroad.
2 *Perhaps* she wasn't taking a bath.
   She *may* not have been taking a bath.
3 *Perhaps* he has been/was studying.
   He *may* have been studying.
4 *I think* she has lost her way.
   She *must* have lost her way.
5 *I suppose* he has left Austria.
   He *must* have left Austria.
6 *I think* he was in Germany.
   He *must* have been in Germany.
7 *It is certain that* he'll fail.
   He *is bound to* fail.
8 *It is certain that* she (has) attended the
   ceremony.
   She *is certain to* have attended the ceremony.
   She *must* have attended the ceremony.
9 *I must* reject this plan.
   I have no option but to reject this plan.
   I will have to reject this plan.
10 *I don't think* she's forgotten.
   She *can't* have forgotten.
11 *I'm sure he isn't* lying to us.
   He *can't* be lying to us.
12 *It wasn't necessary* for you to buy so many roses as
   you did.
   You *needn't have* bought so many roses.
13 *Was it necessary* for her to behave like that?
   Did she need/have to behave like that?
14 *It wasn't necessary* for me to walk to work as he gave
   me a lift.
   I *didn't need to* walk to work as he gave me a lift.
15 *There's no need* to correct the tests today.
   Don't bother to correct the tests today.
   It isn't necessary to correct the tests today.
   You *needn't* correct the tests today.
   You *don't need* to correct the tests today.
16 *He isn't obliged* to tell you the truth.
   He *needn't* tell you the truth.
   He *doesn't need/have to* tell you the truth.
17 *It is important* for you to learn to drive.
   You *need/have to* learn to drive.
18 *Are exams* compulsory at this school?
   Do you have to sit for exams at this school?
19 *Senior students don't have* to take tests.
   It's optional for senior students to take tests.
   It's not compulsory for senior students to take tests.

20 *It is against the rules* to write your answers in ink.
   You *mustn't* write your answers in ink.
21 *It is forbidden* to speed in the city centre.
   You *mustn't* speed in the city centre.
   Under no circumstances should/must you drive fast in
   the city centre.
22 *He couldn't* go out because it was raining.
   The rain prevented him from going out.
23 *It is advisable to* speak politely to your teachers.
   You *should* speak politely to your teachers.
   You *had better* speak politely to your teachers.
24 *It would be* a good idea to go on a diet.
   You *had better* go on a diet.
   You *should/ought to* go on a diet.
   It is advisable to go on a diet.
   It's a good idea to go on a diet.
25 *Why didn't* you consult your lawyer?
   You *should have* consulted your lawyer.
26 *Let's* work out the details.
   Shall we work out the details?
   Why don't we work out the details?
27 *Shall* I help you with the dishes?
   Would you like me to help you with the dishes?
28 *Could* you come on Monday?
   Would Monday be convenient for you?
   How does Monday suit you?
29 *May I* borrow your car?
   Do you mind if I borrow your car?
   Would you mind if I borrowed your car?
   Could I borrow your car, please?
   I was wondering if I could borrow your car.
30 *Would you like* to open an account?
   Would it interest you to open an account?
   Would you be interested in opening an account?
   How would you/do you feel about opening an
   account?
   How about opening an account?
31 *She is unlikely* to pass her exams.
   It is unlikely/not likely that she'll pass her exams.
   There's little likelihood/possibility of her passing her
   exams/that she'll pass her exams.
   It's doubtful whether she'll pass her exams.
32 *He is likely to* win the prize.
   It is likely that he will win the prize.
   It is very possible that he will win the prize.
   He could certainly win the prize.
   There is every likelihood that he will win the prize.

6 *Complete the second sentence so that it has a similar meaning to the first sentence using the word given. Do not change the word given. You must use between three and eight words, including the word given.*

1 Jeff, shall we go out tonight?
how
Jeff ....
.... tonight?

2 It is very possible that he'll be promoted.
every
There ....
.... promoted.

3 It is certain that he will return this afternoon.
bound
He ....
.... this afternoon.

4 He wasn't able to understand the radio message because of interference.
impossible
The interference on the radio ....
.... the message.

5 Why haven't you signed this form at the bottom?
sign
Weren't ....
....at the bottom?

6 Could he have been telling the truth?
likely
Is ....
.... the truth?

7 Could you come on Saturday?
suit
How ....
.... you?

8 How do you feel about going on an excursion?
like
How ....
.... on an excursion?

CONVERSATIONAL GRAMMAR

7 *Choose the correct item.*

1 "I'm freezing."
"You .... more warmly."
A could dress   C may have dressed
B should have dressed D must have dressed

2 "Oh, this looks familiar."
"I .... it to you before."
A had to show   C needn't have shown
B may have shown   D didn't need to show

3 Louisa is still in Palma, so you .... her at the library.
A couldn't see   C weren't able to see
B mustn't have seen   D can't have seen

4 "Whose are these keys?"
"Oh they're Mary's; she .... them."
A must have left   C ought to be left
B should have left   D might be left

5 "Do you think Sally will be offered a place at the University?"
"Definitely; in fact, she's very likely .... the scholarship."
A that she will get   C that she gets
B to be getting   D to get

6 "Kelly's late; that's not like her."
"She .... about your date."
A might forget   C might have forgotten
B could be forgetting D could forgotten

8 *Complete the second sentence so that it has a similar meaning to the first sentence using the word given. Do not change the word given. You must use between three and eight words, including the word given.*

1 You don't have to inform the agency beforehand.
compulsory
It ....
.... the agency in advance.

2 May I borrow your typewriter?
mind
Do ....
.... your typewriter?

3 You won't be able to enter the country unless you have a visa.
prevented
Passengers without a visa ....
.... the country.

4 You mustn't start writing before the test starts.
rules
It ....
.... until the test has started.

9 *Read the text below and think of the word which best fits each space. Use only one word in each space.*

COSMETIC SURGERY

Until half a century **(0)** *ago*, the basic physical structure you were born with, **(1)** .... you suffered an accident, was the one you died with. Apart from normal wear **(2)** .... tear or the possibility of a broken nose or **(3)** .... disfigurement, you did not expect to change your appearance drastically.

However, people have not always been happy with **(4)** .... lot and have often wanted to see something different when they look at themselves in the mirror. Fortunes have been **(5)** .... by selling wigs and miraculous wrinkle removers. Magazines have been full of advice on **(6)** .... to disguise the shape of your face by applying blushers and foundations **(7)** .... the day these products were invented.

Then fresh hope appeared in the form of cosmetic surgery. Most general practitioners warn their patients not to expect their lives to be transformed when they **(8)** .... their noses remodelled or their ears tucked back; nevertheless, there is a constant supply **(9)** .... willing victims streaming **(10)** .... the plush clinics of the knife-wielders.

It **(11)** .... the people in the public eye who normally have the **(12)** .... drastic changes made. However, many ordinary people dream of looking dramatically different, save for years to make their dream **(13)** .... true, and are willing to put up with the inevitable swelling, scarring and black eyes. **(14)** .... some people sell stories to the tabloid press about how their lives have changed, many others are sadly disappointed with the results, **(15)** .... it may even have left them looking considerably worse than they did before.

PHRASAL VERBS 1

10 *a) Match the phrasal verbs in bold with the definitions given.*

1 Perhaps you could hold your questions until the end of the lecture rather than keep **breaking in**.
2 The two countries have **broken off** diplomatic relations.
3 War in the Falklands **broke out** in 1982.
4 The car **broke down** just as we were leaving the house.
5 When accused, she **broke down** and confessed her guilt.
6 **Breaking into** a smile, Tim said "Happy birthday."
7 **Breaking through** poverty barrier she became a world-famous scientist.
8 Since they did nothing but quarrel, they decided to **break up**.

a to end sth suddenly
b to stop functioning
c to end a relationship
d achieve success despite obstacles or difficulties
e suddenly start doing sth
f to begin suddenly (of war, disease, fire etc)
g to lose control of oneself
h to interrupt

1 .... 3 .... 5 .... 7 ....
2 .... 4 .... 6 .... 8 ....

b) What other meanings can you find for the following? **break down, break out, break up** *Use each meaning correctly in a sentence.*

PHRASAL VERBS 2

11 *Replace the words in bold with one of the phrasal verbs in the correct form from the list below.*

- break through • bear out • balance against
- blow up • bank on • brush up • blow over
- become of • build up • book up

0 What **has happened to** John?
I haven't seen him for ages.   *has become of*

1 Over the years he **has accumulated** an impressive collection of artefacts from all over the world. ....

2 Your request for greater financial support has to be **assessed in relation to** the claims from other departments. ....

3 He may come tomorrow but don't **depend on** it. ....

4 Their disagreement about where to spend their holidays soon **stopped and was forgotten**. ....

5 The restaurant was fully **reserved** so we went to another. ....

6 I accept your excuse. His statement **supports the truth of** your story. ....

7 Fortunately, no one was in the car when it **exploded**. ....

8 I must **improve** my Italian before going to that meeting in Rome. ....

9 After days of rain, the sun finally **became visible** from behind the clouds. ....

What are the different uses of **burn down** *and* **burn up**? *Use each meaning correctly in a sentence.*

....
....
....
....
....
....
....

IDIOMS/FIXED PHRASES 1

12 *Match the idioms/fixed phrases with the definitions.*

0	black and blue all over	a	fed up
1	by and large	b	very lively
2	behind bars	c	sudden clever idea
3	full of beans	d	show neither profit nor loss
4	drop a brick	e	be very expensive
5	browned off	f	covered with bruises
6	a brainwave	g	suddenly and unexpectedly
7	out of the blue	h	in prison
8	break even	i	on the whole
9	cost a bomb	j	do/say sth tactless

0 *f*   2 ....   4 ....   6 ....   8 ....
1 ....   3 ....   5 ....   7 ....   9 ....

IDIOMS/FIXED PHRASES 2

13 *Look at Appendix 2 and explain the following idioms/fixed phrases in bold.*

1 Stop **beating about/around the bush** and come to the point.

2 You should **take the bull by the horns** and go and see him right now.

3 The name **rings a bell** but I can't remember who she is.

4 The scandal was **laid bare** by an ambitious journalist.

5 Tom is the teacher's **blue-eyed boy/golden boy**.

6 His life was hanging **in the balance**. We didn't know if he would live or die.

7 I'm afraid I'm **broke**. I can't lend you any money.

8 He's been in everyone's **black books** since he was caught cheating in the exam.

9 He decided **to make a clean breast of it** and tell his wife exactly what had happened.

10 The takeover came as **a bolt from the blue**.

11 Everything should be set out **in black and white** so that there will be no room for misunderstanding.

12 He's always playing practical jokes on us; I think it's time we **got our own back**.

13 My parents' attitude towards the less fortunate, really **makes my blood boil**.

14 It's going to rain; I **feel it in my bones**.

15 The researchers realised they had been **barking up the wrong tree** when the first results came back negative.

16 It might be a good idea to **butter up the boss** before you ask for a rise.

17 **Don't hold your breath** waiting for him; he'll never show up!

18 The student was **caught red-handed** cheating in the physics exam.

19 John's injury **dealt a blow** to his hopes of getting onto the Olympic swimming team.

20 I'm glad to **see the back** of those terrible children.

IDIOMS/FIXED PHRASES 3

14 *What sort of person would you describe as*

1 a chip off the old block?

....

2 a wet blanket?

....

3 big-headed?

....

4 above board?

....

PREPOSITIONS

15 *Look at Appendix 5 and fill the blanks with the correct preposition.*

0 Please take care *of* your sister while I'm out.

1 You have no choice .... the matter. You have to do what he says.

2 Your alibi is consistent .... our report.

3 Does this CD belong .... anyone?

4 He aimed .... the target, squeezed the trigger and fired.

5 The board was agreeable .... the proposal.

6 You're very careless .... locking the house; anyone could walk in.

7 She was bored .... the tedious conversation and tried to change the subject.

8 If you concentrated more .... your school work, your grades would improve.

9 My mother is confined .... a wheelchair so she doesn't go out very much.

10 She didn't like flying and was apprehensive .... making the journey alone.

11 If you can bear .... me a little longer, I'll give you all the information together.

16 *Look at Appendix 5 and choose the best alternative.*

1 Did you notice the **for sale/on sale** sign outside the house next door?

2 There's no point trying to talk to Stuart; he's totally **absorbed by/absorbed in** that magazine.

3 The agent is believed to have been **in possession of/in the possession of** the documents all along.

4 The social worker received an anonymous letter, warning him not to **meddle with/meddle in** other people's business.

5 As soon as the leopard came **in sight/on sight**, the hunter pulled the trigger.

6 This letter is to **advise you of/advise you on** the fact that your overdraft currently stands at £6,435.

7 Some people believe that the end of the world is **at hand/in hand**.

8 The most upsetting part of her relationship with her parents was that they rarely **supported her with/supported her in** her decisions.

9 Even though they knew each other **on sight/by sight**, they had never exchanged words.

10 When the magician was asked the secret of his trick, he **responded with/responded to** a secretive smile.

17 *Complete the second sentence so that it has a similar meaning to the first sentence, using the word given. Do not change the word given. You must use between three and eight words, including the word given.*

1 His father was very angry with him when he heard he had damaged the car.
blew
His father ....
.... he had damaged the car.

2 His speech was so confusing that nobody could understand what he was talking about.
baffled
Everyone ....
.... speech.

3 Jenny's birthday is on the same day as the Queen's.
coincides
Jenny's ....
.... Queen's.

4 Some children treat their younger siblings badly.
cruel
Some ....
.... younger siblings.

5 He bought a new jacket without having planned to.
spur
He bought ....
.... moment.

6 Initially, losing one's job can seem awful; afterwards it can work out well, for some people.
blessing
Losing one's job has proved ....
.... some people.

7 He's a pleasant man socially, but he's a tough businessman.
bargain
He's a pleasant man ....
.... business.

8 He has an obsession about the dishonesty of lawyers.
bee
He ....
.... dishonesty of lawyers.

9 The young actress was very nervous before the audition.
butterflies
The young actress ....
.... audition.

10 She was just about to pass out when someone offered her a seat.
verge
She was ....
.... when someone offered her a seat.

11 Simon couldn't remember ever having met the woman.
recollection
Simon ....
.... ever having met the woman.

12 Malcolm has finally decided to leave his job at the bank.
hand
Malcom has ....
.... at the bank.

13 He got up very early this morning.
crack
He ....
.... this morning.

14 He didn't seem to consider anything to be as important as winning that medal.
matter
Nothing ....
.... winning that medal.

15 The conference will now take place at a later date.
postponed
The conference ....
.... a later date.

16 The diplomat has been arrested because it is believed he had been spying for his government.
suspicion
The diplomat has been arrested ....
.... for his government.

17 Cindy must be ill; she ate very little of her lunch.
touched
Cindy must be ill; ....
.... her lunch.

FIXED PHRASES

make common cause with sb:	act together to achieve aim
rise to the challenge:	act and be successful even though sth is new
give chapter and verse:	give every exact detail
hold/keep in check:	control; prevent from becoming too powerful
big cheese (inf):	person with important job/position
take sth on the chin (inf):	bravely accept criticism, punishment etc
chop and change (inf):	keep changing (your mind)
strike a chord:	make sb feel sympathy/enthusiasm
claim to fame:	thing which makes sb unusual/important
come clean (inf):	admit the truth; confess
steer/stay clear of:	avoid sb/sth
part company with (f):	end association
of no/little consequence (f):	of no value/ importance
cut corners:	be less thorough
not all it's cracked up to be (inf):	not as good as people say it is/overestimated
cramp one's style (inf):	restrict one's behaviour in some way

18 *Complete the sentences using one of the fixed phrases in an appropriate form.*

1 When his boss criticises his work, Jason never complains and ....

2 Firefighting teams worked relentlessly throughout the day and managed to .... the fire ....

3 The teachers decided to .... the administration in the school and together press for a salary increase.

4 Sarah seems unable to make a final choice about her future career. She keeps ....

5 Ted likes to think of himself as a celebrity but his only .... is that he attended a banquet at Buckingham Palace.

6 The employee reluctantly .... about breaking the new computer and confessed to his boss.

7 If you want to lose weight permanently, you should .... food containing a lot of fat.

8 He had to .... his partner due to their strong disagreement.

9 In his attempt to meet the deadline he .... and handed in a poor presentation.

19 *Choose the correct item.*

1 Gavin will .... to the challenge of his new promotion.
A raise   C ride
B rise   D arise

2 I found the information for the project in the encyclopedia but I couldn't give .... and verse on it.
A chapter   C poem
B unit   D extract

3 Mr Simkins is the big .... in the company as he has just been promoted to the position of Managing Director.
A bread   C cheese
B apple   D meat

4 Speaking about his long battle with illness struck a .... with the audience.
A wire   C string
B rope   D chord

5 Whether you attend the lecture or not is of little .... to me.
A consequence   C care
B result   D circumstance

6 Having seen the film that won the Oscar, I was disappointed as it wasn't all that it's .... up to be.
A creased   C lined
B cracked   D valued

7 I prefer to practice the violin alone in my bedroom as having other members of the family listen really .... my style.
A restricts   C obstructs
B impedes   D cramps

20 *Match the phrases and explain the proverbs.*

a)
0	Too many cooks	a	is worth two in the bush.
1	Actions speak	b	has a silver lining.
2	A stitch in time	c	louder than words.
3	A bird in the hand	d	catches the worm.
4	Too many chiefs	e	but it pours.
5	The early bird	f	spoil the broth.
6	Make hay	g	and not enough Indians.
7	Every cloud	h	crying over spilt milk.
8	It never rains	i	while the sun shines.
9	There's no use	j	saves nine.

0   f   2 .... 4 .... 6 .... 8 ....
1 .... 3 .... 5 .... 7 .... 9 ....

b)
1	Better late	a	before they hatch.
2	Time and tide	b	shouldn't throw stones.
3	Absence makes the heart	c	keeps the doctor away.
4	People in glass-houses	d	on the other side (of the fence).
5	All's well	e	wait for no man.
6	An apple a day	f	than never.
7	Don't count your chickens	g	killed the cat.
8	The grass is always greener	h	grow fonder.
9	A new broom	i	sweeps clean.
10	Curiosity	j	that ends well.

1 .... 3 .... 5 .... 7 .... 9 ....
2 .... 4 .... 6 .... 8 .... 10 ....

2b English in Use

21 *This is a detective's preliminary report concerning a robbery at a museum. Read it and complete the following press release using no more than two words for each blank. The words you need do not occur in the detective's report. The first one has been done for you.*

The museum guard went off duty at 9.30 and the replacement was delayed and did not arrive until 10 pm. When I was called to the scene of the crime there weren't any fingerprints but a wrench had been left behind by the robbers. Only the two most valuable paintings had been taken so I assume the robbers knew about art. At first I suspected James Smith but I was later told he was in jail at the time of the crime. Customers in the café opposite the museum possibly witnessed something and I hope they come forward as soon as possible. Witnesses' identities will be kept confidential.

The museum robbery **(0)** *might/could have* taken place at around 9.45 pm. The robbers **(1)** .... worn gloves as no fingerprints **(2)** .... at the scene of the crime. Evidence **(3)** .... that they had forced entry into the museum with a tool. The robbers were obviously **(4)** .... about art because only paintings of exceptionally high **(5)** .... were stolen. James Smith was an immediate **(6)** .... but he was found to have been in police **(7)** .... at the time of the robbery. The police believe customers in a nearby café **(8)** .... witnessed the **9)** .... get in **(10)** .... with Westford Police Station without **(11)** .... All witness statements will be **(12)** .... in the strictest **(13)** ....

WORD USAGE

22 *Read the text below. Use the word given in capitals at the end of some of the lines to form a word that fits in the space in the same line.*

PRECIOUS METAL

Gold has several qualities that have made it a commodity of **(0)** *exceptional* value throughout history. It is attractive in colour, durable to the point of virtual **(1)** ...., and usually found in nature in a **(2)** .... pure form. The history of gold is **(3)** .... by that of any other metal because of its value in the minds of men from earliest times.

Because it is visually pleasing it was one of the first metals to attract human **(4)** .... Examples of elaborate gold workmanship, many in nearly perfect condition, survive from ancient Egyptian, Minoan, Assyrian, and Etruscan artisans, and gold has continued to be a highly **(5)** .... material out of which jewellery and other **(6)** .... objects are crafted.

The era of gold production that followed the Spanish discovery of the Americas in the 1490s was probably the greatest the world had witnessed to that time. The **(7)** .... of mines by slave labour and the looting of Indian palaces, temples, and graves in Central and South America resulted in a(n) **(8)** .... influx of gold that literally unbalanced the **(9)** .... structure of Europe. Until today the world remains **(10)** .... by the allure of gold.

EXCEPTION
DESTROY
COMPARE
EQUAL

ATTEND

FAVOUR
DECOR

EXPLOIT

PRECEDENT
ECONOMY
CAPTIVE

23 *Choose the correct item.*

0 Ann's injuries took a long time to .... completely and she has been left with several scars.
A cure C heal
B remedy D treat

1 The picture looked very impressive but in fact it had been .... from another.
A imitated C emulated
B copied D faked

2 The meat was so .... that I didn't have to cut any fat off.
A slim C skinny
B lean D slender

3 The archeologist was amazed to see that the body hadn't .... at all.
A mouldered C wasted
B rotted D decomposed

4 I'm used to being woken in the morning by the birds .... outside my window.
   A snarling   C bleating
   B howling   D twittering

5 Car prices in the UK are high in .... to other European countries.
   A reference   C relation
   B affinity   D connection

6 We put some .... of bread out every day for the birds.
   A chips   C cubes
   B crumbs   D slivers

7 The ingredients included .... cheese for the topping.
   A chopped   C minced
   B shredded   D grated

8 This is a good hair dye but the colour gradually .... after a few weeks.
   A fades   C disappears
   B vanishes   D pales

9 It was impossible for me to make a decision, so I .... a coin.
   A tossed   C flung
   B threw   D cast

COLLOCATIONS

24 *Complete the expressions with words from the list below.*

   • flout • devour • imitate • mow • raze
   • concede • squirm • interrupt • heal

0 to *squirm* with   5 to .... the grass
  embarrassment   6 to .... a
1 to .... a wound.   speech
2 to .... defeat   7 to .... the law
3 to .... a meal   8 to .... sb's
4 to .... a city   behaviour

25 *Think of one word only which can be used appropriately in all three sentences.*

0 • One doesn't need to be an expert to *appreciate* the beauty of classical music.
  • He seems confident that houses in this area will *appreciate* in value in the next few years.
  • I'll always *appreciate* your help and support.

1 • The talented writer was renowned for his .... sense of humour.
  • Alan's .... cough kept him up all night.
  • The recent .... spell is worrying to farmers.

2 • She knew she would be expected to .... for her indiscretion.
  • They decided to .... a visit to the bank manager to arrange an overdraft.
  • The trick, when bargaining, is not to .... a higher price than is necessary.

3 • Let me give you a .... of advice about how to make a favourable impression at the interview.
  • By nightfall, there was still no .... of the missing hikers.
  • Dan knew Steven could not be trusted to keep his ....

4 • After she had .... as an MP for thirty years, she resigned to live a quiet life in the country.
  • The player .... the ball over the volleyball net.
  • We were .... fresh cucumber sandwiches and lemonade by the hostess.

5 • The most memorable .... we visited was the Piazza Navona.
  • I am the only one in my family whose .... is normal.
  • When the road sign came in ...., I realised I only had a few kilometres of my journey to go.

6 • My grandmother's face is lined with .... and the hardships she has had to endure.
  • It's been an .... since we last saw each other.
  • Some people believe that the .... of chivalry has come and gone.

7 • Joanne's .... in the art competition won first prize.
  • He gained .... to the football match by climbing over the wall of the stadium.
  • The last .... in the balance sheet was dated 11th September.

8 • Where once had stood a busy shopping centre was now only an empty ....
  • Technology has made rapid progress in a very short .... of time.
  • Aunt Vera's living room is so crowded with furniture that there is no .... to move.

PREPARING FOR PART 5

SUMMARY WRITING II Paraphrasing and Linking Information

26 a) *Read the following passages and then read the following summary question.*

In the 1960s television hit *Route 66* when two young men in a Corvette set out looking for adventure. Who better than another '60s icon, Peter Fonda, who played Captain America in the counterculture classic *Easy Rider*, to narrate and host *Route 66: Main Street America*?

This vivid history of America's fabled highway traces its transformation from a twisting two-lane road into a 2,400-mile highway that crosses eight states and three time zones. **(A) Route 66 opened in 1926 to facilitate faster trade (B) and provide drivers with a safe, paved road from Chicago to Los Angeles.** Nowadays, however, the route has been eclipsed by new superhighways like I-40. Along the abandoned sections of the old Route 66, nothing remains but ghost towns and tumbleweed.

Through archival film and the collections of Dust Bowl survivors, this film revisits a time when Route 66 was the road of dreams. **(C) In the 1930s, a decade which saw the largest migration in US history, Americans suffering from a devastating drought in the Great Plains gave Route 66 a new function. They packed their meagre belongings and drove west along the highway to the promised land: California.**

The Nipissing Road was one of a network of roadways devised by the government in 1850 to facilitate the settling of land between the Ottawa River and Georgian Bay. **(D) Flourishing lumber companies made extensive use of the road as a means to access the huge areas of virgin forest in the vicinity, (E) although the government had originally planned it to assist the new settlers.**

By 1877, the Nipissing Road was also open between Lake Rosseau and Lake Nipissing. The stage coach, which arrived three times a week, brought settlers, who built the village of Nipissing. However, the boom in the town was short-lived, as the greedy lumber companies quickly decimated the surrounding forests. The fertile prairies to the west called out to the settlers and, en masse, they heeded the call and set out for greener pastures.

Behind them they left farms and villages which were quickly overrun by bush and vegetation. Of the many original settlements in the region, only four have survived.

In a paragraph of between 50 and 70 words, summarise the various purposes and functions performed by Route 66 and Nipissing Road.

b) *Read the summary below.*

(0) Route 66 supplied a safe way to travel over a huge distance, *in addition to* (1) providing a fast trade route. *Moreover,* (2) it was used by the people of the Great Plains to migrate to California after the 1930s drought. (3) The Nipissing Road, *on the other hand,* was built to help settlers move to certain areas, *but* (4) was also used by lumber companies who took advantage of the forests around it.

c) *Match the numbered items of the summary with the **bold** parts they paraphrase. Item 0 has been done for you.*

0 *B*   1 ....   2 ....   3 ....   4 ....

d) *Which of the words in italics perform each of the following functions?*

Introduce an idea which contrasts with the previous one?   *but*
Introduce a sentence which adds a point?   ....
Add a point to a sentence?   ....
Indicate that we begin to discuss the second of two subjects?

27 *Paraphrase and link the sentences in bold in the following paired passages to answer each question.*

(1) Shirley Bassey was born on January 8, 1937, in Cardiff's Tiger Bay. She was the youngest of seven children. Shirley established herself as a singer in cabaret which soon led to a recording contract with Phillips. **She scored a Top Ten hit with *The Banana Boat Song*** in 1957, and soon found transatlantic fame with her first Bond theme, *Goldfinger* (although it failed to make the UK top 20).

(2) Ella Fitzgerald was born in Newport News, Virginia, on April 25, 1918. She broke into the music business by winning a 1934 talent show at Harlem's Apollo driving band Theatre, then joined Chick Webb's driving band, becoming his featured vocalist at the Savoy Ballroom. **In 1938 she had her first big hit, a novelty tune based on a nursery rhyme, *A Tisket A Tasket***, followed by *Undecided* in 1939. When Webb died that year, Fitzgerald led the band until 1942, then launched herself as a solo artist.

(3) Repetitive strain injury can create microtrauma in joints and the adjacent soft tissue, and can lead to osteoarthritis in later years. **If your job involves squatting, heavy physical labour or occupational knee bending, or if you have a history of regular sports participation, look out for symptoms and do not ignore them.** Even long hours at the computer can strain and perhaps prematurely age your hands. **Pause for at least five minutes every half hour and use ergonomic keyboards with wrist supports.**

(4) Arthritis affects people differently, and the treatment for each patient varies. Most therapies include a combination of medication to control pain and reduce inflammation, exercise to maintain joint movement and strengthen muscles, and periods of relaxation. Your doctor can recommend a treatment programme that fits your individual needs. **Until a cure is found, eating healthy food, taking regular exercise and avoiding tobacco is the best way to cope with the disease.**

1 *What were the first big hits of each of the singers discussed in the passage?*

....
....
....
....
....
....

2 *What advice for preventing and treating arthritis is given in the two passages above?*

....
....
....
....
....
....

(5) According to mythology, at one point the Celtic god Nuada was the King of the Tuata. **However, during the First Battle of Magh (which was fought by the Tuata and their rivals, the Fir Bolg), Nuada's arm was severed from his body.** This wound immediately disqualified the god from the rank of king, and he would have had to abdicate if it had not been for the clever god Dian Cecht. He made a silver arm to replace the one that Nuada had lost, and **it was at this time** that the god received the title "Nuada Argetlam", or "Nuada of the Silver Arm".

(6) Jupiter was the Roman sky god, the equivalent of the Greek god Zeus. The cult of the Jupiter Optimus Maximus ("the best and greatest") began under the Etruscan kings, who were expelled from Rome around 507 BC. At first, Jupiter was associated with the elements, especially storms, and lightning, but he later **became the protector of the Roman people and was their powerful ally in war, allegedly assisting the Roman warriors to defeat many enemies.**

3 *What do the two passages tell us about each god's contribution to war?*

....
....
....

2c Practice Test Two

Paper 3 Use of English

PART 1

Read the text below and think of the word which best fits each space.

TIME TO RELAX? HOW?

One of **(0)** *the* greatest problems with holidays, **(1)** .... from the usual travel complications and accommodation difficulties, **(2)** .... the expectations people have of **(3)** .... When we go on holiday we expect to leave all the stresses and strains of our daily lives **(4)** .... us. We imagine we will be able to escape to **(5)** .... a degree that we even tend to believe, consciously or not, that we can change our own personalities and become completely different people. The average business-person, tense, preoccupied, short-tempered, **(6)** .... to relax, envisages herself/himself **(7)** .... , from the moment of locking the office door, a radically different **(8)** .... of person: carefree, good-humoured, ready to relax and enjoy whatever adventures present **(9)** .... In practice, we take ourselves with us **(10)** .... we go, and the personality that is shaped **(11)** .... years of stress and tension is almost impossible to shake off **(12)** .... a moment's notice. It is no wonder so many holidays are a disappointment, no **(13)** .... how smoothly they go or how lovely the weather is. In fact, the frequent problems that crop **(14)** .... during the average holiday are probably a welcome distraction **(15)** .... the nagging feeling that we are not enjoying ourselves as much as we should.

PART 2

Read the text below. Use the word given in capitals at the end of some of the lines to form a word that fits in the space in the same line.

FLAMENCO DANCE

The essence of flamenco is song, often accompanied by the guitar and improvised dance. Music and dance can be placed into specific groups. These **(0)** *categorisations/categories* are usually located across a continuum with subjects dealing with the profound to those that are light-hearted. **(16)** ...., the themes of death, anguish and despair, in contrast to love, gaiety and the countryside are **(17)** .... In flamenco dance, the men's steps are intricate, with toe and heel clicking. Footwork in women's dancing is of less importance, with the **(18)** .... use of hands and body taking **(19)** .... In the dance, the arm, hand and foot movements closely resemble those of classical Hindu dance. Essential to traditional flamenco is the performer's interpretation of the dance **(20)** .... by the emotion of the music. Performances are often accompanied by rapid hand clapping, finger snapping and **(21)** .... shouts. The dancers themselves frequently employ finger snapping in complex rhythms including the use of castanets. This dance form was **(22)** .... in the 19th century, when Romany people first began to perform in cafés. In this environment, **(23)** .... from the traditional form occurred. Unfortunately, the pressures of the **(24)** .... stage meant that rehearsed routines replaced the **(25)** .... of the original flamenco performances.

	CATEGORY
	TYPE
	DRAMA
	GRACE
	PRECEDE
	HINDER
	COURAGE
	PROFESSION
	DEPART
	COMMERCE
	SPONTANEOUS

PART 3

Think of one word only which can be used appropriately in all three sentences.

0 • One doesn't need to be an expert to *appreciate* the beauty of classical music.
   • He seems confident that houses in this area will *appreciate* in value in the next few years.
   • I'll always *appreciate* your help and support.

26 • We saw the animal .... back as the hunter approached.
   • You should .... the curtains at dusk to stop mosquitoes coming into the house.
   • He waited for the taxi to .... up to the pavement before attracting the driver's attention.

27 • He .... the waiters, even though the service was appalling.
   • The rubbish from the dustcart was .... into the landfill.
   • The glass .... over and smashed on the floor.

28 • She began to .... as Tom related the embarrassing incident.
   • In pursuit of a new image, she decided to .... her hair.
   • .... your narrative with more adjectives which will hold the reader's attention.

29 • Her .... in the conspiracy was comparatively minor.
   • Jeanette Duffy was overjoyed to hear that she had got the .... of Juliet.
   • Forensic examination revealed that a vital .... of the plane was missing.

30 • We had to hire an extra .... to help us with the sheepshearing this year.
   • The loose, flowing script left me in no doubt as to whose .... had penned the letter.
   • It was pointless denying it; they knew I'd had a .... in their downfall.

31 • In the 18th century, the River Thames was a stinking trough of .... water.
   • He got fired on account of his persistent use of .... language.
   • Since he was evidently already in a .... temper, I avoided provoking him further.

PART 4

Complete the second sentence so that it has a similar meaning to the first sentence, using the word given. Do not change the word given. You must use between three and eight words, including the word given.

0 Nobody spoke when the teacher asked who was to blame.
   remained
   Everyone *remained silent when the teacher asked who the culprit was.*

32 Ian is sure he was right to turn down the job.
   regrets
   Ian ....
   .... the job.

33 They have decided to go to Crete for the summer.
   intention
   It ....
   .... for the summer.

34 The meeting was held in the Town Hall.
   took
   The ....
   .... Town Hall.

35 Mum says it was stupid of me to give up French.
   idiot
   Mum says ....
   .... French.

36 I only came to see you.
   sole
   My ....
   .... you.

37 Is it likely that you will move before July?
   chances
   What ....
   .... July?

38 She was pleased that he didn't get the job.
   help
   She ....
   .... he didn't get the job.

39 Not many people went to the last match of the season.
   turnout
   There ....
   .... the last match of the season.

PART 5

*For questions **40-44** read the following texts. For questions **40 - 43** answer with a word or short phrase. You do not need to write complete sentences. For question **44**, write a summary according to the instructions given.*

Tropical seas are renowned for their variety of colour and fascinating marine life. Coral reefs have a unique place in this aquatic world and indeed their surrounding environment. Despite its "plant like" appearance, coral is actually a marine animal of the invertebrate species having no spinal columns, like jellyfish. Coral reefs are sensitive ecosystems, which are under threat from human and natural elements alike. Reefs have formed over millions of years, and their scientific study teaches us many things about the complex changes that our environment has undergone through the ages. Coral reefs are indeed an

line 9 —— invaluable living record of our natural history, a snapshot in time.

The body of the coral consists of a polyp - a hollow, cylindrical structure which attaches its lower end to a surface. The free end is a mouth which gathers food and acts as a "stinger" paralysing unsuspecting prey. The continual growth of new buds, or developing polyps, cause the old ones underneath to die. The skeletons remain, however, creating a colony of corals, later developing into a reef. It is this fragile structure which forms an essential natural filter which removes detritus impurities, providing a clean habitat for marine plants and animals.

Reefs grow faster in clear water and in the warm temperatures of tropical oceans are generally found at depths less than 46 metres, where sunlight penetrates, a necessary condition for corals to thrive and grow. Waves also carry food, nutrients and oxygen to the reef. Shallow, warm, tropical waters with strong wave action are ideal conditions for these unique organisms to flourish.

40 How are coral reefs a 'snapshot in time'? (line 9)

....

....

41 What key role does an old 'polyp' have?

....

....

line 3 —— Have you ever dreamt of going to a tropical island, lounging on the warm sand, feasting your eyes on an outburst of orangey-pink corals while snorkelling in the sea? Just below the rush of foaming waves lies a hubbub of marine life. Coral reefs are one of nature's masterpieces.

Apart from their unsurpassed beauty, reefs are essential to people in many ways. Corals remove and recycle carbon dioxide, hindering gas emissions causing global warming. Reefs also protect land and coastal dwellers from harsh oceans and floods as well as providing a rich food source for fisheries. Tropical reefs are also the favourite attraction for thousands of tourists flocking to view this living sea garden, injecting a welcome income to local economies.

Sadly, they are now under threat of extinction due to natural disasters and human intervention. One major problem is ocean pollution caused by oil slicks and untreated sewage. Pollutants are let out into the water and poison corals. Deforestation, absurd as it may seem, is also detrimental to coral reefs. Topsoil from cleared tropical forests is washed down rivers into the coast and settles on reefs, smothering the corals and blocking out the sunlight crucial for reefs to live. Extensive fishing and the use of dynamite have destroyed many reefs, while the poaching of coral items for the souvenir and jewellery trade continues at a devastating rate. Urgent measures need to be taken at a global level so that corals continue to decorate tropical coasts for future generations.

42 Explain the phrase "a hubbub of marine life" (line 3).

....

....

43 How does deforestation affect coral reefs?

....

....

44 In a paragraph of between 50 and 70 words, summarise the reasons given in the texts for the importance of coral reefs to people and the environment.

....

....

....

....

....

....

....

....

TENSES OF THE INFINITIVE

Active Voice			Passive Voice	
	Regular Verb	Irregular Verb	Regular Verb	Irregular Verb
Present Present Con. Perfect Perfect Con.	(to) cook (to) be cooking (to) have cooked (to) have been cooking	(to) write (to) be writing (to) have written (to) have been writing	(to) be cooked – – – (to) have been cooked – – –	(to) be written – – – (to) have been written – – –

The full infinitive is used

- after certain verbs
  advise, afford, agree, allow sb, appear, be allowed, compel, decide, encourage, expect, hope, intend, invite, manage, pretend, proceed, promise, refuse, remind, seem, tell, tend, etc
  *He **advised** me **to take** a rest.*

- after certain adjectives
  amazed, angry, delighted, difficult, disgusted, easy, first, glad, happy, last, likely, obliged, sad, sorry, supposed, surprised, unable, etc
  *I was **glad to hear** he had been promoted to manager.*

- with impersonal construction + adjective
  *It was **nice of** him **to send** you roses.*

- with only and just (unsatisfactory result)
  *He phoned **only to say** that he wouldn't be coming.*

- in expressions such as: to tell you the truth, to cut a long story short, to be honest/fair, etc
  To tell you the truth, I haven't seen him since Monday.

- after certain nouns (pleasure, nuisance, nightmare, etc)
  *It's a **pleasure to see** you.*

- after question words (who, where, what, etc)
  *I don't know **what to do**.*

- with too and enough
  *She's **too** old **to drive** a car. (negative)*
  *He's old **enough to drive** a car. (positive)*

The bare infinitive is used

- with modals (can, could, may, might, shall, should, must, will, would)
  *He **can go** if he wants to.*

- with need, dare (as auxiliary verbs)
  *You **needn't work** today.*
  *I **daren't talk** to him.*

Notes

a dare expressing courage or lack of courage can be followed by bare or full infinitive
  *I **don't dare (to) tell** her the truth.*
  *He **dared (to) attempt** it again.*

b dare expressing threats, warning, anger, etc is followed by bare infinitive
  *Don't you **dare lie** to me again!*
  *How **dare** you **speak** to me like that!*

c dare expressing challenge is followed by full infinitive
  *I **dare** you **to climb** up that tree.*

- with had better/would rather/would sooner
  *You'd **better go** to bed.*

- with make (= force), let (= allow), see, hear, smell, feel, watch, notice (in active voice)
  *He **let** me **watch** TV.*

Note

Notice, make, see, hear, tell, watch in passive voice are followed by full infinitive.
  *The baby was **made to eat** all his soup.*

- after why (not) to make suggestions
  *Why **not meet** again some day?*
  (Why don't we meet...)

Notes
- too + adj/adverb + full infinitive (negative)
  adj/adverb + enough + full infinitive (negative)
  enough + noun + full infinitive (positive)
  so + adjective + as + full infinitive
- When the subject of the verb is not the same as the subject of the infinitive we indicate it by using object forms.

He is **too young to get** married.
He isn't **old enough to get** married.
He's got **enough money to get** married.
She was **so gullible as to believe** his story.

I would like **him/John** to come.

INFINITIVE AND PRESENT PARTICIPLE WITH VERBS OF PERCEPTION AND OTHER PHRASES

| see hear listen watch | **+ bare infinitive** (complete action) | I **saw** her **lock** the car and **put** the key in her bag. |
| | **+ present participle** (incomplete action/action in progress) | I **saw** her **walking** down the street. |

go, come (when used to refer to physical activities)		He **went skiing** last winter.
spend/waste time	**+ present participle**	He **spent** an hour **fixing** the tap.
be busy		He **was busy cleaning** the car.

CONVERSATIONAL GRAMMAR

1 Choose the correct item.

0 "I haven't heard from Hugo recently. Is he around?"
"Yes, but he's thinking of going .... in the French Alps soon."
A to trek   C to be trekking
B trekking ⓑ   D trek

1 She didn't know who .... to for help.
A turning   C having turned
B to have turned   D to turn

2 "Where's Anne?"
"She's busy .... the washing up."
A doing   C have done
B be doing   D to do

3 "The Government appear to have made up their minds at last."
"It's about time! They've spent months .... this issue."
A debating   C having debated
B to debate   D have been debating

4 "I don't think he will admit to his fault."
"I agree. It takes courage .... the truth."
A to reveal   C revealing
B reveal   D to be revealing

5 No matter what Jo said she couldn't make him .... her point.
A to see   C to be seen
B see   D have seen

6 "So, whose fault was it? Jane's or Brian's?"
"........ fair, they were both partly to blame."
A Being   C To be
B To have been   D Having been

7 I can't believe Peter was .... naive as to trust her.
A so   C as
B too   D enough

8 Sarah is honest and hard-working but she tends .... a little stubborn at times.
A be   C being
B to be   D to have been

9 "She was great, wasn't she?"
"Absolutely. I can't recall the last time I heard her .... such a an inspiring speech."
A deliver   C to be delivering
B to deliver   D has been delivering

TENSES OF THE –ING FORM

	Active Voice	Passive Voice
Present	cutting	being cut
Perfect	having cut	having been cut

The -ing form is used after	
prepositions	
detest, dislike, enjoy, fancy, hate, like, loathe, love, prefer, resent (*hate, like, love, prefer* when used in the conditional are followed by full infinitive)	
begin, cease, commence, finish, start, stop (these verbs, except *stop* and *finish*, can also be followed by an infinitive with no difference in meaning)	+ -ing form
it's no use/good, it's (not) worth, there's no point (in), feel like, can't stand, can't help, be/get used to, be/get accustomed to, have difficulty (in), in favour of	
admit, anticipate, appreciate, avoid, consider, defer, delay, deny, endure, entail, escape (= avoid), envisage, evade, forgive, imagine, incur, involve, keep (= continue), look forward to, mention, mind, miss, pardon, postpone, practise, prevent, recall, recollect, report, risk, save, shirk, suggest, understand, etc	

Note
When the subject of the verb is different from the subject of the -ing form we indicate it by using object forms or possessives (more formal).
*I hate **him/his/Jerry's** interrupting me.*

VERBS TAKING INFINITIVE OR –ING FORM WITHOUT A CHANGE IN MEANING

- begin, start, continue, cease, commence, omit
  *He **continued listening** to the radio.*
  *He **continued to listen** to the radio.*
  Note
  The **-ing** form is not used after the continuous form of these verbs.

- advise, allow, permit, recommend, intend followed by an object take a **full infinitive** whereas they take an **-ing** form when not followed by an object (**intend** can also take a gerund whether the object is mentioned or not)
  *He **allowed us to eat** in the classroom.*
  *He **allowed eating** in the classroom.*
  *He **recommended us to take** plenty of exercise.*
  *He **recommended (our) taking** plenty of exercise.*

- sth needs/requires/wants can be followed by an -ing form or by **a passive infinitive**
  *The car **needs servicing/to be serviced**.*

2 *Put the verbs in brackets into -ing form or the correct form of infinitive.*

0 The police allowed him *to leave* **(leave)** after he had made a statement.

1 She advised us .... **(take)** the short cut through the woods to save time.

2 The doctor recommended .... **(follow)** a diet of fresh fruit and vegetables.

3 There's no use .... **(postpone)** your visit; you'll have to go sooner or later.

4 I don't mind .... **(help)** you with your homework.

5 This room needs .... **(tidy)** before we can use it.

6 He omitted .... **(tell)** us about the meeting.

7 Jane started .... **(have)** bad dreams after being in the car accident.

VERBS TAKING INFINITIVE OR –ING FORM WITH A CHANGE IN MEANING

- **forget + to-infinitive** = not remember to do sth when you intend to
  I forgot to visit the museum.
  forget + -ing form = not to recall
  I'll never forget visiting that museum.

- **go on + to-infinitive** = stop one action and start another
  They first discussed the items on the agenda and then went on to discuss the budget.
  go on + -ing form = continue
  He went on playing the piano in spite of the neighbour's complaints.

- **like + to-infinitive** = find sth good to do
  I like to go to the market very early in the morning so that I can select the best vegetables.
  like + -ing form = enjoy
  I like swimming; it's my favourite pastime.
  would like to + infinitive = want to
  I would like to meet your friend; he sounds interesting.

- **mean + to-infinitive** = intend to
  She means to discuss the matter with the headmaster.
  mean + -ing form = involve, entail
  It means changing the original plans.

- **propose + to-infinitive** = intend
  I propose to build three more classrooms.
  propose + -ing form = suggest
  I propose trying that new Chinese restaurant.

- **regret + to-infinitive** = be sorry to have to do sth
  I regret to inform you that your application has been rejected.
  regret + -ing form = feel sorry about a past action
  I regret buying this car because it is always breaking down.

- **remember + to-infinitive** = not forget to do sth when you intend to.
  Remember to lock the door before you leave the house.
  remember + -ing form = recall
  She remembers locking the door before leaving the house.

- **try + to-infinitive** = attempt
  We tried to persuade him not to go, but he wouldn't listen.
  try + -ing form = do as an experiment
  They tried advertising their business in the local newspaper.

- **stop + to-infinitive** = stop sth temporarily, in order to do sth else
  She stopped to talk to her neighbour as she was taking her dog for a walk.
  stop + -ing form = finish, stop permanently
  They stopped talking when the teacher came into the class.

- **(be) understood + to-infinitive** = give the impression
  He is understood to agree that negotiations are necessary.
  understand + -ing form = to understand sb else's feelings or actions
  I can understand his feeling angry about their decision.

- **want + to-infinitive** = wish
  I want to extend my visa.
  want + -ing form = need sth done
  The battery's flat; it wants recharging.

- **dread + to-infinitive** = be afraid (specific)
  I dread to think how much he may suffer.
  dread + -ing form = to fear greatly (general)
  I dread going to the doctor.

3a Grammar: Infinitive –ing Form

- **hate + to-infinitive** = hate what one is about to do
  I hate to interrupt you but I need some help.
  hate + -ing form = feel sorry for what one is doing
  I hate causing you inconvenience.

- **be sorry + to-infinitive** = regret sth/feel regret
  I am sorry to hear of his illness.
  be sorry for + -ing form = apologise
  I am sorry for shouting at you.

- **be afraid to + to-infinitive** = the subject is too frightened to do sth
  She was afraid to drive the car.
  be afraid of + -ing form = the subject fears that the action expressed by the gerund may happen
  She didn't want to drive the car; she was afraid of causing an accident.

- **be ashamed to + infinitive** (the infinitive refers to a subsequent action)
  She was ashamed to admit that she had lied.
  be ashamed of + -ing form (the gerund refers to a present or previous action)
  She's ashamed of lying, and swears she'll never do it again.

- **would prefer + to-infinitive** (specific action)
  I would prefer to be left alone just now.
  prefer + -ing form (general)
  I prefer swimming to running.
  prefer + to-infinitive (general)
  He prefers to study at night.

- **can't/couldn't bear + infinitive** (specific)
  I can't bear to tell him the bad news.
  can't/couldn't bear + -ing form (general)
  I can't bear telling people bad news.

CONVERSATIONAL GRAMMAR

3 *Choose the correct item.*

1 His colleagues secretly tried .... his advancement in the company.
   A blocking   C block
   B to block   D to be blocking

2 I propose we .... the speeches until the end of the event.
   A leaving   C leave
   B to leave   D be leaving

3 Would you rather .... at home or regular hours in an office?
   A to work   C worked
   B work   D working

4 "Are you coming to the wedding?"
   "Yes but I would prefer not .... to the reception afterwards."
   A going   C having gone
   B to go   D to have gone

5 "Everything I do fails; I'm a walking disaster."
   "I suggest you .... complaining and count your blessings."
   A stopping   C to have stopped
   B stop   D to stop

6 "Have you made your decision yet?"
   "I'd prefer .... right now, if you don't mind."
   A not answer   C not to answer
   B not answering   D to not answer

7 "I thought you liked a challenge!"
   "Not the kind that involves .... off a bridge with a rubber band round my ankles!"
   A jumping   C to jump
   B jump   D to jumping

8 "Has Paul been told yet?"
   "Not yet. I dread his .... out!"
   A to find   C finding
   B find   D to be finding

9 "I refuse to write the report."
   "How dare you .... the boss's instructions!"
   A to defy   C to be defying
   B defying   D defy

10 "Is there something wrong?"
   "Yes, but I'm afraid .... you because you'll be angry."
   A of telling   C to tell
   B telling   D tell

4 *Put the verbs in brackets into the **-ing form** or the correct form of the **infinitive**.*

1 The architect resented .... **(modify)** the design at such a late date.
2 If you want to learn to ride, you must first try .... **(maintain)** control of the horse.
3 She's certain to want to come to the party but I very much doubt she'll wish .... **(participate)** in the dancing.
4 I suggest you .... **(consult)** a specialist for a second opinion before having the operation.
5 They began .... **(argue)** at breakfast and are still quarrelling now.
6 I don't support .... **(use)** live animals for experiments under any circumstances.
7 Daniel intends .... **(take)** a gap year between school and university and wants to travel around Europe.
8 It was strange that the file went missing, because he distinctly remembered .... **(put)** it in the cabinet before he left.
9 I hate .... **(say)** this, but I think you've overstepped the mark this time.
10 I vaguely recall .... **(meet)** him in 1999 at a teaching seminar.
11 The flowers need .... **(arrange)** and the cake needs to be baked.
12 Concerning my eldest son, I wouldn't even venture a guess as to what he is planning .... **(do)**.

5 *Put the verbs in brackets into the **-ing form** or the correct form of the **infinitive**.*

Like many people, I dislike **(0)** *having* **(have)** someone **(1)** .... **(look)** over my shoulder while **(2)** .... **(read)** my newspaper on the bus. I find it difficult **(3)** .... **(prevent)** myself from **(4)** .... **(say)** something sarcastic to the onlooker as surely, **(5)** .... **(peruse)** one's newspaper is a private affair. To my mind, **(6)** .... **(invade)** a reader's space in this way is rather like **(7)** .... **(invite)** oneself **(8)** .... **(join)** a private conversation. We seldom seem **(9)** .... **(tolerate)** rudeness of this kind in ordinary circumstances. I consider my precious few minutes with a newspaper exactly that – mine!

6 *Put the verbs in brackets into the **-ing form** or the correct form of the **infinitive**.*

It is difficult **(0)** *to understand* **(understand)** why millions of cinema–goers queue for hours **(1)** .... **(obtain)** tickets to see the latest "blockbuster", only **(2)** .... **(discover)** that the film is a bitter disappointment. **(3)** .... **(pay)** scant regard to reliable reviews, they appear **(4)** .... **(prefer)** **(5)** .... **(place)** their trust in extravagant claims made by the film promoters. These are the marketers whose sole purpose is **(6)** .... **(boost)** ticket sales, thereby **(7)** .... **(line)** the pockets of the film makers and **(8)** .... **(ensure)** a tidy profit, **(9)** .... **(enable)** them **(10)** .... **(produce)** yet another film of equally poor quality. So, if you're anxious **(11)** .... **(know)** whether you're likely **(12)** .... **(get)** value for money, and if the last film you saw was a real let-down, try **(13)** .... **(read)** what the critics say, first.

7 *Put the verbs in brackets into the **-ing form** or the correct form of the **infinitive**.*

You know that dreadful feeling: **(0)** *sleeping* **(sleep)** through the alarm clock and then **(1)** .... **(worry)** that you'll be too late **(2)** .... **(meet)** your friend for coffee or **(3)** .... **(get)** to work on time. Few people have reason **(4)** .... **(stop)** and wonder how many others might also be **(5)** .... **(hurry)** to various destinations at that moment **(6)** .... **(know)** they will probably miss their appointments. Although you might not be a particularly punctual person, you may still be tempted **(7)** .... **(ask)**, why British social lives are so often ruled by the clock. Perhaps we would all benefit from **(8)** .... **(slow)** down and **(9)** .... **(follow)** the examples of southern Europeans. In Greece for example, punctuality frequently obeys the laws of "rubber time", **(10)** .... **(allow)** for flexibility and the reassuring thought that nobody worries too much if you arrive a little later than expected.

STRUCTURAL CONVERSION ◄

1 *Driving fast is dangerous.*
   It is dangerous to drive fast.
2 *She is too young to get married.*
   She isn't old enough to get married.
3 *He couldn't help noticing that she was upset.*
   It didn't escape his attention that she was upset.
4 *The prospect of a short holiday fills me with pleasure.*
   I look forward to (having) a short holiday.
5 *It's quite unnecessary to answer his letter.*
   Answering his letter is quite unnecessary/pointless.
   There's no point (in) answering his letter.
   It's no use answering his letter.
6 *It was difficult for her to believe that she had won.*
   She had difficulty (in) believing that she had won.
   She could hardly believe that she had won.
   She found it difficult to believe that she had won.
7 *Would you be so kind as to pass the salad?*
   Do/Would you mind passing the salad?
   Could you pass the salad, please?
8 *It took me an hour to do my hair.*
   I took an hour to do my hair.

Doing my hair took (me) an hour.
I spent an hour doing/on my hair.
9 *Do you intend to go/going to her party, tomorrow?*
   Will you be going to her party tomorrow?
   Are you thinking of going to her party tomorrow?
10 *It's out of the question to expect me to apologise.*
   I have no intention of apologising.
   Fancy even suggesting that I apologise!
   I don't mean/intend to apologise.
   I most certainly won't apologise.
11 *Mary objects to lying.*
   Lying is something that Mary objects to/hates/loathes.
12 *I'm not in the habit of waking up early.*
   I'm not used to waking up early.
13 *He made me open my suitcase.*
   I was made to open my suitcase.
14 *I can't remember reading this novel.*
   I have no recollection of reading this novel.
15 *It's a waste of time trying to make yourself understood.*
   It's not worth trying to make yourself understood.

8 *Complete the second sentence so that it has a similar meaning to the first sentence, using the word given. Do not change the word given. You must use between three and eight words, including the word given.*

1 I refuse to pay the bill.
   intention
   I have ....
   .... the bill.

2 He is too irresponsible to run the department.
   charge
   He is not ....
   .... of the department.

3 Sheila is worried about the proposed changes at work.
   prospect
   The ....
   .... worry.

4 Would you please keep your mobile phone switched off during the flight.
   mind
   Would you ....
   .... the plane is airborne.

5 We waited on the bus for an hour before the engine was fixed.
   took
   They ....
   .... while we waited on the bus.

6 Ian was not used to doing such strenuous training.
   habit
   Ian was ....
   .... strenuously.

7 You should always wear a seatbelt.
   unwise
   It is ....
   .... a seatbelt.

8 I apologise but I completely forgot about our appointment.
   confess
   I must ....
   .... my mind.

9 There's a possibility that you may be able to get a grant.
   eligible
   We are pleased ....
   .... a grant.

10 At least make an attempt at the exercise. It might not be as difficult as you think it is.
   try
   If you ....
   .... it easier than you think.

11 Perhaps a high-fibre diet will do you good.
   benefit
   You ....
   .... high-fibre diet.

12 He continued his speech, even though they all appeared disinterested.
   on
   He ....
   .... that they all appeared disinterested.

13 Sonia's preference is for a nine-to-five job.
   rather
   Sonia ....
   .... from nine to five.

14 I will probably have to get my car serviced soon.
   need
   My car ....
   .... soon.

15 It is believed that the two rival companies have agreed to the merger.
   through
   The two rival companies ....
   .... the merger.

16 Nadia said nothing because she was afraid of offending them.
   fear
   Nadia remained silent ....
   .... offence.

17 It was very nice of you to let us know about the change in venue.
   appreciate
   We ....
   .... change.

18 He didn't have a clue what it would be like to live in the country.
   envisage
   He ....
   .... out of town.

19 If you invest all your savings in this scheme you may lose them.
   risk
   You run ....
   .... if you invest them in this scheme.

20 I don't really want to go to the reception.
   feel
   I ....
   .... to the reception.

21 I bet you wouldn't swim that far out!
   dare
   I don't ....
   .... that far out!

22 When he locked the door, the telephone rang.
   just
   He ....
   .... the telephone ringing.

23 Your sending her flowers in hospital was a thoughtful gesture.
   kind
   It ....
   .... in hospital!

24 I couldn't help noticing how friendly he's been towards you recently.
   not
   His ....
   .... my notice.

25 I am delighted to make your acquaintance.
   pleasure
   It is ....
   .... you.

CONVERSATIONAL GRAMMAR

9 *Choose the correct item.*

1 "How much time do I have to make my choice?"
   "I suggest you .... a quick decision."
   A having made   C made
   B to make   D make

2 "I'm sure you miss the island, having lived there for so long."
   "Yes, I often imagine .... it again."
   A seeing   C having seen
   B to see   D to be seeing

3 "So, what did the President have to say?"
   "He mentioned pension reform and went on .... that he would reduce unemployment figures."
   A adding   C to be adding
   B add   D to add

4 "Did you enjoy your picnic?"
   "Yes, we had a great time and on the way home we stopped .... the sunset."
   A to admire   C to have admired
   B admiring   D admire

10 *Read the text below and think of the word which best fits each space.*

FOREVER ON THE PHONE

A hundred years ago, the principal means **(0)** *of* communication for individuals and for businesses was **(1)** .... letter and telegram, but nowadays telephones are used constantly in private houses, offices and factories. This is certainly the **(2)** .... widespread and convenient way for people to communicate with one another.

With the telephone, business deals can be arranged and completed rapidly. In **(3)** ...., financial centres and stock exchanges, **(4)** .... constant use of the telephone system, can be assured **(5)** .... getting the very latest, up-to-the-minute information about the **(6)** .... changing currency and share values. This type of information is essential **(7)** .... economic stability worldwide.

The telephone network also provides a direct line into the homes of friends and relatives. For old and infirm people, and for those lonely people living on their **(8)** ...., the telephone is a friend. At **(9)** ...., families are often scattered, not only throughout the country but also throughout the world. **(10)** .... a few minutes' conversation with a loved one, who may be thousands of miles away, is a source of great comfort **(11)** .... us.

Of course, very often the telephone can be a nuisance. Some will say that it intrudes too **(12)** .... on people's privacy by ringing at the **(13)** .... inconvenient times.

On the **(14)** ...., though, the changes brought about by the introduction of the telephone have been **(15)** .... great benefit to everyone. The telephone has helped to bring people closer in a difficult world and has made life, for many, much easier and much more enjoyable.

PHRASAL VERBS 1

11 *Look at Appendix 1 and fill in one of the prepositions below, then give a synonym for each phrasal verb.*

- up • off • on • about • in • round
- out • over • through

0 The rioting was brought *about* by a huge increase in the price of bread.

1 Let's all chip .... and buy her a gift.

2 He brought .... the business deal through sheer persistence.

3 His new song caught .... right away and entered the top ten the week after its release.

4 Don't forget to bring .... the matter of the new park at the council meeting.

5 CBN has just brought .... a new CD of a collection of songs from the sixties.

6 Tradition has been carried .... into our time in many ways.

7 He was brought .... by his grandmother as he had been orphaned at an early age.

8 We brought the unconscious woman .... with smelling salts.

9 The cold weather has brought .... his cough again.

10 That law was brought .... to protect tenants from being exploited by their landlords.

11 The young actress carried .... the performance without a hitch.

12 Carry .... with your work, please. There's no time to waste.

13 The soldier carried .... his orders, doing exactly what he had been told to do.

14 Negotiations between the Union and the management have been carrying .... for months without a result.

15 He will carry his plan .... despite all your objections.

16 She is always carrying .... like a lunatic when she loses something.

17 She was walking too quickly for me to catch .... with her.

What's the difference between **charge to** and **charge with**?

....
....
....
....
....
....

PHRASAL VERBS 2

12 Match the phrasal verbs in bold with one of the definitions given.

0	I'll **call at** the travel agency to collect our tickets.	**a** to cancel	0	f
1	She **was cleared of** the charges of negligence but some people still believe she's guilty.	**b** to conscript	1	....
		c to ask to return	2	....
2	As soon as John reached Vienna he **was called back** to Paris.	**d** to run away	3	....
3	His condition **calls for** immediate medical attention.	**e** to brighten up (of the weather)	4	....
4	The meeting **was called off** due to the chairman's illness.	**f** to visit briefly	5	....
5	You'd better **call in** a solicitor before writing your will.	**g** to get rid of unwanted things	6	....
6	My cousin **was called up** at the age of 19 and died in Vietnam a year later.	**h** to remove, tidy	7	....
		i to cause one to go on strike	8	....
7	The union **has called out** its members to try to get a better deal.	**j** to find innocent	9	....
8	The bully **cleared off** when he saw the teacher approaching.	**k** to consult	10	....
9	They **cleared out** the garage to make room for their new car.	**l** to require	11	....
10	It's been raining all morning but it seems **to be clearing up** now.			
11	If you **cleared away** all these books, we'd have room to eat.			

IDIOMS/FIXED PHRASES 1

show one's true colours:	reveal one's character
lost cause:	hopeless situation or case
chair a meeting:	preside over a meeting
off colour:	slightly unwell
have the cheek (inf):	dare to do sth unreasonable/ annoying
get a bit hot under the collar:	get angry/upset
keep one's chin up (inf):	not be discouraged
with flying colours:	with great success
get a problem off one's chest:	confide in sb
different as chalk and cheese:	very different
call sb names:	insult sb
play one's cards right:	act cleverly

What is meant by **"don't count your chickens before they are hatched"**?

....
....
....

13 Fill in the blanks with one of the idioms/fixed phrases.

0 Trying to make them understand how teenagers think is a *lost cause*. They are so conservative.

1 Paul was asked to .... as the director was away on business.

2 Laura passed her exam .... She came top of the class.

3 He .... when he started throwing his weight around at work.

4 I don't know how he .... to moan about my spelling when his is even worse.

5 You look .... Would you like me to call a doctor for you?

6 John managed to .... despite his chronic illness.

7 If you .... and speak nicely to your father, he might take you to the fair this afternoon.

8 Bert and Tom are as different as ....
.... It's hard to believe that they are brothers!

9 Those boys are very rude to me. They are always
....

10 Instead of just sitting there feeling bad, why not talk about it and .... ?

11 She ....
when a colleague started criticising her work.

IDIOMS/FIXED PHRASES 2

a wild-goose chase:	hopeless pursuit
be caught red-handed:	be caught while committing a crime/doing sth wrong
crocodile tears:	false tears
a piece of cake:	(sth) easily done
down the drain:	wasted/lost
down in the dumps:	not cheerful
on the dole:	receiving unemployment benefit/social security
go to the dogs:	fail/deteriorate
a red-letter day:	a very important day
let sleeping dogs lie:	avoid mentioning a subject or taking action which could cause trouble

14 *Fill in the blanks with one of the idioms/fixed phrases.*

0 Fred thought the test was *a piece of cake*; he has no doubt that he has passed it.

1 I have plenty of spare time but very little money because I am ....

2 Kate is feeling .... because her boyfriend has left her.

3 12 June is .... for my sister. It's the day she launched her own business.

4 Looking for Susan in New York is simply ....; she could be anywhere.

5 You can't fool me with your ....; I know you're not really upset.

6 Please don't bring up that old argument with Joe when you see him. Just ....

7 While some people claim the country is ...., others think the new government will be able to improve matters.

8 The little boy .... taking the last piece of cake from the tin.

9 All the money I'd invested went .... when the stockmarket crashed.

PREPOSITIONS

15 *Look at Appendix 5 and fill in the blanks with the correct preposition.*

0 The children were late and had to make a dash *for* the school bus.

1 The woman exulted .... her son's success as a writer.

2 We'll have to economise .... heating or we won't be able to pay the bill.

3 I dream .... becoming a millionaire and buying a big yacht.

4 The student was eligible .... a full grant to study at university.

5 The employee showed total disregard .... the company rules and was dismissed.

6 The driver was distracted .... the commotion and didn't notice that the traffic lights had changed.

7 John was so engrossed .... the film that he forgot about the cake that was in the oven.

8 We were totally entranced .... the prima ballerina's dancing.

9 The doctor told me I was deficient .... iron and would have to take supplements.

10 Michael was delighted .... his promotion to office manager.

16 *Look at Appendix 5 and fill in the blanks with the correct preposition.*

0 We sold our house *at* a profit; we made £2,000.

1 He put the car .... gear and drove off.

2 She's working as a waitress .... the time being, but her ambition is to become an actress.

3 I've met Elizabeth Taylor .... the flesh. I even shook her hand.

4 She's been .... a diet for weeks, but she hasn't lost much weight.

5 We have a car .... loan until ours has been repaired.

6 Strictly .... the record, his work is below standard.

7 The workers have been .... strike for three weeks.

8 I realised something was .... of the ordinary when Ann didn't show up for work today.

9 We were shocked when she called him an idiot .... his face.

10 He was .... pain after the operation.

11 .... times he wishes he had never become a doctor.

12 .... all accounts, he is the best basketball player in the association.

17 *Complete the second sentence so that it has a similar meaning to the first sentence, using the word given. Do not change the word given. You must use between three and eight words, including the word given.*

1 Have you ever thought of changing jobs?
 mind
 Has ....
 .... jobs?

2 These two cars are not in the same class at all.
 comparison
 There ....
 .... cars.

3 He never stops criticising people.
 limit
 There ....
 .... people.

4 It's not our habit to eat so early.
 used
 We ....
 .... so early.

5 What do you think of his appearance?
 strike
 How ....
 .... you?

6 That man has no pity whatsoever.
 devoid
 That man ....
 .... pity.

7 He is likely to be promoted.
 cards
 It is ....
 .... promoted.

8 We were elated by the birth of our first grandchild.
 moon
 We ....
 .... was born.

9 Employees failing to abide by the rules will be dismissed on the spot.
 sack
 Employees failing to abide by the rules ....
 .... immediately.

10 Our boss criticises our work all the time.
 fault
 Our boss ....
 .... work.

11 I don't mind whether you come in the morning or the afternoon.
 difference
 It ....
 .... in the morning or the afternoon.

12 Women outnumber men by two to one in Greece.
 twice
 There ....
 .... in Greece.

13 It's quite likely he will resign soon.
 chance
 There's ....
 .... will resign soon.

14 As soon as she saw my flatmate, my mother decided she didn't like him.
 dislike
 My mother ....
 .... my flatmate.

15 Could you have a quick look at my essay before I give it in?
 cast
 Could you ....
 .... before I hand it in?

16 My father has been healthier since he moved to the country.
 improved
 My ....
 .... since he moved to the country.

17 The public reacted angrily to the minister's remarks.
 drew
 The ....
 .... the public.

18 The company has changed a lot since the new management took over.
 undergone
 The company ....
 .... since the new management took over.

19 Frances is unlikely to be promoted.
 prospect
 There's ....
 .... promoted.

20 The minister's actions do not conform at all to his pre-election promises.
 contrast
 The minister's actions ....
 .... his pre-election promises.

FIXED PHRASES

put a damper on:	ruin sth or make it less enjoyable
be in the dark about sth:	be unaware of sth
don't give up your day job (inf):	continue to do sth you know rather than trying sth new
in broad daylight:	in full view of the public/easily seen
deal a blow to sb or sth:	cause sb great difficulty or spoil their plans
be on the defensive:	protect oneself because one feels insecure or threatened
by definition:	having a quality simply because of what it is
(for) donkey's years (inf):	(for) a very long time
on the dot:	punctual, exactly on time
lend an ear:	listen to sb in a careful and sympathetic way
play it by ear:	act in a situation by responding to events rather than according to plan
ease off:	reduce in degree, speed or intensity
at the cutting edge:	at the forefront of (eg. technology)
on edge:	tense/nervous/anxious
to no effect (f):	unsuccessful; ineffective
(not) see eye to eye with sb:	(dis)agree with sb
have an eye for:	be good at judging, the worth/quality of sth
more to sth/sb than meets the eye:	sth/sb is more important/interesting than is first seen

18 *Complete the sentences using one of the fixed phrases in an appropriate form.*

1 Todd hadn't prepared for his T.V. appearance, so he had to .... and improvise.
2 John's losing his money and passport on the first day .... on his holiday.
3 Julia's really been .... waiting for the results of her university entrance exam.
4 Breakfast will be at 7 am ....; latecomers will go hungry!
5 She's been .... at work ever since she was criticised by her boss for losing an important contract.
6 Despite being identical twins, Deidre and Donna don't .... on everything.
7 Mrs Gibson is an extremely shrewd shopper and .... a bargain.
8 Initially Brian appears shy and introspective but there's ....

19 *Choose the correct item.*

1 I know you have a good voice and have ambitions to be an opera singer but don't give up your day .... yet!
A situation   C job
B work   D place

2 I am in the .... as to where Chris was last night.
A shade   C pink
B dark   D black

3 Breaking his leg dealt a .... to his chances of becoming a professional footballer.
A thump   C hit
B strike   D blow

4 Jane is a sympathetic listener. She lent me a(n) .... when I lost my job.
A mind   C ear
B mouth   D eye

5 Let's make a dash for the train now as the rain seems to be .... off.
A easing   C reducing
B slowing   D running

6 Our firm is so successful because it is at the cutting .... of computer technology.
A limit   C verge
B fringe   D edge

20 Read the following letter and, using the information given, complete the following reply by writing the missing words in the correct spaces. The words you need do not occur in the letter. The first one has been done for you. Do not use more than two words for each blank.

Dear Mary,

I can certainly understand your problem, as anyone who has been brought up in a family environment can. But I must say I think you are underestimating your parents' concern and understanding. If they appear to be interfering in your personal concerns, it is only because they consider themselves to be wiser and more experienced than you are. If you dislike being questioned, you must convince your parents by your actions that you are to be trusted. You can encourage them to trust you by being honest and dependable, and if you feel unfairly treated, consider discussing the problem with them. It is extremely important not to hesitate to approach your parents with any problem you may have. If you trust them, they are more likely to trust you.

Claire

Well, I have just received an answer to my letter to Claire. In it she says that she can understand **(0)** *my situation* as she has experienced **(1)** .... problems herself. However, she **(2)** .... to tell me that I didn't **(3)** .... my parents' **(4)** .... me. The fact that they seem to interfere in **(5)** .... is only because they regard themselves as being **(6)** .... and experienced than I am. She goes on to say that if I **(7)** .... all their questions, I **(8)** .... to make them **(9)** .... me by my actions. It **(10)** .... that I should make them trust me by acting **(11)** .... and **(12)** .... and if I ever feel that they are **(13)** .... me, then I **(14)** .... talk it over with them. She **(15)** .... my not hesitating to **(16)** .... to them by discussing any problem that I may have. It **(17)** .... to trust them because then it is **(18)** .... that they'll trust me too.

WORD USAGE

21 Read the text below. Use the word given in capitals at the end of some of the lines to form a word that fits in the space in the same line.

ALL WORK AND NO PLAY...

Playing is a serious business. Children engrossed in a make-believe world, fox cubs play fighting, or kittens teasing a ball of string, aren't just having fun. Play may look like a **(0)** *carefree* and exuberant way to pass the time before the hard work of **(1)** .... comes along, but there's much more to it than that. For a start, play can be dangerous and costs some animals their lives. It is also extremely **(2)** .... in terms of energy. Nature tends not to waste energy so there must be a reason for this dangerous and strenuous activity.

Playing is a **(3)** .... for the development of intelligence. Current theory posits that more of the brain is involved in play than was previously believed. Play certainly seems to **(4)** .... higher cognitive processes because it involves complex **(5)** .... of playmates, ideas of reciprocity and the use of **(6)** .... signals and rules.

It is already known that juveniles denied the opportunity for play lose the ability to apply social rules when they do interact with their peers. Children destined to suffer mental illnesses as adults engage in precious little social play early in life. The effect of depriving normal children of play is still **(7)** ...., but the implication is that **(8)** .... and learning abilities could be adversely affected. With **(9)** .... beginning earlier and becoming **(10)** .... more exam-oriented, the time afforded to play is obviously being reduced. What the result will be is likely to cause concern.

CARE
ADULT

COST

REQUIRE

ACT
ASSESS
SPECIAL

KNOW
CREATE
SCHOOL
INCREASE

22 *Fill in the blanks with one of the following words:*

- heritage • inheritance • legacy • will

0 The two brothers of the family fell out over the *inheritance* when the head of the family died.

1 The family were called to the solicitor's office for the reading of their grandfather's ....

2 The old man's back trouble was the .... of a childhood fall from a horse.

3 The Acropolis is part of Greece's national ....

4 His .... will be held in trust until he is an adult.

23 *Choose the correct item.*

0 He was .... intensively for two weeks before the tennis tournament.
A practised   C learned
(B) coached   D taught

1 Our journey was .... by the icy roads, which forced us to drive very slowly.
A obstructed   C barred
B impeded   D blocked

2 Before the parachute jump he was carefully .... in safety procedures.
A shown   C presented
B instructed   D familiarised

3 She .... her daughter to the care of a babysitter for the evening.
A entrusted   C confided
B consigned   D resigned

4 The engineer .... the machine with a hammer and, miraculously, it roared back to life.
A slapped   C whacked
B smacked   D punched

5 Fighting among rebel soldiers .... last night and a curfew has now been imposed on the city.
A enhanced   C heightened
B aggravated   D intensified

6 While other companies collapsed in the economic recession, Cartwright Ltd. .... and share prices rose.
A earned   C profited
B exploited   D gained

7 Rebecca .... her fiancé across the face during an argument and walked out of the restaurant.
A smashed   C struck
B slapped   D punched

8 The judge's ruling .... a wave of protest campaigns across the country.
A provoked   C launched
B instigated   D commenced

9 Although she was able to walk with the aid of crutches, having a broken ankle .... her movements considerably.
A barred   C intervened
B hindered   D blocked

10 The Oscar winning actress simply .... charm and professionalism in her acceptance speech.
A exuded   C expunged
B excluded   D extricated

COLLOCATIONS

24 a) *Fill in **investigate**, **explore**.*

0 *explore* a jungle
1 .... a possibility
2 .... a town
3 .... Mr Smith
4 .... a crime
5 .... an idea
6 .... an ocean
7 .... an allegation
8 .... the cause of sth
9 .... an area for oil

b) *Fill in **weak**, **feeble**.*

1 .... tea
2 .... attempt
3 .... boy
4 .... eyesight
5 .... voice
6 .... smile
7 .... defence
8 .... heart
9 .... supports
10 .... bones
11 .... light
12 .... case

25 a) Fill in *interval, intermission, break*.

1 .... between school lessons
2 .... for coffee
3 .... in the middle of a film
4 .... in conversation
5 .... for lunch
6 .... between two acts of a play

b) Fill in *keen, enthusiastic*.

1 .... eye
2 .... on music
3 .... about travelling
4 .... response
5 .... sense of smell
6 .... greeting
7 .... swimmer

26 Collocate the expressions with words from the given list.

- curb • betray • cuddle • ~~stagger~~ • accuse
- marvel • charge • sprinkle • disperse
- blab • slip

0 to *stagger* under the weight of sth
1 to .... a crowd
2 to .... one's behaviour
3 to .... the baby
4 to .... on the ice
5 to .... the secret
6 to .... sb of lying
7 to .... with sugar
8 to .... sb with careless driving
9 to .... sb's trust
10 to .... at the view

27 Think of one word only which can be used appropriately in all three sentences.

0 • One doesn't need to be an expert to *appreciate* the beauty of classical music.
  • He seems confident that houses in this area will *appreciate* in value in the next few years.
  • I'll always *appreciate* your help and support.

1 • Adrienne has problems buying comfortable shoes due to her .... feet.
  • The soda we were served was ...., so we complained to the barman.
  • This phone company charges a .... rate of 40 p per minute for all calls to the US.

2 • The model moved with such .... that she appeared to float across the stage.
  • She was given a week's .... in which to pay the outstanding debt.
  • It's hard to believe that she didn't even have the .... to apologise after it was proved she had made the mistake.

3 • The antique shop, as it turned out, was merely a .... for his spying activities.
  • If it's very cold tonight, put an extra .... on your bed.
  • To be honest, I bought the book because it had an attractive ....

4 • 30% of the company's .... of olive oil is solely for export to Europe.
  • What did you think of the amateur drama group's .... of 'Hamlet'?
  • Everyone in full time education will be offered cheap rail fares on .... of their student union cards.

5 • The loud .... from the pistol caused me to start in surprise.
  • Look at this interesting news .... about the fall in unemployment.
  • Sally's school .... was better this term, which pleased her parents.

6 • He made his .... on the fashion industry in the 1970s.
  • The university student was delighted with her .... in the final examination.
  • It was a .... of the child's developing independence that he didn't want to sit with his father on the train.

7 • The policeman .... the angry protester against the wall to stop him escaping.
  • Grandmother recalled that, for her wedding, the hairdresser .... her hair up to create an elaborate display of curls and braids.
  • He eventually .... the blame on his sister, though she was quite obviously innocent.

PREPARING FOR PART 5

SUMMARY WRITING III Paraphrasing

28 *Choose the best paraphrase of the bold parts of each passage. There is an example.*

Pepper was one of Egypt's major sources of trade revenue well before the birth of Christ. In 180 BC, Alexandria was the greatest spice trading port in the Mediterranean, with one of its entrances known as "Pepper Gate". Pepper remained highly valued merchandise throughout the centuries and was a desirable commodity. **(0) In 410 AD, Alaric the Visigoth demanded 3,000 pounds of pepper as ransom from Rome, and two years later he forced the city to pay 300 pounds in annual tribute. (1) In 1672, Elihu Yale started a pepper-exporting business in India. It provided him with a fortune, part of which he used to found Yale University. (2) World trade in black pepper continues to soar today, with an all-time high of 290 million pounds in 1999.** A hot business indeed.

(0) a Alaric the Visigoth forced Rome to pay him a large ransom in pepper.

  b In 410 AD, Rome was forced to pay a large ransom and an annual tribute in pepper to Alaric the Visigoth.

  ⓒ In the 5th century AD, Alaric the Visigoth forced Rome to pay him a ransom and an annual tribute in pepper.

(1) a In 1672, Elihu Yale started making great profits from trading in pepper and founded Yale University.

  b Elihu Yale founded Yale University with the profits he made from his pepper-exporting business.

  c Elihu Yale made great profits trading in pepper, and founded Yale University in 1672.

(2) a Pepper trade today is extremely profitable and amounts to 290 million pounds per year.

  b Pepper trade today is extremely profitable and continues to be as profitable as it was in the past.

  c Pepper trade today is extremely profitable, with 290 million pounds being traded in 1999.

Many of the boarding schools built after 1870, particularly in London, were designed in a newly-fashionable style known as the Queen Anne Style. **(3) This was a nickname for a style loosely associated with buildings built long before the reign of Queen Anne. (4) It was popular because it was thought to have a friendly look, better suited for children than the severity and gloom of the Gothic style of early nineteenth century architecture.** The passing of the Education Act of 1870 making elementary education compulsory meant that many extra school places had to be found, particularly in the big cities. As the school buildings often had to fit onto a small plot of land, urban schools at this time were often two or three storeys high. This changed with the onset of the new century, **(5) when many schools built between 1900 and 1935 were not constructed in the centre of cities, but in the suburbs, where land was available for the playing fields required for sports lessons.**

(3) a The Queen Anne style was not developed during Queen Anne's reign.

  b The Queen Anne style was not very popular during Queen Anne's reign.

  c The Queen Anne style was a nickname for buildings that were built prior to Anne becoming Queen of England.

(4) a Queen Anne style buildings had a friendlier appearance than Gothic buildings.

  b Children preferred Queen Anne style schools because they looked friendly.

  c Building schools in the style of Queen Anne made them popular with children.

(5) a Schools between 1900 and 1935 were no longer built in the Queen Anne style.

  b The need for sport at school meant that early twentieth-century schools took up more space.

  c All schools built between 1900 and 1935 were in the suburbs and had playing fields.

I can't recall the exact moment when my father realised that our family needed a car and made the decision to buy one. I do know it had taken him an awfully long time. **(6) He had always been so devoted to his horses and he could never see how such a costly investment could help him around the farm.**

But slowly things began to change; perhaps he had grown weary of having to hitch up the horses every time he needed to use the old wagon. Maybe he noticed that my mother rather enjoyed it when the neighbours offered her a car ride into town; then, of course, he couldn't help but notice that the McCoys on the adjoining farm were using a car to help with farm work; **(7) I think the last straw was when he learnt that his younger brother had bought a car for his family.**

One night, over supper, my father sombrely announced that it was time we bought a car. My brother and I were thrilled. Finally, we were going to become part of the ever-growing number of car owners. **(8) The next day, my practical father methodically went about shopping for just the right vehicle.**

(6)
a The writer's father liked his horses, and did not understand how a car could help him in his work.
b The writer's father liked his horses so much that he didn't really want a car.
c The writer's father was so devoted to his horses that he refused to accept that he needed a car.

(7)
a The writer's father's younger brother persuaded him to buy a car.
b When he discovered his younger brother had bought a car, the writer's father finally decided that he should get one.
c The family of the writer's father's younger brother encouraged him to buy a car.

(8)
a The writer's father bought a car the next day.
b The writer's father was practical and methodical and went shopping for a car the next day.
c The writer's father carefully started looking for an appropriate car the next day.

In 1920, a famous Hawaiian swimmer, Duke Kahanamoku, formed the first surfing club in Waikiki. **(9) It took a relatively long time (the best part of 30 years) for surfing to go from a strange coastal pastime to a major sporting industry.** However, by the mid-1950s there were international competitions and surfing events held in several places around the world, with participation from countries as diverse as England, Madagascar, Iceland and Cyprus. **(10) Post-war prosperity and the commercialisation of surfboard manufacturing played important parts in the development of this new sport.**

(11) The end of the 1960s saw a change in the image of the surfer portrayed in the media. The surfer no longer had the reputation of being idle and lazy, drifting from coast to coast. Instead, he became the symbol of a healthy and glamorous lifestyle. The seventies saw surfing as a sport which expressed freedom and progress, and surfers became global travellers, looking for good waves in countries that had never seen a surfboard and, in the process, re-mapping and renaming many of the world's remote coastlines.

(9)
a A relatively long time passed before surfing was accepted as a sport of major importance.
b Surfing was considered a sport for strange sportsmen.
c Surfing was a strange coastal pastime before it became a recognised sport.

(10)
a After the war, surfing developed commercially.
b After the war, people had more money and surfboards began to be manufactured as a business.
c Post-war prosperity and the commercialisation of surfing helped the sport develop.

(11)
a By 1960, the surfer's image had changed.
b Surfers were no longer seen as time-wasters in the sixties.
c The media stopped seeing surfers as time-wasters in the late 60s, and began to portray them more favourably.

3c Practice Test Three

Paper 3 Use of English   Time: 1 hour 30 minutes

 PART 1

Read the text below and think of the word which best fits each space. Use only one word in each space.

QUEEN VICTORIA

Victoria first learned of her future role as a princess **(0)** *during* a history lesson when she was 10 years old. **(1)** .... four decades later, Victoria's governess recalled that the future queen reacted to the discovery **(2)** .... declaring, "I will be good". This combination of earnestness and egotism marked Victoria **(3)** .... a child of the age that bears her name. **(4)** .... was an era of industrialisation and colonial expansion **(5)** .... had not happened before. By the end of her reign, about a third of the known world was **(6)** .... her rule. **(7)** ...., the queen herself was resistant to technological change **(8)** .... while mechanical and technological innovation was reshaping the face of European civilization. **(9)** .... significantly, Victoria was a queen determined to retain political power; yet she presided **(10)** .... the transformation of the sovereign's political role into a ceremonial **(11)** .... and thus helped to preserve the English monarchy. When Victoria became queen, the political role of the crown was by **(12)** .... means clear or defined; nor **(13)** .... the permanence of the throne **(14)** .... When she died, the change in the monarch's roles was one of social **(15)** .... than of political focus.

 PART 2

Read the text below. Use the word given in capitals at the end of some of the lines to form a word that fits in the space in the same line.

PROTECTING YOUR RIGHTS

Copyright is the inalienable, **(0)** *legally* secured right to publish, reproduce, and sell the   **LEGAL**
matter and form of a literary, musical, dramatic, or artistic work. Copyright is designed
(16) .... to protect an artist, publisher, or other owner against any   **SPECIFIC**
(17) .... copying of his works – as by reproducing the work in any   **AUTHORISE**
material form, publishing it, performing it in public, filming it, broadcasting it, causing
it to be distributed to **(18)** .... or making any adaptation of the work.   **SUBSCRIBE**
A copyright supplies a copyright holder with a kind of **(19)** .... over   **OWN**
the created material, which assures him of both control over its use and the monetary
benefits derived from it. **(20)**................................., copyrights grew out of the same   **HISTORY**
system as royal patent grants, by which certain authors and printers were given the
(21) .... right to publish books and other materials. The   **EXCLUDE**
(22) .... purpose of such grants was not to protect authors' or   **BASE**
publishers' rights but to raise government revenue and to give governing authorities
control over **(23)** .... contents. The Statute of Anne, passed in   **PUBLIC**
England in 1710, was a **(24)** .... in the history of copyright law   **MILE**
as it recognised that authors should be the **(25)** .... beneficiaries   **PRIME**
of copyright law. Today, the Berne Convention of 1886 and the Universal Copyright
Convention of 1955 protect rights on an international level recognised in all countries.

PART 3

Think of one word only which can be used appropriately in all three sentences.

0 • One doesn't need to be an expert to *appreciate* the beauty of classical music.
  • He seems confident that houses in this area will *appreciate* in value in the next few years.
  • I'll always *appreciate* your help and support.

26 • Dora wanted exactly the right .... of blue for the walls of her bedroom.
  • In summer, people with a pale complexion always need some kind of ....
  • The artist's particular use of colour and .... helped to create an atmosphere of foreboding in the painting.

27 • Be sure to .... the details in case they are needed at a future date.
  • Both male and female members of the tribe .... their teeth to points, maintaining a centuries-old tradition.
  • I watched the soldiers .... past me on their way to the barracks.

28 • She was hoping a reply to her job application would arrive in the morning ....
  • The dog had been tied to a .... outside the building waiting for its owner.
  • Jo was glad to be offered the new ....

29 • I used to think she was .... and trustworthy – but I was wrong.
  • The offer will remain .... until the date specified.
  • I've completely run out of ideas, so I'm .... to suggestions.

30 • A mean spirit is .... as a severe character failing by some people, as it shows a lack of openness and generosity.
  • If she wins the next tournament, she will be .... as number one in the world.
  • Sotheby's .... my grandmother's chest of drawers highly.

31 • The .... between Manchester United and the home team was disrupted by unruly fans.
  • Joan and Bob are so well suited that everyone says they are an ideal ....
  • Even the world grand master was no .... for the computer at chess.

PART 4

Complete the second sentence so that it has a similar meaning to the first sentence, using the word given. Do not change the word given. You must use between three and eight words, including the word given.

0 Nobody spoke when the teacher asked who the culprit was.
  remained
  Everyone *remained silent when the teacher asked who the culprit was.*

32 You will have to give up the whole idea.
  option
  You .... the whole idea.

33 Victory was stolen from the sprinter at the finish of the race.
  robbed
  The sprinter .... line.

34 Most of the committee voted for the proposal.
  favour
  The .... the proposal.

35 Don't you think there is an odour of burnt meat in the kitchen?
  smell
  Doesn't .... kitchen?

36 They have definitely agreed to lend us the money.
  committed
  They .... the money.

37 Do you have to wear a uniform at school?
  compulsory
  Is .... at school?

38 Don't pay any attention when she complains.
  notice
  Don't .... complaints.

39 They remain close friends, despite having had many arguments.
  fallen
  They .... have had many arguments.

PART 5

*For questions **40-44**, read the following texts. For questions **40 - 43**, answer with a word or short phrase. You do not need to write complete sentences. For question **44**, write a summary according to the instructions given.*

Parents hope their encouragement will make their children more motivated to achieve academic success, but despite their best efforts, they often end up frustrated and puzzled at their failure to effectively inspire. What is good, effective motivation? Recent investigations of parental motivational practices have revealed two main kinds – 'intrinsic motivation', where enjoyment of learning is emphasised, and 'extrinsic motivation', where parents reward their children on achievement.

line 6 ——

Many parents may be shocked by the results of this study, which found common practices adopted by pushy parents, like external rewards for academic success (for example, gifts of money, or the withdrawal of privileges contingent on academic results) actually produced lower levels of academic curiosity and enjoyment of school work among children, in turn leading to lower achievement. The lesson from this research is that, if parents want their children to be academically motivated, they should emphasise the enjoyability of school work, rather than the benefits which will accrue from the rewards of academic success. In other words, they should encourage their children not to see academic tasks as work at all, but more like play.

line 18 ——

This has important implications for anyone engaged in trying to achieve change through motivation, including psychologists. A whole new debate has been opened regarding whether they should use punishment and reward less, and instead accentuate the pleasurable aspects of change as a means to encourage children to attain academic success.

40 In your own words, explain what the term "extrinsic motivation" means as it is used in line 6.

....

....

41 What does the word "This" refer to in line 18?

....

....

There I was, a parenting advisor, making a really stupid parenting mistake – not listening to my child. It was a cold winter afternoon and my entire extended family were crowded into our house – 4 kids, 9 adults. Where did I go wrong? Well, to a non-parent this may seem trivial, but I'm sure those with young children will understand. It was time for my five-year-old, Lily, to be off to her ballet class. She complained that her tummy was sore, but being aware of her tendency to occasionally try and get out of regular tasks when her cousins are around, I dismissed her whimpering and drove her to her class.

I had only been back for twenty minutes or so, when I got a phone call from the ballet school. I was asked to go and pick Lily up because she had been sick. I can assure you that the ten-minute drive back to the school was probably the absolutely worst ten minutes of my entire life.

Lily put her seatbelt on, looked at me through the mirror and asked me why I hadn't listened to her. I felt awful. I admitted to her that I had been wrong. I said that I should have been more sensitive to her feelings and not so concerned about what "needed to be done". By the end of the night she said "I love you", hugged me, and went to sleep. Not I. In fact, I'm still feeling guilty.

Sometimes we find it hard to accept that, as parents, we are not perfect and will make mistakes. We should all try to understand why we make our mistakes, take responsibility for them and apologise. Tell your child why you did what you did, and promise to do things differently next time. Although it doesn't mean that you won't feel bad after making a silly parenting mistake, it will help your child get over the incident much faster than you will.

42 Why did the writer not believe her daughter when she said her "tummy was sore"?

....

....

43 Why was the drive back to the ballet school the writer's "absolutely worst ten minutes" of her life?

....

....

44 In a paragraph of between 50 and 70 words, summarise the advice to parents contained in the two passages.

....

....

....

....

....

....

....

....

We form the passive voice by putting the verb **to be** into the same tense as the active verb and adding the past participle of the active verb. The object of the active verb becomes the subject of the passive verb. The subject of the active verb becomes the "**agent**" of the passive verb and is preceded by "**by**". The **agent is omitted** when it is a) **a pronoun**, b) words like **one, someone, people, etc**, c) **easily understood**. *(Someone destroyed the evidence.* → *The evidence was destroyed.)* Most transitive verbs can be used in the passive.

Tenses	Active Voice	Passive Voice
Simple Present Simple Past	*The assistant **types** reports.* *The assistant **typed** reports.*	*Reports **are typed** (by the assistant).* *Reports **were typed** (by the assistant).*
Present Continuous Past Continuous	*The assistant **is typing** reports.* *The assistant **was typing** reports.*	*Reports **are being typed** (by the assistant).* *Reports **were being typed** (by the assistant).*
Present Perfect Past Perfect	*The assistant **has typed** reports.* *The assistant **had typed** reports.*	*Reports **have been typed** (by the assistant).* *Reports **had been typed** (by the assistant).*
Simple Future Future Perfect	*The assistant **will type** reports.* *The assistant **will have typed** reports.*	*Reports **will be typed** (by the assistant).* *Reports **will have been typed** (by the assistant).*
Conditional Conditional Perfect	*The assistant **would type** reports.* *The assistant **would have typed** reports.*	*Reports **would be typed** (by the assistant).* *Reports **would have been typed** (by the assistant).*
Present Infinitive Perfect Infinitive	*The assistant ought **to type** reports.* *The assistant ought **to have typed** reports.*	*Reports ought **to be typed** (by the assistant).* *Reports ought **to have been typed** (by the assistant).*
Gerund Perfect Gerund	*The assistant hates people **asking** her **to type** reports.* *The assistant remembers her boss **having asked** her **to type** reports.*	*The assistant hates **being asked to type** reports.* *The assistant remembers **having been asked to type** reports. (by her boss)*

Notes

- Conversational and informal English often replaces the passive form with an active form with **get**. The **get - passive** is normally used in constructions without an agent.
  *Mary **got** hit.*
  *He **got** cut.*

- **Have + object + past participle** can be used colloquially to replace a passive verb when we want to talk about an accident or misfortune.
  *She **had her leg broken**. (Her leg **was broken**.)*

Use

The passive voice is used:
- when the person who performs the action ("agent") can easily be understood, or is unknown.
  *He **has been arrested**. (=The police have arrested him.)*
  *A new government **has been elected** (= easily understood: by the citizens).*

- when it is necessary to express sth more formally.
  Some people think the Minister was involved in the conspiracy to overthrow the government. → ***It is thought that the Minister was involved** in the conspiracy to overthrow the government./**The Minister is thought to have been involved** in the conspiracy to overthrow the government.*

- when we are interested in the **action itself** rather than the person who performs it.
  *The new hospital **will be opened** tomorrow (by the Minister of Health).*

- when we mean to be tactful by not naming the agent.
  *All my shampoo **has been used**. (instead of: You've used all my shampoo!)*

FURTHER POINTS ON THE PASSIVE VOICE

- *Make, hear, see, help* are followed by **to + infinitive** in the passive voice.
  He made her leave. → *She was made **to leave**.*

- *Let* becomes *was/were allowed to* in the passive. When the subject of *let* and the object of the infinitive that follows *let* are the same, then *let*, when used in the passive voice, is followed by a **reflexive pronoun + bare passive infinitive**.
  She let me go out. → *I **was allowed to** go out.*
  Don't let him tease you. → *Don't **let yourself be teased**.*

- The passive voice with verbs of reporting such as *assume, believe, consider, feel, know, report, say, think, understand,* etc is formed in two ways. a) **It + passive verb + that - clause** b) **subject + passive verb + to - infinitive**.
  They believe she is a spy. → *It is believed that she is a spy.*
  They believe she is a spy. → **She is believed to be** a spy.*

- Verbs which take two objects such as *allow, ask, give, lend, send,* etc have two passive forms.
  He showed me the way to the door. → *I **was shown** the way to the door.* **The way to the door was shown** to me.*

- Passive voice can take **by + agent** or **with + instrument** (a person is involved), **material, past participles** (such as **filled, packed** etc).
  *It was cut **with a knife**. (by someone)*
  *Ice cream is made **with milk**.*
  *The stadium was filled **with thousands of spectators**.*

- Verbs followed by a certain preposition take the preposition immediately after them when put into the passive voice.
  *She **accused** me **of** lying.* → *I **was accused of** lying.*

- *Prepositional verbs of movement* when turned into the passive voice change to other synonymous verbs which take no preposition.
  *Columbus **reached/arrived in** America in 1492.* → *America was **reached** (NOT arrived in) by Columbus in 1492. The royal couple **entered/went into** the room arm in arm.* → *The room was **entered** (NOT gone into) by the royal couple arm in arm.*

- *Modals* do not change in the passive voice. We change the **active infinitive into passive infinitive**.
  *They **can't repair** the building.* → *The building **can't be repaired**.*

---

1 *Turn the following sentences from **active** into **passive**, or vice versa.*

1 Susan will have redecorated her flat by the end of the month.
....
....

2 Which car did the family eventually choose?
....
....

3 The bus timetable is going to change during the summer period.
....
....

4 You must return all books to the library within a week.
....
....

5 Lucy is known to have applied for the manager's position.
....
....

6 Don't let them take advantage of you.
....
....

7 Will all the new students be made to learn a second language?
....
....

8 He wasn't allowed to leave the premises.
....
....

9 The government department should have sent all the necessary forms.

....

....

10 The toddler dislikes being forced to eat breakfast.

....

....

11 Peter believes he has left his wallet in his jacket pocket.

....

....

12 Don't let the gloomy weather depress you.

....

....

13 I just don't like people staring at me.

....

....

2 *Turn the following from **active** into **passive** where necessary.*

1 When Hilary joined the production team, her manager introduced her to important contacts in the industry, and before long she was promoted to head of department.

....

....

....

....

2 The shops have lowered their prices for the sales. The difficulty is that the credit card company has cancelled my credit card, so I can't buy anything.

....

....

....

....

3 Sally says that Harvard University has offered her a place on their Bachelor of Arts course, but she's decided to reject it as Radcliff has admitted her too.

....

....

....

....

4 Lucy gave me a novel in which someone stole Monet's *Water Lilies* from the National Gallery.

....

....

....

....

5 The ATM withheld my card last night, so now I'll probably get it back on Monday. I just hope the machine doesn't discharge my card over the weekend.

....

....

....

....

6 Most people believe that the government should do more to protect the local environment. I don't think they are doing enough to encourage people to recycle.

....

....

....

7 From the manner in which the committee spoke of Madeline Adams, you would have thought they were going to promote her, but instead of that they've just dismissed her.

....

....

....

8 It appears they have diagnosed her symptoms as influenza, but they are testing her for suspected pneumonia as well.

....

....

....

9 My car's battery went flat and they had to tow it to a mechanic. I will have to pay for the tow truck charges, but if they have to replace the battery I won't have to pay because the guarantee still covers it.

....

....

....

....

10 When they appointed Therese as head chef of the restaurant, they gave her permission to add any new dishes, so she may replace their existing menu.

....

....

....

CONVERSATIONAL GRAMMAR

3 *Choose the correct item.*

1 She was anxious .... for the post of the Personal Assistant to the Director in the recently affiliated Jacobs Sussard Company.
   A to select   C to be selected
   B to have selected   D to be selecting

2 "Why are the Newtons asking for loan repayment modifications?"
   "Because their house .... in the flood."
   A was damaged   C had damaged
   B damaged   D was being damaged

3 "How's the new town planning project going?"
   "Oh, there's still a lot ...."
   A having done   C to be done
   B has been done   D have done

4 "How did his speech go?"
   "With all the noise outside, he couldn't .... himself heard."
   A make   C be made
   B be making   D have made

5 "Did you hear anything about last month's Barclays' robbery?"
   "Yes eventually the robbers .... given a ten-year sentence."
   A were not being   C were not to be
   B were   D were not have been

STRUCTURAL CONVERSION

1 *It is said* that this poem was written by Elytis.
   This poem was written by Elytis, so it is said.
   Elytis is said to have written this poem.
   This poem is said to have been written by Elytis.
   They say (that) this poem was written by Elytis.
   They say that Elytis wrote this poem.

2 *Nothing* more can be done about this matter.
   There's nothing more to be done about this matter.
   With regard to this matter, there's nothing more to *be done.*

3 *Someone* fitted her new costume.
   Her new costume was fitted.
   She was fitted for her new costume.
   She had her new costume fitted.

4 *They don't allow* speeding in the city.
   Speeding isn't allowed in the city.
   Speeding is forbidden in the city.

5 *I'd love you* to take me out.
   I'd love to be taken out (by you).

6 *He lets people* laugh at him.
   He lets himself be laughed at.

7 *Your contract says* that you are to be present by 8 am every day.
   You are expected to be present by 8 am every day, according to your contract.

8 *Her story didn't* deceive me.
   I wasn't taken in by her story.

9 *He wore a hat so that* no one would recognise him.
   He wore a hat to avoid being recognised.

10 *I love people* asking for my autograph.
    I love being asked for my autograph.
    I love it when I'm asked for my autograph.

11 *They couldn't* hear him.
    He couldn't make himself heard.

12 *They saw* him enter the building.
    He was seen to enter/entering the building.

13 *Who made* this dress?
    Who was this dress made by?

14 *No actor* can be expected to remember all the names of the plays he has acted in.
    No one can expect an actor to remember all the plays he has acted in.

4 *Complete the second sentence so that it has a similar meaning to the first sentence, using the word given. Do not change the word given. You must use between three and eight words, including the word given.*

1 She allows her colleagues to take her attention from her work.
   distracted
   She ....
   .... by her colleagues.

2 She locked the door so that nobody would disturb her.
   avoid
   She ....
   .... disturbed.

3 We can't do much for him now.
   little
   There ....
   .... now.

4 I believe parking is prohibited in this area.
   permit
   I don't think ....
   .... in this area.

5 No student can be expected to know every word in the book.
   students
   Nobody ....
   .... in the book.

6 The agreement states that you are to pay the installment once a month.
   according
   You ....
   .... to the agreement.

7 I don't like it when people I don't know very well ask me personal questions.
   being
   I ....
   .... people I don't know very well.

8 His claim that he didn't know anything didn't deceive me.
   taken
   I ....
   .... he didn't know anything.

9 Using notes is forbidden in this examination.
   allowed
   Notes ....
   .... in this examination.

10 I'd hate them to forget about me.
   left
   I'd ....
   .... out.

11 Allegedly, this book was written by two people.
   said
   This ....
   .... two people.

5 *Choose the correct item.*

1 "How was your dinner?"
   "A great success! Our guests ate the appetizers, the two main courses and the dessert. There was literally nothing ...."
   A to be left   C have left
   B left   D has been left

2 "Is there any news about the ex-President?"
   "Well, he's reported .... the country last night."
   A to be leaving   C to have left
   B that he left   D to leave

3 "What do you think of Uberto Eco's novel *The name of the rose*?"
   "Well, it .... widely regarded as his best, but to tell you the truth I'm not crazy about it."
   A has been   C is being
   B was   D is

4 "Did you enjoy your graduation ceremony?"
   "Oh yes; I didn't like .... photographed all the time, though."
   A being   C to have been
   B having been   D it to be

5 "How was your first day in your new job?"
   "Extremely embarrassing! We were .... present ourselves and talk about our previous work experience."
   A been asked to   C being asked
   B asked   D asked to

6 *Underline the correct item.*

0 He hates being **asked**/asking to sign autographs.
1 The new wing of the museum will be **open/opened** tomorrow by the Minister of Culture.
2 It is said that the new cinema complex **will have been/to be** completed by the summer.
3 He recalled **having/having been** severely bitten by insects the last time he was in the area.
4 The walls of our classroom were filled **with/by** colourful pictures.
5 This machinery has been **wore/worn** out by constant use.
6 This old house hasn't been **lived/lived in** for years.
7 The author is said **that he spent/to have spent** a fortune on his new villa.

7 *Read the text below and think of the word which best fits each space. Use only one word in each space.*

ENTERTAINING PEOPLE

When the human capacity **(0)** *for* amazement, thrill, and suspense approaches **(1)** .... limits, a circus unleashes its clowns **(2)** .... freshen the atmosphere and recondition the spectator's mind for the next act. **(3)** .... tradition, there are several varieties of clowns, **(4)** .... the elegantly-costumed white-faced clown who appears rather severe and domineering, to the happy-go-lucky grotesque variety, **(5)** .... exaggerated make-up and costumes are more outrageous and less predictable, to the dejected, down-and-out "tramp" character, popularised **(6)** .... all by the American, Emmett Kelly. In 19th century circuses it was usual for clowns to entertain audiences with songs and long monologues, in **(7)** .... they sometimes offered words of wisdom **(8)** .... politics and current events or quoted Shakespeare. More recently, especially in Russian circuses, a **(9)** .... number of clowns have attempted to strike **(10)** .... in new directions, abandoning traditional costumes and make-up and developing **(11)** .... natural characters. The great Russian clown, Oleg Popov, **(12)** .... appear in the ring wearing a minimum **(13)** .... make-up and only a slightly unconventional wardrobe. He impersonated an incompetent buffoon **(14)** .... was forever trying to mimic the acts of the legitimate performers. Frequently, he almost succeeded – **(15)** .... only after sufficient bungling – to make his performance a comedy.

PHRASAL VERBS 1

8 *Look at Appendix 1 and fill in one of the prepositions or adverbs from the list below, then give a synonym for each phrasal verb.*

- about • round • off • across • through
- down to • to • into • out • up • up with
- by • up to • forward • on • over • in
- round to • out in

1 They've come .... our way of thinking at last.

2 He came .... a collection of valuable old coins in the attic.

3 How did you come .... this painting? It's a Picasso, you know.

4 This diamond ring came .... me from my great-grandmother.

5 After she was hit on her head by the cricket ball, it took her several minutes to come ....

6 How much did the supermarket bill come .... this week?

7 Did the new play at the National Theatre come .... your expectations?

8 Those tomato seeds I planted in the spring haven't come .... yet.

9 He came .... several thousand pounds when his grandfather died.

10 The party went .... rather well. Everyone seemed to have enjoyed themselves.

11 The students are coming .... very well in Maths this term.

12 It came .... that Sue's husband had been arrested for speeding.

13 I don't know what's come .... him; he's been acting very oddly lately.

14 He came .... a rash after eating a kilo of strawberries.

15 Her latest novel is coming .... in paperback soon.

16 Long hair for men is coming .... again. More and more men are starting to wear their hair long.

17 After the flood, hundreds of volunteers came .... with offers of assistance.

18 We don't know yet how we'll solve the problem but I'm sure someone will come .... a solution soon.

19 Most of the companies which managed to come .... the economic crisis are now operating very successfully.

20 I'm not sure how the accident came .... but I suspect somebody was being careless.

PHRASAL VERBS 2

deal in:	trade in sth
deal with:	tackle a problem, cope with
do away with:	abolish; get rid of
do down:	criticise
be done for:	be in serious trouble
do out of:	deprive of
do up:	fasten (a coat etc)
do with:	need/would like
do without:	manage in spite of lack of sth
drive at:	imply, suggest

9 Fill in the correct phrasal verb.

0 Can you *do up* my dress, please?

1 I'm ....! Here comes my teacher and she'll see I should be in my Maths lesson.

2 The law limiting the amount of foreign exchange you can take out of the country should have been .... years ago.

3 I'm really thirsty. I could .... a cup of tea.

4 What were you .... when you said you might not see Mark for some time?

5 He .... antique furniture and paintings.

6 The old man was .... his life savings by a confidence trickster.

7 Surely you can .... sugar in your coffee for once?

8 How do you .... a class when they are constantly unruly?

9 You shouldn't .... your classmates just because they didn't pass their exam.

IDIOMS/FIXED PHRASES 1

10 Match the idioms/fixed phrases with the definitions.

0	keep an eye on sth	a	have a feeling that sb is talking about one
1	be green		
2	take it easy	b	within the rules
3	feel one's ears burning	c	manage to look serious
4	(keep) a straight face	d	be inexperienced
5	be worn out	e	very quickly
6	one's flesh and blood	f	guard/protect sth
7	fair and square	g	insist
8	in a flash	h	be very tired
9	put one's foot down	i	family member
		j	not work too hard, relax

0   f   2 ....   4 ....   6 ....   8 ....
1 ....   3 ....   5 ....   7 ....   9 ....

Now make sentences using the above idioms.

0 ....
1 ....
....
2 ....
....
3 ....
....
4 ....
....
5 ....
....
6 ....
....
7 ....
....
8 ....
....
9 ....
....

IDIOMS/FIXED PHRASES 2

11 Look at Appendix 2 and explain the meaning of the idioms/fixed phrases in bold.

1 There were so many **gatecrashers** at the party that I didn't even recognise the people I had invited.

2 My teacher and I **got off on the wrong foot** in the first lesson but now we are good friends.

3 Don't **take her for granted**; she won't be here for ever.

4 After I broke up with my fiancé, I was comforted by the fact that **there are plenty more fish in the sea**.

5 Most politicians **have the gift of the gab**.

6 "It's all Greek to me," she said as the professor was explaining the new maths problem.

7 In politics, there is always a little **give and take**.

8 I **heard it through/on the grapevine** that we are going to get a rise next month.

9 When he met Jennifer he instantly **fell head over heels in love** with her.

10 He **put his foot in it** when he told Sally about the surprise party they were planning for her.

11 I was asked to make a speech but I couldn't speak because I **had a frog in my throat**.

PREPOSITIONS

12 *Look at Appendix 5 and fill in the blanks with the correct preposition.*

0 My cousin has a flair *for* languages and can speak more than six.

1 The factory owner is not in the habit of fraternising .... his workers.

2 All the animals in the forest fled .... the fire.

3 If you have a grievance .... the company, please lodge a formal written complaint.

4 My car is guaranteed .... rust for eight years.

5 The teacher told me to stop fidgeting .... and to sit still and concentrate.

6 I was furious .... my sister .... her always borrowing my clothes without my permission.

7 His glee .... the news of his success was a joy to see.

8 You mustn't grieve .... one trivial mistake.

9 He has a fixation .... becoming the best doctor in the world.

10 She does nothing but fret .... her being overweight yet never tries to diet.

11 His fidelity .... the firm has won him great respect.

12 He is always gloating .... his meteoric rise as an actor.

13 He is certainly good .... maths, if not much else.

13 *Look at Appendix 5 and fill in the blanks with the correct preposition.*

1 Her sales methods have been criticised as being .... odds with company policy.

2 I found the ring in the street purely .... luck.

3 I didn't go to see him .... fear of catching his cold.

4 That house has been up .... sale for two years.

5 Come to the party, ... all means.

6 We regard this atrocity as an offence .... humanity.

7 .... all, I spent £500 on holiday.

8 Margot prefers not to buy goods .... credit.

9 He went to the meeting .... disguise so as not to be recognised.

10 There were a lot of problems at the beginning of the school year, but .... the end everything was all right.

11 He was so surprised by the news that he was .... a loss for words.

12 Our teacher was .... a bad mood today; he shouted .... everyone.

13 Try to get the photograph .... focus this time.

14 They were .... the trail of the Yeti when the blizzard started.

15 .... answer to your question, the meeting will take place next Tuesday.

14 *Complete the second sentence so that it has a similar meaning to the first sentence, using the word given. Do not change the word given. You must use between three and eight words including the word given.*

1 "That meal would have satisfied a king!" he exclaimed.
fit
"That ....
....!" he exclaimed.

2 No matter what he does, people don't seem eager to work on the project.
generate
He doesn't seem ....
.... the project.

3 There are hardly any people in the centre of the city in August.
virtually
The centre ....
.... in August.

4 The war has caused emigration to increase.
resulted
The war ....
.... emigration.

5 The board had a secret meeting in order to discuss changes in company policy.
doors
The board ....
.... company policy.

6 She will probably come before the end of next month.
likelihood
In ....
.... of next month.

7 It is usual for young children to ask a lot of questions.
apt
Young ....
.... questions.

8 I won't stay overnight; I don't want to put you to any trouble.
impose
I won't stay overnight; ....
.... you.

9 The manager is investigating your complaint.
looked
Your ....
.... manager.

10 She often exaggerates how much she earns.
tendency
She ....
.... how much she earns.

11 Anne has decided to buy fewer clothes from now on.
cut
Anne has decided to ....
.... from now on.

12 Mary always ignores her parents' advice.
notice
Mary ....
.... her parents' advice.

13 I was just about to ring him when he called.
point
I was ....
.... he called.

14 Her mother smiled with delight when Sarah gave her the flowers.
lit
Sarah's ....
.... when she gave her the flowers.

15 His sudden outburst was not consistent with his character.
keeping
His sudden ....
.... his character.

16 Nothing would induce him to leave the house without locking the door.
circumstances
Under ....
.... without locking the door.

17 Since he retired, his main pastime has been gardening.
spent
Since he retired ....
.... gardening.

18 Marie has the annoying habit of losing her keys.
forever
Marie ....
.... keys.

19 The board of directors will not meet again until the end of the year.
held
A meeting of the board of directors ....
.... the end of the year.

20 A new arrangement over working conditions has been made between the management and the Union.
struck
The management ....
.... over working conditions.

FIXED PHRASES

be/have at one's fingertips:	be/have easily available/ have free access to
blow a fuse:	become very angry/ lose one's temper
come to the fore:	become important or popular
put on a brave face/put a brave face on a situation:	try to hide one's disappointment
without fail:	do sth no matter what
few and far between:	scarce/rare
in the flesh:	in person
in full flow:	(talking) at length
bear fruit:	be successful
on the face of it:	judging by how sth appears
point the finger of suspicion:	blame sb for sth
see fit:	think suitable or right
flat broke:	penniless
not have the foggiest idea:	not know sth at all
get cold feet:	be nervous or frightened because sth might fail
by/from force of habit:	used to doing sth without thinking

15 *Complete the sentences using one of the fixed phrases in an appropriate form.*

1 Daphne is feeling anxious and is .... about changing her job.

2 As Jane was the only one in the office everything .... at her for the broken window.

3 Why are you accusing me of breaking the window? I haven't .... what you are talking about.

4 The chances of winning the Lotto are unfortunately ....

5 I have tea and cereal every day for breakfast ....

6 Living in the city centre means that you have all the necessary amenities ....

7 The deadline for the project is June 1st ....

8 .... the economy seems to be improving but in reality there is the possibility of a recession.

16 *Choose the correct item.*

1 After buying an expensive new penthouse Marianna was flat ....
  A shattered   C smashed
  B broke   D torn

2 The new political party came to the .... after the general election.
  A front   C side
  B back   D fore

3 On the eighth day of the strike the Minister .... fit to make a statement.
  A saw   C looked
  B showed   D appeared

4 Harry blew a .... when his holiday was cancelled.
  A switch   C fuse
  B plug   D socket

5 Despite her poor exam results, Alice put a .... face on the situation.
  A tough   C courageous
  B brave   D bold

6 I was thrilled to meet Paul Mc Cartney in the .... when I sat next to him at the theatre.
  A meat   C flesh
  B blood   D vein

17 *Find the mistake and correct it.*

0 There are many underprivileged ~~childs~~ in the world.   *children*

1 He refused that he had been there at the time of the accident.   ....

2 She did very good in the test.   ....

3 He enjoys listening to the works of classic composers.   ....

4 Her eyes have the same colour as her mother's.   ....

5 You can divide this box of sweets between the three of you.   ....

6 As a conclusion, I'd like to say thank you for you help.   ....

7 The committee is consisting of twelve members.   ....

8 There were a continuous flow of traffic into the town centre.   ....

9 The cooker in this restaurant is renowned for his excellent cuisine.   ....

10 He purchased several items, which cost £200 all together.   ....

11 You may have to bear the price of any damage.   ....

12 All the passengers and crew were dead in the plane crash.   ....

13 I want to catch plane BA413.   ....

14 The employee was dismissed for denying to work overtime.   ....

15 He was rushed to hospital because he had it difficult to breathe.   ....

16 They took a quiet, candlelit dinner together.   ....

17 The tormented woman sees horrific nightmares every night.   ....

18 No one of the accident victims pulled through.   ....

19 As a team we must work well together and help each another.   ....

20 Her parents' attitude had a bad affect on her.   ....

21 She did three mistakes in one sentence.   ....

22 She was considering to give up her career.   ....

23 Her parents would not let her to stay out late.   ....

24 Skiing is her best activity. ....

25 Everyone of my two sisters is a teacher. ....

26 He stopped tying his shoe-lace on the way up the steps. ....

27 I have written three letters from this morning. ....

18 *Match the items from column A with those from column B and then fill in the blanks with the correct idiom.*

Column A		Column B	
0	as tough as	a	a dog
1	as silent as	b	a rake
2	as right as	c	a sheet
3	as sick as	d	old boots
4	as strong as	e	a cucumber
5	as thin as	f	a post
6	as white as	g	the grave
7	as cool as	h	chalk and cheese
8	as deaf as	i	a horse
9	as different as	j	rain

0 *d*   2 ....   4 ....   6 ....   8 ....
1 ....   3 ....   5 ....   7 ....   9 ....

0 You couldn't make her cry if you tried. She's *as tough as old boots.*

1 You'll have to speak louder; he's ....

2 She turned .... when he told her the news about the accident.

3 Let him carry the trunk. He's ....

4 You may not feel well now, but you'll be .... in a few days.

5 I promise to be .... about your secret.

6 Why is she dieting? She's already ....

7 After eating twelve chocolate bars, he was ....

8 Although everyone else was shaking with nerves, Betsy was ....

9 John and his brother are not at all alike; they're .....
....

19 *Read the following notes on a school excursion and complete the announcement below, using no more than two words to fill each blank. The words you need do not occur in the notes. The first one has been done for you.*

Dates:	15-17 March
Destination:	Stratford-upon-Avon – Special study excursion – Shakespeare's historical plays
Accommodation:	two per room, (breakfast & dinner incl.)
Price:	£59.00
Extras:	lunch, pocket money, museums
Advice:	Notify secretary by end of next week if going. Guests may come if space allows. Meet at school entrance 8 am 15/3

Limpton School wishes **(0)** *to announce* this year's Special Study Excursion to Stratford-upon-Avon, **(1)** .... number of Shakespeare's historical plays are **(2)** .... this season. The excursion is **(3)** .... take **(4)** .... 15th - 17th March, and coach, room – double **(5)** .... with **(6)** .... board – theatre tickets and a guided tour **(7)** .... in the price of £59. Students will be **(8)** .... to pay for one meal per **(9)** ...., museum **(10)** .... fees and any personal expenses. The secretary must **(11)** .... by the end of next week if students **(12)** .... go. Guests may be **(13)** .... space is available. Departure will be at 8 am, 15th March from the school entrance. **(14)** .... information **(15)** .... obtained from the secretary.

20 Use the following notes to prepare a short health guide for tourists travelling abroad. Write in complete sentences for each numbered set of notes, using connecting words and phrases as appropriate. You must use all the words in the same order as the notes. You may add words and change the form of words where necessary. The first point has been expanded for you in the example.

0 Inquire – travel agent's – vaccinations necessary – country visit.

Inquire at a/your travel agent's which vaccinations are necessary for the country you are visiting.

1 Utmost importance – take holiday insurance – duration holiday.

....
....
....
....

2 Not advise drink local tap-water/bottled water easy available local supermarkets – or able take supply – sterilising tablets.

....
....
....
....

3 Well-advised – take anti-mosquito device or similar type – repel – insects.

....
....
....

WORD USAGE

21 Read the text below. Use the word given in capitals at the end of some of the lines to form a word that fits in the space in the same line.

THE ART OF GIVING AND TAKING

Gift exchange, which is also called **(0)** *ceremonial* exchange, is the transfer of goods or services that, although regarded as **(1)** .... by people involved, is part of the expected social **(2)** .... Gift exchange may be distinguished from other types of exchange in several respects: the first offering is made in a generous manner and there is no haggling between donor and **(3)** ....; the exchange is an expression of an existing social relationship or of the establishment of a new one that differs from **(4)** .... market relationships; and the profit in gift exchange may be in the sphere of social relationships and prestige rather than in material advantage.

The gift-exchange cycle entails **(5)** .... to give, to receive, and to return. Sanctions may exist to induce people to give, **(6)** .... or loss of prestige resulting from a failure to do so. **(7)** .... to accept a gift may be seen as rejection of social relations and may lead to enmity. The reciprocity of the cycle rests in the necessity to return the gift; the prestige associated with the appearance of **(8)** .... dictates that the value of the return be **(9)** .... equal to or greater than the value of the original gift. Alongside its obvious economic functions, gift exchange is a **(10)** .... expression of social relations.

CEREMONY
VOLUNTEER
BEHAVE

RECEIVE
PERSON

OBLIGE
APPROVE
REFUSE

GENEROUS
APPROXIMATE
SIGNIFY

22 *Choose the correct item.*

0 I'm very sorry, but these .... are out of stock at the moment.
(A) goods   C commodities
B wares   D supplies

1 Each .... of the house must pay his own tax.
A dweller   C settler
B resident   D inhabitant

2 My father has decided to .... a beard to cover a small scar he has on his chin.
A rear   C breed
B bring up   D grow

3 The farmer makes money by .... pedigree horses.
A bringing up   C breeding
B nurturing   D growing

4 For months I sat with my binoculars watching a bird .... its young.
A rear   C bring up
B breed   D grow

5 "He .... my rubber, miss!" shouted the boy.
A acquired   C abducted
B ripped off   D swiped

6 My grandmother was a lovely person who .... pleasure from helping others.
A gathered   C deduced
B derived   D collected

7 You were really .... when you paid $100 for those shoes. They're not even leather!
A swiped   C pinched
B ripped oft   D pilfered

8 Many forest – .... animals were killed in the fire.
A dwelling   C inhabiting
B residing   D settling

9 This city has four million ....
A residents   C inhabitants
B dwellers   D settlers

COLLOCATIONS

23 *Fill in the following collocational grid.*

	soldiers	cards	geese	lions	monkeys	wolves	fish	ants	bees	cows	grapes	sheep
a gaggle of												
a shoal of												
a pride of												
a swarm of												
a colony of												
a herd of												
a flock of												
a pack of												
a troop of												
a school of												
a bunch of												

24 *Think of one word which can be used appropriately in all three sentences.*

0 • One doesn't need to be an expert to *appreciate* the beauty of classical music.
  • He seems confident that houses in this area will *appreciate* in value in the next few years.
  • I'll always *appreciate* your help and support.

1 • So what .... of action do you propose to follow?
  • Throughout the .... of history, we see that people do not learn from their mistakes.
  • The river followed a meandering .... and finally flowed into the sea.

2 • The conservatory door had a glass .... in its centre.
  • A .... of experts on the environment will discuss the depletion of the ozone layer.
  • Lights were flashing urgently on the aeroplane's control ....

3 • Sylvia was out in the meadow, ... wild flowers.
  • Floyd is so quarrelsome; he is always .... fights with his schoolmates.
  • .... the winning entry from so many impressive paintings in the competition was no mean task.

4 • China is likely to be a great military .... in the future.
  • As soon as it came into ...., the government set about reforming the National Health Service.
  • Because fossil fuel supplies are fast running out, alternative sources of .... will have to be found.

5 • The .... of the law requires an incisive mind, as well as legal training.
  • Ruby's constant .... resulted in her receiving the Young Pianist of the Year award.
  • It was his .... to wear a hat whenever he went out in the sun.

6 • In the days before electricity, my grandmother had a wood-burning kitchen .... to do the cooking .
  • You'll find a wide .... of clothes and household goods in our autumn sale.
  • The mountain .... extends over three countries.

7 • I .... the parcel I sent you because I didn't want it to get lost.
  • Gloria .... for a course to learn pottery at the college yesterday.
  • The fact that he had been insulted suddenly .... on his face when he flushed with anger.

8 • Joe's .... temper makes everybody avoid him.
  • The .... curry made me reach for the iced water.
  • The .... news is that the Prime Minister intends to resign.

9 • Despite being in her fifties, Jocelyn has hardly a .... on her face.
  • The patient .... of people waiting in the queue at the bank shuffled slowly forward.
  • A tree had fallen across the railway .... in the storm, making train cancellations inevitable.

10 • Although the two women look remarkably alike, there is no family .... between them.
  • A .... on my beautiful gold chain broke and I lost it.
  • There is no .... between the minister and the spy ring, despite the rumours which are circulating in the government.

11 • I wish she would turn down the .... on the TV as the noise is disturbing me.
  • .... one deals with European history up to 1500 AD.
  • Dough should be left to rise until its .... doubles.

12 • When learning to drive, you are taught to check your .... mirror before setting off.
  • The bird's .... was clearly broken so we took it to a vet.
  • The east .... of the stately home was built in the 15th century.

PREPARING FOR PART 5

MEANING AND USAGE I

25 *Choose the correct answer to each question.*

Dreams of similar or identical content experienced by two or more people are sometimes reported between therapists and clients. The English Society for Psychical Research in the 19th century collected dozens of accounts of shared dreams. However, the interest in the subject waned as scientists suggested that these reports proved little more than "the power of biased imagination when applied to coincidence".

The guidelines for writing scary books for children are fairly clear-cut, but I was never aware of how books affect children until I had two of my own. Many parts of scary stories which the adult mind understands as "inoffensive" can seem frightening to a child.

She walked into the room wearing a bright red evening gown. On her head there was what looked like a slaughtered albatross, or was it a hat?

His flat was in a terrible state. There was rubbish everywhere and the floor was covered in wrappers. His fridge had been broken for two weeks – I looked inside and a piece of chicken said hello to me.

Nobody could have predicted the disaster. Nobody could have done anything to prevent it, even if they had predicted it. The once glorious city lay in ruins: the tall, proud buildings had become rubble, the majestic statues outside the city hall lay shattered on the dusty ground, and the once busy highways were torn apart as though they were made of paper.

0 Why does the writer put the phrase "the power of... coincidence" in quotation marks?
  A He is using it to imply something else.
  B He is reporting someone else's exact words.
  C He is implying that he disagrees with the statement.

1 Why does the writer put the word "inoffensive" in quotation marks?
  A He is suggesting that we may be wrong in describing certain parts of children's stories as "inoffensive".
  B He is reporting someone else's exact words.
  C He is implying that adults mean something else when they use the term "inoffensive".

2 What does the writer mean by the phrase "On her head... or was it a hat?"
  A The woman's appearance confused him.
  B He is being ironic about the woman's appearance.
  C He is admiring the woman's hat.

3 Explain the use of the phrase "a piece of chicken said hello to me."
  A The writer is implying that the man kept living things in his fridge.
  B The writer is implying that there was a toy chicken inside the man's fridge.
  C The writer is humorously describing the spoilt food in the man's fridge by implying that it had come to life.

4 Explain the use of the phrases "proud buildings" and "majestic statues".
  A The writer is trying to convey the extent of the disaster by telling us the fate of the things that the city was once proud of.
  B The writer is implying that there is some pride left in the city, despite the disaster.
  C The writer is criticising the inhabitants of the city as being arrogant.

High-tech toxicology tests are being devised to monitor foods for bacteria before they go onto the supermarket shelf. However, the best processing in the world cannot protect us from ourselves: more than 75% of reported food poisoning cases can be traced to improper food handling and preparation by consumers.

Many of us are confronted with kids who "throw a wobbly" on a regular basis. Sometimes we handle it well, sometimes we don't. The first step to helping your child work through a crying fit is understanding what's going on with him. This series of articles can help you deal with crying fits and other emotionally challenging experiences.

Keeping pace with the times, Liverpool FC have launched their own TV station. Its programmes feature news bulletins about events affecting the club, news reports from the training centre and, of course, live matches.

In the meantime, Manchester United's own TV station has shown profits of £16 million in the first six months of its operation. Newcastle United TV is also doing well, with profits of £2.5 million in its first three months.

Researchers have cooked up a coating that's much harder and slicker than Teflon. The new substance, called NFC (standing for "Near-Frictionless Carbon"), is thought to be the slickest carbon-based material in the world.

Sir,
Your article about continuing to drive past one's middle age (January 22, *Driving On Through Time*) was an insult to thousands of people over 65 who are still driving their cars efficiently and safely. On what evidence does Harry Mills base his claim that "eyesight is bound to deteriorate after 65"? He assumes things before examining any facts, and that has to be the definition of putting the cart before the horse.

Plane-spotters, flight simulator fans and other aviation freaks can now practise their hobby on the World Wide Web. Visit **http://www.airliners.net** for a 260,000 – picture collection of aircraft taking off, landing, flying and taxiing, or try **http://webevents.broadcast.com/simuflite** to listen to the conversations that take place between air traffic control and the pilots of departing or arriving flights.

5 Explain the use of the phrase "the best processing in the world cannot protect us from ourselves".
   A The writer urges us to prepare food in a hygienic manner regardless of how it has been processed.
   B The writer is sceptical about toxicology tests.
   C The writer fears that incidences of food poisoning will rise.

6 What is the meaning of the phrase "throw a wobbly"?
   A Suddenly become frustrated, angry and lose your temper.
   B Suddenly become ill.
   C Suddenly become tired.

7 Why does the writer use the phrase "keeping pace with the times"?
   A He is implying that Liverpool FC took very little time to set up their own TV station.
   B He is implying that Liverpool FC are following a trend.
   C He is implying that other teams will do the same.

8 What does the phrase "cooked up" mean as it is used by the writer?
   A discovered
   B developed
   C invented

9 Explain the phrase "put the cart before the horse".
   A Assume that all people over a certain age have poor eyesight, as does the writer of the article to which this letter refers.
   B Do things in the wrong order, as in making an assumption before examining any evidence.
   C Deliberately insult somebody in order to provoke them, as in the article the writer is referring to.

10 Explain the phrase "aviation freaks".
   A People who are afraid of flying.
   B People who like studying and collecting information about aircraft and flying.
   C People who are interested in strange-looking aircraft.

85

Paper 3 Use of English   Time: 1 hour 30 minutes

PART 1

Read the text below and think of the word which best fits each space. Use only one word in each space.

ISLAND LIFE

Life **(0)** *on* a small island may **(1)** .... very inviting to the tourists who spend a few weeks there in the summer, but the realities of living on **(2)** .... is virtually a rock surrounded by water are quite different from what the casual visitor imagines. **(3)** .... in summer the island villages are full of people, life and activity, **(4)** .... the tourist season is over many of the shop owners shut **(5)** .... their businesses and return to the mainland to spend the winter in town. **(6)** .... to say, those who remain on the island, **(7)** .... by choice or necessity, face many hardships. One of the worst of these is isolation, with **(8)** .... many attendant problems. When the weather is bad, which is often the **(9)** .... in winter, the island is entirely cut off; this means not only that people **(10)** .... have goods delivered but also that a medical emergency can be fatal **(11)** .... someone confined to an island. At **(12)** .... telephone communication is cut off, which means that **(13)** .... word from the outside world can get **(14)** .... Isolation and loneliness are basic reasons why so many people have left the islands for a better and more secure life in the mainland cities, in **(15)** .... of the fact that this involves leaving "home".

PART 2

Read the text below. Use the word given in capitals at the end of some of the lines to form a word that fits in the space in the same line.

A BUILDING OF CLASS

The Crystal Palace was a glass-and-iron exhibition hall in Hyde Park, London, that housed the Great Exhibition of 1851. The structure was taken down and **(0)** *rebuilt* (1852-1854) at Sydenham Hill, where it survived until 1936. In 1849   BUILD

Prince Albert, husband of Queen Victoria and president of the Royal Society of Arts, invited **(16)** .... from all over the world to participate in   EXHIBIT

an **(17)** .... Plans were developed, and the necessary   EXPOSE

funds speedily raised, so the **(18)** .... exhibition   MEMORY

opened in the Crystal Palace on May 1, 1851. The Crystal Palace was a

(19) .... construction of an intricate network of slender iron   REMARK

rods sustaining walls of clear glass. With more than 13 km of display tables, the

number of **(20)** .... was about 14,000, nearly half of whom   PARTICIPATE

were non-British. The **(21)** .... of millions of visitors generated   ATTEND

a **(22)** .... profit and a closing ceremony was held on October 15.   SIZE

The Crystal Palace established an **(23)** .... standard   ARCHITECT

for later international fairs and exhibitions, which likewise were housed in glass

buildings resembling conservatories. On the night of November 30, 1936, it was

virtually destroyed by fire; the towers that remained **(24)** ....   DAMAGE

were finally demolished in 1941 because they were deemed a dangerous

(25) .... for incoming German bombers.   LAND

PART 3

Think of one word only which can be used appropriately in all three sentences.

0 • One doesn't need to be an expert to *appreciate* the beauty of classical music.
  • He seems confident that houses in this area will *appreciate* in value in the next few years.
  • I'll always *appreciate* your help and support.

26 • Documents of a highly .... nature are jealously guarded in the government archives.
  • From a young age, Ian had been .... to other people's feelings.
  • The planetarium's telescope is so .... that only trained specialists are permitted to use it.

27 • Eric swam only one .... of the pool before cramp and fatigue brought his exercise to an end.
  • The director is renowned for making films that exceed three hours in ....
  • She bought a .... of lilac velvet with a view to making the dress herself.

28 • As a trainee, he has to survive on a modest salary, though he .... a little extra on commission.
  • The boss .... him do overtime every day.
  • A Japanese company .... the electronic components found in this product.

29 • The company was .... on the principles of trust, integrity and reliability.
  • It was a good idea to have .... Information Technology into the syllabus.
  • By working hard Bill .... up his savings and managed to buy a car.

30 • Intricate stone carvings decorate the steps at the .... of the monument.
  • The tourists used the village as a .... to tour the surrounding countryside.
  • Oil is used as a .... to which fragrances are added for the purpose of massage.

31 • The troops at the .... had to endure lack of food and comforts for many months.
  • When the baby lay on his .... he started to cry.
  • Michelle maintained a brave .... as her way of dealing with personal tragedy.

PART 4

Complete the second sentence so that it has a similar meaning to the first sentence, using the word given. Do not change the word given. You must use between three and eight words, including the word given.

0 Nobody spoke when the teacher asked who the culprit was.
  remained
  Everyone *remained silent when the teacher asked who the culprit was.*

32 Some people accept that life is full of problems.
  resigned
  Some people .... full of problems.

33 He makes too many mistakes to be considered for promotion.
  frequent
  His .... be considered for promotion.

34 He will not be put off taking that trip to China.
  deter
  Nothing .... trip to China.

35 Neil is unreliable and often breaks his promises.
  goes
  Neil is unreliable and .... promises.

36 Virtue is of little value in a corrupt government.
  counts
  Virtue .... government.

37 Could you tell me where the lobby is?
  direct
  Could .... lobby?

38 Margaret is said to be a very good cook.
  reputation
  Margaret .... very good cook.

39 Reality shows on TV are extremely popular at the moment.
  flavour
  Reality shows on TV .... at the moment.

PART 5

For questions **40-44** read the following texts. For questions **40 - 43** answer with a word or short phrase. You do not need to write complete sentences. For question **44**, write a summary according to the instructions given.

It is staggering to think that Heathrow Airport, which is now almost a self-contained city with a population of 60,000 workers, started life as a small grass airfield. It was initially privately owned by the Fairey company and used mostly for test flying. London's commercial flights took off from nearby Heston and Hanworth Park airfields.

World War II changed the course of Heathrow's history. In 1944 it was requisitioned by the Air Ministry to be developed as a major transport base for the Royal Air Force. It was never to be. Before the work was completed the war ended, and thus surfaced the prospect of a huge expansion in civil aviation.

line 8

London needed a large airport with modern equipment and the partly-built site at Heathrow was ideal. One runway was ready for use, and when the Ministry of Civil Aviation took it over in 1946 a tented terminal was quickly put in place and a new chapter began. As air traffic boomed, the airport found itself with an ever-increasing demand for passenger facilities. By the mid-50s, restaurants, cafés and shops had attached themselves to the airport.

Next came the new Oceanic terminal handling long-haul carriers, a function it still performs as Terminal 3, followed by the opening of Terminal 1 in 1968. Increased congestion in the central area led to the construction of Terminal 4 in 1986 on the south side of the airport, a modern facility but an inconvenient 10-20 minute transfer from the heart of Heathrow.

The pressures on London's principal airport keep mounting. The extension of the city rail link to the airport central area is now open and Heathrow is fighting hard to build yet another passenger terminal in the face of local objections. Today's battles are tomorrow's history at the grass airfield which became a worldwide name.

40 Why was the plan to turn Heathrow into a major base for the Royal Airforce "never to be" (line 8)?

....

....

41 What are the advantages and disadvantages of Heathrow Airport's Terminal 4?

....

....

Nottingham Victoria station began operating on May 24, 1900. Main line services from London to Sheffield had already been passing through it for over a year.

The construction was on a grand scale - around 750,000 cubic metres of sandstone rock was excavated from the cavernous site. Some 1300 houses and 24 public buildings previously on the site had to be demolished. The site was approximately 13 acres in size and 690 metres long, and had an average width of 110 metres with a tunnel at each end of it for access. Great Central and Great Northern Railways shared the station, which constituted legal grounds for not naming it Nottingham Central. The name which was finally agreed upon was Nottingham Victoria.

The train traffic that passed through included London-Manchester expresses, local services, cross-country services as well as freight trains. The two railways that shared the station offered a superb network of lines to almost every destination in Great Britain.

line 16 —— Nottingham Victoria was a comfortable, friendly and luxurious station, in which the city of Nottingham took pride. Unfortunately, its heyday did not last long. By the mid 1960s, Great Central Railways was in decline. Services were being cut and the trains themselves were old and unreliable. As passenger numbers fell, Great Northern Railways also started using the station less and less. The last through service from Nottingham to London ran on September 3, 1966.

The station was finally closed on September 4, 1967. People watched as the bulldozers tore the prestigious building down. The whole demolition took less than a day and a half. The clock tower was spared, but does not blend into its modern surroundings of shopping centres, restaurants and cafés, and stands as an odd monument to a once truly great station.

42 Why was the name "Nottingham Victoria" chosen for the station?

....

....

43 What does the term "its heyday" mean (line 16)?

....

....

44 In a paragraph of between 50 and 70 words, give an account of the two sites discussed in the passages as they are today.

....

....

....

....

....

Direct speech is the exact words someone said or wrote.
Reported speech is retelling exactly what someone said or wrote, without using their actual words.

There are three types of Direct Speech which can be reported:	A. statements B. questions C. commands/requests

Direct Speech		Reported Speech
• STATEMENT "The plane will be late," they said.	→	• THAT-CLAUSE They said **(that)** the plane **would be late.**
• QUESTION "Why are you late?" she asked. "Are you feeling well?" he asked me.	→ →	• WH-CLAUSE or IF-CLAUSE She asked **why I was late.** He asked me **if I was feeling well.**
• COMMAND/REQUEST "Don't touch it!" he said. "Turn on the light, please,"he said.	→ →	• TO-INFINITIVE He told me **not to touch it.** He asked me **to turn on the light.**

The most common reporting verbs are **say**, **tell** and **ask**.

• We use **say** with or without **to + personal object** in direct speech but without **to + personal object** in reported speech.
"I don't know what to do," he **said** to Mary.
He **said** (that) he didn't know what to do.

• We use **tell** in direct and reported speech with a **personal object**.
"I don't know where the café is", she **told me**.
She **told Mary** to wait outside the Principal's office.

Notes

• We can use **say + infinitive**.
The teacher **said to study** harder.

• We cannot use **say about**. We can use **tell sb/speak/talk about** instead.
He **told us/spoke/talked about** his experiences travelling in Canada.

• We use **ask** in reported questions and commands.
He said to me, "Please don't move!"
He **asked** me not to move.
He said, "Do you like strawberries?"
He **asked** me if I liked strawberries.

There are some common expressions with **say**, **tell** and **ask**. These are:

say	say good morning etc, say a few words, say no more, say one's prayers, say sth, say so, say for certain, etc
tell	tell the truth, tell a lie, tell sb the time, tell sb one's name, tell sb's fortune, tell a story, tell a secret, tell sb so, tell sb the way, tell one from another, tell the difference, etc
ask	ask a favour, ask the time, ask a question, ask the price, etc

1 *Fill in the blanks with* **say**, **tell**, **speak** *or* **ask** *in the right form.*

0 "I don't think he will be on time," he *said*.
1 Mark likes .... about his schooldays.
2 She .... the price of the hairdryer that was in the sale.
3 He .... goodbye to his mother and left for school.
4 Father used to .... us a story before we went to bed.
5 Sharon .... me to help her with her homework.
6 "I can't .... her secret," she .... to me.
7 I think he will come but I can't .... for certain.

CHANGING FROM DIRECT INTO REPORTED SPEECH

- **Verb tenses** change as follows:

Direct Speech		Reported Speech
Simple Present		Simple Past
"I **can't stand** that boy," she said.	→	She said (that) she **couldn't stand** that boy
Present Continuous		Past Continuous
"I'm **having** a nice time," she said.	→	She said (that) she **was having** a nice time
Present Perfect Simple		Past Perfect Simple
"I've **booked** my summer holiday," he said.	→	He said (that) he **had booked** his summer holiday.
Present Perfect Continuous		Past Perfect Continuous
"I've **been waiting** for you all morning," he said.	→	He said (that) he **had been waiting** for me all morning
Simple Past		Past Perfect
"I **failed** my driving test," he said.	→	He said (that) he **had failed** his driving test.
Simple Future		Conditional
"I'll **tidy** my room tomorrow," she said.	→	She said (that) she **would tidy** her room the next day.
Future Continuous		Conditional Continuous
"I'll **be working** in Paris next year," he said.	→	He said (that) he **would be working** in Paris the following year.

Note: *Past Perfect Simple* and *Continuous* do not change their forms in Reported Speech.

- The following words also change:

Direct Speech		Reported Speech
this/these		that/those/the
here		there
come		go
bring		take
He said to me, "**Come** and look at **this** bird."	→	He told me to **go** and look at **that** bird.
She said to me, "Stand **here** and wait for me."	→	She told me to stand **there** and wait for her.

- **Pronouns** and **possessive adjectives** change according to the meaning of the sentence.

Direct Speech		Reported Speech
He said, "I can't do it **myself**."	→	He said (that) **he** couldn't do it **himself**.

- **Time expressions** change as follows:

Direct Speech	Reported Speech
tonight	that night
now	then, at that time, at once/immediately
now that	since
today	that day
yesterday	the day before, the previous day
tomorrow	the day after, the following day, the next day
tomorrow morning	the morning after, the following morning/the next morning
last night	the night before, the previous night
the day before yesterday	two days before
the day after tomorrow	in two days time/in two days
this week/month/year	that week/month/year
last week/month/year/Monday etc	the previous week/month/year/Monday etc
next week/month/year/Monday etc	the following week/month/year/Monday etc
two days/years etc, ago	two days/years etc, before
"He left **last week**," she said.	→ She said (that) he had left **the previous week/the week before**.

THERE IS NO CHANGE IN THE VERB TENSES IN REPORTED SPEECH WHEN:

	Direct Speech	Reported Speech
• the sentence expresses a general truth or permanent states and conditions.	My mother said, "It **gets** dark earlier in the winter."	My mother said (that) it **gets** dark earlier in the winter.
• the introductory verb is in the Present, Future or Present Perfect tense.	She **says/will say/has said**, " I **can cook** well."	She **says/will say/has said** (that) she **can cook** well.
• the verb of the sentence is in the Unreal Past (e.g. 2nd type conditionals, wishes, it's time, would rather, suppose, as if)	He said, "I **would rather go** out for dinner." She said, "**It's time** we **went** home."	He said (that) he **would rather go** out for dinner. She said (that) **it was time** they **went** home.
• the following verbs are used: had better, could, would, used to, needn't have, should, might and ought to.	Her boyfriend said, " I really **ought to go** home." She said, "**I'd better consult** the doctor this evening."	Her boyfriend said (that) he really **ought to go** home. She said (that) she **'d better consult** the doctor that evening.
• there is Past Simple or Past Continuous in a Clause of Time.	She said, "**When I was swimming, I got** cramp."	She said (that) **when** she **was swimming**, she **got** cramp.
• the sentence expresses sth which is believed to be true. In this case the verb tense can either change or remain unchanged. However, if the sentence expresses sth which is not true, then the verb changes.	He said, "Ethiopia **is** a third-world country." (true) He said, "Ethiopia **is** a highly developed country." (false)	He said (that) Ethiopia **is/was** a third-world country. He said (that) Ethiopia **was** a highly developed country.
• it is up-to-date reporting.	Anne said, "I**'ve got** a headache."	Anne said (that) she**'s got** a headache.

2 *Rewrite the following sentences in reported speech.*

0 "Don't walk on the white carpet!" said the mother to her son.
The mother told her son not to walk on the white carpet.

1 "Egypt has a very long recorded history, "she said.
....
....

2 "Do you think Terence will join us for dinner tonight?" Joanne asked me.
....
....

3 Peter said, "The waiter has made a mistake with the bill."
....
....

4 "Stop picking on your younger sister, will you?" he said to his daughter.
....
....

5 "Would it be possible to extend my club membership?" Adrienne asked the manager.
....
....

6 "I have no intention of lending Nick my car," said Diane.
....
....

7 "What did the car dealer tell you?" Isabelle asked me.
....
....

8 "When I entered the house, there were footprints on the floor," she said to me.
....
....

9 "I'd rather not leave before Leo arrives," Anna said.
....
....

MODAL VERBS IN REPORTED SPEECH

Modal verbs generally remain unchanged in reported speech. Some of them, however, change as follows:

must	Direct Speech	Reported Speech
• When **must** expresses **obligation**, it changes into **had to** (when the sentence in direct speech refers to the **present**) or **would have to** (when the sentence in direct speech refers to the **future**).	He said, "You **must** try harder."	He said (that) I **had to** try harder.
	He said, "I **must** get my hair cut."	He said (that) he **would have to** get his hair cut.
• When **must** expresses **advice**, **duty** or **logical assumption**, it does not change or it changes into **should**.	He said, "You **must** try that new restaurant." (advice)	He said (that) I **must/should** try that new restaurant.
	He said, "You **must** always lock the door before you leave." (duty)	He said (that) I **must/should** always lock the door before I leave/left.
	He said, "You **must** be tired." (logical assumption)	He said (that) I **must** be tired.
• **mustn't** usually remains unchanged or it is expressed by **wasn't to/weren't to/couldn't** or a **negative infinitive**.	He said to me, "You **mustn't** enter that room."	He told me (that) I **mustn't/wasn't to/couldn't** enter that room. or He told me **not to enter** that room.

can changes into:	Direct Speech	Reported Speech
• **could** when the sentence in direct speech refers to the **present**.	He said, "I **can** help you."	He said (that) he **could** help me.
• **would be able to** when the direct sentence refers to the **future**.	He said, "I **can** finish it tomorrow."	He said (that) he **would be able to** finish it the following day.

shall changes into:	Direct Speech	Reported Speech
• **offered** when it expresses **willingness** to do sth.	He said, "**Shall** I open the door?"	He **offered** to open the door.
• **should** when it asks **for advice**.	He said, "What **shall** I do?"	He wondered what he **should** do.
• **would** when it is used to **ask for information**.	He said, "When **shall** we arrive?"	He asked when they **would** arrive.

needn't changes into:	Direct Speech	Reported Speech
• **didn't need to/didn't have to** when the sentence in direct speech refers to the **present** or remains the same.	She said, "You **needn't** worry."	She said I **didn't need to/didn't have to/needn't** worry.
• **wouldn't have to** when the sentence in direct speech refers to the **future**.	She said, "You **needn't** give me a lift tomorrow."	She said I **wouldn't have** to give her a lift the following day.

may changes into:	Direct Speech	Reported Speech
• **might** when it expresses **probability**.	He said "It **may** snow tonight."	He said it **might** snow that night.
• **might/could** when it expresses **permission or concession**.	He said "You **may** go."	He said I **might/could** go.

3 *Rewrite the following sentences in reported speech.*

1 The waitress said, "Shall I put the leftover pizza in a doggy bag for you?"

....

....

2 My boss said, "You needn't attend the meeting tomorrow."

....

....

3 The supervisor said, "You mustn't overlook such a serious mistake again."

....

....

4 Margaret said to the airhostess, "When shall we be landing?"

....

....

5 Martin said, "I can give you a definite answer next Friday."

....

....

6 My lawyer said, "You needn't give me your final answer now."

....

....

7 Peter said, "I may not finish my project in time."

....

....

8 The chairperson said, "We must meet again on Saturday afternoon."

....

....

9 The assistant chef said, "What shall I do with the extra pastry dough?"

....

....

10 He said, "You must be very hungry."

....

....

EXCLAMATIONS – "YES" AND "NO" SHORT ANSWER – QUESTION TAGS

A. Exclamations are introduced in reported speech by **exclaim, say** or **give an exclamation,** with an exclamation of **surprise/horror/disgust/delight, thank, wish, call,** etc. They usually become statements when reported and the exclamation mark becomes a full stop.

Direct Speech		Reported Speech
She said, "Happy Birthday!"	→	*She **wished** me (a) happy birthday.*
"Yuk!" she said when she saw the mouldy cake.	→	*She **gave an exclamation of disgust** when she saw the mouldy cake.*
He said, "You idiot!"	→	*He **called** me an idiot.*

B. **"Yes"** and **"No"** short answers are expressed in reported speech by **subject + appropriate auxiliary/introductory verb.**

Direct Speech		Reported Speech
"Will you come with me? he said. *"Yes", I said.*	→	*He asked me if I would go with him and I said **I would**.*
"Can I have a pay rise?" he said. *"No", the boss replied.*	→	*He asked (the boss) if he could have a pay rise and/but the boss **refused/said he couldn't**.*

C. Question Tags

Question tags are omitted in reported speech. However, we can use the verb **reminded** as a suitable introductory verb in order to retain their effect.

Direct Speech		Reported Speech
"This isn't the first time she has made this mistake, ***is it?"*** *he said.*	→	*He **reminded** me that it wasn't the first time (that) she had made that mistake.*

94

4 *Turn the following sentences into reported speech.*

1 "Will you lend me your car?" he said. "No," his father said.

....

....

2 "What a wonderful present!" Frances said.

....

....

3 "Well done! That was a wonderful performance," she said to them.

....

....

4 She said, "Be careful with that knife! It's very sharp!"

....

....

5 "Good luck with the test," he said.

....

....

6 "That's revolting!" he said when he tasted the soup.

....

....

7 "The curry we ate at the restaurant made us ill, didn't it?" Joe said. "It certainly did;" Elizabeth replied.

....

....

....

8 "You liar!" she said to him.

....

....

9 "Will you remind me to phone Jim later?" he said. "Yes," I said.

....

....

INTRODUCTORY VERBS

Introductory Verbs	Direct Speech	Reported Speech
agree demand offer promise + infinitive refuse threaten	"Yes, I'll take the job." "I must be informed of your decision now." "Shall I help you?" "I will write to you next week." "No, I won't tell you the answer." "Slow down or I'll get out of the car."	He **agreed** to take the job. He **demanded** to be informed of my decision immediately. He **offered** to help me. He **promised** to write to me the next/ following week. He **refused** to tell me the answer. He **threatened** to get out of the car if I didn't slow down.
advise allow ask beg command encourage forbid instruct + sb + infinitive invite order permit remind urge warn want	"You should see a doctor." "You can leave early." "Please, don't shout at me." "Please , please, don't punish me." "Turn around slowly!" "Go on, buy yourself a new car!" "You mustn't talk during the test." "Turn left at the traffic lights." "I'd like you to come to my wedding." "Stop talking at once!" "You may enter the palace." "Don't forget to post the letters." "Think about it very seriously." "Don't believe a word." "I'd very much like you to come."	He **advised** me to see a doctor. He **allowed** me to leave early. He **asked** me not to shout at him. He **begged** me not to punish him. He **commanded** her to turn around slowly. He **encouraged** me to buy a new car. He **forbade** us to talk during the test. He **instructed** me to turn left at the traffic lights. He **invited** me (to go) to his wedding. He **ordered** me to stop talking. He **permitted** me to enter the palace. He **reminded** me to post the letters. He **urged** me to think about it very seriously. He **warned** me not to believe a word. He very much **wanted** me to go.

5a Grammar: Reported Speech

accuse sb of, admit (to), apologise for, deny, insist on, suggest } + gerund	"You lied to me."	He accused me of lying/having lied to him.
	"Yes, I'm the culprit." "I'm sorry I missed the meeting."	He admitted (to) being the culprit. He apologised for having missed the meeting.
	"I didn't lose the tickets." "You must let me help you."	He denied losing/having lost the tickets. He insisted on me/my letting him help me.
	"Let's go to the park!"	He suggested going to the park.
complain to sb about + gerund/noun	"You're always late to work!"	He complained to me about my lateness/being late to work.
agree, claim, complain, deny, exclaim, explain, inform sb, promise, suggest } + that-clause	"Yes, it is a foolish idea." "I've never seen her before."	He agreed that it was a foolish idea. He claimed that he had never seen her/never to have seen her before.
	"You never listen to me." "No, I didn't see the accident." "What a horrible colour!" "Cheating in exams is a very serious matter." "The cheque for the car is in the post."	He complained that I never listened to him. He denied that he had seen the accident. He exclaimed that it was a horrible colour. He explained that cheating in exams was a very serious matter. He informed me that the cheque for the car was in the post.
	"I'll be very careful." "You ought to try harder."	He promised that he would be very careful. He suggested that I should try harder.
explain to sb + why/how + clause	"That's how I recognised the film star."	He explained to me how he had recognised the film star.
wonder where/what/why/how + clause (when the subject of the introductory verb is **not the same** as the subject in the indirect question)	He asked himself, "Why is she unhappy?"	He wondered why she was unhappy.
wonder where/what/why/how + infinitive (when the subject of the infinitive is the **same** as the subject of the verb)	He asked himself, "Where shall I buy her present from?"	He wondered where to buy her present from.

5 Rewrite the following sentences in reported speech, using an appropriate introductory verb.

1 "Would you like to come to a show with me tonight?" he said.
....
....

2 "Shall we buy some new furniture for the study?" she said.
....
....

3 "He's always moaning about his mother-in-law," she said.
....
....

4 "I'll give you the money back tomorrow," she said.
....
....

5 She asked herself, "When shall I see him again?"
....
....

6 "Give us the money or we'll reveal your secret," the blackmailers said to her.
....
....

7 "Don't forget you have a doctor's appointment at 11am," I said to him.

....
....

8 "Please, please, give me one more chance," the boy said to me.

....
....

9 "You will attend your aunt's wedding," my father said.

....
....

10 "It was John who wrote this graffiti on the wall," said his brother.

....
....

11 "Why don't we postpone the meeting for tomorrow?" the boss said.

....
....

12 "We know you were lying in your testimony," the policeman said.

....
....

MIXED TYPES OF REPORTED SPEECH

In everyday conversation, we use a mixture of statements, commands and questions. When changing them into reported speech, we can connect them with the following linkers: **and, as, adding that, and he added that, because, but, since, and he/she went on to say, and he/she continued, explaining that,** etc or **the introductory verb in present participle form**. Language features such as *oh, well* etc, which are used in direct speech, are omitted in reported speech.

Direct Speech	Reported Speech
"Oh, it's very cold," he said. "Shall I close the window?" →	He remarked that it was very cold **and** offered to close the window. (Oh is omitted.)
"He can't come," she said. "He has a meeting." →	She said that he couldn't go **as/because/since** he had a meeting.
"Why don't you buy a Mini?" he said. "They're very economical to run." →	He suggested that I should buy a Mini, **explaining that** they **are/were** very economical to run.

6 *Turn the following into reported speech.*

1 "I know that John's an adventurous businessman," Paul said. "I'd never have expected him to get mixed up with such a notorious firm, though."

....
....
....
....

2 "When I first came here," Susan said, " I had a hard time with the language, but now that I've been here for five years, I find I can communicate without any difficulty."

....
....
....
....

3 She went on to say, "I usually only teach beginner's classes but since we're understaffed at the moment, I have to take an advanced class too."

....
....
....
....

4 "I hope," he said, "that you'll consider taking over the shop when I retire as you've developed an excellent eye for antiques. And that's quite a compliment, I assure you, coming from me."

....
....
....
....

5 "Who are you going to leave the house to?" I asked
my uncle. "Perhaps," I went on, "you should leave it
to Sarah as she seems to be the most attached to it."

   ....
   ....
   ....
   ....
   ....

6 "Don't imagine that just because I've criticised you, I
don't think you're a good musician," he said to me.
"With enough practice, I have no doubt that you will
be able to work as a professional."

   ....
   ....
   ....
   ....

7 "Is he going to accept the job offer," she asked, "or
will he just continue to stagnate here until it's time
for him to retire?"

   ....
   ....
   ....
   ....

8 "I've heard her say that she may give up her job
and open a restaurant," he said. "She's certainly a
good enough cook to do it."

   ....
   ....
   ....
   ....

9 "I needn't have bothered to buy a spare tyre," she
said, "as I didn't have to change the old one after
all."

   ....
   ....
   ....
   ....

10 "I couldn't believe my ears when I heard they'd split
up," she said to me. "Could you phone Jane to see
if it's really true?"

   ....
   ....
   ....
   ....
   ....

11 "Oh, it looks as if we'll have to cancel the meeting
if Julia is going to be away," he said. "Do you know
when she'll be back?"

   ....
   ....
   ....
   ....

12 "What do you think about going to a new
restaurant tonight?" he said to his wife. "I've just
read about one that's meant to be very good."

   ....
   ....
   ....
   ....

13 "By the way, if anyone rings while I'm out," she told
her secretary, "please take a message and tell them
that I won't be here until tomorrow afternoon."

   ....
   ....
   ....
   ....

14 "I might be able to come," he said to Sarah,
"although I won't be able to let you know until
tomorrow."

   ....
   ....
   ....
   ....

15 "Shall I pass on the news to the staff," I asked him,
"or would you prefer I didn't until you've had a
chance to confirm it with the boss?"

   ....
   ....
   ....
   ....

16 "Alright, I made a terrible mistake but I really didn't
do it on purpose," she said.

   ....
   ....
   ....
   ....

7 *Rewrite the following dialogue in reported speech.*

Mr Jones: Mr Smith, would you come into my office, please?

Mr Smith: Certainly, sir.

Mr Jones: Look, we have a problem with the office Christmas party. Mrs White was organising it, but she has been taken ill.

Mr Smith: Would you like me to arrange it instead?

Mr Jones: That would be wonderful! And you'll definitely get a gift basket for yourself and your wife for your extra work.

....
....
....
....
....
....
....
....
....
....

8 *Rewrite the following passage in direct speech.*

The postman asked Mr Wood to sign for the parcel, explaining that it had been sent by Recorded Delivery. Mr Wood exclaimed that it was the gardening book he had been waiting for, and wondered whether the postman was interested in gardening. The postman said that he was very keen on it and that he had a very large garden that was difficult to look after. He asked if Mr Wood could give him any advice on the subject, and Mr Wood offered to lend him the book. The postman accepted his offer gladly and thanked him.

....
....
....
....
....
....
....
....
....
....
....
....

CONVERSATIONAL GRAMMAR

9 *Choose the correct item.*

1 "What lie did Liz tell you this time?"
"She claimed .... before she was two."
A that she could write   C about writing
B to writing   D that she write

2 "What was Bob yelling about?"
"He warned .... touch that wire."
A me to not   C that I don't
B that I not   D me not to

3 "So, how is Anne getting to the airport?"
"She said that her brother .... her a lift."
A would have given   C should give
B would give   D could be given

4 "Did they find out who had taken the money?"
"Yes. Robert finally admitted .... it all."
A to spend   C to have spent
B have spending   D to having spent

5 "Why do you look so upset?"
"Mum refused .... after my flat while I'm away."
A my looking   C to looking
B to look   D me to look

6 "What did the dietician say to Angela?"
"He advised .... down on fats otherwise she would develop heart problems in later life."
A to cut   C her to cut
B that she cuts   D her cut

7 "What did Ivan suggest?"
"He suggested .... on an excursion tomorrow."
A going   C we to go
B us to go   D to going

8 The firefighter ordered .... the building at once.
A to everyone evacuating   C to be evacuated
B everyone to evacuate   D evacuating

9 "What's the matter with Terry and Paula?"
"They said that if the business continued to do so badly they .... sell the house."
A would have to   C had to
B must   D should

10 "How did Gina react when she arrived at her surprise birthday party?"
"She exclaimed .... a wonderful surprise."
A to be   C being
B that it was   D to being

5a Grammar: Reported Speech

10 *Rewrite the following dialogue in reported speech.*

Sally: I'm sorry to bother you, Jackie, but I've run out of sugar. Do you think I could borrow some?
Jackie: Yes, of course. Brown or white?
Sally: I'd rather have white. Do take some money for it, please.
Jackie: Don't be silly! I won't accept any money.
Sally: Well, alright, if you insist. What about me buying you some more tomorrow?

....
....
....
....
....
....
....
....
....
....

11 *Rewrite the following passage in direct speech.*

The doctor told/asked Mr Green to sit down and tell him what was wrong. Mr Green replied that he had a pain in his knee, which hurt when he walked and he complained it was keeping him awake at night. The doctor asked him to roll up his trousers and explained that he needed to examine his knee. Mr Green enquired whether it was anything serious, and the doctor assured him that he had just strained a muscle and advised Mr Green to rest his leg adding it would be better in a few days. The doctor warned him not to walk on it otherwise he could do some permanent damage to it.

....
....
....
....
....
....
....
....
....
....

12 *Complete the second sentence so that it has a similar meaning to the first sentence, using the word given. Do not change the word given. You must use between three and eight words, including the word given.*

1 "I don't approve of people who tell lies," he said.
disapproval
He ....
.... tell lies.

2 She refused to go to bed until she had seen her favourite soap opera.
insisted
She ....
.... she went to bed.

3 "Should I ask for help or do it myself?" Jeff wondered.
himself
Jeff ....
.... do it himself.

4 "No, I didn't laugh at him," Danny said.
laughed
Danny ....
.... at him.

5 "That's the way the radiator should be installed," the shopkeeper said to us.
how
The ....
.... install the radiator.

6 "Let's go to the planetarium next Saturday," he said.
going
He ....
.... Saturday.

7 "The food is awful here," George said.
about
George ....
.... there.

8 "Honestly, I will wash up for you this evening," Max told his mother.
do
Max ....
.... evening.

9 "I'd really like it if you could come sailing with us," Terry said to me.
me
Terry ....
.... with them.

10 "Shall I help you with your research?" Jenny said.
to
Jenny ....
.... research.

13 *Read the text below and think of the word which best fits each space. Use only one word in each space.*

A SPORTING GOAL FOR WOMEN

Football is traditionally, a man's sport, **(0)** *but* now the women are muscling in on their act, or so it **(1)** .... So many top male footballers have been transferred **(2)** .... astronomical sums of money that the game has become more a high-powered business than a sport. This is **(3)** .... the women come in, more motivated, more interested in the game **(4)** .... than in promoting themselves and generally better behaved both **(5)** .... and off the pitch, **(6)** .... a strong contrast to **(7)** .... male counterparts' greed and cynicism. Indeed, according to FIFA, the world football governing body, the future of football belongs to women, and the organisation has **(8)** .... out to actively promote women's football. Perhaps, in **(9)** .... of the fact that women are half the world's population, this is how it should be. In the USA, many members of national women's football teams are **(10)** .... known than male footballers, and some professional female players in **(11)** .... North America and Europe have attracted lucrative sponsorship deals. Generally, two problems beset women's football: the need to be **(12)** .... more seriously and for more funding to be made available. **(13)** .... these have been achieved **(14)** .... with the blessing of FIFA, we should see footballers who are accessible, co-operative, decent and sporting in **(15)** .... of the spoiled mercenary star boys of sport.

PHRASAL VERBS 1

14 *Look at Appendix 1 and fill in the blanks with one of the prepositions or adverbs from the box below, then give a synonym for each phrasal verb.*

• out of • off • into • for • back • on • up • down on • in • out • at • up on

0 The government have decided to cut *back* expenditure on health services.

1 He was cheated .... his full holiday entitlement due to a change in company policy.

2 I truly feel .... you in your terrible misfortune.

3 The interviewer kept cutting .... when the Minister was trying to answer the question on environmental policy.

4 Sales of records and cassettes have dropped .... considerably this year.

5 She's trying to get on with her schoolmates but she doesn't really fit ....

6 Their house was cut .... from the village by the flooding river.

7 Winter is coming. It's getting darker and the days are really starting to draw ....

8 He had to draw .... his savings to pay his rent after he was made redundant.

9 I wish you wouldn't fly .... me like that every time I make a mistake.

10 The limousine drew .... in front of the theatre and the actress got out.

11 Yes, I've already heard the news. Simon dropped .... to tell me this morning.

12 During the power workers' strike the electricity was cut .... at regular intervals.

13 He was forced to drop .... college when his father died.

14 The unforeseen expense on the new house ate .... my savings but it was worth it.

15 He was told to cut .... sugar and fats or he would suffer serious health problems.

16 This composition would be better if you cut .... the second paragraph.

17 They've fitted .... their kitchen with new cupboards.

18 She drew the lecture .... to nearly three hours although it was only supposed to last an hour.

19 I'm afraid their business is on the verge of folding .... due to a lack of orders.

20 We'll have to organise a union meeting if we want to head .... a strike.

21 Could you check .... the children and see what they're up to?

22 We had to wait to check .... at the hotel as the receptionist was not at his desk.

23 All guests should check .... by 12 o'clock or they will be charged for an extra day.

PHRASAL VERBS 2

15 *Match the phrasal verbs in bold with the definitions given.*

0 The soldiers **fell back** when the enemy appeared on the horizon.
1 During the war many men **joined up** in order to defend their country.
2 She **fell back on** her own ingenuity when all else failed.
3 John **fell for** Susan at first sight. They got married a month later.
4 The roof of the house **fell in** during the earthquake.
5 To avoid an argument, she **fell in with** her husband's plans.
6 When Tom saw the food he **fell on** it and ate it greedily.
7 Attendance **has fallen off** severely during the Christmas period.
8 They always **fall out with** each other over the household accounts.
9 Their holiday plan **fell through** when the children became ill.

a to fall in love with sb
b to decline
c to agree
d to fail to happen
e to retreat
f to quarrel
g to collapse
h to attack
i to join the army
j to turn to sth for help

0 *e* 1 .... 2 .... 3 .... 4 .... 5 .... 6 .... 7 .... 8 .... 9 ....

IDIOMS/FIXED PHRASES 1

16 *Look at Appendix 2 and explain the following idioms/fixed phrases in bold.*

1 Linda must be lacking in **grey matter** if she can't understand this.
2 She has lived here so long that she knows the town **like the back of her hand.**
3 Would you **hold your horses** and stop complaining? I'll be ready as soon as I can!
4 All the praise he's got from his teachers has **gone to his head**; now he thinks he's the best student in the school.
5 I'd appreciate it if you could **lend me a hand** with these bags; I can't carry them all by myself.
6 Kristina **had her hands full** after giving birth to triplets.
7 When he failed the exam for the third time, he **lost heart** and decided not to try again.
8 Mary is **hand in glove with** her supervisor, and as a result knows everything that's going on in the office.
9 When they heard the sound of police sirens, the burglars **took to their heels** and managed to escape.
10 I heard the news **straight from the horse's mouth**; John himself told me he was planning to change jobs.
11 I daren't tell him my plans; I know he's incapable of keeping things **under his hat.**
12 He **has so much time on his hands** now that he's retired that he's taken up several new hobbies.
13 As the politician hadn't had the chance to prepare a speech, he had to deliver one **off the cuff.**
14 She **had her heart in her mouth** all the time the firemen were trying to rescue her child from the building.
15 A torch **comes in handy** when you go on a camping trip.
16 Talking this matter over again is just **flogging a dead horse**; we can't have anything new to discuss.
17 Someone is going to have to do something about the violence at football matches before the situation completely **gets out of hand.**
18 You have to drive a car a number of times before you **get the hang of it.**
19 You should be careful about criticising her as she always **takes** it **to heart.**
20 She was **a bit of a dark horse**; nobody knew she was a published poet.
21 Everyone says Maria **struck gold** when she married her millionaire husband.

IDIOMS/FIXED PHRASES 2

break the ice:	ease the tension when one first meets people
the tip of the iceberg:	small evident part of a much larger concealed situation
ill at ease:	embarrassed, uncomfortable
the ins and outs:	the details of an activity
have many irons in the fire:	to have a lot of plans/ possibilities in progress at the same time
be in for the high jump:	be about to be punished
have a job:	find sth difficult to do
stew in one's own juice:	suffer the consequences of one's own actions
keep up with the Joneses:	compete with others in status/material goods
before one can say Jack Robinson:	extremely quickly

17 *Fill in the blanks with one of the idioms/fixed phrases above.*

0 George has so *many irons in the fire* that if he decides not to accept the sales job he has the pick of at least seven other positions.

1 It's your own fault you got the sack; now you ....

2 When someone threatened to report him to the police, Peter was out of the house ....

3 Having worked for the firm for years, she knew all the .... of company policy.

4 The children who broke the window will .... when their father finds out.

5 When she introduced her two friends, she tried to .... by mentioning the interests they had in common.

6 Our neighbours do their best .... by buying the latest model car and most expensive furniture.

7 She .... making the pastry as she had never done it before and had no recipe to follow.

8 He was .... at the party as he didn't know anyone who was there.

PREPOSITIONS

18 *Look at Appendix 5 and fill in the blanks with the correct preposition.*

0 You should not use aerosols because they're harmful *to* the environment.

1 Surgeons operated .... her last night; her condition is said to be satisfactory.

2 The teacher was deaf .... Nick's explanation of why he hadn't done his homework.

3 It was so cold in the tent that the children had to huddle up .... to keep warm.

4 She haggled .... the shopkeeper over the price of the souvenir.

5 We still haven't heard .... the insurance company about our claim.

6 Commuters found themselves faced .... a lengthy public transport strike.

7 I've received an invitation .... the annual nurses' conference in Glasgow.

8 Mr Smith is becoming increasingly impatient .... this class as they never pay attention.

9 I'm indebted .... my husband for his support in my new business venture.

10 The computer in the reception is inferior .... the one in my office.

11 He says he's feeling a bit .... colour today.

12 .... regard to your request, I'm afraid there's nothing I can do about it.

13 She wasn't allowed in the cinema because she was .... age.

14 The castaways were stranded .... an island for nearly a week.

15 He is a solicitor .... profession.

16 This coat was .... a sale when I bought it so it was very cheap.

17 He is .... arrears with his loan repayments.

18 I will lend you the money .... condition that you pay it back within the month.

19 Strawberries are only .... season in May and June.

20 He is an expert .... name only; he actually knows very little about the subject.

19 Complete the second sentence so that it has a similar meaning to the first sentence, using the word given. Do not change the word given. You must use between three and eight words, including the word given.

1 Everyone was in a deep sleep when the fire started.
sound
Everyone ....
.... broke out.

2 She doesn't know whether she should marry him.
minds
She ....
.... him.

3 She sued the newspaper as the article they'd written about her had damaged her reputation.
injurious
She sued the newspaper as ....
.... her reputation.

4 Seeing the damage to his car, Jerry became furious.
beside
Jerry ....
.... he saw the damage to his car.

5 He was dismissed for neglecting his work.
led
His ....
.... dismissal.

6 She looks exactly like her mother. They could be taken for twins!
exact
She's ....
.... her mother.

7 His illness was serious but he managed to recover from it.
of
In ....
...., he managed to get over it.

8 They promised me they would come.
word
They ....
.... come.

9 The occasional cream cake won't do you any harm.
now
A ....
.... won't do you any harm.

10 He resented the way she spoke to him.
exception
He ....
.... she spoke to him.

11 There is a bus to the station every half hour on Saturdays.
intervals
There is a bus to the station ....
.... on Saturdays.

12 We found her manner rather off-putting.
by
We ....
.... her manner.

13 No matter how much he was criticised, his confidence was not affected.
amount
No ....
.... his confidence.

14 Jane goes abroad a lot in the course of her job.
involves
Jane's ....
.... abroad.

15 How will the changes affect the company?
implications
What ....
.... the company?

16 They have no idea why Lena resigned.
mystery
It's ....
.... Lena resigned.

17 They should have given us more time to finish the work.
insufficient
We ....
.... to finish the work.

18 The concert was cancelled because of the strike.
in
The strike ....
.... cancelled.

19 I happened to see James as he walked past the door.
caught
I ....
.... he walked past the door.

20 He made an attempt to solve the equation but he couldn't do it.
go
He ....
.... but he couldn't do it.

FIXED PHRASES

gain ground:	make progress/become more popular
beat sb at their own game (inf):	to defeat/do better than sb in an activity considered their strength
give the game away:	reveal a secret or one's feelings
throw down the gauntlet:	challenge sb
gild the lily:	spoil sth beautiful by additions
fit like a glove:	fit perfectly
move the goalposts:	change the rules or demands of a situation
have a lot going for you:	have a lot of advantages in your favour
as good as:	practically, very nearly
up for grabs (inf):	available to those who are interested
dig one's own grave:	cause one's own failure
grind to a halt:	slowly stop/come to an end
come/get to grips with:	consider seriously and start to take action
get off the ground:	begin or start functioning
come to grief:	sth is unsuccessful
make a go of sth:	have some success
for good:	permanently
stick to one's guns:	keep to your opinion

20 *Complete the sentences using one of the fixed phrases in an appropriate form.*

1 For a new invention .... a lot of time and money is needed.
2 If you are computer literate, you .... in the workplace nowadays.
3 When inflation reached double figures the government had to .... the problem.
4 The new Pension Act .... eliminates some of the basic rights of pensioners.
5 You'll .... if you tell Peter about his surprise birthday party.
6 The patient was told that he .... with his unhealthy diet.

7 The lawyer knew that to win his case he had .... the prosecuting counsel ....
8 All Sue's efforts to keep the business going .... and she was forced to declare herself bankrupt.
9 She had been unhappy in her marriage for some time but decided .... for the sake of her children.

21 *Choose the correct item.*

1 For busy people in today's society, lifestyle management is gaining ....
A points   C ground
B speed   D terrain

2 We at Buyrite throw down the .... to competitors to match us for price, quality and service.
A mitten   C sword
B gauntlet   D hat

3 Every time the government meets their demands, the union leaders move the ....
A lamp-posts   C bus stops
B goalposts   D roadblocks

4 The designer refuses to gild the ...., preferring clean, simple lines for his creations.
A lily   C rose
B flower   D daisy

5 During pioneer days a lot of land in the United States was up for ....
A gain   C taking
B promotion   D grabs

6 With fuel in short supply, machinery in the factory slowly ground to a(n) ....
A halt   C pause
B stop   D end

7 This lovely new dress fits like a ....
A treat   C gown
B gauntlet   D glove

8 The teacher was adamant and stuck to his .... about the date of the final exam.
A weapons   C thumb
B guns   D neck

9 David decided that smoking was ruining his health and so gave it up for ....
A all   C good
B always   D once

22 *This is a part of a speech given by an election candidate, followed by the newspaper report printed the next day. Complete the report, using no more than two words to fill each blank. The words you need do not appear in the speech. The first one has been done for you.*

A " ...And so, ladies and gentlemen, I would like you to know that if I am elected, I will do everything in my power to ensure that the voters of this constituency will be fully and fairly represented in all phases of the governmental process. While your beliefs have been misrepresented, if not completely neglected, in the past, I shall consider it my duty to make your voices heard in the corridors of Whitehall as they have never been heard before, clearly stating the dissatisfaction which you have every right to feel. Furthermore, I shall consider my duty unfulfilled until I have done everything in my power to remove every cause of your dissatisfaction and resentment. I thank you, ladies and gentlemen, and I look forward to what I hope will be many fruitful meetings where together we can resolve the problems of this great country."

B Mr Whyte concluded his speech **(0)** *addressing* his listeners and **(1)** .... them that he would do all he could to assist them as their **(2)** .... He referred to **(3)** .... misrepresentations and neglect of the voters' beliefs and **(4)** .... to bring to the Government's **(5)** .... their dissatisfaction, which, he said, was quite **(6)** .... He **(7)** .... to say that he would not be **(8)** .... until he had done everything **(9)** .... to **(10)** .... the situation. After thanking the **(11)** .... he expressed **(12)** .... that in future he would be able to **(13)** .... with his constituents in meetings which would **(14)** .... worthwhile results.

WORD USAGE

23 *Read the text below. Use the word given in capitals at the end of some of the lines to form a word that fits in the space in the same line.*

HEALING FLOWERS

Flowering plants were **(0)** *primarily* cultivated for their fragrance, as well as	PRIMARY
their **(1)** .... and beauty. In the last two decades this situation	USE
has changed in that currently plants and their flowers are being subjected to the	
rigours of intensive scientific research in an attempt to **(2)**	VEIL
their secrets. Although it is a **(3)** .... recent undertaking,	RELATIVE
(4) .... have already scoured some of the most obscure	RESEARCH
regions of the globe in search of the ultimate curing, healing and rejuvenating	
(5) .... specimens. Ancient tribal traditions and healing	BOTANY
recipes have also been researched as a means of identifying the potential	
(6) .... properties of flowers and plants. Flora has been	CURE
researched for centuries in order to **(7)** .... a continuous	SURE
supply of the ingredients that have been proven to be **(8)**	EFFECT
in providing remedies offering **(9)** .... The latest	RELIEVE
technologies are employed in parallel to this ancient knowledge to identify	
chemical profiles and **(10)** .... Modern plant	CHARACTER
breeding makes it possible for new and improved plants to be added to the list	
of previously discovered specimens. In this marriage of science and nature, a	
new market of products is now available to whet consumer appetite.	

COLLOCATIONS

24 *Fill in* **lost, stray**.

0 *lost* money
1 .... dog
2 .... property
3 .... opportunity
4 .... bullet
5 .... cat
6 .... child
7 .... hope
8 .... youth
9 .... lock of hair

25 *Fill in* **produce, generate**.

1 .... cars in a factory
2 .... discussion
3 .... new jobs
4 .... warmth/power
5 .... offspring
6 .... bad feelings
7 .... a play

26 *Fill in the collocational grid.*

	fake	counterfeit	forged	mock	false
money					
fur					
cream					
painting					
pearls					
document					
passport					
jewellery					

27 *Think of one word only which can be used appropriately in all three sentences.*

0 • One doesn't need to be an expert to *appreciate* the beauty of classical music.
   • He seems confident that houses in this area will *appreciate* in value in the next few years.
   • I'll always *appreciate* your help and support.

1 • The clock's .... has luminous hands and numbers, which shine in the dark.
   • Matilda made a .... as she swallowed the foul-tasting medicine.
   • Slowly, the climber inched his way up the jagged .... of the cliff.

2 • Angela keeps her .... by constantly dieting and exercising.
   • When I saw the .... on the cheque I gasped with astonishment.
   • A key .... in producing any new legislation is the Prime Minister.

3 • The charismatic speaker .... his audience with enthusiasm.
   • Jake's boss .... him for his laziness and lack of initiative.
   • The potter .... the huge vases.

4 • The government has been .... to withdraw the controversial education bill.
   • I could see that the door to my office had been .... and my papers were missing.
   • The leading actor's performance was not natural at all and came over as melodramatic and ....

5 • Martin felt a .... of satisfaction at having been of help in the charity drive.
   • Her brisk walk in the crisp autumn countryside had given Zoe's face a healthy pink ....
   • The coal fire gave off a soft .... which created a romantic atmosphere in the room.

6 • And with a .... of two goals to nil, Barmworth are very likely to win the cup.
   • Police are following up a new .... in an effort to solve the baffling case.
   • Rick Shears is the male .... in this exciting, action-packed adventure.

7 • The .... and delicate movements of a ballerina are a wonder to watch.
   • Hazel's .... green jumper matched her eyes.
   • After a .... supper, they retired to bed.

8 • The date of the church garden fete has been .... to July 30th.
   • During the writer's early childhood, her family .... to the country.
   • The soprano's rendering of the aria .... the audience to tears.

9 • With his pinstripe suit, dark tie and bowler hat, Mr Prescott was clearly a man who was part of the ....
   • All food and drinks bought here must be consumed inside this ....
   • The .... of a working party to look into immigration was the first item on the government's agenda.

PREPARING FOR PART 5

BACK REFERENCE I

28 *Look at the following extracts and, in the spaces provided, write what each word or phrase in bold refers to. Two items have been done for you.*

0 The Jones family always shopped at the local U-Save supermarket. As valued customers, **(1) they** were offered a year's supply of breakfast cereal. Then they phoned all of their friends to tell them about **(2) it**.

1 *The Jones family.*
2 *Being offered a year's supply of cereal.*

1 Statistics indicate that, within the last year, there have been more businesses established than in the past five years. In fact, in **(1) this period**, more than five thousand small businesses have opened **(2) their** doors to customers in the metropolitan area alone. If **(3) this trend** continues, economists say that the country's international debt will be paid off in less than ten years.

1 ....
2 ....
3 ....

2 John Keats' mother died of tuberculosis in 1810. He long suspected that he had **(1) the illness** himself and moved to Rome to avoid the severe English climate. Despite **(2) this**, he succumbed to **(3) the dreaded disease** in 1821.

1 ....
2 ....
3 ....

3 Jack met Ellie in the autumn while working for her brother, **(1) who** owned a small carpentry shop. It was **(2) at this time** that he realised he wanted to spend the rest of his life with her. **(3) This** gave him the courage to ask for her hand in marriage.

1 ....
2 ....
3 ....
....

4 The assembly line was first used by Henry Ford in his car factory. He felt that **(1) this mode of production** would be beneficial to both workers and consumers. He was correct in the sense that reduced labour costs were passed along as savings to **(2) the latter**, but unfortunately **(3) it** also meant that **(4) the former** were robbed of any sense of personal job fulfilment.

1 ....
2 ....
3 ....
4 ....

5 Every year, hundreds of toddlers are poisoned by swallowing pharmaceutical drugs. In spite of **(1) this**, parents still fail to take precautions and put **(2) these potentially harmful substances** in safe places. If only **(3) they** would take a few moments to store medicines in locked cupboards or up on high shelves, **(4) such casualties** could be avoided.

1 ....
2 ....
3 ....
4 ....

6 There are two major legal prerequisites for the termination of employment; compensation and fairness of dismissal. **(1) The first** dictates that termination does not occur until an employee has been paid in full the amount of legal compensation (see section 26 below for how **(2) this amount** is calculated). **(3) The second** places two preconditions: that the employer has given the employee two written warnings that his or her employment will be terminated unless he or she conforms to clearly stated conditions; and that, after **(4) these warnings**, the employer notifies the employee about the termination of employment 30 days prior to **(5) it** .

1 ....
2 ....
3 ....
4 ....
5 ....

7 Drawing on the memoirs of the survivors of the Titanic, Wilson tells the tale of **(1) this short-lived man-made wonder**. Along with Wilson's deep knowledge of the structure of **(2) the ship**, **(3) these accounts** provide a new kind of insight into the disaster.

1 ....
2 ....
3 ....

8 Henry VIII was a more popular monarch than his father **(1) who** had had the reputation for being ruthless. **(2) This** was not strictly true as **(3) he** had had to implement harsh measures to guarantee the stability of the throne.

1 ....
2 ....
3 ....

9 Anton Diabelli, an Austrian, is known to have been the composer of the waltz on which Beethoven wrote **(1) his** 33 variations for the piano. Diabelli had originally intended to become a priest, and entered a Bavarian monastery **(2) for this purpose**. He left for Vienna in 1803, when **(3) it was** secularised. **(4) There**, he found employment as a piano and guitar teacher.

1 ....
2 ....
3 ....
4 ....

10 From the moment a patient is diagnosed as suffering from diabetes, he must follow a diet which will be designed to help him reach and maintain a suitable body weight. In some cases, sufferers of **(1) this disease** may require a daily dose of insulin. **(2) This** is because some forms of diabetes prevent the body from producing enough of **(3) this hormone**.

1 ....
2 ....
3 ....

11 By 1919, there were nearly 9 million cars registered in the United States. **(1) That year** alone, Henry Ford's Motor Company sold close to a million new cars. To the American people, the benefits of owning a car were obvious; no matter where or how **(2) you** lived, **(3) it** provided freedom to explore the world beyond your local community.

1 ....
2 ....
3 ....

12 Sharp Claw Software, **(1) one of the major players** in multimedia software development, is seeking a highly qualified and experienced machine code programmer. The successful candidate will have at least 3 years of experience in multimedia programming, and **(2) he** must be London-based. Experience in sales or marketing is preferred. **(3) The post** comes with an attractive remuneration package, bonuses and a company car.

1 ....
2 ....
3 ....

13 In many ways, Hemingway views his heroine Jig as superior to **(1) her** boyfriend. Unlike **(2) him**, she refuses to disguise or belittle the situation in which they find **(3) themselves**. Jig faces up to the sad fact that, after the crisis, their relationship will never be the same and that the two of them will have to go **(4) their** separate ways. In one particular scene, **(5) the writer** suggests that Jig's boyfriend is both weak and naive.

1 ....
2 ....
3 ....
4 ....
5 ....

14 *Shakespearean Tragedies II* is available to semester 5 or semester 7 students who are majoring in English Literature or Theatre Studies. The course will examine all aspects of Shakespeare's writing, with particular focus on the dramatic devices **(1) it** utilises. How **(2) these plays** were understood in Shakespeare's own day is also an important part of **(3) this course**, as is what we know about the way Elizabethan actors interpreted and portrayed **(4) his** characters. The course consists of 12 seminars (the attendance of **(5) which** is compulsory) and 24 lectures. A detailed course outline is available at the departmental secretary's office. A list of set books and suggested background reading may also be found **(6) there**.

1 ....
2 ....
3 ....
4 ....
5 ....
6 ....

5c Practice Test Five

Paper 3 Use of English

Time: 1 hour 30 minutes

PART 1

Read the text below and think of the word which best fits each space. Use only one word in each space.

STARTING A CONVERSATION

It is **(0)** *often* said that the British talk about the weather more than any **(1)** .... people in the world; some extremists claim that they talk about **(2)** .... else. But in fact, **(3)** .... in countries with far less changeable climates than Britain's, the weather is an endless, **(4)** .... not varied, source of conversational fodder. This seems **(5)** .... natural when you consider that the weather is one of the few things we all have in **(6)** .... It affects our senses, and **(7)** .... our moods, so directly and, at times, so intensely that it is natural we **(8)** .... talk about it. After several days **(9)** .... sometimes weeks of dark, gloomy weather, a bright day tends to bring **(10)** .... the best in everyone; people recognise the relief in others' expressions which they feel in themselves, and find **(11)** .... hard to resist commenting on a change **(12)** .... is having such an evident **(13)** .... on everyone. "Nice day, isn't it?" is much more than simply a comment on the state of the weather; it is a comment on the human state **(14)** ...., an acknowledgement that the tenability of our place in the universe relies on the existence of a community **(15)** .... human feeling.

PART 2

Read the text below. Use the word given in capitals at the end of some of the lines to form a word that fits in the space in the same line.

AROUND THE GLOBE

National Geographic Magazine is a **(0)** *monthly* magazine of geography,	MONTH
archaeology, anthropology, and **(16)** ...., providing the	EXPLORE
armchair traveller with literary and **(17)** .... accounts and unexcelled	FACT
photographs and maps to comprehend those **(18)** .... The	PURSUE
magazine was founded in 1888 and is still published by a non-profit	
corporation, the National Geographic Society. The original **(19)**	INTEND
of the society was for the **(20)** .... to be oriented toward	PERIOD
the United States, but the nature of its articles soon made it a magazine with a	
(21) .... view. Under the editorship of Gilbert Hovey Grosvenor,	GLOBE
it attained a circulation of 1,000,000 by 1926. National Geographic was one	
of the first magazines to **(22)** .... colour photographs of	PRODUCE
undersea life, views from the stratosphere, and animals in their natural habitat.	
The magazine became world famous for its **(23)** .... illustrated	BEAUTY
articles of the various geographic regions of the world. Its features include	
(24) .... information on the environmental, social, and cultural	SUBSTANCE
aspects of the areas covered and their peoples. Proceeds from the magazine	
help support its **(25)** .... expeditions.	SCIENCE

PART 3

Think of one word only which can be used appropriately in all three sentences.

0 • One doesn't need to be an expert to *appreciate* the beauty of classical music.
  • He seems confident that houses in this area will *appreciate* in value in the next few years.
  • I'll always *appreciate* your help and support.

26 • Police .... has revealed that the spy escaped to a country from which he cannot be extradited.
  • Are these cave paintings proof that an alien .... once visited our planet?
  • Martha is a brilliant student but doesn't show much .... in her everyday life.

27 • When the publishers rejected her first novel, Celeste felt such a .... disappointment that she burst into tears.
  • As you know, Gary is a .... sportsman who loves football, basketball and cricket.
  • He ground the knife blade to give it a .... edge.

28 • Press any .... to start the computer.
  • Scientists think they have found the .... to some hereditary diseases.
  • It was an awful performance, with the soloist singing in the wrong ....

29 • The .... Party has been in power for ten years now.
  • The woman was suffering from excruciating .... pains on her way to hospital.
  • Sometimes women are used as cheap .... by some unscrupulous employers.

30 • The discussions to find a peaceful solution to the uprising took place against a .... of continuing violence.
  • You shouldn't be ashamed of your working-class ....
  • The fabric she chose has got pink roses on a pale blue ....

31 • An .... number of players is needed to begin the game.
  • I don't eat sweets very often but I enjoy the .... bar of chocolate.
  • That's .... ; I'm sure I left my glasses here, but they're gone.

PART 4

Complete the second sentence so that it has a similar meaning to the first, using the word given. Do not change the word given. Use between three and eight words, including the word given.

0 Nobody spoke when the teacher asked who the culprit was.
  remained
  Everyone *remained silent when the teacher asked who the culprit was.*

32 The lecturer is an expert on modern art.
  wide
  The ....
  .... art.

33 He behaved in an incomprehensible way at the party.
  beyond
  His ....
  .... comprehension.

34 I consider him my worst enemy.
  look
  I ....
  .... enemy.

35 May is bound to pass her exam.
  foregone
  It ....
  .... her exam.

36 Len tried to do the exercise, but without success.
  matter
  No ....
  .... do the exercise.

37 Only Paul succeeded in acquiring high grades.
  failed
  Everyone ....
  .... high grades.

38 The director decided that the cost of relocation was too high.
  conclusion
  The director ....
  .... was too high.

39 The company tried unsuccessfully to secure a bank loan.
  avail
  The company's ....
  .... a bank loan.

111

PART 5

For questions **40 - 44** *read the following texts. For questions* **40-43**, *answer with a word or short phrase. You do not need to write complete sentences. For question* **44**, *write a summary according to the instructions given.*

Scottish writer Iain Banks was born in Dunfermline, Scotland, on February 16th, 1954. He has written over 30 novels, the subject matter of which varies from crime detective stories to traditional science fiction and cyber-culture narratives. His novels focus on the story rather than the setting, but Scottish places and people do feature widely.

Justice and morality, along with an on-going exploration of how people understand their place in the world, are some of his prevalent themes. In *The Bridge* (1986), Banks presents us with a brilliant novel of self-discovery, as the central character struggles to rebuild his memory after an accident, but does not like the lying, cunning person he discovers he was. In *Canal Dreams* (1990), the female protagonist confronts fears from her past, and finds herself morally obliged to defeat them and take charge of her life in a dramatic manner, saving
line 13 —————— the lives of others as she does so.

Nor is the element of the fantastic absent from Banks' work. In *The Player of Games* (1988), the central character is the champion in a world where there is no disease or disaster, only endless games. When he accepts a challenge from a distant, foreign empire, he discovers what "the Game" is all about.

Modern critics rank Iain Banks as one of the greatest living writers in the world, his books having been read by over 10 million people in 12 different languages. The University of Stirling awarded him an honorary doctorate in 1997.

40 What do we learn about the subject matter of Iain Banks' novels?

....

....

41 What does the phrase "as she does so" refer to in line 13?

....

....

In Iain Banks' latest novel, *Complicity*, Cameron Colley is a Scottish newspaper reporter, with a casual attitude toward life and a deep commitment to his profession, his motto being "let's cover the story". As the story begins, Colley gets a series of disturbing phone calls from an anonymous informant who can never stay on the phone long enough to tell him very much, but hints at world-wide conspiracies and other mysterious ploys.

Interleaved with the sections that acquaint us with Colley are extracts that describe premeditated assaults from the point of view of an unnamed perpetrator. These attacks turn out to be punishments that very cleverly fit "crimes" which have in the past been committed by the victims.

I'm reluctant to reveal too much of this fine plot, but I can say that it thickens as it becomes clear that Colley's informant knows a lot about the situation. He is wrongly arrested for the crimes, but begins to realise that the real culprit is someone very close to him. Colley tries to discover his identity by delving deep into his own past, and thus begins to question his own morality and values.

The mood of the story is hip, clever, cynical but bright, and both Banks and his character are very funny throughout; fans of both Hunter Thompson and Martin Amis are especially encouraged to try this one.

42 Why is the writer "reluctant to reveal much of this fine plot"?

....

....

43 What can we infer about novels by Hunter Thompson and Martin Amis?

....

....

44 In a paragraph of between 50 and 70 words, summarise the examples of Iain Banks' writing about morality found in the two passages.

....

....

....

....

....

....

....

....

ADJECTIVES

Adjectives describe people, places, things, ideas, etc. They have only one form in all genders, singular and plural, and can be placed before nouns or after verbs such as **appear, keep, make, feel, sound, smell, look, taste**, etc.

She is a **pretty** girl.	It smells **horrible**.
They are **hard-working** students.	Keep **quiet**, please!

Most common adjectives (**large, long, heavy, late**, etc) do not have a particular ending. However, there are certain common endings for adjectives which are formed from nouns and verbs. These are:

- able	fashion**able**	- ous	courag**eous**	- ist	rac**ist**
- al	classic**al**	- esque	pictur**esque**	- less	care**less**
- ant	petul**ant**	- ful	care**ful**	- like	business**like**
- ar	angul**ar**	- ian	Canad**ian**	- ly	friend**ly**
- ary	imagin**ary**	- ible	poss**ible**	- ory	introduct**ory**
- ate	fortun**ate**	- ic	histor**ic**	- ous	fam**ous**
- en	wood**en**	- ical	histor**ical**	- some	quarrel**some**
- ent	depend**ent**	- ious	hilar**ious**	- y	luck**y**
- ean	Shakespear**ean**	- ish	redd**ish**		

The most common prefixes used with adjectives are:

a -	**a**moral	im -	**im**possible	pre -	**pre**mature
ab -	**ab**normal	in -	**in**tolerant	pro -	**pro**-American
anti -	**anti**-aircraft	ir -	**ir**regular	sub -	**sub**tropical
dis -	**dis**honest	mal -	**mal**nourished	super -	**super**human
extra -	**extra**curricular	non -	**non**-stop	un -	**un**true
hyper -	**hyper**sensitive	over -	**over**grown	under -	**under**manned
il -	**il**legal	post -	**post**-modern		

1 *Write the adjectives made from the following words.*

day	*daily*	rust	....	energy	....
victory	....	accident	....	sun	....
base	....	responsibility	....	hesitate	....
fear	....	affection	....	circle	....
use	....	life	....	glory	....
beauty	....	fool	....	humour	....

2 *Use the word given in capitals to form a word that fits in the space in the same line.*

1 I was told that the information I was looking for was classified and .... to the public. ACCESS
2 His .... business methods have gained him a bad name. SCRUPLE
3 Jane's .... behaviour towards her superiors led to her dismissal from the job. RESPECT
4 The manager was so .... with his work that he failed to notice me standing there. OCCUPY
5 The child was emaciated and .... after being abandoned by its parents. NOURISH
6 "Her hand writing is ....; how does she expect me to read it?" LEGIBLE
7 Special schools are recommended for .... children. ADJUST
8 The city of Athens is known to be noisy, ... and polluted. POPULATE
9 The European Union is trying to .... salaries in all countries. STANDARD
10 The idea of moving to the countryside was .... to him as he was used to living in the city. APPEAL

Notes on Adjectives

- Compound adjectives are formed with:

present participles	*long-standing* debt, *long-playing* record
past participles	*self-employed* carpenter, *candle-lit* restaurant
cardinal numbers + nouns	*one-year-old* girl, *three-day* course, a *£30* pair of shoes
prefixes and suffixes	*non-stop* show, *waterproof* watch
well, badly, ill, poorly + participles	*well-paid* clerk, *ill-fitting* shirt, *poorly-paid* assistant

- Some adjectives ending - ly look like adverbs (friendly, motherly, lonely, lovely). These adjectives form their adverbs by adding the word *way/manner/fashion*.
  She behaved in a very friendly way/manner/fashion.

- Some adjectives such as **poor, late** and **old** have different meanings, according to where they are placed in the sentence.
  My grandfather is very old. (in years)
  Tony is an old friend of mine. (I've known him for a long time)

- Certain adjectives can be used with **the** to represent a group as a whole:
  the rich, the dead, the young, the unemployed, the homeless, the blind, etc

- Present and past participles can be used as adjectives.
  Present participles describe **the quality of** a noun.
  annoying behaviour (What kind of behaviour? annoying)
  Past participles describe **how the subject feels**.
  annoyed teacher (How does the teacher feel? annoyed)

- Nouns describing *materials, substances, purpose,* and *use* can be used as adjectives, but they do not have comparative or superlative forms and cannot be modified by **very**.

a *cotton* shirt	a *gold* necklace		a *wooden* table (not *wood table)
a *silver* brooch	a *summer* dress	but	a *woollen* coat (not *wool coat)
a *stone* wall	a *chopping* board		

  However, there are adjectives derived from the above nouns. These adjectives have a metaphorical meaning.
  silky hair (hair like silk), *golden* hair, *silvery* moon, *stony* look etc

- There are certain adverbs such as **above, upstairs, downstairs, inside,** etc which can be used as **adjectives**.
  an upstairs room   the *downstairs* bathroom   the *above* rule   the *inside* page etc

- **Little, old** and **young** are often used in fixed adjective-noun combinations, so they are always placed next to the noun they modify.
  This young man spends too much money.   *That little girl seems to be lost.*

- Adjectives which describe absolute qualities such as **left, right, single, correct, equal, absent,** etc do not have comparative or superlative forms.

3 *Make compound adjectives to describe the following:*

1 A boy who has straight hair. ....
2 A woman with green eyes. ....
3 A dog which barks constantly. ....
4 A car that moves fast. ....
5 A parent who has a broad mind. ....
6 A table with three legs. ....
7 A teacher with good qualifications. ....
8 A student who speaks French. ....
9 A workshop which lasts four hours. ....
10 A room with poor lighting. ....

4 *Fill in the appropriate **present** or **past participle**.*

1 That's a most .... (**irritate**) noise, isn't it?
2 Thankfully, the results of the survey were thoroughly .... (**encourage**).
3 The news came as a shock to everyone. The community was .... (**devastate**).
4 It was .... (**exhilarate**) to be back in San Francisco after such a long time.
5 Hamilton's novel was .... (**inspire**) by a real person.
6 It was very .... (**move**) to see such true love and devotion.

5 Underline the correct item.

1 Father drove us to the station in **stone/stony** silence.
2 It would be a good idea to pack one or two pairs of thick **woollen/wool** socks.
3 The lake looked magnificent in the **silvery/silver** moonlight.
4 Jenny got a beautiful **gold/golden** brooch for her birthday.
5 Monica visited her aunt in her **summer/summery** house in Majorca.
6 The actress was wearing a stunning long **silky/silk** dress.

ORDER OF ADJECTIVES

A general guide to the ordering of adjectives is given below. However, this cannot always be strictly followed since when there is more than one adjective in a sentence, it is rather difficult to say in exactly what order they should be placed, as this depends on the speaker's feeling or intention.

	number	opinion	size/ weight	age	shape	colour/ temperature	verb/ participle form	origin/ nationality	material	noun
all/both/	three	nice	small		round	brown	carved		wooden	tables
half/first	one		large	old	rectangular			Chinese		mirror

Notes

• When two or more adjectives of the same category are used, the more general adjective comes before the more specific one.
  a kind, gentle man

• Commas are only used to separate adjectives which are equally important; they are never used to separate the final adjective from the noun it modifies.
  a long, distinguished career   *a rare, colourful bird*

6 Put the adjectives into the correct order.

1 The screenplay was written by a(n) (**eccentric, French, brilliant**) writer.

2 The flower girl wore a (**satin, pretty, white**) dress at the wedding ceremony.

3 I'm going to the (**spring, Asian, annual**) festival on Sunday.

4 The fruit tart is made with (**red, fresh, delicious**) strawberries.

5 The company has produced a new sports car with (**leather, maroon, soft**) seats.

6 Corals are (**microscopic, orangey-pink, tropical**) sea animals.

ADVERBS

Adverbs usually describe a verb, but they can also modify adjectives, nouns, sentences or other adverbs.

That is, adverbs tell us **how** (adverbs of manner), **when** (adverbs of time), **where** (adverbs of place), **how often** (adverbs of frequency), **to what extent** (adverbs of degree) **something happens or is.**

She entered the room **slowly**. (how? adverb of manner)
She left **yesterday**. (when? adverb of time)
The people **next door** are very unfriendly. (where? adverb of place)
She **usually** goes shopping on Fridays. (how often? adverb of frequency)
He was **absolutely** right in what he said. (to what extent? adverb of degree)

- **Adverbs of manner** are usually formed by adding **- ly** to the adjective.
  clever - clever**ly**   bad - bad**ly**   careful - careful**ly**

- There are also **adverbial phrases**. They are usually formed with a **preposition + noun**: at the cinema, in a mess, in the restaurant etc **but** again and again, now and then, here and there

- Spelling of - **ly** adverbs

quick	-	quick**ly**	basic	-	basic**ally**	
beautiful	-	beautifu**lly**	sly	-	sly**ly**	**but** extreme - extreme**ly**
capable	-	capab**ly**	busy	-	bus**ily**	

- Adjectives/Adverbs with the same form

best	cold*	easy*	fine*	inside	low	right*	thick*	wide
cheap*	daily	extra	first*	last	monthly	slow*	thin*	wrong*
clear*	dear	fair*	free*	late	past	straight	tight*	yearly
	direct	far	further	long	quick*	sure*	weekly	etc
	early	fast	hard	loud*			well	
			high					
			hourly					

He is a **fast** driver.	→	He drives **fast**.
That was a **cheap** blouse.	→	I bought that blouse **cheap**. (colloquial)
She was the **first** guest to arrive.	→	She arrived **first**.

The adverbs having an asterisk (*) can also be found with the - ly form. In this case, they are usually placed before verbs, participles or adjectives. Otherwise they are less formal.

Speak **clear**! (less formal)
Speak **clearly**, please.

7 Complete the sentences with a suitable **adjective** or **adverb** from the list above.

0 They charged me ....*extra*.......... because my luggage was overweight.

1 He's a .... worker, and he works .... as well.

2 You must draw the lines very ....

3 I'd like you to slice the meat very ....

4 I answered two of the questions ....

5 They stayed .... the office to discuss some .... information.

6 She held .... to the rope.

7 Go .... down the road and you'll see the bank on the .... side.

8 He stopped .... when he saw the .... cat in the road.

9 He pays rent ...., but we pay on a .... basis.

10 I wish you wouldn't talk so ....

Adverbs with two forms and different meanings.

direct = by the shortest route
directly = immediately

hard = in a hard way
hardly = scarcely

high = to a high level
highly = very much

short = suddenly
shortly = not long, soon

right = correctly, exactly
rightly = wisely

deep = going a long way down
deeply = greatly

free = without charge or cost
freely = willingly

wide = fully
widely = very much

last = after all others/most recently
lastly = finally

late = after the usual time
lately = recently

pretty = fairly
prettily = in a pretty way

WORD ORDER OF ADVERBS OF MANNER, PLACE AND TIME

When there is more than one time adverb, the one expressing a shorter time period precedes the one which expresses a longer period.

subject + verb (+ object)	manner	place	time	
			shorter period	longer period
He ate his breakfast	quickly	in the kitchen	at 7:00	yesterday.

subject + verb of movement (+ object)	place	manner	time
He left	home	hurriedly	at 7:30

time (when it is not the main focus of the message)	subject + verb (+object)	place	manner
Every weekend	he goes	to the office	by car.

Adverbs of frequency are usually placed after the auxiliary verb or before the main verb, but in short answers they precede the auxiliary verb.
I have **never** seen such a huge lion.
"She is late for work again". "Yes, she **always** is".
He **sometimes** goes to the cafeteria after work for a coffee.

Adverbs of degree usually go before the words they modify.
She types **quite** fast.
He gave me **only** £1.

Certain adverbs such as probably, evidently, obviously, actually, certainly, presumably, undoubtedly, etc can be placed at the beginning of a sentence or in the same position as adverbs of frequency.
Obviously, she suffers a lot.
I'll **certainly** be on time.

8 *Underline the correct word.*

0 The <u>direct</u>/directly road to the new airport saves a lot of travelling time.
1 Residents may visit the museum **free/freely**, but tourists will have to pay.
2 She worked very **hard/hardly** to get that promotion.
3 The arrow fell **short/shortly** of the target.
4 We walked **deep/deeply** into the forest, following the tracks of the deer.
5 Police described the situation as "**high/highly** dangerous", and warned the public not to approach the area.
6 You've **hard/hardly** eaten anything! Do have some more!
7 The winner of the dance competition will **short/shortly** be announced.
8 I was **deep/deeply** touched by everyone's concern after my accident.
9 The teacher was **right/rightly** upset when the students refused to do their homework.
10 The sword passed **right/rightly** through the knight's armour.
11 After the flood, the water levels remained very **high/highly** for several days.
12 We went **direct/directly** to the manager as soon as we realised what had happened.

9 *Put the adverbs in the right place in the following sentences.*

0 She is on time for work. **(never)**
She is never on time for work.
1 They go out for dinner. **(seldom)**
....
....
2 Peter is bragging about how rich he is. **(always)**
....
....
3 He won an expensive car. **(unexpectedly/ amazingly/yesterday)**
....
....
4 I get the feeling of "déjà vu", that something has happened before. **(sometimes)**
....
....

5 A speech was delivered and the film was shown. **(first/later)**
....
6 There's been talk of people getting laid off. **(lately, too much)**
....
....
....
7 If you use the buses, it's a good idea to buy a bus pass. **(frequently)**
....
....
8 People ask me whether I prefer living here to living abroad. **(often)**
....
....

10 *Complete the second sentence so that it has a similar meaning to the first sentence using the word given. Do not change the word given. You must use between three and eight words including the word given.*

1 It is impossible to keep up with Sharon as she shows great diligence.
diligent
Sharon ....
.... keep up with her.
2 She was surprised when he suddenly asked her to marry him.
took
His ....
.... surprise.
3 He decided to have an early night because he was exhausted.
go
He ....
.... because he was exhausted.
4 His boss had a very high opinion of him.
highly
He was ....
.... his boss.
5 The boxer dealt a hard blow to the punchbag while training.
hit
The boxer ....
.... while training.

Regular Comparisons

one-syllable adjectives	Positive	Comparative	Superlative
	small	smaller (than)	the smallest (of/in)
	sad	sadder (than)	the saddest (of/in)
	nice	nicer (than)	the nicest (of/in)
two-syllable adjectives	happy	happier (than)	the happiest (of/in)
more than two syllables adjectives	intelligent	**more** intelligent (than)	the **most** intelligent (of/in)

Note

Two-syllable adjectives ending in - **er**, - **ly** or - **y** usually form their comparative and superlative by adding - **er** or - **est** to the positive form, whereas those ending in - **re** or - **ful** take **more** and **most**.
clever - *cleverer* - *cleverest,* *careful* - *more careful* - *most careful*

one-syllable adverbs	Positive	Comparative	Superlative
	fast	faster (than)	the fastest (of/in)
two-syllable adverbs	early	earlier (than)	the earliest (of/in)
compound adverbs	quickly	**more** quickly (than)	the **most** quickly (of/in)

Note

Compound adverbs are adverbs which are formed by adding - **ly** to the adjective form: *careful - carefully*

Irregular Comparisons

Positive	Comparative	Superlative
bad/badly	worse	worst
good/well	better	best
little	less	least
many/much	more	most
far	farther (of distance only)	farthest
	further	furthest
old	older	oldest
	elder (never used with **than**)	eldest (of members of a family, only implying seniority of age)

Types of Comparisons and Similarities

- **as ...as - not as/so/such ...as**
  *He is **as** stubborn **as** a mule.*
  *It's **not such** hard work **as** I thought.*
- **the + comparative ...the + comparative**
  ***The older** he gets, **the more** forgetful he becomes.*
- **comparative + and + comparative**
  *The lecture was becoming **more and more boring**.*
- **such + ...as + noun/pronoun/clause**
  *I've never seen **such** a nice baby **as** theirs.*
- **the same... + as (pro)noun + clause**
  *She has **the same** blouse **as** the one you gave me.*
- **less + positive degree + than**
  *Pam is **less helpful than** John.*
- **the least... + positive degree + of/in**
  *She was **the least interested** of all.*

- **comparative + than + clause**
  *He is **more tired than** he looks.*
- **prefer + gerund + to + gerund = like doing** (general)
  *I prefer **dancing to singing**.*
  prefer + to - infinitive + rather than + bare infinitive (general)
  *I prefer **to walk** to school **rather than** take the bike.*
- **would prefer + to - infinitive + rather than + bare infinitive** (specific)
  *I would prefer **to swim rather than** sunbathe.*
- **would rather/sooner + bare infinitive + than + bare infinitive = would like to**
  *I'd **rather/sooner be** a doctor **than (be)** a teacher.*
- **clause + as if + clause**
  *She looks **as if** she's in pain.*

- clause + whereas/while/but + clause (comparison by contrast)
  *She can hide her feelings **whereas/while/but** he is like an open book.*
- very + positive degree (+ noun)
  *This is a **very difficult** task.*

- much/far/even/rather + comparative (+ noun)
  *This is a(n) **much/far/even/rather** more difficult task.*
- any/no/a lot/a little/a bit + comparative
  *This task is **not any/no/a lot/a little/a bit** more difficult.*
- by far + the + superlative (+noun)
  *This is **by far** the most difficult task.*

As is used
- for what sb or sth really is (jobs or roles).
  *She works **as** an air-hostess. (She is an air-hostess)*
- before *clauses/phrases*
  *I'll do **as you say**.*
- in certain expressions: as usual, as ... as, as much, such as.
  *He came late **as usual**.*
- after **accept, describe, be known, class, refer to, use, regard**.
  *She is **regarded as** an authority on Physics.*

Like is used
- for what sb or sth is not really but looks or is like. (similes)
  *She works **like** a slave. (She's not a slave)*
- with **nouns/pronouns/- ing.**
  *It was **like travelling** in a spaceship.*
- after **sound, smell, look, feel** + noun.
  *It feels **like velvet**.*
- after **negative expressions**.
  *There is no place **like** home.*

11 Complete the second sentence, so that it has similar meaning to the first sentence using the word given. Do not change the word given. You must use between three and eight words, including the word given.

1 Wiltshire is older than most other counties in England.
   one
   Wiltshire ....
   .... England.

2 More students pass their exams at the new language school than the others in the area.
   rate
   The new language school ....
   .... the other schools in the area.

3 Comparative literature is an intriguing subject, whereas linguistics is less so.
   fascinating
   Comparative literature ....
   .... than linguistics.

12 Fill in the blanks with **as** or **like**.

1 Pam behaved .... an idiot at the party ....
   usual.

2 Jason is not .... active .... he used to be; he doesn't play .... much sport .... he did when he was at high school.

3 My cherry cake wasn't such a disaster .... I'd thought it would be, but it didn't taste anything .... my mother's.

4 This is .... far .... the tour goes. It looks .... if the bus has run out of fuel.

5 If Jane were .... her sister, she wouldn't have behaved .... rashly .... she had.

6 Ken's ambition to work .... a fashion designer was soon shattered; his creations lacked originality and looked .... last year's designs.

CONVERSATIONAL GRAMMAR

13 Choose the correct item.

1 "So, what do you think of his new novel?"
   "It's definitely .... than his previous one."
   A most controversial   C far controversial
   B more controversial   D much controversial

2 This car is .... of the two models in the showroom.
   A the more modern   C more modern
   B the most modern   D one of the most modern

3 She was chosen as one of .... dressed women in the world.
   A a better   C most best
   B the better   D the best

4 "There's a great film on at 11 tonight!"
   "I wish it started ...... because I'm too tired to stay up and watch it."
   A more early   C the earliest
   B more earlier   D earlier

5 John is ...... the five children.
   A oldest than   C the oldest of
   B the older of   D the oldest than

STRUCTURAL CONVERSION

1 *I've never* tasted such a delicious dish.
   It's the most delicious dish I've ever tasted.
2 *If you buy a big* house, you'll pay a lot of money.
   The bigger the house you buy, *the more* money you'll pay.
3 *She is more* helpful than her sister.
   Her sister isn't as helpful as she is/her.
4 *Can't you find* an easier exercise than this?
   Is this the easiest exercise you can find?
5 *That dress is like* Jane's.
   That dress is similar to Jane's.
6 *That skirt is the same as* this one.
   That skirt and this one are alike.
7 *The German car is much* better *than* this one.
   This car can't compare to the German one.
   There is no comparison between this car and the German one.
8 *Can you describe* your cousin to me?
   Can you tell me what your cousin *looks like?*

9 *He is the* fastest runner of all.
   No other runner is *as* fast *as* he is/him.
10 *Tony has the same number* of pens *as* Chris.
   Chris has as many pens *as* Tony.
11 *A DVD player is much more* expensive *than* a TV set.
   A DVD player is far/a lot more expensive *than* a TV set.
   A TV set is much/far less expensive *than* a DVD player.
12 *A new car is twice as expensive as* a second-hand one.
   A new car is twice the price of a second-hand one.
   A second-hand car is half the price of/*half as* expensive *as* a new one.
13 *She gave an* ironic smile.
   She smiled ironically.
14 *Sheila has a friendly* smile.
   Sheila smiles in a friendly way.
15 *I'd prefer* to go home now.
   I'd sooner go home now.

14 Complete the second sentence so that it has a similar meaning to the first sentence, using the word given. Do not change the word given. You must use between three and eight words, including the word given.

1 I prefer teaching to working in an office.
   sooner
   I'd ....
   .... in an office.
2 The new mixer is much better than the old one.
   comparison
   There ....
   .... the new one.
3 If you work late tonight, you'll be tired tomorrow.
   later
   The ....
   .... you'll be tomorrow.
4 He gave him a fatherly talk.
   talked
   He ....
   .... way.
5 Couldn't the newspaper have printed a better headline?
   could
   Was that ....
   .... print?
6 I would never expect Mary to behave rudely.
   not
   It's ....
   .... rude.

7 Can you describe the picture to me, please?
   looks
   Can ....
   ...., please?
8 He is an exceptionally good driver in hazardous conditions.
   well
   He ....
   .... conditions.
9 I've never heard such a ludicrous claim.
   ridiculous
   It's ....
   .... heard.
10 It's great to go home after a long day.
   like
   There's ....
   .... after a long day.
11 She's got as much money as I have.
   amount
   She's got ....
   .... have.
12 John and his father look very similar.
   image
   John is ....
   .... father.

15 *Read the text below and think of the word which best fits each space. Use only one word in each space.*

CHEKHOV

Anton Chekhov was a Russian playwright and short story writer **(0)** *born* in Taganrog in 1860. In 1879, he became a medical student in Moscow, later qualifying **(1)** .... a doctor. With a needy family to support, Chekhov **(2)** .... to writing, contributing short humorous stories and sketches **(3)** .... popular newspapers. His major work **(4)** .... to come towards the end of his short life – Chekhov died of tuberculosis in 1904 – his reputation resting chiefly **(5)** .... four plays, *The Seagull, Uncle Vanya, The Three Sisters* and *The Cherry Orchard*, written in 1896, 1899, 1901 and 1904 **(6)** .... All four works, while gloomy and pessimistic **(7)** .... tone, blend a poetic atmosphere **(8)** .... a sympathetic treatment of characters **(9)** ...., unable to break **(10)** .... of the vicious circle that they find **(11)** .... in, are trapped in unfulfilling lives which they feel **(12)** .... powerless and dispirited to change. They **(13)** .... be regarded as symbolic **(14)** .... the torpor and stagnation of late nineteenth century Czarist Russia. **(15)** .... realism is a product of Chekhov's scientific training and experience as a provincial doctor. They remain masterpieces of Russian literature.

PHRASAL VERBS 1

16 *Look at Appendix 1 and fill in one of the prepositions or adverbs below, then give a synonym for each phrasal verb.*

- at • off • down • round • up to • by • ahead • across • off with • along • on • away with
- through • round to • out of • over • about • on with

0   What are you getting *at*? I can't understand what you're trying to say.
1   I only get .... watching TV when the children are in bed.
2   Instead of being given a ticket, the driver got .... a warning.
3   She's having trouble getting .... with her sprained ankle.
4   Do you get .... with your colleagues?
5   If you don't get those invitations .... today, they'll never arrive on time.
6   How are you getting .... at school?
7   He has a talent for getting the most complicated ideas ....
8   I've been trying to get .... for ages but the line is always engaged.
9   This awful weather is really getting me ....
10 My father is always getting .... me about my clothes.

11 If you aren't well organised, you'll never get ....
12 I don't know how he gets .... cheating on his tests.
13 Stop talking and get .... your work, will you?
14 She has barely enough money left to get ....
15 I wish I could get .... going to this wedding but I have no choice.
16 News of their "secret" wedding got .... fast.
17 She says she won't help us, but we'll soon get .... her.
18 I don't know if she'll ever get .... her husband's death.
19 What are the children getting .... in the garden?

PHRASAL VERBS 2

give away:	reveal
give in:	1) deliver
	2) yield
give off:	send out/emit
give out:	1) announce
	2) come to an end
give up:	1) stop
	2) admit defeat
give oneself up:	surrender
hype up:	exaggerate the value of sth

IDIOMS/FIXED PHRASES 1

keep oneself to oneself:	live quietly, privately
fine kettle of fish:	confused state of affairs
make a killing:	have a sudden, great success/profit
bring to one's knees:	destroy/humble
in the know:	well-informed
keep one's fingers crossed:	hope that sth will turn out well
pull sb's leg:	tease or trick sb
make/earn a/one's living:	earn money
sleep like a log:	be sound asleep

17 *Fill in the blanks with the correct preposition or adverb.*

0 The chemicals give *off* toxic fumes, so be extremely careful when using them.

1 The teacher reluctantly gave .... to the students' request to change the date of the exam.

2 The athlete has decided to give .... amateur competition and become a professional.

3 The man was forced to give himself .... to the police.

4 She unintentionally gave .... the secret of the surprise party.

5 Haven't you given .... your application form yet?

6 Eventually their savings gave .... and they were forced to apply to the state for assistance.

7 I can't guess the answer. I give ....!

8 On the news last night it was given .... that the Prime Minister had resigned.

9 They have hyped this car .... to such an extent that it should be the biggest seller of the year.

18 *Fill in the blanks with one of the idioms/fixed phrases*

1 She .... all the time they were announcing the winners of the contest, hoping that her brother would get a prize.

2 Although she enjoys an occasional evening out with friends, as a general rule she ....

3 Starting with only a few thousand pounds, Tom .... on the stock market and within a year was a millionaire.

4 The enemy were .... by a surprise air attack.

5 She .... as a freelance journalist.

6 The tap is dripping, the bath's overflowing, the plumber's on holiday; what a .... this is!

7 David .... I'm not sure if he'd hear a bomb drop.

8 If you want to know about the new film you should ask someone who is .... like a critic.

IDIOMS/FIXED PHRASES 2

the lion's share:	the biggest part/portion
turn over a new leaf:	make a new start
on the level:	honest/sincere
drop sb a line:	send sb a letter
go to any lengths:	do anything necessary to get sth you want
shed light upon:	give new/further information
make light of:	treat sth as unimportant
bury one's head in the sand:	avoid or ignore reality/responsibility
come to a head:	reach a critical point

19 *Fill in the blanks with one of the idioms/fixed phrases*

1 I wouldn't have any doubts about trusting him; I'm sure he's completely ....
2 You shouldn't .... other people's problems, even if you don't consider them to be very serious.
3 Although she had several people to help her, Susan still did .... of the work.
4 John has a tendency to .... whenever he's faced with problems instead of facing up to them.
5 As he wanted to go to university, David decided .... and study harder.
6 Their research has .... some aspects of the reproduction of cancer cells, but there is still much to be discovered.
7 The differences between management and the workers .... when the Union called a strike.
8 If you have time, ... while you're on holiday. I'd love to hear from you.
9 That man would .... to get his own way.

PREPOSITIONS

20 *Look at Appendix 5 and fill in one of the prepositions below.*

0 I'm sure there's a jinx *on* this dress. Whenever I wear it I have a terrible time.
1 Terry McWoddle has been named .... the new chairman of the football club.
2 Several flights were delayed and so the departure lounge was jam-packed .... angry travellers.
3 The harassed mother juggled .... four bags of shopping, a pushchair and a dog in the middle of the busy high street.
4 Many vegetarians argue that there is no justification .... eating meat in this day and age.
5 I've been asked to key this information .... the computer immediately.
6 The businessman insisted that he had no knowledge .... the missing currency.
7 When I was abroad I longed .... a traditional English Sunday lunch.
8 My husband's always lazing .... while I'm always busy.
9 The donkey climbed the steep track laden .... bags of oranges.
10 Sarah is jealous .... her sister because she is much more popular.
11 She is looking .... for a new job, but hasn't found anything yet.
12 No one is kinder .... children than he is.
13 I think we should limit this discussion .... the facts.
14 My uncle lectures .... the History of Art at the university.
15 You mustn't judge people .... the way they dress.
16 Their new baby is being named .... his father.
17 The man kept his child .... his side throughout the journey.
18 He's not very clever academically but he's good .... D.I.Y.

6b English in Use

21 *Complete the second sentence so that it has a similar meaning to the first sentence, using the word given. Do not change the word given. You must use between three and eight words, including the word given.*

1 You could let someone else use your old clothes.
recycle
Why ....
.... old clothes?

2 Severe weather conditions have had a serious effect on traffic.
affected
Traffic ....
.... conditions.

3 She decided to start her own business because she wanted to be independent.
with
She decided to start ....
.... independent.

4 The loss of the account was not our fault.
blame
We ....
.... the account.

5 She said she was worried about the problem of pollution.
concern
She ....
.... pollution.

6 Tom's presence at parties adds to everyone's enjoyment.
soul
Tom ....
.... the party.

7 Linda did not agree with me about the closure.
share
Linda ....
.... the closure.

8 The government's retraining programme proved to be unsuccessful due to lack of funds.
met
The government's ....
.... due to lack of funds.

9 The lease on my flat is valid until the end of the year.
renewal
The lease on my flat ....
.... the end of the year.

10 I always get your boys mixed up.
between
I ....
.... your boys.

11 She wants success more than anything else.
outweighs
Her ....
.... anything else.

12 There are fewer males than females in our country.
in
Females ....
.... in our country.

13 Mark didn't get home until just before dawn yesterday.
hours
Mark didn't get ....
.... yesterday.

14 Sheena can be bad-tempered in the mornings.
tendency
Sheena ....
.... in the mornings.

15 The latest developments have made them decide to postpone their visit.
view
They have decided ....
.... the latest developments.

16 He hated the way the media scrutinised his private life.
came
He hated ....
.... from the media.

17 The current champion has been beaten in this year's tournament.
suffered
The current ....
.... in this year's tournament.

18 The civil service has completely changed under the present government.
undergone
The civil service ....
.... under the present government.

19 Charles has potential but he hasn't exploited it yet.
use
Charles ....
.... yet.

20 Some services may be running late due to bad weather.
subject
Some services ....
.... due to bad weather.

FIXED PHRASES

meet (sb) halfway:	come to an agreement/ compromise
come under the hammer:	sth is sold at auction
let your hair down:	relax and enjoy yourself
to make/lose money hand over fist:	acquire/lose a lot of money very quickly
give sb a free hand:	allow sb to do as they wish
(know sth) off-hand:	(know sth) without asking or looking it up
have to hand it to sb:	admire sb and think they deserve praise
keep out of harm's way:	keep out of danger
fly off the handle:	lose your temper very suddenly
do sth at the drop of a hat:	be willing/happy to do sth; do sth quickly
not to make head (n)or tail of sth:	not to understand sth at all
make headway:	make progress
take heart from sth:	feel encouraged by or optimistic about sth
make a hash of sth (inf):	do sth very badly
to one's heart's content:	(do) as much or as often as one wants
strike/hit home:	(of situation) be accepted as real even though it is painful/ achieve the intended effect
after hours:	outside regular business hours

22 Complete the sentences using one of the fixed phrases in an appropriate form.

1 Sally couldn't .... the instruction for operating the lawnmower.

2 Alice .... her final exam and failed her degree.

3 Let's .... if we can't agree on this.

4 When soldiers are on leave they forget about the army's rigid discipline and ....

5 You .... Larry for tirelessly working with the disabled.

6 All medication must be .... if you have young children.

7 To withdraw cash from your bank account .... you can use an ATM card.

8 Some recently found paintings attributed to Picasso are .... next week.

23 Choose the correct item.

1 It was only when he had been unemployed for six months that Neil's situation hit ....
A base   C home
B down   D back

2 Investors have taken .... from the improving economic situation.
A heart   C consolation
B courage   D meaning

3 I can't tell you .... the population of Prague, but there's an encyclopedia in the cupboard.
A in hand   C at hand
B off-hand   D on hand

4 The government is making little .... in its fight to beat inflation.
A headway   C improvement
B advance   D forward

5 Once at the skating rink, Ivan was allowed to skate to his heart's ....
A happiness   C contentment
B content   D delight

6 The art teacher gave the children a free .... in their creative compositions.
A offer   C hand
B gift   D kick

7 After making several bad business deals the company was losing money hand over ....
A finger   C thumb
B wrist   D fist

8 Maggie is so moody and unpredictable. She's apt to fly off the .... without any real cause.
A handle   C catch
B strap   D belt

127

24 *Find the mistake and correct it.*

0 The cake has two pounds of dried ~~fruits~~ in it.   *fruit*
1 He returned at home shortly before midnight.   ....
2 He made his fortune dealing in antique furnitures.   ....
3 She doesn't mix with other people very good.   ....
4 He won't be back for another one and a half week.   ....
5 In the other hand, many employees support his decision.   ....
6 Hardly had he began to speak when someone interrupted him.   ....
7 Society shouldn't punish these people too hardly.   ....
8 If I work much long at the computer, I get a headache.   ....
9 Which judge will listen to the case?   ....
10 Here Jane comes at last!   ....
11 Last night we went to a new club. It's name is "Roxy".   ....
12 He is renowned for writing historic novels.   ....

25 *Match column A with column B and then fill in the blanks with the correct idiom/fixed phrase.*

Column A	Column B	Answers
0 as clear as	a lead	0 *e*
1 as fresh as	b life	1 ....
2 as hard as	c a mule	2 ....
3 as heavy as	d a rock	3 ....
4 as large as	e a bell	4 ....
5 as stubborn as	f a beetroot	5 ....
6 as steady as	g nails	6 ....
7 as thick as	h a daisy	7 ....
8 as red as	i thieves	8 ....

0 She has a lovely voice; It's *as clear as a bell*.
1 I never expected to actually meet such a great actress, but when I arrived at the party, there she was ....
2 Although she had been up all night, after a short nap she looked ....
3 He's nice enough as a neighbour, but as a businessman he's ....
4 Those boys are .... You hardly ever see them apart.
5 When she realised her embarrassing mistake, she turned ....
6 I don't think I can move this sofa. It's ....
7 You'll never convince John to do it if he doesn't want to. He's ....
8 Compared with her shiftless, unreliable husband she's ....

26 *Match column A with column B and then fill in the blanks with the correct idiom/fixed phrase.*

Column A	Column B	Answers
1 as safe as	a a glove	1 ....
2 eat like	b a ton of bricks	2 ....
3 fit like	c a house on fire	3 ....
4 have a memory like	d houses	4 ....
5 go/come down (on sb) like	e wildfire	5 ....
6 get on like	f a sieve	6 ....
7 spread like	g a leaf	7 ....
8 shake like	h a horse	8 ....

1 I'm afraid I've forgotten your name again. I ....
2 She was so nervous that her hands ....
3 Although James and Julie are very different types of people, they ....
4 If your mother finds out you haven't been doing your homework, she'll ....
5 I thought the suit would be too small for me, but it ....
6 It's no wonder he's fat, he ....
7 Don't worry about losing money; this investment is ....
8 Thanks to thorough press coverage, the scandal .... .Everyone knew about it the next day.

27 *In most lines of the following text there is a spelling or punctuation error. Read the numbered lines 1-16 and then write the correct form in the spaces provided for your answers. Some lines are correct. Indicate these lines with a tick (✓). The first one has been done for you.*

AN ANNUAL HAZARD

0	With Europe facing the most serious 'flu epedemic in years	*epidemic*
1	the World health Organisation is warning the public, especially	....
2	the sick and elderly, to have an innoculation now.	....
3	Health experts warn that this winters' outbreak could be as	....
4	severe as the one in 1989 which killed 25,000 people in	....
5	Britian alone.	....
6	WHO has stressed the importance of vaccination; and several	....
7	countries are already taking precautions to ensure that those in	....
8	high-risk categories, such as diabetics and those with heart or	....
9	lung complaints, are vaccinated.	....
10	Nearly all previous strains of 'flu are known to have origenated in	....
11	China and the Far East, and wheras in the past infection spread	....
12	slowly across the world, in these days of mass air travel rapide	....
13	global infection is a great threat?	....
14	Sweden has reported cases of para-influenza, effecting mainly	....
15	children, and danish doctors have recorded 1,500 cases of 'flu	....
16	in the past week.	....

WORD USAGE

28 *Read the text below. Use the word given in capitals at the end of some of the lines to form a word that fits in the space in the same line.*

CAPRI

One of the most **(0)** *frequently* visited areas in Italy is the island of Capri in the southern part of the country. — **FREQUENT**

(1) .... in prehistoric times, the island later became a Greek colony and then a resort of emperors in the early years of the Roman Empire. During the 10th century the **(2)** ...., fearing pirate raids, moved from seaside **(3)** .... to the present towns, Capri (east) and Anacapri (west), high above the shore. It changed hands between the French and the British several times during the Napoleonic Wars, before being returned to the Kingdom of the Two Sicilies in 1813. Stone **(4)** .... has been found in one of the caves with which the rocky shores of Capri abound: the most **(5)** .... of these is the Blue Grotto, rediscovered in 1826 and **(6)** .... only by boat. Sunlight entering through the water that fills most of the entrance gives it an **(7)** .... blue light, hence its name. Since the second half of the 19th century, Capri has **(8)** .... become one of the most popular resorts in southern Italy, famous for its magnificent **(9)** .... and the mild climate in which vegetation flourishes despite the **(10)** .... amount of water.

— HABITAT
— POPULATE
— SETTLE
— ART
— NOTE
— ACCESS
— ORDINARY
— GRADE
— SCENE
— SUFFICE

6b English in Use

29 *Choose the correct item.*

0 My neighbour has threatened to .... over our dispute about property boundaries.
   A take legal aid   C try me
   Ⓑ take legal action   D bring me to trial

1 He managed to .... the flow of blood by tightly bandaging the wound.
   A restrain   C check
   B curb   D inhibit

2 Mr Wright is being .... for fraud at the Old Bailey courthouse, this afternoon.
   A taken to court   C summoned
   B tried   D charged

3 The heavy rain lashed down .... throughout the night without letting up.
   A continually   C perpetually
   B continuously   D eternally

4 We intend this to be a(n) .... project, taking us into the next decade.
   A constant   C steady
   B incessant   D ongoing

5 As long as you have the most .... ingredients for the recipe, you can make do without the other things.
   A critical   C essential
   B crucial   D vital

6 A(n) .... proportion of the population did not vote in the last elections.
   A essential   C grave
   B significant   D fundamental

7 When a former secret agent tried to publish his memoirs, the government had certain parts of the book ....
   A forbidden   C disallowed
   B prohibited   D censored

8 Benjamin Britten, the composer, is probably most .... for his opera "Peter Grimes".
   A famous   C remarkable
   B conspicuous   D distinguished

9 .... scientists from around the world met in London to discuss a revolutionary new drug.
   A Eminent   C Prestigious
   B Elevated   D Noteworthy

COLLOCATIONS

30 a) *Fill in postponed, delayed.*

0 The plane has been *delayed* in Munich.
1 The meeting was .... due to the absence of the chairman.
2 The picnic was .... because of bad weather.
3 I was .... in the traffic.
4 We .... our journey.

b) *Fill in extend, expand.*

1 .... a hand
2 .... a deadline
3 .... a product range
4 .... a road
5 .... a business
6 .... a deadline
7 .... a piece of furniture
8 .... one's services

31 *Collocate the expressions with words from the given list.*

- repress • abide by • hold • relish • control
- cling to • secure • stick to • bar

0 to *decline* an offer
1 to .... someone's hand
2 to .... the rules
3 to .... an idea
4 to .... one's feelings
5 to .... someone from a club
6 to .... someone's release
7 to .... the question
8 to .... a crowd
9 to .... an old habit

32 *Think of one word only which can be used appropriately in all three sentences.*

0 • One doesn't need to be an expert to *appreciate* the beauty of classical music.
   • He seems confident that houses in this area will *appreciate* in value in the next few years.
   • I'll always *appreciate* your help and support.

1 • Because of her red hair and .... complexion, she avoided sunbathing.
   • Though unable to give an exact figure, he gave us a .... idea of how much the trip would cost.
   • He was informed that the merchant was an astute but .... businessman.

2 • During the battle, the entire area .... to the French.
 • While journeying through tropical regions, he .... ill after drinking contaminated water.
 • As the manager had predicted, production .... by 10% due to staff reductions.
3 • I .... down the numberplate of the speeding vehicle.
 • They .... that Mr. Ponsonby had chosen not to wear a dinner jacket for the formal banquet.
 • The speaker .... in closing that a solution to the problem of the thinning ozone layer was still no nearer to being found.
4 • The traffic .... extended for three kilometres.
 • Martha was in a terrible .... and didn't know what to do.
 • Try some of my blackberry ....; it's delicious!
5 • The song Auld Lang Syne is an old .... in most parts of the UK.
 • The two year-old, ridden by Richard Guest, is the .... in next week's Cheltenham Gold Cup.
 • The Earl of Essex had notoriety as the .... of Queen Elizabeth.
6 • A farmer himself, Tom holds that solitude and fresh air are two of the best .... of country living.
 • Graceful and statuesque, her beauty was accentuated by her well-defined facial ....
 • Ornithologist Ted Mannings noted that there had been some excellent .... on wildlife in the news recently.
7 • The peacock strutted around proudly, the .... of his tail a beautiful sight.
 • I'm a great .... of country and western music.
 • Switch on the .... if you are cooking in the kitchen.
8 • In his haste to locate the exit, he accidentally .... the torch directly into my eyes.
 • After five applications of soap and oil, the newly polished saddle .... in the sun.
 • In secondary school, she .... athletically but was academically poor.

9 • Transfixed by the gargantuan lizard, he gazed in .... terror at the television screen.
 • Aware that his life depended on it, the young man dived from the .... cliff into the water below.
 • .... black tights were all the rage when my mother was young.
10 • The majestic .... in the distance was none other than Mount Everest.
 • Stephen is in the fifth .... and he is going to do A Levels next year.
 • The government will have to enact some .... of wages policy if it wants to beat inflation.
11 • Going to gymnastics classes gives you good muscle ....
 • Don't you dare speak to me in that ....!
 • I've been trying to ring you all day, but I just get the engaged ....
12 • It's vital that your attention remain .... on your goals.
 • She got in the car, ... her safety belt and drew away from the kerb.
 • Feeling increasingly nervous about his role as best man, he .... the rose to the lapel of his jacket.
13 • They were married secretly in a .... ceremony to avoid the glare of publicity.
 • Even if you are not helpful, you can at least be .... in your replies.
 • Humphrey had been a .... servant for many years.
14 • So many things .... our attention these days that we are unable to see to them all.
 • Henry does not .... to be an authority on tropical fish, but he knows a lot about them.
 • Every year landmines .... many innocent people's lives.
15 • As stones cascaded past his head, he held .... to the rope to avoid falling.
 • He's just lazy, and I am .... running out of time and patience with him.
 • You would be best advised to leave for the airport as .... as possible.

PREPARING FOR PART 5

WORKING WITH "ECHOED IDEAS" II

33 *Read the passages and answer the following questions. One question has been answered for you.*

Medium-sized businesses are spending more and more money on in-house computer technicians, said a report by the National Technology Board published in last Friday's *Evening Times*.

According to Timothy Archibald, spokesman for the National Technology Board, "this is happening not only because of the **(0) increasing demand for round-the-clock operating computers,** but also because the practice of calling in a computer technician whenever there is a problem with them has become very costly in the last three years." The report states that a London-based freelance computer technician will charge anything from £150 to £300 an hour for maintenance work. An in-house technician's salary averages around £28,000 per year, so it is the more economical option for businesses that rely on computers extensively.

"**(1) The more sophisticated computers get, the higher the risk of losing precious work through bad maintenance,** and business managers seem to be aware of this", said Archibald.

Remember the eighties? The first PCs were structured in such an ingeniously simple way that serious technical problems were rare, and treating your machine well was all you had to do to make sure it continued to work properly.

How things have changed! **(0) Your computer is on all the time now, working away into the small hours when you've long gone to get some well-deserved rest.** It has become about a hundred times more powerful, a thousand times more complicated and equally more prone to malfunctioning if you don't care for it properly. Maintenance has become an expert's job.

Starting from £185 a month, you can benefit from the services of Conway Electronics' computer maintenance experts, who will visit you weekly to make certain that your equipment is functioning (and will continue to function) properly. No more lost work because of crashes, no more delays caused by poor software setups, no more costly repairs due to damaged parts.

Call Conway Electronics now on 0800 - 180 - 180 to arrange a free consultation.

Conway Electronics
Because your business matters!

(0) *Which sentence in the second passage echoes the idea that there is an "increasing demand for round-the-clock operating computers" expressed in the first passage?*
"Your computer is on all the time now, working away into the small hours..."

(1) *Which sentence in the second passage echoes the idea that "the more sophisticated computers get, the higher the risk of losing precious work through bad maintenance" expressed in the first passage?*

....
....
....

Long ago, virtually nothing was known about diabetes and **(2) this terrible illness went undiagnosed and untreated;** as a result, the majority of its victims were left to their own fate and **(3) died long before their time**. Now, in these days of medical enlightenment, a combination of healthy diet and pharmaceutical drugs allow the diabetic a chance of a long, normal life. Until recently, the prevailing belief had been that the diabetes sufferer should be put on a high-protein, low-carbohydrate diet. Times have changed and now most experts advocate a high-fibre, high-carbohydrate diet.

Many members of the Tudor family suffered mysterious, premature deaths. Of Henry's six siblings, only three grew to adulthood and nobody could identify the strange, debilitating disease, which steadily ate away at their health. A recently posed theory seems to offer a plausible explanation. The symptoms of their disease, which Henry also displayed, indicate that they were suffering from severe uncontrolled diabetes.

(2) Which sentence in the second passage echoes the idea that diabetes "went undiagnosed and untreated" expressed in the first passage?

....

....

(3) Which sentence in the second passage echoes the idea that diabetes sufferers "died long before their time" expressed in the first passage?

....

....

EAST-END WAREHOUSE DESTROYED IN FIRE

LEITH - Fire fighters were called to the scene of a large blaze at the Menzies Transport warehouse in Broomridge Road late last night. Due to the lateness of the hour, **(4) only a skeleton staff was working in the building**. A security guard and a warehouse worker were rushed to Edinburgh Royal Infirmary suffering from smoke inhalation. John Collins, spokesman for the fire department, said that "the fire was most likely caused by faulty wiring". Menzies Transport are being charged with negligence as the structure did not meet with government safety standards and **(5) the fire alarm was not in proper working order**.

POLICE WITNESS STATEMENT

Incident 107/3/8/200- Attending Officer, DC Arthur Haley, 446-2211

I had just completed my midnight rounds and returned to the guard house when I thought I smelled smoke. I knew that there were only a few people on that shift in the warehouse that night. I went to the main entrance of the building and checked to see if the metal door was hot. It was, so I immediately phoned the fire brigade. Next, I desperately tried to sound the alarm. I had been telling my superiors for months that the glass on it was broken and that it needed fixing. All I can say is, that it's amazing nobody was killed.

Signed: Peter Merson. Security Guard

(4) Which sentence in the second passage echoes the idea that "only a skeleton staff was working in the building" expressed in the first passage?

....

....

(5) Which sentence in the second passage echoes the idea that "the fire alarm was not in proper working order" expressed in the first passage?

....

....

6c Practice Test Six

Paper 3 Use of English

Time: 1 hour 30 minutes

Read the text below and think of the word which fits each space. Use only one word in each space.

BEWARE OF VITAMINS!

Vitamins are good for our health, aren't they? Perhaps not. New research suggests that **(0)** ......*rather*...... than ward off disease, high doses of certain vitamins may **(1)** .... more harm than good and could even put you in an early grave. A variety of recent studies suggest that **(2)** .... from improving health, these vitamins, **(3)** .... taken in very high doses, may actually increase the risks of cancer and a range **(4)** .... debilitating diseases, a discovery that has sent the medical world into a spin. Scientists are unsure **(5)** .... to why vitamins, so essential to health, can be toxic in high doses. The most likely explanation is that the body is only equipped to deal with the levels found naturally in the environment. If the intake is too far **(6)** .... the normal range, then the body's internal chemistry can be shunted out of alignment. **(7)** .... this means is that the commercially sold vitamins and **(8)** .... provided by nature are not always compatible. The commercial forms may interfere with the body's internal chemistry **(9)** .... 'crowding out' the **(10)** .... natural and beneficial forms of the nutrients. The vitamins obtained **(11)** .... food are also allied **(12)** .... a host of other substances which may moderate **(13)** .... augment their activity in the body. The latest advice **(14)** .... to eat a balanced diet to ensure you get all the nutrients you need, and if you must take supplements make **(15)** .... you take the lowest recommended dose and follow the instructions on the bottle.

Read the text below. Use the word given in capitals at the end of some of the lines to form a word that fits in the space in the same line.

A TASTE FOR SUCCESS

Founded in 1892, the Coca-Cola Company is today engaged **(0)** *primarily* in the manufacture **PRIME**
and sale of the famous carbonated beverage that is a **(16)** .... institution in the **CULTURE**
United States and a symbol around the world of American tastes.

The drink was **(17)** .... in 1886 by an Atlanta pharmacist, John S. Pemberton; **ORIGIN**
his bookkeeper, Frank Robinson, chose the name for the drink and penned it in the flowing
script that became the Coca-Cola trademark. Pemberton originally touted his drink as a tonic
for most common **(18)** .... He sold his syrup to local soda fountains, and, with **AIL**
advertising, the drink became **(19)** .... successful. By 1891 another **EXPECT**
Atlanta pharmacist, Asa Griggs Candler had secured complete **(20)** .... **OWN**
of the business for a total cash outlay of $2,300 and the exchange of some proprietary rights.
In 1899 the Coca-Cola Company signed its first **(21)** .... with an independent **AGREE**
bottling company, which was allowed to buy the syrup and produce, bottle, and distribute the
drink. Such licensing deals formed the basis of a unique distribution system that now
(22) .... most of the American soft-drink industry. The post-World War **CHARACTER**
II years saw **(23)**...................................... in the packaging of Coca-Cola and also in the **DIVERSE**
development or **(24)** .... of new products. Today, Coca-Cola stands as **ACQUIRE**
one of the most **(25)** .... of US businesses. **PROSPER**

PART 3

Think of one word only which can be used appropriately in all three sentences.

0 • One doesn't need to be an expert to *appreciate* the beauty of classical music.
  • He seems confident that houses in this area will *appreciate* in value in the next few years.
  • I'll always *appreciate* your help and support.

26 • The sentry remained at his .... throughout the night.
  • Your cheque must still be in the ....
  • Tony stubbed his toe against a wooden .... yesterday and it still hurts.

27 • In "A Christmas Carol", Scrooge starts by being .... with his money.
  • It is .... to criticise people unfairly.
  • The .... score of a pass candidate is 60%.

28 • Mr Portman was in his .... writing a report.
  • The press .... will give you further details.
  • The Prime Minister has been in .... for five years.

29 • On a .... day, there is a spectacular view across the valley.
  • Mike earns a .... thousand pounds a week.
  • It is .... to everyone that the government will have to call elections soon.

30 • Janice decided to wear the dress with the red and white ....
  • There were dark clouds in the sky and .... of rain were beginning to fall.
  • Eating too much chocolate can give you ....

31 • Jess made a .... to be more organised in future.
  • There is little hope of an early .... to the miners' strike.
  • The U.N. has passed a .... to establish irrigation schemes in developing countries.

PART 4

Complete the second sentence so that it has a similar meaning to the first sentence, using the word given. Do not change the word given. You must use between three and eight words, including the word given.

0 Nobody spoke when the teacher asked who the culprit was.
  remained
  Everyone *remained silent when the teacher asked* .... who the culprit was.

32 She said she disapproved of eating meat.
  her
  She ....
  .... meat.

33 Mr Jones was shocked to hear that his son had failed his exam.
  came
  It ....
  .... hear that his son had failed his exam.

34 I never thought of borrowing money from him.
  occurred
  It ....
  .... from him.

35 Rhonda's not very keen on foreign food.
  care
  Rhonda ....
  .... foreign food.

36 Ray's good work record enabled him to get promotion.
  strength
  Ray ....
  .... good work record.

37 Travellers may bring as much luggage as they require.
  amount
  There ....
  .... travellers may bring.

38 The government has tried to make the incident seem less serious.
  played
  The government ....
  .... of the incident.

39 We couldn't understand the film at all.
  sense
  We could ....
  .... the film.

135

PART 5

For questions 40 - 44 read the following texts. For questions 40 - 43, answer with a word or short phrase. You do not need to write complete sentences. For question 44, write a summary according to the instructions given.

As puzzling as it may seem, landfill sites may provide a solution to global warming. Researchers state that burying wood and paper locks large amounts of carbon under the earth. This process, unlike other methods of garbage disposal, prevents carbon from seeping into the atmosphere resulting in the acceleration of global warming. Some countries have proposed to have landfills count as "carbon sinks" under the 1997 Kyoto Protocol to curb greenhouse gas emissions. This might have the effect of inciting countries to bury their carbon waste in order to burn more fossil fuels; an ironic twist to landfills' newly found environmental potential.

Researchers in the US Forest Products Laboratory have concluded that most of the carbon found in paper and wood products doesn't rot. An estimated 70% of carbon from paper, and 97% from wood, is permanently sealed underground. Requests by some countries to enlist landfills have been taken to the UN's Intergovernmental Panel on Climate Change (IPCC), which triggered an inquiry into the complex interchanges of carbon between air and land. However, environmentalists are still concerned about the ecological impact of landfills. Research continues.

40 Why does the writer say that burying used wood and paper could be "an ironic twist to the landfills' newly found potential"?

....

....

41 When paper and wood are buried, what happens to most of the carbon they contain?

....

....

I must admit I was taken aback by the landfills article in the June edition of your publication. I am rather sceptical about the newly acquired wisdom on the environmental benefits of landfills as "carbon sealers" which would miraculously decelerate global warming. As an active member of a global environmental group, I have campaigned over the years for the restriction of gas emissions and have carefully looked into various governmental policies. It is well known that countries are desperately looking for ways to circumvent respecting carbon emission rate limits, which were imposed by the 1997 Kyoto Protocol. I can just
line 9 — envisage industry using this as an excuse to continue burning fossil fuels, with devastating consequences.

This is bound to have negative effects on recycling. Paper production might increase under the excuse of its harm-free disposal, and recycling paper might be abandoned at an industrial level. The long struggle to establish recycling as part of everyday life is threatened with failure, as any excuse to retreat from
line 15 — recycling, which has always carried the stigma of being non-profitable, would be attractive to manufacturers.

I strongly urge a thorough investigation of long-term effects of this research, or we might find ourselves inside a vicious carbon cycle.

Harold Brown,
Kent

42 What does the word "this" refer to in line 9?

....

....

43 Explain the phrase "has always carried the stigma of being non-profitable" (line 15).

....

....

44 In a paragraph of between 50 and 70 words, summarise the arguments for and against landfill sites as they are presented in the two passages.

....

....

....

....

....

....

....

....

Type	If-Clause	Main Clause	Use
Type 0 Conditional	If + present simple *If metal **gets** hot,* *If you **stand** in the rain,*	present simple *it **expands**.* *you **get** wet.*	scientific facts general truths laws of nature
Type 1 Conditional	If + present tense (or **should** + bare infinitive: more doubtful or polite) *If it **rains**,* *If you **should see** him,*	future imperative (instruction, advice) ought to (advice) had better (advice) } + infinitive should, must may, can *we'll **stay** at home.* *give him my message.*	real situation (likely to happen in the present or future)
Type 2 Conditional	If + past tense *If I **were** you,* *If he **were** here,*	would could } + should } infinitive might *I would tell her the truth.* *(advice)* *he **could help me**. (imaginary situation)*	advice or imaginary situation in the present or future (unreal or unlikely to happen)
Type 3 Conditional	If + past perfect *If he **had worked** harder,*	would could (ability/ permission } + have + p.p. should (advice) might (possibility) *he **would have been promoted**. (unfulfilled plan)*	imaginary situation in the past (regrets, unfulfilled plans, wishes impossible to fulfil, criticism)

Notes

- *Future tense* (will/would) with a future meaning is never used in **if**-clauses.
  However, **will/would** can be used to express polite requests or insistence.
  *If you **will wait** for a moment, I'll wrap it for you. (request)*
  *If you **will go on** chatting, I'll send you out of the classroom. (insistence)*

- The *if*-clause can either precede or follow the main clause. When the if-clause precedes the main clause, we put a comma after it. When the main clause comes first, no comma is used to separate the two clauses.
  If he is still in Paris, he may visit us. (He may visit us if he is still in Paris.)

- **unless** (=if not) is used in first conditional sentences.
  Unless he gets a promotion, he'll resign.

- When referring to imaginary or unreal situations, *suppose* can be followed either by Simple Past or Past Perfect for present or past situations respectively. *Suppose*, however, can be followed by Simple Present to express a situation which may happen in the future, or to introduce suggestions.
  *Suppose she **had** married the film star, do you think she'd be happy?*
  *Suppose she **is** on holiday, how shall we contact her?*

- In reported speech, the verb tenses of first conditional sentences change in the usual way, whereas those of second and third conditional do not follow the usual changes with the verb tenses remaining unchanged.

  *"If I **am** back early, we**'ll go** out for dinner," he said.*
  *He said that if he **were/was** back early, we **would go** out for dinner.*
  *"If I **were** you, I **wouldn't say** that," he said.*
  *He said that if he **were** me, he **wouldn't say** that.*
  *"If he **had been** ill, he **wouldn't have come** to work," she said.*
  *She said that if he **had been** ill, he **wouldn't have come/gone** to work.*

- Other expressions used in place of *if* are the following: **on condition that, even if, even though, when, provided (that), providing (that), as long as, suppose, supposing, since, as, unless (if not), but for + gerund/noun, in case + Present** (for the present) or **Past** (for the past).

  If the Mayor comes, we'll hold a meeting. (He may come or he may not.)
  When the Mayor comes, we'll hold a meeting. (He will definitely come.)
  Even if the Mayor doesn't come, we'll hold a meeting. (Whether he comes or not doesn't affect the result).

Provided (that)	
Providing (that)	the Mayor comes, we'll hold a meeting; (We'll only hold a meeting if he comes.)
As long as	
Unless	the Mayor comes, we won't hold a meeting. (We'll only hold a meeting if he comes.)
Suppose	the Mayor comes, we'll hold a meeting (It is unlikely that he will come, but if he does, we'll
Supposing	hold a meeting.)
Since	the Mayor can't come, we won't hold a meeting. (the fact that he can't come means that we
As	can't hold a meeting.)

  In case *the Mayor comes, we'll prepare for a meeting. (It is unlikely that he will come, but we'd better be ready for the event as it's not impossible that he will.)*

INVERSION IN IF-CLAUSES

When there is **should, were** or **had** in the if-clause, the subject and the auxiliary verb can be inverted and *if* is omitted.

*If he **should** ring, tell him to come at 7.00.*
***Should** he ring, tell him to come at 7.00.*
*If I **were** you, I wouldn't say that.*
***Were** I you, I wouldn't say that.*
*If I **had** known earlier, I wouldn't have done such a thing.*
***Had** I known earlier, I wouldn't have done such a thing.*

MIXED CONDITIONALS

A mixed conditional sentence makes use of one type of if-clause and a different type of main clause.

If-clause		Main Clause	
Type 1	If she *is* honest,	she *would have told* the truth	Type 3
Type 2	If she *knew* the truth,	she *would have told* me.	Type 3
Type 3	If she *had accepted* his proposal,	she *would be married* now.	Type 2
Type 2	If he *missed the train*,	he *will be* late.	Type 1

1 *Put the verbs in brackets into the correct tense.*

1 If ....were.... **(be)** you, I .... **(not/listen)** to his lies.

2 If he .... **(not/eat)** that sandwich, he would not have suffered from food poisoning.

3 Father Christmas won't bring you any presents unless you .... **(be)** a good girl.

4 As long as you .... **(do)** your best, no one will criticise you.

5 He put the answerphone on in case anyone .... **(want)** to leave him a message.

6 Supposing we ....**(be/stop)** by the police, what .... **(we/say)**?

7 If you .... **(tell)** me you were cold, I .... **(put)** the fire on.

8 What .... **(we do)** if John hadn't helped us?

9 If she were rich, she .... **(not/have)** to work.

10 Go and see a doctor in case you .... **(have)** a serious illness.

11 You won't understand this unless you .... **(pay)** attention.

12 What .... **(you/give)** me if I .... **(keep)** your secret?.

13 Even if he .... **(beg)** me I would not help him.

14 If this case .... **(go)** to trial, it will cause a national outcry.

15 Supposing no one .... **(invent)** the silicon chip, ... **(things/be)** different now?

2 *Write the correct conditional for the following sentences.*

1 He hasn't got a free weekend. He would have visited us, then.

....
....

2 He has made a lot of friends. He isn't lonely now.

....
....
....

3 You are soaked. Why didn't you bring an umbrella with you?

....
....

4 He can't be in trouble. He would have called by now.

....
....

5 He has lost his security pass. He won't be allowed to enter the building.

I ....
....

6 They can't have caught the ferry. Otherwise they would be here by now.

....
....
....

7 He must eat meat. He asked for a steak.

....
....

8 She isn't reliable. She would never have let you down.

....
....

9 They didn't ban hunting. The tiger is endangered.

....
....

10 Aren't you sure? Why did you agree to it then?

....
....

11 My father loves Shirley Bassey. He bought all her records.

....
....

12 He is a pessimist. He always looks on the black side.

....
....

-- STRUCTURAL CONVERSION ◄--------------------------------

1 *If you don't drive* carefully, you'll have an accident.
Unless you drive carefully, you'll have an accident.
You won't have an accident **provided that** you **drive** carefully.
As long as you drive carefully, you won't have an accident.
Drive carefully **or else** you'll have an accident.

2 *You had better* take his advice.
If I were you, I'd take his advice.
Were I you, I'd take his advice.
You should take his advice.

3 *Should she come*, tell her to wait for me.
If she should come, tell her to wait for me.

4 *As he couldn't* afford a holiday, he stayed at home.
He couldn't afford a holiday, so he stayed at home.
If he had been able to afford a holiday, he wouldn't have stayed at home.
He stayed at home because he couldn't afford a holiday.

5 *Since* he doesn't have any qualifications, he can't find a job.
If he had qualifications, he could find a job.
As he doesn't have any qualifications, he can't find a job.

6 *If it hadn't been for* my mother's generosity, I wouldn't have my car now.
But for my mother's generosity I wouldn't have my car now.

7 *Suppose he phoned* you, what would you tell him?
If he phoned you, what would you tell him?
What would you tell him if he phoned you?

8 *If you help* me, I'll help you.
I'll help you provided (that) you help me.

9 *Suppose* he marries her?
What if he marries her?

10 *Suppose* the teacher caught you cheating in the test?
What would you do if the teacher caught you cheating in the test?

11 *If he had been* on time, we wouldn't have missed the bus.
Had he been on time, we wouldn't have missed the bus.

12 *If you won* the lottery, what would you do?
Should you win the lottery, what would you do?
If you were to win the lottery, what would you do?

13 *If she were rich*, she would buy a villa.
Were she rich, she would buy a villa.

14 *If I had been you*, I wouldn't have accepted his offer.
If I had been in your shoes, I wouldn't have accepted his offer.
If I had been in your position, I wouldn't have accepted his offer.

15 *I'm not rich*, so I can't afford a long holiday abroad.
If I were rich, I could afford a long holiday abroad.

16 *I didn't go* out because I had a lot of work to do.
If I hadn't had a lot of work to do, I would have gone out.

17 *She must be* out since she didn't answer the phone.
If she were in, she would have answered the phone.

18 *She must have lived* in France because she has a perfect French accent.
If she hadn't lived in France, she wouldn't have a perfect French accent.

3 *Complete the second sentence so that it has a similar meaning to the first sentence using the word given. Do not change the word given. You must use between three and eight words, including the word given.*

1 If I were him, I would not be late for the interview.
better
He ....
.... the interview.

2 You won't be punished provided you admit it was your mistake.
long
You won't be ....
.... to your mistake.

3 Since he is an only child, his parents have spoiled him.
not
If ....
.... his parents wouldn't have spoiled him.

4 If I had been you, I would have punished him.
shoes
If ....
.... have punished him.

5 If you revise all your notes, you'll pass the exam.
provided
You'll pass ....
.... all your notes.

6 If it wasn't for the good pay, I wouldn't stay in this job.
but
I wouldn't ....
.... pay.

141

7a Grammar: Conditionals

7 If you don't get to work on time, you'll be given the sack.

punctual

Unless ....

.... the sack.

8 As you've got a high temperature, you'd better go to the doctor's.

were

If I ....

.... about your high temperature.

9 As I couldn't answer any of the questions, I walked out of the Maths exam.

so

I couldn't ....

.... out of the Maths exam.

10 But for his help, I wouldn't be in my current job.

got

If it hadn't ....

.... my current job.

11 If Mary were feeling well, she would have come to Tom's party.

since

Mary must ....

.... to Tom's party.

12 If someone gave you a free airline ticket, where would you travel to?

to

If you ....

................................., where would you travel to?

CONVERSATIONAL GRAMMAR

4 *Choose the correct item.*

1 "Should I eat that?"
"If I .... you, I wouldn't."
A would have been   C were
B would be   D had been

2 "Thank God we came across that policeman!"
"Oh, yes! What .... done if you hadn't?"
A would you have   C had you
B were you to have   D will you have

3 "So, are you going to buy it or not?"
"If it .... so expensive, I would."
A were   C hadn't been
B weren't   D isn't

4 "Why do you have to get a taxi to work?"
"Well, if I didn't live so far away, I .... to."
A wouldn't have   C wouldn't have had
B hadn't had   D didn't have

5 .... pay attention in class, you won't pass the test.
A If you didn't   C If you don't
B Unless you don't   D Unless you wouldn't

6 "Why don't we ask Martin to chair the meeting?"
"Well, suppose .... to ask him, do you think he would accept?"
A were we   C we had been
B we were   D had we been

7 If he .... as honest as you believe, he wouldn't have done that.
A were   C would have been
B would be   D have been

8 "What would you do in my place?"
"Were .... treated like that, I'd complain to the manager."
A I to be   C I have been
B I to had been   D to I be

9 What would you do if you .... rich?
A have been   C would be
B were   D would have been

10 What would you buy, provided .... the money?
A had you   C have you
B you had   D you would have

11 .... you go on talking, he'll ask you to leave.
A Unless   C When
B If   D Suppose

12 "Why are you screaming?"
"If you burn yourself, it .... you know!"
A would have hurt   C have hurt
B hurts   D hurt

13 .... I been informed, I'd have attended the meeting.
A Should   C Had
B Were   D Would

14 "......... you were ill, we wouldn't have come."
"Don't be silly! I always enjoy your company."
A Were we to know   C Should we have known
B Had we known   D Had we to know

15 Suppose they .... at home, what shall we do?
A aren't   C hadn't been
B weren't   D won't be

5 Read the text below and think of the word which best fits each space. Use only one word in each space.

WHAT'S OUT THERE?

In 1969, Neil Armstrong was the first man **(0)** *to* land on the moon. If earthlings can take part in intergalactic travel, then why can't life forms from other planets do the same? Is Earth the only inhabited planet in the universe? How can we be so sure of **(1)** ...*whether*... the existence or the non-existence of extraterrestrial life?

On 24th June, 1947, Kenneth Arnold reported seeing nine silvery objects moving rapidly through the sky near Mount Rainer, Washington. Obviously he had no proof **(2)** ...*other*... than his testimony, but this sparked **(3)** ...*such*... an epidemic of apparent spottings of "unidentified flying objects". In June and July of the same year, a **(4)** *announce*... of 850 sightings of spaceships were reported.

Ufology had **(5)** ...*grown*... root and was spreading prolifically. The latest Gallup poll conveyed that twenty percent of the British and sixty percent of the American populations believed in the existence of UFOs. In **(6)** ...*Europe*..., a French group claimed that we only hear **(7)** ...*realistically*... one in every 38,400 alien visits to Earth. Clearly, these figures do not prove the existence of life **(8)** *elsewhere*... in the cosmos, but they do prove that belief in humanoids is international and widespread.

In alleged encounters with alien life, one **(9)** ...*encounter*... of five leaves some trace behind, such as burnt ground, footprints, powdery residues or metallic fragments. One group of ufologists studied thousands of cases and **(10)** ...*arrive*... to the conclusion that there were four main **(11)** ...*groups*... of extraterrestrial existence; small humanoids, experimental animals, humanlike entities and robots. However, Hilary Evans of the British UFO Research Association admits **(12)** *consciously*... the inadequacies of all findings and testimonies. Some UFO witnesses lie, either deliberately or unconsciously. So, with little **(13)** ...*more*... than the word of an apparent eye witness to consider, evidence for the existence of alien life forms is far **(14)** ...*from*... conclusive.

Who knows, perhaps somewhere in this cosmos, another species **(15)** ...*are*... deliberating on the existence of the Earthling.

PHRASAL VERBS 1

6 Look at Appendix 1 and fill in one of the prepositions or adverbs below, then give a synonym for each phrasal verb.

• with • up • through • round • down • off • into • for • down with • on • in for • on with

0 Let's go ...*through*... the plan once more to make sure it's all clear.

1 Does the shed go .... the house or should I pay extra?

2 She had to cancel her holiday when she went .... the flu.

3 She's gone .... all her savings since she lost her job.

4 I don't know what's going .... next door but they're being very noisy.

5 I'm planning to go .... the poetry competition this year.

6 Suddenly the fire alarm went ....

7 The Prime Minister promised to go .... the matter of lowering inflation.

8 Those shoes are going ...*for*... next to nothing. I've never seen such a good sale.

9 I don't think there's enough fruit to go ...*on*... . Could you get some more?

10 His proposals didn't go ...*down*... very well at all; in fact they were all rejected.

11 He paused to answer the phone, and then he went .... what he was doing.

12 New blocks of flats are going .... everywhere, destroying the character of the township.

PHRASAL VERBS 2

hold back:	1) delay (tr) 2) prevent development 3) withhold
hold in:	control (oneself/feelings)
hold off:	1) keep at a distance 2) delay
hold on:	wait
hold out:	1) last 2) resist
hold out for:	wait to get sth desired
hold out on:	keep a secret from sb
hold over:	postpone
hold up:	1) delay 2) rob

7 *Fill in the correct preposition(s) or adverb.*

1 Can't you hold .... those reporters until I've finished the rehearsal?

2 He is a talented actor but his lack of ambition holds him ....

3 Although they tried, they couldn't hold .... their laughter.

4 Hold .... a minute while I get something from my room.

5 They offered to buy her a BMW but she's holding .... a Porsche.

6 Some Japanese soldiers refused to believe the war was over and held .... in the jungle for years.

7 Due to the chairman's illness, the meeting was held .... till the next week.

8 Strike action held .... trains and buses all day yesterday.

9 He says he knows nothing about the missing documents but I'm sure he's holding .... me.

10 Our water supplies held .... for three weeks when we were marooned in the desert.

Make sentences using a) **hold back**, b) **hold off** and c) **hold up** meaning **"delay"**.

....

....

....

....

....

....

IDIOMS/FIXED PHRASES 1

feel down in the mouth:	feel discouraged/depressed
get a move on:	hurry up
work a miracle:	make sth almost impossible happen
slip one's mind:	forget about sth
put words into one's mouth:	pretend that sb had said sth that they hadn't actually said
make hay while the sun shines:	take advantage of favourable circumstances
cry over spilt milk:	grieve over sth that can't be put right
give the green light to sth/sb:	give permission to proceed with sth
cross one's mind:	occur to one/have a sudden idea

8 *Fill in the blanks with one of the idioms/fixed phrases.*

0 She's always *crying over spilt milk* when she should be getting on with her life.

1 The surgeon seemed to have ....
.... when he succeeded in separating the Siamese twins.

2 He ....
when he said I was willing to help. I simply haven't got the time to.

3 He ....
when he heard he'd failed all his exams.

4 I know you told me about the meeting, but it completely ....

5 The Mayor ....
.... the builder to construct a new shopping centre on the outskirts of town.

6 Would you ....?
We've only half an hour before the bus leaves.

7 It never ....
that she might be offended by what I said.

8 Life is short, so ....

IDIOMS/FIXED PHRASES 2

a night owl:	person who enjoys staying up late
in a nutshell:	briefly, in a few words
have an early night:	go to bed early
be second to none:	be the best
hit the nail on the head:	say exactly the right thing
lose one's nerve:	lose courage
null and void:	invalid/not legally binding
every nook and cranny:	everywhere
make a name for oneself:	become famous/respected for sth
get on one's nerves:	irritate/annoy sb

9 Fill in the blanks with one of the idioms/fixed phrases.

1 You .... when you called him the slowest worker on earth. I've never seen anyone do so little.
2 Paul is such ....; I don't think he ever goes to bed before 3 or 4 in the morning.
3 My cousin Rebecca has .... as a neurosurgeon. She's considered the best in London.
4 I think I'll .... tonight as a dog kept me awake last night.
5 She cleaned .... of the house before she was satisfied that it was spotless.
6 He was planning to ask his boss for a rise, but when it came to the point he .... and didn't do it.
7 That pianist is .... in his interpretation of Mozart's music.
8 I haven't really taken to him; actually ...., I think he's unbearable.
9 Endless telephone calls in the evening ....
10 The contract was declared .... when it was found that one of the parties had been forced to sign.

10 Look at Appendix 5 and fill in the blanks with the correct preposition.

1 I muddled .... the jigsaw pieces and the children did the puzzle again.
2 I waved at a complete stranger in the street whom I mistook .... my cousin.
3 Nobody likes Rick because he's so mean .... money.
4 I asked the assistant which make .... hi-fi he recommended.
5 All the evidence militated .... a conclusion in our favour.
6 I was born in Britain but was naturalised .... Italy.
7 I've been asked to notify the personnel department .... my new address.
8 The doctor is not noted .... his tact when it comes to dealing with patients.
9 The swimming pool attendant was negligent .... his duties and the little girl almost drowned.

11 Look at Appendix 5 and fill in the blanks with the correct preposition.

1 They spent the summer .... a cruise travelling round the world.
2 We are .... favour of abolishing experiments on live animals.
3 When they got home, their house was .... fire.
4 .... her boss's request, she has worked overtime nearly every day this month.
5 They estimated the candidates' popularity .... means of opinion polls.
6 .... a guess, I'd say he weighs about 70 kilos.
7 Very short skirts worn with thick woollen tights are .... vogue at the moment.
8 She was brought up .... a farm so she is used to living in the countryside.
9 Paul has been .... leave from work for the past month.
10 .... second thoughts, I don't think I want to go to the concert.

145

12 Complete the second sentence so that it has a similar meaning to the first sentence, using the word given. Do not change the word given. You must use between three and eight words, including the word given.

1 Some friends nominated him as a spokesman.
forward
Some friends ....
.... spokesman.

2 They may have escaped through the back door.
getaway
They ....
.... back door.

3 You've been looking miserable all day.
moon
You've ....
.... all day.

4 She is a person who always lets you down.
on
You ....
.... her.

5 Why did you behave so rudely?
point
What ....
.... so rudely?

6 He suffers from headaches and insomnia.
prone
He ....
.... insomnia.

7 There are more than six hospitals in this city.
excess
There are ....
.... in this city.

8 A rejection of their offer would have been unwise.
accepted
Not ....
.... unwise.

9 Mike has a more complex personality than you may think.
depths
Mike ....
.... than you may think.

10 To look at him, you would think he was poor.
judging
You would think ....
.... him.

11 The salesman promised me the cooker would be delivered today.
assurance
The salesman ....
.... be delivered today.

12 How did he explain his lateness?
explanation
What ....
.... his lateness?

13 Before the new manager took over, sales were half what they are now.
doubled
Sales ....
.... took over.

14 For further information, contact the accommodation officer.
obtained
Further ....
.... the accommodation officer.

15 We can't possibly imagine how we're going to afford a new car.
remotest
We ....
.... we're going to afford a new car.

16 If I help you now, don't assume I'll help you next time.
count
If I help you now, ...
.... next time.

17 She's angry that she is constantly overlooked for promotion.
resents
She ....
.... promotion.

18 People often mistake me for my elder sister.
confuse
People often ....
.... sister.

19 The brochure doesn't say anything about its parking facilities.
makes
The brochure ....
.... its parking facilities.

FIXED PHRASES

from/since time immemorial:	for a long time/throughout history
take the initiative:	be the first person to act
add insult to injury:	make things even worse
make inroads into:	affect sth negatively or destructively
to all intents and purposes:	practically/in effect
in the interests of:	in order to achieve a certain aim
in the interim:	in the meantime
take issue with sb:	disagree and start arguing
have/get itchy feet:	have a strong desire to travel
be in jeopardy:	be in danger
in a jiffy:	quickly
jog one's memory:	make one remember sth
jump for joy:	extremely pleased or happy
reserve judgement on sb/sth:	postpone giving an opinion before more is known
do sb/sth justice:	reproduce sb/sth accurately and show how good they are
rough justice:	unfair or unjust treatment
(be) on an even keel:	working or progressing steadily, to regularise sth
on a knife-edge:	situation where nobody knows what will happen next/extremely exciting
knock sb dead:	impress sb greatly
tie oneself in knots:	get confused
safe in the knowledge:	confidently (because a prior condition has been met)

13 *Complete the sentences using one of the fixed phrases in an appropriate form.*

1 Salaries are paid at the end of the month but .... a small advance may be arranged.

2 I always .... when speaking in public.

3 In an effort .... Jo was shown pictures of the place where she was found.

4 After an operation you don't fully recover for a while so you shouldn't expect to feel .... for a few weeks.

5 Cinema-goers and critics alike ....by the special effects in Spielberg's "Jurassic Park".

6 Students are requested, ... hygiene, not to bring food into the lecture hall.

7 Being out of work for so long has .... the money he was keeping for a rainy day.

8 The delighted children .... when they heard they were going camping.

9 I don't think Julia's wedding photos .... I think she looked much more attractive on her wedding day.

10 Alan .... his daughter over her coming home from the party in the early hours of the morning.

14 *Choose the correct item.*

1 Greg has, to all intents and ...., finished his degree course, with the exception of his final dissertation.
   A reasons   C aims
   B purposes   D proposals

2 I'll reserve .... on Ben Shipley's latest novel until I've read it.
   A condemnation   C criticism
   B thought   D judgement

3 Always having had .... feet, Delia is off again, backpacking round India.
   A itchy   C sore
   B scratchy   D light

4 It was .... justice for Ted to receive a parking fine when he was at the doctor's.
   A poetic   C small
   B only   D rough

5 He slammed my hand in the car door and, to add insult to ...., didn't stop to apologise.
   A damage   C injury
   B harm   D infamy

6 We were all on a .... -edge until the very end of the Hitchcock film.
   A razor   C cliff
   B knife   D chair

147

7 Those stones have been here since time ....
A immemorable   C immemorial
B immortal   D innumerable

8 Enjoy your "Sunway" cruise, safe in the .... that everything has been taken care of.
A knowledge   C awareness
B recognition   D fact

9 This shoe repairer is so quick that he can sole and heel your shoes in a(n) ....
A moment   C jiffy
B hurry   D instant

10 Not wearing a seatbelt in the car can put your life in ....
A jail   C hazard
B jeopardy   D risk

11 The manager was not at work so his secretary took the .... herself and confirmed the deal.
A initiative   C risk
B issue   D biscuit

15 *Find the mistake and correct it.*

0 The cyclist claims that a car is not important ~~for~~ him.   *to*
1 On 1st July we went to London on train. ....
2 Please have your passports ready in arrival at the airport. ....
3 She was wearing an expensive suit made from silk. ....
4 He works forty hours in week. ....
5 Some people consider instant coffee to be inferior than filter coffee. ....
6 Police is seeking further information about the incident. ....
7 He intends to run as President a second time. ....
8 She has very interested ideas on psychic phenomena. ....
9 He told us all about the journey he did in great detail. ....
10 He is ardent in his admiration of all kind of sport. ....
11 She remarried her late husband ten years after their divorce. ....
12 They've lately purchased a new hi-fi system. ....
13 His latest film became a great success soon after his death. ....
14 She left from the cinema in a confused state of mind. ....
15 Can I lend your car this evening? ....
16 A person who says lies habitually must at least, have a good memory. ....
17 I've been leaving in Britain for two years. ....

16 *In most lines of the following text there is a grammatically incorrect item. Read the numbered lines 1-16 and then write the correct form of the word in the spaces provided for your answers. Some lines are correct. Indicate these lines with a tick (✓). The first one has been done for you.*

TRANSYLVANIAN TRIP

0 Dracula lives! A small travel agent in Budapest is offering "a   *agency*
1 Transylvanian adventure for bloodthirsty travellers". At £200 ....
2 tourists can enjoy a four-days excursion to Transylvania on the ....
3 trail of the 15th century tyrant, nicknamed Vlad the Impaler, which ....
4 achieved notoriety for his custom of sticking people onto spikes, ...
5 a punishment which he inflicted at thousands of prisoners ....
6 and loyal subjects like. ....
7 Visitors keen on get the feel of the "terror of the living dead" can ....
8 lunch in the house were the Count lived and stroll through ....
9 cemeteries with a guide who is an inexhaustible source of ....

10 informations concerning the myth of vampirism. ....

11 "We're putting all the emphasis in atmosphere," explains the ....

12 tour organiser, but by doing such, the agency is wandering off ....

13 the real trail of Vlad the Impaler. The castle of Poienari does not, ...

14 for example, feature on the programme, to be naturally less ....

15 impressive that Bram, which is a caricature of a vampire's ....

16 castle but one where Vlad never put foot. ....

17 *Match the phrases, then explain the proverbs.*

Column A	Column B	
0 A drowning man	a before you leap.	0 *e*
1 A leopard	b and shame the devil.	1 ....
2 When the cat's away	c is another man's poison.	2 ....
3 The proof of the pudding	d never changes its spots.	3 ....
4 Tell the truth	e will clutch at a straw.	4 ....
5 People who live in glass houses	f shouldn't throw stones.	5 ....
6 Look	g flock together.	6 ....
7 Nothing ventured,	h the mice will play.	7 ....
8 One man's meat	i nothing gained.	8 ....
9 Birds of a feather	j is in the eating.	9 ....

18 *Use the following notes to write an article about criminal trial procedure in Britain. Write complete sentences for each numbered set of notes, using connecting words and phrases as appropriate. You must use all the words in the same order as the notes. You may add words and change the form of words where necessary. The first point has been expanded for you in the example.*

0 Under the British judicial system - if - a person charge - serious offence - he/she have stand trial.
   Under the British judicial system, if a person is charged with a serious offence he or she has to stand trial. ....

1 Mean - he/she - have - appear - court - a judge and jury.
   ....
   ....

2 During trial - the accused - also - know - the defendant - have right - be represent - a lawyer/another lawyer be also present - act for the crown - try - secure - a conviction.
   ....
   ....
   ....
   ....
   ....

3 Start trial - the accused - stand - dock - plead guilty - not guilty.
   ....
   ....
   ....

4 If the accused - plead - "not guilty" - trial proceed /witnesses - be called - evidence/all evidence be hear - jury retire - reach verdict/least 10 - jury - must be - same opinion.
   ....
   ....
   ....
   ....
   ....
   ....

5 Jury - find - accused - not guilty, he/she acquit/ if - other hand, the accused - find - guilty, it be up - judge -sentence.
   ....
   ....
   ....
   ....
   ....

6 Depend - serious - offence - sentence - may - fine, suspend - sentence - prison term.
   ....
   ....
   ....

WORD USAGE

19 *Read the text below. Use the word given in capitals at the end of some of the lines to form a word that fits in the space in the same line.*

AFRICAN TALES

A dilemma tale is a **(0)** *traditional* African form of short story whose ending is either open   **TRADITION**
to conjecture or is **(1)** .... ambiguous, thus allowing the audience to   **MORAL**
comment or speculate upon the correct solution to a **(2)** .... problem   **TIME**
posed in the tale. **(3)** .... issues raised involve conflicts of   **TYPE**
(4) ...., the necessity to choose a just response to a difficult situation, and the   **LOYAL**
question of where to lay the blame when several parties seem equally guilty. An example
has a tortoise as the **(5)** .... character. Tortoise wishes to be thought of as an equal   **CENTRE**
in strength and authority to Hippopotamus and Elephant. When his **(6)** ....   **BOAST**
reach their ears, however, they snub him by saying he is only a small **(7)** ....   **SIGNIFY**
being. So Tortoise challenges both the powerful animals to a tug of war and through a trick
pits them against each other, thus winning from each the **(8)** .... consent that   **GRUDGE**
he is their match. The audience must decide exactly how **(9)** .... the three of   **LIKE**
them are. As the example shows, dilemma tales function both as **(10)** ....   **INSTRUCT**
and entertainment, and they help to establish social norms for the audience.

20 *Choose from the sets of synonyms the word which is most appropriate in each case.*

0 Sue spent weeks in hospital after being seriously .... in a car crash.
A ruined   C injured
B impaired   D damaged

1 When she lost her temper, she .... the vase her ex-husband had brought her.
A snapped   C broke off
B clipped   D smashed

2 Floods have completely .... the farmer's crops.
A injured   C harmed
B damaged   D ruined

3 I .... the notice-board quickly, looking for second-hand cars for sale.
A scanned   C scrutinised
B peered at   D inspected

4 The forensic expert .... the evidence looking for particles of skin.
A scanned   C glimpsed at
B scrutinised   D peered at

5 My brother is always .... me about my hooked nose.
A harassing   C getting on at
B pestering   D teasing

6 The border guards have been accused of .... refugees.
A pestering   C harassing
B getting on at   D teasing

7 My young nieces kept .... me to buy them sweets.
A teasing   C getting on at
B pestering   D harassing

8 I .... a plate when I was washing up, but it can still be used.
A chipped   C snapped
B smashed   D shattered

9 The windscreen .... into a thousand pieces when the car hit a lamp-post.
A smashed   C snapped
B shattered   D cracked

COLLOCATIONS

21 *Fill in hire, borrow, rent.*

1 .... £50
2 .... a flat
3 .... a car
4 .... a hall
5 .... a pencil
6 .... a boat
7 .... a lawyer

22 *Complete the expressions with words from the given list.*

• work • shiver • contaminate • evaluate • alter • glimpse • devastate • peer • bluff • cope with

1 .... your way out of a difficult situation
2 .... a cow out of a moving train
3 .... to earn a living
4 .... a problem
5 .... a river
6 .... at the small print
7 .... sb by giving bad news
8 .... the damage at £1,000
9 .... with cold
10 .... a dress

23 *Fill in the collocational grid.*

	secretary	medication	system	cure	speech	insect repellent
effective						
efficient						
efficacious						
defective						

24 *Think of one word only which can be used appropriately in all three sentences.*

0 • One doesn't need to be an expert to *appreciate* the beauty of classical music.
   • He seems confident that houses in this area will *appreciate* in value in the next few years.
   • I'll always *appreciate* your help and support.

1 • You should use a high .... of oil to protect your car engine.
   • Mickey re-sat the maths exam to improve his ....
   • For civil service positions the .... depends on both qualifications and length of service.

2 • We are always pleased to be of .... to our customers.
   • Mother brought out the lovely willow pattern tea ....
   • A short .... was held to celebrate the renewal of their marriage vows.

3 • A van suddenly .... out in front of Roy's car, forcing him to brake.
   • The movie was .... on location and includes some amazing African scenery.
   • The Spice Girls .... to fame within a very short time.

4 • Peggy took off her hat to reveal a .... of red curls.
   • The .... of the explosion shattered windows in many surrounding buildings.
   • It came as a .... to me to discover that Simon was leading a double life.

5 • Pete is on night .... at the moment, but I'll take a message for him.
   • The recent increase in inflation has triggered a .... in government plans.
   • She put a cloak over her thin cotton ...., as the night was chilly.

6 • A new .... of talks took place about reducing the harmful effects of CFCs on the ozone layer.
   • How about a .... of golf before tea?
   • There was a .... of thunderous applause as the star came onto the stage.

7 • Beryl was in a bad mood and spoke to him in a .... tone.
   • Watch that bread knife; it has a very .... edge.
   • These lemon sweets are too .... for my taste.

8 • Everyone knows that one good .... deserves another.
   • They suddenly came to a sharp .... in the road.
   • When Tim jumped out from the shadows like that, he gave her a nasty ....

9 • The refugees are finding it difficult to .... to their new surroundings.
   • The management has revised company policy to .... the demands of its workers.
   • The hotel is not large enough to .... the star and his entourage.

PREPARING FOR PART 5

IDENTIFYING WRITER'S TONE I

25 *Read the following extracts, and choose the adjective which best describes the writer's tone. An example has been done for you.*

0 I can understand the need for street signs which warn about farm animals crossing the streets in Cumbria which go through vast areas of farmland. However, I have difficulty in distinguishing the need for two kinds of signs, one for sheep, and one for cows. If each poses a different kind of danger to motorists, why don't we have warning signs about bulls, chickens or goats?

A aggressive   (B) tongue-in-cheek   C critical

1 The substantial drop in profits can be attributed to poor low level management. The four assistant managers failed in maintaining our rate of production. Their excuse of being short-staffed is insufficient. I recommend their swift dismissal.

A critical   B dispassionate   C descriptive

2 Although there are many variations of the European vine in the Medoc area, there is actually only one species. The American vine, on the other hand, is a result of cross-breeding more than twenty-four species.

A enthusiastic   B patronising   C informative

3 If you are attempting the climb for the first time, please be aware of the level of difficulty involved. Proper footwear, suitable clothing and quality equipment are essential. Hiring a guide is also advisable.

A instructive   B strict   C kind

4 Over the years, the Salvation Army has helped to feed, shelter and clothe multitudes of poor people. A pound may not mean much to you, but to the homeless it means a hot meal and a clean bed. When an Army member comes to your door, please give generously.

A appealing   B stern   C helpful

5 Isn't it fantastic being a working mum? You can feel the self-satisfaction (not to mention the physical exhaustion) gained from working all day and then returning home to do another eight or nine hours looking after the kids and the house!

A spirited   B sarcastic   C disheartening

6 Whenever I telephone that office, I have to wait for at least ten minutes before being connected to the switchboard. Then I'm put on hold, having to listen to a tape of bland muzak whilst waiting for someone to have the courtesy to deal with my enquiry. When someone deigns to pick up the phone, invariably I am told that I have been put through to the wrong department and I have to repeat the whole performance. It's totally unacceptable from a renowned, international organisation.

A irate   B informative   C enthusiastic

7 Classical music offers an individual an experience in sensuous delight. Of course, those who are ignorant of this as an art form will fail to appreciate its aesthetic value.

A combative   B apathetic   C patronising

8 The Regent restaurant in Bridge Street has done nothing to justify the cost of a meal for two, which you can expect to set you back around £90. The lack-lustre service, bland cuisine and dingy decor will be enough to make sure you never return.

A critical   B humorous   C tentative

9 The True Progress Party has suffered a humiliating defeat at the hands of the electorate. They have fewer seats in Parliament than at any other time in their history. I doubt that they will ever recover to be a viable political force again.

A demeaning   B consoling   C gloomy

10 Please do not hesitate to contact Doctors Without Frontiers if you wish to find out more about our work. Use the free-phone number below, or e-mail us at info@dwf.com.

A uninformative   B neutral   C unpalatable

11 For years, local residents have been voicing a need for additional recycling bins in their area. Every year, just before elections, the obligatory promises are made, and every year just after elections, the promises are broken.

A desperate   B disillusioned   C aggressive

12 The gap between the haves and have-nots is forever widening. It's really time that something was done to redress the balance. We should take to the streets to demonstrate and even use force to make our feelings known. A few smashed cars or shop windows is nothing compared to what the poor have to tolerate.

A aggressive   B bemused   C collected

13 Alarming statistics indicate that the number of early school-leavers is increasing, and that a high percentage of students who leave institutions of learning without having received a certificate are male. If unreversed, this trend may have serious knock-on effects: increased unemployment among the male population will lead to more working mothers, and could subsequently cause a significant drop in the birthrate.

A cautionary   B bantering   C dry

14 In attendance at last night's gala premier was no other than Alice Grace. With hubby number two nowhere in sight, the star of this year's Oscar winning film laughed and lived it up with escort film producer Jim Myers.

A informative   B gossipy   C aggressive

15 We would like to apologise, because here, at Norwich General Auto, despite our love of cars, we haven't got any good salesmen. We are not assertive, we are not persuasive, and we don't sell as many cars as we could. Going against the most fundamental of marketing principles, we prefer to make friends with the people we sell to. And we have so many old clients that keep popping in for a coffee and a chat that we decided to build a little addition to our branch. Come for a cup of free coffee at our brand-new cafeteria, and let's talk about cars. And we'll let others talk about the most fundamental of marketing principles.

A nonchalant   B kind   C informal

16 Basketball fans were treated to a rare performance last night from the likes of veteran players Mike Reilly and Phil Tops, two of this sport's greats. Those at Madison Square Garden also caught a glimpse of what rookie Tony Pitson is destined to become as he soared through the air, sinking basket after basket.

A insinuating   B uncompromising   C enthusiastic

Paper 3 Use of English

Time: 1 hour 30 minutes

PART 1

Read the text below and think of the word which best fits each space. Use only one word in each space.

DANGERS OF TECHNOLOGY

Much has been heard recently **(0)** *about* possible health hazards, including memory loss and brain tumours, from the use of mobile phones. With the possible half a billion mobile phones in **(1)** .... throughout the world, in Britain **(2)** ...., one person in four owns one, **(3)** .... is worrying enough, even if, so far, no concrete evidence has come to **(4)** ....

One study by Dr. Alan Preece and his team at Bristol University has shown, however, in a report in the International Journal of Radiation Biology, that tests on volunteers demonstrated no effect on **(5)** .... short-term memory or attention span. Subjects **(6)** .... exposed to microwave radiation for **(7)** .... to thirty minutes, but the one noticeable effect was positive **(8)** .... than negative; the subjects reacted more rapidly in one test **(9)** .... a visual choice. One explanation of **(10)** .... is that following the transmissions, a warming of the blood led to increased bloodflow.

For the experiment, places were chosen where the signal was good and the microwave dose light, and then where the signal was poor and the dose **(11)** .... higher. The subjects were tested for recall and mental alertness **(12)** .... exposure to microwaves characteristic of analogue phones, digital phones or no phones at all, without knowing **(13)** .... they were exposed to.

It is, of course, early days **(14)** .... and the sample may not be large **(15)** .... to generalise from. More research needs to be done.

PART 2

Read the text below. Use the word given in capitals at the end of some of the lines to form a word that fits in the space in the same line.

A WORRYING DISEASE

Rubella, also called German measles, is an epidemic **(0)** *viral* disease of mild course. **(16)** .... study of epidemics in Germany in the 19th century gave rise to the popular name of the disease. Although rubella may occur in young children, **(17)** .... to the disease is more commonly seen in older children and young adults.

Usually the **(18)** .... rash is the first sign noted. **(19)** .... of the lymph glands in the neck, behind the ears, and perhaps elsewhere in the body is **(20)** .... Although it is certainly not pleasant to suffer from rubella, **(21)** .... are rare. A day or so of bed rest and a light diet with plenty of fluids is the only **(22)** .... required in most cases. In 1941 it was discovered that rubella early in pregnancy may be **(23)** .... to the health of the foetus, especially the eyes and heart. Years later it was demonstrated that infants may be born with active rubella and may manifest many additional **(24)** .... In fact, it has been found capable of causing extensive damage to almost any organ of the infant's body. Methods of **(25)** .... have been recommended in the hope of stamping out the virus from the environment.

VIRUS
INTENSE

SUSCEPTIBLE

COMFORT
LARGE
CHARACTER
COMPLICATE
TREAT

THREAT

NORMAL

IMMUNE

PART 3

Think of one word only which can be used appropriately in all three sentences.

0 • One doesn't need to be an expert to *appreciate* the beauty of classical music.
  • He seems confident that houses in this area will *appreciate* in value in the next few years.
  • I'll always *appreciate* your help and support.

26 • The system was not .... to deter tax evaders.
  • Hiring a lawyer was a .... attempt to frighten us into giving them what they want.
  • Investing in property at such a time was a .... risk that paid off.

27 • Dolphins are often seen to follow in the .... of ships.
  • In certain parts of Ireland they still hold a .... to mourn the dead.
  • The hurricane left a trail of devastation in its ....

28 • His work .... him so much that he forgot to eat dinner.
  • She had only .... half of the information contained in the manual.
  • Many of the smaller colleges have been .... into the main university.

29 • Elizabeth's reassuring response put Lynne's mind at ....
  • The doctor told his stressed patient that he needed more ....
  • Settling himself comfortably with his head on the head ...., the passenger fell fast asleep.

30 • Branwen had got herself into such a ...., that she didn't know what to do.
  • The colonel was eating his lunch in the officer's ....
  • Clean this room up immediately - it's a complete ....

31 • Be careful with the faulty .... on that bracelet or you might lose it.
  • One .... about the new public transport scheme is that it will need large subsidies.
  • The fishermen were pleased to have such a large .... of fish.

PART 4

Complete the second sentence so that it has a similar meaning to the first sentence, using the word given. Do not change the word given. You must use between three and eight words, including the word given.

0 Nobody spoke when the teacher asked who the culprit was.
  remained
  Everyone *remained silent when the teacher asked who the culprit was.*

32 He owes his life to that surgeon.
  indebted
  He .... life.

33 There wasn't a single ticket left for the concert so we couldn't go.
  sell-out
  The .... couldn't go.

34 You have the ability to do really well in your career if you make an effort.
  mind
  You could do really well .... it.

35 The news of the merger really surprised the staff.
  taken
  The staff .... by the merger.

36 I expected the film to be good, but it wasn't at all.
  live
  The film .... at all.

37 A cup of tea is the most refreshing drink of all.
  match
  There's .... as a refreshing drink.

38 Everyone was shocked by the success of the novel.
  shock
  The success of the novel .... everyone.

39 It was impossible for Roy to keep the appointment.
  way
  There .... the appointment.

155

PART 5

For questions **40 - 44**, read the following texts. For questions **40 - 43**, answer with a word or short phrase. You do not need to write complete sentences. For question **44**, write a summary according to the instructions given.

During the latter part of the 18th century in Britain, owners of factories and businesses scoured the country for orphans and children of poverty-stricken parents, obtaining their services for the minimal cost of maintaining them. In some cases, children as young as five or six were forced to work from 13 to 16 hours a day.

As early as 1802, a handful of social reformers were striving for legislative change which would address the worst features of the child labour system. Despite their efforts, society tended to turn a blind eye to the plight of the child labourer and, as a result, conditions steadily declined. The disregard shown for these children by the general populace led to further social evils, which included an increase in illiteracy, ever-deepening impoverishment, and many children becoming diseased or crippled.

line 15 — Only when the people's social conscience developed did reforms begin to take place. By the mid-1800s, British society was showing growing concern over the brutality of child labour. In 1878, legislation was passed which raised the minimum age for employees to ten, restricted working hours to a maximum of twelve per day and made every Saturday a half holiday.

40 What were the results of the public's turning a blind eye to child labour?

....

....

41 Explain the phrase "legislation was passed" in line 15.

....

....

Charles was one of thousands; there was nothing unusual in the early nineteenth century about a twelve-year-old boy going to work. Six shillings a week was not a bad wage for a boy, and the hours at the warehouse were not prolonged. He began at 8 in the morning and finished at 8 in the evening, with a break of one hour for dinner and half an hour for tea.

line 6 ——— The blacking warehouse was a crazy tumbledown old place, abutting on the river at Hungerford Stairs. Dirty and decayed, its cold rooms and rotten floors resounded with the squeaking and shuffling of the rats swarming down in the cellars. Charles sat and worked by himself in a recess of the counting house. His task was to cover the pots with paste-blacking, first with a piece of oilpaper, then with a bit of blue paper. Then he was to tie them round with a string, and then clip the paper close and neat until it looked as smart as a pot of ointment from an apothecary's shop.

But the separate working place was inconvenient, and his small work table was moved downstairs to the common workroom. He wasn't too young to know that he would be slighted and despised if he couldn't work as well as the others, so, despite his unhappiness, he soon made himself quick and efficient.

42 What does the phrase "a crazy tumbledown old place" mean? (line 6)

....

....

43 What does the second paragraph tell us about the conditions Charles worked in?

....

....

44 In a paragraph of between 50 and 70 words, summarise how society viewed child labour.

....

....

....

....

....

....

....

....

UNIT 8a Grammar: Wishes - Unreal Past

Form	Use
I **wish** (**If only**) + past simple *I **wish** he **were/was** here now.*	regret about a present situation which is unreal, impossible or unlikely
I **wish** (**If only**) + past perfect *If only he **had behaved** himself at the party last night!*	regret about a past situation
I **wish** (**If only**) + subject + would + present infinitive We never say: <s>I wish I would</s> *I **wish** he **would stop** lying. (I'm fed up with his lies.)* *I **wish** you **would help** me. (Please, help me.)*	complaint/regret about the present; willingness, request; wish about sth not likely to happen; unwillingness; insistence
I **wish** (**If only**) + subject + could + present infinitive *I **wish** I **could speak** French.*	regret about present or future situation caused by lack of ability
I **wish** (**If only**) + inanimate subject + would + present infinitive *If only it **would stop** raining.*	a wish for a change in the future which is not likely to happen

Remember that after *wish* or *if only* we go one tense *back*. This means that we use *Simple Past* to refer to the present and *Past Perfect* to refer to the past.

Notes

- *Wish* expresses a hypothetical desire, *if only* expresses regret or strong desire. Both *wish* and *if only* can be used interchangeably, but *wish* is used for something that may happen, whereas *if only* is used to express that what is wished does not exist.
  *I **wish** she **wasn't/weren't** always late.*
  *If only I **knew** what to do!*

- *Wish* + infinitive = want to (formal).
  *I **wish to** be informed of all the details. (I want to be informed of all the details.)*

- *Wish* + personal object + object is used in some fixed expressions of good wishes.
  *I **wish you** all the best.*

- We use **hope** instead of **wish** for wishes about things that are likely to happen.
  *I **hope** you get the job. (NOT: I <s>wish</s> you would get the job).*

1 *Write a wish for each of the following sentences.*

1 You want to go on holiday this summer, but you haven't got any leave left.

....
....

2 You neglected to have your clothes dry-cleaned.

....
....

3 Louise realised she left her lecture notes at home.

....
....

4 Tim didn't have enough time to go to the bank during his lunch hour.

....
....

5 It was unusually cold, so we couldn't go to the beach.

....

6 Mathilda wanted to be auditioned for the National Ballet.

....
....

7 You didn't put the ice cream in the fridge and now it's spoilt.

....
....

8 You didn't do mathematics in high school and now you regret it.

....
....

9 It didn't occur to you to take wet weather gear on your walking tour in Scotland and now you're drenched.

....
....

10 Your best friend won't lend you her white silk dress because last time you spilt coffee on it.

....

....

....

11 Theresa's dog keeps the neighbours awake because it barks all night.

....

....

12 You have lost your reference from one of your previous jobs and now you need it for an interview.

....

....

13 Dina gets cross because there is a lot of traffic in the street where she lives.

....

....

14 You and your next door neighbour had an argument and now he won't speak to you.

....

....

15 Adrienne saw a beautiful winter coat but it cost one month's pay.

....

....

STRUCTURAL CONVERSION

1 *I wish* I hadn't read the letter.
   If only I hadn't read the letter.
   I regret reading/having read the letter.
   I'm sorry I read the letter.
   It's a pity I read the letter.

2 "*I wish* he would be more patient," she said.
   She complained that he wasn't patient.
   She complained that he was impatient.

3 *I would love to* travel abroad.
   If only I could travel abroad.
   I wish I could travel abroad.

4 *Why don't* you drive more carefully?
   I wish you would drive more carefully.
   Please drive more carefully.
   I'd rather you drove more carefully.
   You'd better drive more carefully.
   It's time you started driving more carefully.
   You would be better off driving more carefully.

5 *It's a pity* I am not wealthy.
   I wish I were wealthy.
   If only I were wealthy.

6 *I want* to see you in my office.
   I wish to see you in my office.

2 *Complete the second sentence so that it has a similar meaning to the first sentence, using the word given. Do not change the word given. You must use between three and eight words, including the word given.*

1 Please, stop talking because I can't concentrate on the film.
   quiet
   I ....
   .... I can't concentrate on the film.

2 Why don't you show me your stamp collection?
   let
   I ....
   .... your stamp collection.

3 You look tired. Why don't you go to bed early tonight?
   better
   You ....
   .... you look tired.

4 Zoe has a job which makes her feel very stressed.
   less
   Zoe ....
   .... job.

5 Meg wants to be left alone because she's upset.
   rather
   Meg ....
   .... she's upset.

6 I regret having committed myself to so many private lessons in the evenings.
   not
   If ....
   .... private lessons in the evenings.

7 He regrets not taking her threats of leaving him seriously.
   wishes
   He ....
   .... of leaving him seriously.

8 I would love to go on a round-the-world trip.
   able
   I ....
   .... round-the-world trip.

159

CONVERSATIONAL GRAMMAR

3 *Choose the correct item.*

0 If only I .... then what I know now!
(A) had known   C could know
B knew   D was known

1 "It's time you .... in bed. It's almost midnight, isn't it?"
"You're right."
A are   C had been
B have been   D were

2 "That trip was a nightmare."
"Yes, I wish we ...."
A went   C hadn't gone
B have gone   D go

3 "I overslept and was late for work again!"
"You'd .... that clock fixed; it hasn't worked for over a week now."
A rather have   C better have
B better to have   D rather had

4 "You missed an exciting start to the football match."
"Yes, it's a pity I .... on time."
A am not   C wasn't
B haven't been   D hadn't been

5 If only I .... the bill; we wouldn't have been cut off.
A paid   C had been paid
B have paid   D had paid

6 "I shouldn't have missed Mary's party."
"It's a pity you ....; we had a lovely time."
A haven't come   C weren't coming
B didn't come   D hadn't come

7 He regrets .... enough time to finish the exercises.
A not to have   C not having
B not have had   D to not have

8 "Do you mind if I tell Mary about your trip?"
"Well, I'd rather you .... anyone else about it."
A wouldn't tell   C not to tell
B didn't tell   D haven't told

9 "You're looking tired."
"I'm exhausted. I wish my neighbours .... loud music when I'm trying to sleep."
A haven't played   C won't play
B wouldn't play   D hadn't played

UNREAL PAST

We can use the *past simple* to talk about imaginary, unreal or improbable situations in the present, and *past perfect* when we refer to imaginary, unreal or improbable situations in the past. This use of the past tenses is called *unreal past*.

Past Simple	Past Perfect
• **conditional type 2** *If I **were** you, I would resign.*	• **conditional type 3** *If I **had been told** earlier, I wouldn't have acted this way.*
• **wishes (present)** *I wish I **were** in London.*	• **wishes (past)** *If only you **hadn't ruined** my dress!*
• **I'd rather/sooner sb ...** (for present situations) *I'd sooner you **answered** me **now**.*	• **I'd rather/sooner sb ...** (for past situations) *I'd rather he **hadn't behaved** like that **last night**.*
• **suppose/supposing** *Suppose you **were fired**, what would you do?*	• **suppose/supposing** *Suppose you **had lost** all your money?*
• **as if/as though** *He behaves as if he **owned** the place!*	• **as if/as though** (when the action of the as if - clause has happened earlier than the action of the main clause) *He looked as if he **had won** the pools!*
• **It's (about/high) time...** *It's time we **left**.*	

Notes

- *Suppose* can be followed by a verb in the present tense to express a situation which may happen in the future or to introduce suggestions.
  *Suppose he **isn't** at work, where shall we find him?*
  *"We haven't got any Coke." "Suppose we **drink** lemonade instead."*
- *As if/as though* can also be used with perfect tenses to express a real comparison.
  *The cottage looks as if it **has been renovated**. (It probably has).*

WOULD RATHER = I'D PREFER

when the subject of *would rather* is also the subject of the following verb

I'd rather +
present bare infinitive   (present/future reference)
perfect bare infinitive   (past reference)

*I'd rather **have** fish for lunch. I like it a lot.*
*I'd rather **have told** him before. He wouldn't have been angry with me.*

when the subject of *would rather* is different from the subject of the following verb

I'd rather +
past simple   (present/future)
past perfect   (past)

*I'd rather you **left** before the guests arrive. They'll be here soon.*
*I'd rather they **had left** earlier. They wouldn't have missed their flight.*

HAD BETTER = SHOULD

I had better + present bare infinitive (present/future)
*We had better **cut down** on fats. (=We should cut down on fats.)*

It would have been better if + Past Perfect (past)
*It would have been better if you **hadn't behaved** impolitely.*

Notes

- prefer + gerund/noun + to + gerund/noun (general)
  *I prefer **orange juice to tomato juice**.*
  *I prefer **swimming to climbing**.*

- prefer + full infinitive + rather than + bare infinitive (general)
  *I prefer **to travel** by car **rather than** (travel) by coach.*

- would prefer + full infinitive + rather than + bare infinitive (specific)
  *I'd prefer **to have** apple pie **rather than have** spinach pie.*

- would rather + bare infinitive + than + bare infinitive (general or specific)
  *I'd rather **sleep than watch** TV.*

CONVERSATIONAL GRAMMAR

4 *Choose the correct item.*

1 "It's a pity Sarah is still unemployed."
"Yes, if only she .... university."
A would have finished   C would finish
B had finished   D finishes

2 I wish I .... their help when it was offered.
A would accept   C had accepted
B have accepted   D accepted

3 Suppose she .... that outrageous story
circulating around the office; she'd be furious!
A has heard   C were heard
B would hear   D had heard

4 "Susan looks ready to cry".
"It looks as if Peter .... her birthday again!"
A had been forgetting   C has been forgetting
B had forgotten   D has forgotten

5 "Why are you glaring at me?"
"You treat me as if I .... your slave."
A were   C have been
B was being   D had been

6 I'd rather you .... the deal in writing by the end
of next week.
A confirmed   C had confirmed
B have confirmed   D confirm

7 "You're looking rather pleased with yourself."
"Suppose your boss .... you a big bonus, you
would too."
A had offered   C would offer
B has been offering D had been offered

8 It's time you .... about your future.
A to think   C thought
B had thought D think

9 If only she .... to her principles, she wouldn't
have been led astray.
A sticks   C had stuck
B stuck   D have stuck

10 "I can't think of a good excuse for being late."
"You .... be honest and tell the truth."
A had better   C would have been
                       better
B would better   D had better to

STRUCTURAL CONVERSION ◄-----------------------------

1 *If you don't* tell the truth, he'll punish you.
You'd better tell the truth *or else* he'll punish you.
2 *If I were you*, I would accept his proposal.
You should accept his proposal.
You'd better accept his proposal.
3 *"You'd better* take a nap," Mother said.
Mother advised me to take a nap.
4 *"You shouldn't be* rude to her," he said to me.
He advised me not to be rude to her.
He suggested that I shouldn't be rude to her.
5 *They asked for a spare key. Why* didn't you give them
one?
They asked for a spare key. You should have given
them one.
6 *There'll be trouble if* he behaves like that again.
He'd better not behave like that again or (else) there
will be trouble.

7 *Why didn't* you tell him so?
It would have been better if you had told him so.
If I were you, I would have told him so.
I'd rather/sooner you had told him so.
I wish you had told him so.
8 *I'd rather* watch TV than listen to music.
I prefer (watching) TV to (listening to) music.
9 *I'd rather* stay indoors than go to the party.
I'd prefer to stay indoors rather than go to the party.
10 *I prefer* to play tennis rather than play polo.
I'd rather play tennis than (play) polo.
I'd sooner play tennis than (play) polo.
11 *I'd rather you* left now.
I'd prefer you to leave now.
12 *It's time you* learnt how to cook.
It's time for you to learn how to cook.
You should learn how to cook.
You must learn how to cook.

5 *Complete the second sentence so that it has a similar meaning to the first sentence, using the word given. Do not change the word given. You must use between three and eight words, including the word given.*

1 Why didn't you take the day off work?
better
It ....
.... the day off work.

2 "You'd better tidy your desk" he said.
to
He ....
.... desk.

3 He'd rather eat with friends than eat alone.
prefers
He ....
....alone.

4 If we don't leave now, we won't catch the train.
or
We'd ....
.... catch the train.

5 It's time you started learning French.
for
It's ....
.... lessons.

6 I prefer to go by car rather than go by coach.
sooner
I ....
.... by coach.

7 You really should learn to drive.
high
It's ....
.... to drive.

8 I'd prefer you to do the washing-up now.
rather
I'd ....
.... now.

CONVERSATIONAL GRAMMAR

6 *Choose the correct item.*

1 She's such a snob; she behaves .... the Queen.
   A as if she has been   C as if she were
   B like she were   D like she was

2 "Have I done something wrong?"
   "I wish you .... more tactful; you're always offending people."
   A were   C were being
   B have been   D had been being

3 I'd rather you .... a noise last night; I couldn't get to sleep.
   A wouldn't make   C didn't make
   B hadn't made   D haven't made

4 If only we .... more people, then we wouldn't be feeling so lonely.
   A had known   C have know
   B knew   D were known

5 It's high time you .... the balcony. It's covered in leaves and dust.
   A cleaned   C had cleaned
   B to be cleaned   D to have cleaned

6 "My washing machine is about to break down."
   "If I were you, ... a new one."
   A I'd bought   C I'll buy
   B I bought   D I'd buy

7 If only they .... their tickets; I've got two spare ones.
   A didn't buy   C wouldn't buy
   B hadn't bought D haven't bought

8 If John .... the train instead of driving, he wouldn't have been late for work.
   A would catch   C caught
   B should catch D had caught

9 Suppose the stock market .... how much money would we have lost?
   A had crashed   C has crashed
   B crash   D would crash

10 Sally would prefer to pursue her studies .... to look for a job.
   A rather than start   C rather than starting
   B to starting   D than to start

7 *Read the text below and think of the word which best fits each space. Use only one word in each space.*

SIGNS OF THE TIMES

We are familiar **(0)** *with* the saying "a picture paints a thousand words" and in the global village the world has become, information in pictorial form is **(1)** .... we turn. Much communication takes **(2)** .... through symbols rather than words, a case in point **(3)** .... airports, where you can see the majority of the thirty-four symbols devised **(4)** .... the American Institute of Graphic Arts in the 1970s. **(5)** .... signs as a knife and fork for a restaurant or a telephone for a phone booth are a boon for **(6)** .... a traveller who does not speak English or use the Latin alphabet. **(7)** .... worldwide "languages" of **(8)** .... kind are musical and mathematical notation, circuit diagrams, road signs and computer icons, **(9)** ...., again, bypass the need for words. Even   label on a garment will carry, in symbols, washing and ironing instructions. All these **(10)** .... to be sufficient to their **(11)** .... restricted worlds but would it **(12)** .... be possible to devise a universal symbolic system of communication independent of **(13)** .... spoken language, culture-free and value-free, as dreamt of by the seventeenth-century philosopher Leibniz? It would seem **(14)** .... Chinese and Japanese pictograms and ancient Egyptian hieroglyphics are sometimes cited as examples of such a system, yet **(15)** .... Japanese script and Egyptian hieroglyphics include sound-base elements and Chinese is often transliterated into romanised sound-based "pin yin" script. In a word, words are inescapable.

PHRASAL VERBS 1

8 *Match the phrasal verbs in bold with the definitions given.*

0 If you **keep at** your French studies, you'll improve.
1 I need to **keep up with** the latest developments in the stock market.
2 If we **keep to** the plan exactly, we're certain to succeed.
3 As I couldn't **keep up with** my classmates, I transferred to a lower class.
4 Don't **keep on at** me about the door; I'll fix it.
5 **Keep up (with)** your work and you'll eventually succeed.
6 The authorities managed to **keep down** rebellious factions with the use of force.
7 **Keep in with** the boss and you'll soon get a promotion.
8 It's time we found out what he's **keeping back** from us.
9 The student **was kept in** for an hour for cheating in the exam.
10 **Keep on** the diet and you'll soon begin to lose weight.

a follow
b progress at the same rate
c continue doing sth
d continue working at
e repress
f detain after normal hours as a punishment
g hide
h stay at an equal level with
i continue to be friendly
j continue talking in an irritating way
k be informed about

0 *d*
1 ....
2 ....
3 ....
4 ....
5 ....
6 ....
7 ....
8 ....
9 ....
10 ....

PHRASAL VERBS 2

lay aside:	put to one side
lay into:	attack (with blows or words)
lay off:	stop doing sth irritating
lay out :	spend
let down :	1) disappoint
	2) lower sth
let in for:	involve in trouble
let in on:	allow sb to share a plan, secret etc
let sb off:	not punish severely
let on:	reveal a secret
let out:	1) make (a garment etc) loose or larger (**opp.**: take in)
	2) utter a cry
let sb through:	allow sb to pass an exam or a test
let up:	become less in degree
let up on:	treat sb less severely

IDIOMS/FIXED PHRASES 1

against all odds:	despite difficulties
get the sack:	be dismissed from one's job
in the offing:	likely to happen
status symbol:	possession thought to show sb's high social rank, wealth, etc
once and for all:	for the last time
white elephant:	useless/unwanted possession
short and sweet:	brief but pleasant (usu ironic)
out in the open:	(of secrets) revealed, known
golden opportunity:	the best chance to gain sth
out and out:	complete, total
in public:	in the presence of other people
get the wrong end of the stick:	misunderstand completely what has been said
throw a party:	have/hold a party
take things to pieces:	dismantle things
grease sb's palm:	bribe sb

9 *Fill in the correct preposition(s) or adverb.*

0 He *laid out* all his savings on that venture which fortunately succeeded.

1 This blouse is too tight for me. I'd better let it ....

2 He let his parents .... by failing his exams.

3 Don't let .... that they're planning to get married. Their parents don't know.

4 I wish you'd lay .... telling me what to do all the time.

5 You should really let .... the children. They can't be perfect all the time.

6 We'll let you .... our plans but don't tell anybody else.

7 Her father laid .... her when she came home two hours late from a party.

8 I let myself .... a lot of trouble when I agreed to help her.

9 If the rain lets ...., we'll be able to play tennis.

10 For the last twenty years, he has been laying .... 15% of his salary for his old age.

11 Your skirt needs taking ....; it's too large.

12 He was let .... with a warning instead of being given a fine.

13 The student let .... a cry of horror when she saw her poor exam results.

10 *Fill in the blanks with one of the idioms/fixed phrases.*

0 This new job is a *golden opportunity* and far too good to turn down.

1 Let's keep this .... – just tell me what you want and then leave. I'm busy!

2 ...., sit down and be quiet or I'll send you out!

3 I always find it embarrassing when people argue ... .

4 ...., he won the national song contest and became quite well-known.

5 What he promised was impossible – he was a(n) .... liar.

6 Being a car mechanic, William loves .... engines ....

7 I'm afraid a recession is ....

8 Now that the scandal is ...., the Minister will have to resign.

9 When the traffic warden gave me a parking ticket, I tried to ...., which only got me into more trouble.

10 It's traditional to .... when you move house.

11 John .... because he was always arriving late to work.

IDIOMS/FIXED PHRASES 2

out of print:	(of books) not available anymore
past one's prime:	growing old/not at your best
come to the point:	reach the main point in a discussion
be out of practice:	lacking practice
off the point:	irrelevant
pop the question:	make a proposal of marriage
part and parcel of:	basic part of
out of the frying pan into the fire:	from a bad situation to a worse/similar one
a bitter pill to swallow:	a difficult fact to accept
fall into place:	become clear

11 *Fill in the blanks with one of the idioms/fixed phrases.*

0 My husband *popped the question* on Valentine's Day in 1974.

1 The book was published in the 1940s and is now ....

2 Moving from that house to this one was a case of .... It's much worse here.

3 I'd love a game of tennis even though I'm ....

4 Failing the exam after so much hard work was ....

5 Everything .... at the end of the film.

6 Since we were discussing unemployment, his comment about football was totally ....

7 I wish he'd .... and stop wasting everyone's time.

8 You're no longer considered .... until you're well into your 60s.

9 Doing the washing-up is .... of being a housewife.

PREPOSITIONS

12 *Look at Appendix 3 and fill in the blanks with the correct preposition(s).*

0 *To* everyone's astonishment, she arrived at the party in a Rolls Royce.

1 Mary was impatient .... the Christmas holidays to arrive.

2 Their school building is .... repair, so they are having lessons in the old library.

3 She was .... the point of leaving when the phone rang.

4 People were chosen .... random to try the new product.

5 .... answer to your question, the meeting will take place next Tuesday.

6 Don't be so impatient .... Sue. She's only 10 and doesn't understand things quickly.

7 .... no account must you open your book during the test.

8 Gill wasn't her usual cheerful self today. She was .... the weather.

9 .... the whole, I think your work is quite satisfactory.

10 As there was little time left, he outlined his plans .... brief.

11 Jam oozed .... the doughnut when she bit into it.

12 He is proud .... his new sports car.

13 The driver was oblivious .... the red light and went straight through it.

14 The schoolchildren were overburdened .... homework.

15 My mother has an obsession .... cleanliness and is forever doing the housework.

16 The surgeon operated .... the woman with the fractured hip.

17 My brother is so mean that he hates to part .... a single penny!

18 The villagers left their homes in the valley and moved to higher grounds as a precaution .... flooding.

19 The shop sent me the cooker .... approval as I wasn't sure it was the model I wanted.

20 He has a proclivity .... being dishonest in business.

21 Mrs Heath pleaded .... her husband not to resign from his job.

13 *Complete the second sentence so that it has a similar meaning to the first sentence, using the word given. Do not change the word given. You must use between three and eight words, including the word given.*

1 Digging in the garden gives me an outlet for my frustrations.
   vent
   Digging ....
   .... frustrations.

2 The TV broadcast the whole of the tennis tournament.
   extensive
   There ....
   .... tennis tournament.

3 She was allegedly the richest singer in Peru.
   claimed
   They ....
   .... singer in Peru.

4 The boys hurled lots of snowballs at their next-door neighbour.
   pelted
   The boys ....
   .... snowballs.

5 She claimed that her success was due purely to luck.
   attributed
   She ....
   .... luck.

6 The first sign of the disease is blurred vision.
   onset
   The ....
   .... blurred vision.

7 Pam didn't understand the situation and so made a terrible mistake.
   stick
   Pam ....
   .... made a terrible mistake.

8 The newspaper was the first to reveal that the politician was a spy.
   exposed
   The politician ....
   .... the newspaper.

9 Sheila has become too big to wear this pullover.
   grown
   Sheila ....
   .... pullover.

10 There are a lot of people out of work in this town.
   level
   The ....
   .... in this town.

11 We forgot to include the cost of accommodation in our holiday budget.
   allow
   We ....
   .... in our holiday budget.

12 We need to find a new market if the company is to survive.
   on
   The ....
   .... market.

13 They say he owes a lot of people money.
   debt
   He's said ....
   .... a lot of people.

14 Unless we can obtain more information, we can't process your claim.
   forthcoming
   Unless ....
   ...., we can't process your claim.

15 The judge concluded that the accident was the result of reckless driving.
   cause
   The judge concluded that ....
   .... accident.

16 The redevelopment programme needs to be supported by the local council.
   backing
   The redevelopment programme ....
   .... the local council.

17 Rick's boss says he thinks Rick is doing a wonderful job.
   praise
   Rick's boss ....
   .... Rick.

18 The company is introducing a new dress code on the first of the month.
   force
   A ....
   .... on the first of the month.

19 Marcus hasn't got very far with his dissertation.
   made
   Marcus ....
   .... his dissertation.

20 No one could explain why she suddenly disappeared from the area.

for

There ....

.... from the area.

FIXED PHRASES

by and large:	to a great extent/generally
larger than life:	exaggerated
on its last legs (inf):	in weak or poor condition/ needing replacement
lay it on thick (inf):	exaggerate
lay sb low:	make sb ill or weak, confine them to bed
improve by/in leaps and bounds:	improve/increase very rapidly
do sth at length:	take a long time to do/do sth in great detail
follow/obey to the letter:	follow (e.g. instructions) exactly without question
on the level (inf):	sincere, truthful
make light of sth:	treat sth as though it is not serious when in fact it is
bring into line with:	make sb/sth comply with a standard/behaviour
draw the line:	refuse to do/tolerate sth
put sth on the line (inf):	risk, endanger
be lost on sb:	have no effect on sb/not to be understood by sb
not for love nor money:	by no means/for no reason
like it or lump it (inf):	whether you like it or not
leave sb in the lurch (inf):	abandon/let sb down

14 *Complete the sentences using one of the fixed phrases in an appropriate form.*

1 Barbara was .... by a nasty bout of gastroenteritis.

2 The new taxation law .... the country .... the rest of Europe.

3 I read through the recipe and .... for a successful outcome.

4 Martha's piano playing is improving .... these days.

5 The irony of the situation .... Ted.

6 .... would I go bungee-jumping.

7 I will reluctantly work on Saturdays but I .... on Sundays.

8 Sean always attempts to .... the fact that he has a serious illness. He never complains.

9 The chairman spoke .... at the board meeting about the proposal of the company.

15 *Choose the correct item.*

1 The optician says you have to wear glasses, like it or .... it.

A jump   C dislike

B lump   D loathe

2 You will be putting your life on the .... if you take up skydiving.

A ground   C lane

B way   D line

3 His friends and family left him in the .... when he went bankrupt.

A church   C end

B lurch   D street

4 There are more people employed, by and .... in the service sector than in manufacturing nowadays.

A large   C by

B all   D through

5 Tara was really laying it on .... about her accident at work.

A fine   C thick

B broad   D thin

6 Were you on the .... when you said you had resigned from work?

A wagon   C flat

B level   D town

7 Stars of the Hollywood silver screen tended to be larger than ....

A life   C reality

B drama   D ever

8 Judging from the noise it is making, the washing machine is on its last ....

A gasp   C resort

B breath   D legs

16 *Match column A with column B, then fill in the correct idioms/fixed phrases.*

Column A		Column B			
0	as plain as	a	the hills	0	*d*
1	as keen as	b	a lamb	1	....
2	as fit as	c	mustard	2	....
3	as gentle as	d	the nose on your face	3	....
4	as good as	e	ditchwater	4	....
5	as light as	f	Punch	5	....
6	as miserable as	g	gold	6	....
7	as old as	h	a feather	7	....
8	as dull as	i	a fiddle	8	....
9	as pleased as	j	sin	9	....

0   What do you mean, you can't see she's unhappy? It's *as plain as the nose on your face.*
1   Joan was .... when she learned she'd failed the exam.
2   That magic trick is ....; I've seen it a hundred times.
3   Her cat Rosie is .... She weighs less than a kilo.
4   John was .... to get on with the project. In fact he could hardly wait.
5   Mary was .... when she learned she'd won the lottery.
6   The babysitter said that the children had been .... and that
    she hoped to have children just like them.
7   The dog looked vicious, but in reality it was ....

WORD USAGE

17 *Read the text below. Use the word given in capitals at the end of some of the lines to form a word that fits in the space in the same line.*

SILENT ACTING

Mime and pantomime was a Greek and Roman **(0)** *dramatic* entertainment   DRAMA
representing scenes from life, often in a **(1)** .... manner.   RIDICULE
Currently, the art has evolved into the **(2)** .... of a   PORTRAY
character or the narration of a story solely by means of body movement.

The Greco-Roman mime was a farce that stressed **(3)** ....   MIME
action but which included song and spoken dialogue. In Roman pantomime, unlike
the mime actor, the players wore **(4)** .... masks, which   NUMBER
identified their characters but deprived them of speech and of the use of
(5) .... gestures. Thus hand movements were particularly   FACE
expressive and important. Pantomimus, dressed like a tragic actor in a cloak and long
tunic, usually performed solo **(6)** .... by an orchestra.   COMPANY

In the theatre of China and Japan, mime acquired a role unknown in the West,
becoming a(n) **(7)** .... part of the major dramatic   DISPENSE
genres. In Chinese drama the conventions of gesticulation, as well as the
(8) .... of the stage properties, are immense in scope and   SYMBOL
(9) .... to those unfamiliar with the traditional forms.   COMPREHEND

The high art of modern mime was **(10)** .... philosophically   NOBLE
by such artists as Marcel Marceau, who defined mime as "the art of expressing
feelings by attitudes and not a means of expressing words through gestures."

18 *Choose the correct item.*

0 I left the house in a hurry and my bedroom was
.... with clothes.
  A scattered   C strewn
  B dispersed   D sprinkled

1 We giggled at the sight of Mrs Brown .... down
the road in her six-inch stiletto heels.
  A staggering   C tottering
  B reeling   D stumbling

2 The skaters .... gracefully across the ice.
  A slid   C slipped
  B glided   D skidded

3 The cat slept peacefully .... in the long grass.
  A huddled   C snuggled
  B nestled   D cuddled

4 Mr Wright .... his vegetable garden carefully.
  A tends   C maintains
  B grows   D attends

5 Employees of the company are forbidden to ....
information about the secret formula.
  A betray   C portray
  B divulge   D unveil

6 The soldier didn't .... his comrades even when
he was pressured to do so.
  A betray   C reveal
  B divulge   D disclose

7 The removal men .... the heavy piano up the
stairs with great difficulty.
  A toted   C thrust
  B shoved   D heaved

8 She .... a few clothes into a case and hurried
to the airport.
  A scattered   C piled
  B shoved   D heaved

9 My fear of wasps .... from the fact that I was
severely stung as a child.
  A stems   C generates
  B begets   D commences

10 This year's series of open-air plays .... with a
performance of "Electra".
  A stems   C derives
  B originates   D commences

11 We could hear the monkeys .... long before we
reached their cage.
  A chatting   C prattling
  B chattering   D babbling

12 Jane .... about the surprise party for Sheila and
now the whole idea is ruined.
  A blabbed   C prattled
  B gossiped   D chatted

COLLOCATIONS

19 a) *Fill in* **valuable, precious.**

0 *valuable* stone   **5** .... friend
1 .... advice   **6** .... moment
2 ....   **7** .... antique
    experience   **8** .... jewellery
3 .... metal   **9** .... time
4 .... discovery   **10** .... links

b) *Fill in* **comfortable, convenient.**

1 .... time   **6** ....
2 .... bed   supermarket
3 ....   **7** .... life
    position   **8** ....
4 .... place   bus stop
5 .... excuse   **9** .... room

20 a) *Fill in* **chop, slice, shred.**

0 *slice* bread   **4** .... paper
1 .... cake   **5** .... meat
2 .... wood   **6** ....
3 ....   documents
    tomatoes   **7** .... cabbage

b) *Fill in* **slim, lean, thin.**

1 .... meat   **5** .... chance
2 .... man   **6** .... line
3 .... ice   **7** .... times
4 .... volume   **8** .... harvest

c) *Fill in* **clean, clear.**

1 .... hands   **6** .... wound
2 .... sky   **7** .... day
3 .... sheets   **8** .... knife
4 .... air   **9** .... voice
5 .... weather   **10** .... lines

21 Fill in the blanks with one of the words from the list below in the correct form.

- fire • monitor • enact • broaden • vent
- waive • howl • pamper • ~~meet~~ • issue

0 "If you don't *meet* our demands, we will destroy your business", he said.

1 The booking office hasn't .... my tickets yet.

2 Considering my vast experience, they .... the normal requirements.

3 The doctors .... his progress with sophisticated equipment.

4 The teacher .... his anger on the naughty child.

5 As soon as he .... the gun, the birds flew away.

6 The government .... a law to make recycling compulsory.

7 My father says that reading .... your mind.

8 The dog .... with pain when the cat scratched it.

9 If you .... children, they will grow up spoilt.

22 Think of one word only which can be used appropriately in all three sentences.

0 • One doesn't need to be an expert to *appreciate* the beauty of classical music.
- He seems confident that houses in this area will *appreciate* in value in the next few years.
- I'll always *appreciate* your help and support.

1 • His constant questions surely .... her patience.
- We .... the door, but it was locked.
- His case is being .... at the High Court at the end of the year.

2 • Your .... will follow you on the next flight, sir.
- These exercises are designed to develop the muscles in your ....
- The road was blocked by the .... of a fallen tree.

3 • You have a .... choice. Either you obey the rules or you leave.
- The tennis player beat his opponent in .... sets.
- Pam has beautiful teeth they are pearly white and ....

4 • A wooden .... had been nailed over the broken window pane.
- The local tourist .... is offering several bargain breaks this spring.
- The guesthouse charges £10 per night for room and ...., so it offers good value.

5 • Terence and his friends are a strange, arty .... of people.
- Many of us are not satisfied with their .... and yet do nothing to improve their lives.
- At the auction I bought .... number 3 which was an antique ring.

6 • The whole place .... with music.
- His cruel words still .... in her ears.
- There was something about her story that .... true.

7 • It was a .... fight and the best man won.
- In order to qualify for this position, you must have a .... driving licence.
- She took a .... sheet of paper and began the letter again.

8 • There is no evidence that a rise in the number of the unemployed is connected to the latest crime ....
- A .... of panic swept over her when she realised what she'd done.
- The .... of immigrants into the country is the direct result of its neighbour's famine.

9 • Most of what they serve at that place isn't .... to eat.
- Since his accident he's only .... to do part-time work.
- According to doctors, elderly people should try to keep themselves .... by taking regular exercise.

10 • America .... with Japan in the World Championship.
- Linda is .... to the house all day because she's waiting for a delivery.
- The fortunes of the company are .... to the success of the industry as a whole.

PREPARING FOR PART 5

ANSWERING DETAIL QUESTIONS I

23 a) *Read the following passages and underline the parts where the answer to each of the following questions is contained. The first question has been done for you. Then paraphrase the underlined parts to answer the questions. Answer accurately, but use as few words as possible. Item (0) has been done for you.*

During the period of the Irish dance masters, "stages" were much smaller and quite unorthodox compared to stages today. **(0)** <u>Table tops, dismantled doors, or even barrels</u> were pressed into service as dance surfaces.

The fact that stages have become larger has changed step dancing in two important ways. Firstly, more movement has been introduced into the dance. Secondly, dance steps which require substantial space (flying jumps, for example) have become possible.

Footwear and costumes have also changed. Early descriptions of Irish dancing sometimes note that dancers were barefoot. Soft shoes were introduced around 1920 for girls dancing reels and jigs. Men also used them for a while, but had dropped them by the 1970s. Hard shoes were introduced and bubble heels were invented in 1985 to augment clicking, but they are now prohibited in dance competitions. Step dance rules also state that "authentic Gaelic dress" must be worn in competitions.

0   What examples of "unorthodox" dance surfaces are given in the text?
1   How have larger stages affected Irish dancing?
2   Who were soft shoes mainly made for when they were introduced?
3   What is the purpose of bubble heels?
4   What *two* step dance completion rules are mentioned?

0   *parts of tables, doors and barrels*
1   ....
    ....
2   ....
    ....
3   ....
4   ....
    ....

Brodsworth Hall began being built in 1861, and its construction lasted almost exactly 2 years. Charles Sabine Thellusson, after inheriting a substantial sum of money in a family will, built this country house in the *Italianate* style, replacing an earlier hall on the site.

The south side (which was sunnier) provided comfortable accommodation for the family, while the side facing northward contained the servants' wing and was built reusing materials from the earlier hall.

Different areas of the house segregated the family, their children and their servants. Even the male and female servants slept on different floors and had their own hierarchy depending upon seniority.

Many rooms had a specific leisure function. In addition to a library and study, Brodsworth Hall has a billiard room and a drawing room. After dinner, ladies and gentlemen retired separately. The ladies would go to the drawing room, where music would be played, and the men would go to the billiard room, where they could smoke and discuss mutual interests. For the Thellusson family, these would include racing and sailing.

1   When was the construction of Brodsworth Hall completed?
2   How did Charles Sabine Thellusson fund the construction?
3   Which side of the house did the servants live on?
4   What system of hierarchy did the servants have?
5   What were the after-dinner functions of the drawing room and the billiard room?

1   ....
2   ....
    ....
3   ....
4   ....
5   ....
    ....
    ....

b) *Read the following passages and underline the parts where the answer to each of the following questions is contained. Then paraphrase the underlined parts to answer the questions. Answer accurately, but use as few words as possible.*

> Fear of flying seems to have its roots in an overall fear of loss of control. For some, it can be an uneasiness about not physically being in control of the aeroplane, and others fear a loss of control of their emotions. Some may experience claustrophobia with the closing of the aeroplane door, and others become less and less comfortable the further they get from home.
>
> The psychological function of fear is to alert us, physically and emotionally, to defend ourselves or to take action to protect ourselves from some perceived danger. Lots of juices flow in the body to help us accomplish this task. Under the proper circumstances, this reaction is to our benefit, and the feelings are eased by taking immediate action that solves the situation for the moment.
>
> Anxiety, on the other hand, is activated by thinking or believing that we're in some form of imminent danger. We believe something dangerous is about to happen, even when there's no external verification available. Thinking and knowing get all confused. Suddenly, what we think becomes reality, and our bodies begin to respond. There's considerable difficulty in taking immediate action because the stimulus is internal, not external. If someone throws a rock at me, I can dodge. That's an external problem. If I think someone is going to throw a rock at me, which way do I go and when? That's anxiety.

1 Give two examples of "fear of loss of control".
2 What is the psychological function of fear?
3 How are feelings of fear alleviated?
4 What is the difference between fear and anxiety?

1 ....
   ....
2 ....
   ....
3 ....
   ....
4 ....
   ....

8c Practice Test Eight

Paper 3 Use of English

PART 1

Read the text below and think of the word which best fits each space. Use only one word in each space.

ANCIENT ADORNMENTS

To some, **(0)** *the* wearing of jewellery for adornment may appear self-indulgent. If **(1)** ...., it is a self-indulgence common to all ages and all places. **(2)** .... prehistoric times crude necklaces and bracelets were **(3)** .... fashioned from leather or reeds and strung with berries, pebbles, feathers, shells or animal bones, and decorative thorns or sharp bones were used **(4)** .... clasps. They may have complemented the caveman's fur outfit **(5)** .... been worn as part of a religious ceremony, to indicate superior rank and even as amulets to ward off bad luck. Gradually, ivory, wood and metal took over from **(6)** .... durable materials, and ears, noses and lips **(7)** .... pierced for the insertion of ornaments. **(8)** .... 3500 BC, the discovery **(9)** .... gold heated with fire could be pounded into thin sheets and shaped **(10)** .... objects had revolutionised jewellery-making. Similarly, silver, copper and bronze were now being used. In the late 2000s BC the Egyptians began inlaying jewellery with glass, enamel and precious gemstones, some of **(11)** .... were believed to possess magical properties or bring the wearer good fortune, **(12)** .... now and in the afterlife, as mummies were adorned with them. Slightly later, the Greeks **(13)** .... in for fine filigree metalwork, twisting gold into intricate patterns and rarely using precious stones. **(14)** ...., later were reinstated by the Romans, who **(15)** .... have been the first to use jewelled rings as engagement tokens.

PART 2

Read the text below. Use the word given in capitals at the end of some of the lines to form a word that fits in the space in the same line.

A NEUTRAL COUNTRY

Switzerland is the **(0)** *recipient* of a fair share of stereotype images such as   **RECEIVE**
(16) .... chocolates, kitsch cuckoo clocks, the practice of yodelling and   **RESIST**
(17) ...., serious bankers. Visitors will find a flavour of Germany,   **HUMOUR**
France and Italy, but always **(18)** .... with an intangible essence   **PREGNANT**
that is uniquely Swiss. The Swiss have carefully guarded their lack of involvement in the
20th century. Their only **(19)** .... in WW1 lay in the organising of Red   **PARTICIPATE**
Cross units. Switzerland joined the League of Nations after peace was won, under the
proviso that its inclusion would be financial and economic rather than entailing any possible
military sanctions. Despite the country's long standing **(20)** ....,   **NEUTRAL**
Switzerland maintains a 400,000 -strong civilian army. Every able-bodied male
(21) .... national service. In addition, a whole infrastructure is in place   **GO**
to repel any **(22)** .... including the planned destruction of key roads   **INVASION**
and bridges. It is a sobering thought to realise that those apparently undisturbed mountains
and lakes hide a network of military **(23)** .... The Swiss are   **INSTALL**
generally a law-abiding nation, valuing established forms of demonstrating respect and
courtesy to others. Formal titles are always used and it is **(24)** ....   **CUSTOM**
to greet shopkeepers when entering their shops. Citizens further engender respect, by
(25) .... recycling waste as part of an overall policy to protect   **DILIGENT**
the environment.

PART 3

Think of one word only which can be used appropriately in all three sentences.

0 • One doesn't need to be an expert to *appreciate* the beauty of classical music.
  • He seems confident that houses in this area will *appreciate* in value in the next few years.
  • I'll always *appreciate* your help and support.

26 • Leo gave the other passengers a .... look and went on reading his newspaper.
  • It was .... comfort to the workers to be told that their wage rise would be below the rate of inflation.
  • I was tracking the deer in the wood when suddenly the trail went ....

27 • You have been late every day this week; what is your .... ?
  • Dora is so headstrong; her actions defy all ....
  • Within ...., I am prepared to work overtime.

28 • There was a loud .... when I stupidly stood on my sunglasses.
  • That was a nasty .... you told about your boss, and it wasn't even funny.
  • A large .... appeared in the wall from floor to ceiling after the earthquake.

29 • There was a loud .... as the tea tray and all its contents fell to the floor.
  • We heard the screech of brakes, then saw a terrible car ....
  • A sudden .... in the system meant that all the computers were out of action.

30 • The train left the station, ... momentum as it went.
  • People were .... outside the store, eager to snap up bargains on the first day of the sales.
  • The whole family were out in the orchard .... olives.

31 • The police used .... to disperse the gang of football hooligans.
  • The .... of the explosion destroyed many of the surrounding buildings.
  • His .... of argument persuaded me to change my ideas.

PART 4

Complete the second sentence so that it has a similar meaning to the first sentence, using the word given. Do not change the word given. You must use between three and eight words, including the word given.

0 Nobody spoke when the teacher asked who the culprit was.
  remained
  Everyone *remained silent when the teacher asked who the culprit was.*

32 John took my place while I was at the dentist's.
  stood
  John .... at the dentist's.

33 Most people know that becoming an actor is difficult.
  common
  It .... is difficult.

34 I think you'll have problems if you park here.
  better
  I think .... here.

35 I don't think Patrick has ever been camping.
  best
  To .... been camping.

36 In my opinion, computers are more trouble than they're worth.
  hindrance
  In my opinion, computers .... help.

37 Those gates must be locked before we leave the premises.
  prior
  We .... the premises.

38 Customers will not want to buy this product.
  market
  There .... this product.

39 Fiona said she was against the proposal.
  expressed
  Fiona .... the proposal.

PART 5

*For questions **40-44**, read the following texts. For questions **40-43**, answer with a word or short phrase. You do not need to write complete sentences. For question **44**, write a summary according to the instructions given.*

The first rigid aircraft, the USS Shenandoah, was designed and constructed solely for a military purpose – to infiltrate foreign territory unnoticed and spy on the enemy. In 1917, the US Navy established an air station at Lakehurst, New Jersey, which would serve as both a training and operational centre of lighter-than-air (LAT) aeronautics. When it was realised that rigid and non-rigid aircraft could play an important role in commercial transportation, the site became a development centre for commercial aircraft.

When they designed the Hindenberg, the German aircraft industry had this exact role in mind. A sizeable, fast, versatile civil transport. The Hindenberg was 245 metres in length and of conventional Zeppelin design. It could reach a maximum speed of 135 km/h, and a cruising speed of 126 km/h. It was first launched from Friedrichshafen, Germany, in April 1936, and made the first of its ten scheduled commercial flights during that year. It was the first of its kind to make the cross-Atlantic flight from Germany to the United States.

On May 6, 1937, while landing at the Lakehurst Naval Air Station, the Hindenberg suddenly burst into flames. As a result of the explosion, the hydrogen-inflated craft was completely destroyed and 36 of the 97 passengers on board lost their lives. This terrible disaster shocked the world and marked the end of the use of rigid airships in commercial air transport.

40 Why did the air station at Lakehurst become a development centre for commercial aircraft?

....

....

41 Why was the Hindenberg so important in the history of air transportation?

....

....

The mystery of Amelia Earheart's disappearance has never been solved, and at
line 2 — this late date probably never will be. On June 1, 1937, Amelia Earheart and her
navigator, Fred Nooman, set out to accomplish an unprecedented feat. By
travelling from Florida to California, she hoped to be the first woman to
circumnavigate the globe. Their route took them along the northeast coast of
South America, across Africa over the Red Sea and then to Bandoeng. It was at
this point that their venture was interrupted by bad weather conditions. During
line 8 — this unplanned stopover, Earheart found herself stricken with dysentery and was
unable to continue the flight until June 27.

Three days later, Earheart made her last radio contact with the US Coast Guard.
The communication contained the ominous message "KHAQQ calling Itasca. We
must be on you but cannot see you... gas is running low..." After having
completed 22,000 miles of the 29,000 - mile journey, Earheart seemingly
disappeared from the face of the earth. Despite an extensive operation, no trace
of the plane or its two passengers was ever found.

42 Which phrase justifies the writer's claim that the mystery of Earheart's disappearance "(will) probably never be
(solved)"? (line 2)

....

....

43 What does the phrase "this unplanned stopover" refer to in line 8?

....

....

44 In a paragraph of between 50 and 70 words, summarise the two air tragedies discussed in the two passages.

....

....

....

....

....

....

....

....

RELATIVE PRONOUNS

	subject of the following verb (cannot be omitted)	object of the following verb (can be omitted)	possession (cannot be omitted)
people	**who/that** *He is **the actor**. **He** was awarded the Oscar* *He is **the actor/who/that** was awarded the Oscar.*	**whom/who/that (inf)** *There's **the man**.* *We met **him** yesterday.* *There's **the man (whom/who/that)** we met yesterday.*	**whose** *That's **Mr Brown**. **His** wife died last month.* *That's **Mr Brown, whose** wife died last month.*
things/animals	**which/that** *I bought **a camera**. **It** doesn't work properly.* *I bought a **camera which/ that** doesn't work properly.*	**which/that** *Here's **the dog**. I found **it** in the street.* *Here's the dog **(which/that)** I found in the street.*	**whose/of which (formal)** *There's **the camera**. **Its** lens is broken.* *There's **the camera whose lens/the lens of which** is broken.*

RELATIVE ADVERBS

time	**when** (= in/on which) *The day **when** he first met Jane was the happiest of his life.*
place	**where** (= in/at/on/to which) *That's the centre **where** the conference is being held.*
reason	**why** (= for which) *His laziness was the reason **why** he was dismissed.*

Notes
- *That* can replace *when*, or be *omitted* in an informal style. *I'll never forget the day (when/that) the earthquake happened.*
  That can replace *where*, or be *omitted* only after the words *somewhere, anywhere, nowhere, everywhere, place.*
  Have you got a place (where/that) I can store my schoolbooks?
  That can replace *why* or be *omitted* only after the word *reason. That's the reason (why/that) he lied to you.*

- *That* is never used after commas or prepositions.
  That's the place in which I was born.
  not *That's the place ~~in that~~ I was born.*
  This is Paul, who you spoke to last week.
  not *This is Paul, ~~that~~ you spoke to last week.*

178

DEFINING RELATIVE CLAUSES

A defining relative clause refers to the preceding noun. It gives essential information about it and cannot be omitted, as this could obscure the meaning of the main clause. A defining relative clause cannot be placed between commas.
People are artists. (Which people? Everyone?)
*People **who paint** are artists.*

NON – DEFINING RELATIVE CLAUSES

A non-defining relative clause refers to the preceding noun and gives extra information about it. Therefore, it can be omitted without cause or confusion or changing the meaning of the main clause, and must be put between commas.
*My brother, **who is studying medicine**, will be 24 next week.*

Relatives with Prepositions
The preposition is put in front of **whom** or **which** (formal English). However, it can be put at the end of the relative clause, thus **whom** becomes **who**. In this case **that** (less formal) is more commonly used instead of **who/which**. It is usual, though, to omit **who/which/that** in everyday speech and put the preposition at the end of the relative clause.
*That's the man **with whom** I went to France. (formal)*
*That's the man **who/that** I went to France **with**. (less formal)*
*That's the man I went to France **with**. (informal)*

where:	a	preposition + which	**when:**	a	preposition + which
	b	which/that + clause + preposition		b	that + clause + preposition
	c	clause + preposition (no relative)		c	no relative, no preposition

*That's the house **where** we lived for ten years.*
*a That's the house **in which** we lived for ten years.*
*b That's the house **which/that** we lived **in** for ten years.*
*c That's the house we lived **in** for ten years.*

*1964 is the year **when** I was born.*
*a 1964 is the year **in which** I was born.*
*b 1964 is the year **that** I was born **in**.*
c 1964 is the year I was born.

CONVERSATIONAL GRAMMAR

1 *Choose the correct item.*

1 "He looks familiar."
"He's the author .... novel became a best seller."
A which   C whose
B of which   D whom

2 "Hi Nick. I break bad news. Natalie and James broke up again."
"I know, but it is James .... is to blame this time, not Natalie."
A for whom   C who
B whose   D which

3 "Wendover? Never heard of that town before."
"Well, actually it's the town .... I spent my teen years."
A where   C when
B who   D which

4 "What are you reading?"
"A review of the film .... was on television last night."
A which it   C that it
B where   D which

5 "Which was the most disappointing moment in your career?"
"It was the moment .... I realised that my partner was giving away company secrets to our rivals."
A which   C when
B where   D on which

6 Children always want to know the reason .... things are as they are.
A whom   C which
B why   D who

7 "Is there a problem with the letter?"
"The person .... this letter is addressed no longer lives here."
A who   C to who
B to whom   D whom

8 India is the country .... he spent the early years of his life.
A at which   C where
B that   D on which

2 *Fill in the blanks with the correct **relative pronoun** or **adverb**. Indicate where the relatives can be omitted.*

1 Our new neighbours, who live in the flat .... is just below ours, own the gallery .... is showing the Picasso exhibition.

2 Two weeks ago he went to Chicago .... he met the magazine editor for .... he will be working .... he finishes his training.

3 Kevin Sedgewick, ... stars in this film, comes from the small town .... I lived .... I was studying in England.

4 It was at the dinner on Saturday .... Gary told us about the woman .... claimed that she was his kindergarten teacher.

5 I believe that vitamin C relieves colds quickly, ... is a point .... many doctors disagree on.

6 Angela is a parent .... I met at the school last week. Angela, ... is so interested in children, gave up a successful career to campaign for their rights, ... is certainly praiseworthy.

7 That young man .... you were speaking to at the conference was the one .... mother is the country's best heart surgeon.

8 My Babe Ruth baseball card, ... value has tripled since I bought it twenty years ago, was bought by a collector .... lives in the house .... I grew up.

9 Just as we were getting out of our car, Miss Williams, ... lives two doors away, came with a police officer and asked us if we had seen the couple to .... she had rented a flat.

10 Yesterday was one of those days .... I couldn't find any free parking spots, ... was frustrating considering all the clients I had to meet.

3 *Join the following sentences using **relative pronouns** or **adverbs**.*

1 John and Joe are brothers. They own the café down the street. ....

2 He bought these trousers at a second-hand shop. His best friend owns it. ....

3 That woman is a wealthy heiress. She is wearing dark sunglasses. ....

4 His article was accepted by the editor. He wrote it last week. ....

5 Jim and Maureen are our neighbours. Their daughter has just got married. ....

6 The cinema has recently been renovated. It was designed by a famous architect. ....

STRUCTURAL CONVERSION ◄

1 *This is the building **where** the meeting will take place.*
   *This is the building **in which** the meeting will take place.*
   *This is the building the meeting will take place **in**.*
2 *She **sent** her kindest regards, **which** was thoughtful of her.*
   *It **was** thoughtful of her to send her kindest regards.*
3 *She **is** rather childish, **which** can be irritating.*
   *It **can be** irritating that she's rather childish.*
4 *It **was a shame** that you weren't able to attend the performance.*
   *You **weren't** able to attend the performance, **which** was a shame.*
5 *She received a gift **which** was totally useless.*
   *The **gift** she received was totally useless.*
6 *The **actor** I met was extremely talented.*
   *I **met** an actor **who** was extremely talented.*
7 *That's the Queen. Her reign began in 1953.*
   *That's the **Queen whose** reign began in 1953.*
8 ***Whose** pen is this?*
   ***Who** does this pen belong to?*
   ***To whom** does this pen belong?*
   ***Who** is the owner of this pen?*
9 *He spoke quickly **and** I got confused.*
   *He spoke quickly, **which** confused me.*
10 ***Many students** graduate every year. Most of them come from abroad.*
   ***Many students, most** of whom come from abroad, graduate every year.*
11 ***Shakespeare** wrote the play Othello.*
   ***Othello** is a play (**which/that**) Shakespeare wrote.*
12 ***Dante was born** in that house.*
   *That's the **house** Dante was born in.*
   *That's the **house where** Dante was born.*
13 *I **can't see** any reason **for** their behaving like that.*
   *I **can't see** any reason **why they** behaved like that.*
14 *The **day when** I got married was the happiest of my life.*
   *The **day on which** I got married was the happiest of my life.*
   *The **day** I got married was the happiest of my life.*

---

4 Complete the second sentence so that it has a similar meaning to the first sentence, using the word given. Do not change the word given. You must use between three and eight words, including the word given.

1 Can you tell me who the owner of that car is, please?
   belongs
   Can you tell me ....
   ...., please?

2 This is Thomas Hardy's birthplace.
   town
   This ....
   .... in.

3 It was generous of her to donate so much money to charity.
   amount
   She donated ....
   .... was generous of her.

4 This is the dog which won first prize at Crufts last week.
   awarded
   This is the dog ....
   .... last week.

5 He recommended me for the position, which was very nice of him
   kind
   It ....
   .... for the position.

6 It's unfortunate that the construction of the building will not be finished as originally planned.
   longer
   The construction of the building ....
   .... unfortunate.

7 It was childish of him not to accept my apologies.
   refused
   He ....
   .... of him.

8 He was born in London fifty years ago.
   city
   London ....
   .... fifty years ago.

9 The newspaper editor only accepted one of the ten articles I wrote.
   by
   I wrote ten articles, ...
   .... the newspaper editor.

10 The writer I really admire won the Nobel Prize for Literature.
   admiration
   The writer ....
   .... won the Nobel Prize for Literature.

5 *Read the text below and think of the word which best fits each space. Use only one word in each space.*

DISAPPEARING WORLD

The destruction **(0)** *of* the rainforests is a pressing problem of our times **(1)** .... not one that is regarded equally seriously by everyone. The **(2)** .... affluent nations regard the issue as **(3)** .... of preservation; deforestation must stop. When it comes to the poorer countries, the issue is not so cut and dried. **(4)** .... these people, the rainforests represent a source of economic prosperity, a point that obviously takes precedence **(5)** .... ecological concerns. A solution must be found **(6)** .... the damage caused by the deforestation that is destroying the rainforests becomes irrevocable.

Deforestation is carried out by **(7)** .... involved in the timber industry and also by migrant farmers. The latter occupy an area of land, strip it, farm it **(8)** .... its natural mineral supply is used up and then move on. The land is left useless and exposed and a process of erosion **(9)** .... into effect, washing soil into rivers thereby killing fish and blocking the water's natural course.

The land is not the **(10)** .... victim. Rainforests are a richly populated habitat. In the rainforests of Madagascar there are at **(11)** .... 150,000 individual species of plants and animals which are found nowhere **(12)** .... in the world, and more are being discovered all the **(13)** .... Furthermore, approximately 50% of all endangered animal species live in the world's rainforests. The destruction of the forests effectively represents a complete removal of all these plants and animals. Deprived **(14)** .... their natural environments, they will disappear altogether. Again, this process is irreversible. Man, no **(15)** .... how powerful he considers himself, does not have the power to re-establish the species he is so wilfully destroying.

PHRASAL VERBS 1

6 *Look at Appendix 1 and fill in the missing preposition or adverb from the box below, then give a synonym for each phrasal verb.*

- ahead • onto • back • for • after • up
- out for • to • up to • over • down on
- on • at • into • out

0 Looking *back* on my life I realise I've been very fortunate.

1 In 1917 the Russian working classes rose .... against their masters.

2 She looks .... Mrs Brown's children three days a week.

3 This firm looks .... employees who have initiative.

4 Robert looks .... people who are not as educated as he is.

5 The police are looking .... the matter hoping to find a solution soon.

6 Look .... ! There's a car coming.

7 He looks .... his older brother and follows his example in everything.

8 Look .... this manuscript and tell me what you think of it.

9 Let's make an appointment to look .... the house that is for sale.

10 The hotel room looked .... the swimming pool.

11 Passers-by looked .... as the circus passed through town.

12 They looked .... him to provide funds for the new magazine.

13 We've been looking .... a new flat for months but we haven't found one yet.

14 You'd better look .... the dates in the encyclopaedia.

15 I'm sorry; I haven't had time to look .... your composition yet.

16 Have you looked .... at what you'll be doing in two years' time?

17 Could you please go to the station and look .... my grandmother?

18 He was led .... by her flattery but soon discovered how insincere she was.

19 I don't think we can rule .... this possibility after all.

PHRASAL VERBS 2

7 *Look at Appendix 1 and fill in the missing preposition or adverb from the box below, then give a synonym for each phrasal verb.*

• for • out • up • off with • up for • out
• over • into

0   Can you make ....*out*......... the meaning of this passage?

1   When you make .... the cheque, please make it payable to Mr. R. Smith.

2   The naughty boy made .... the last of the sweets.

3   When they heard the fire alarm, the audience made .... the exit.

4   The boss asked her to make .... the hours she missed last week.

5   I don't know how to make .... my rudeness to him.

6   The committee is made .... of twelve members.

7   She makes .... that she is a successful actress, but in fact she's only played one small role.

8   They want to make the loft .... a study.

9   He made .... the whole story; it was just a figment of her imagination.

10 Her father has made .... all his property to her as she is his only child.

11 After not speaking for several days, they finally made it ....

12 I can't make .... who is in the room, as it's too dark.

13 She never goes out of the house without first making .... her face.

0	.......*understand*.......	7	....
1	....	8	....
2	....	9	....
3	....	10	....
4	....	11	....
5	....	12	....
6	....	13	....

IDIOMS/FIXED PHRASES 1

hit the roof:	get very angry
work to rule:	adhere strictly to the regulations as a form of protest
rack your brains:	think very hard about sth
off the record:	unofficial(ly)
in a rut:	be stuck in a monotonous routine
in the long run:	after a long period of time
it stands to reason:	it is logical
as a last resort:	when all else has failed
put down roots:	settle down
know the ropes:	know all the details of sth

8 *Fill in the blanks with one of the idioms/fixed phrases.*

0   After working in the same office for twenty-seven years with no hope of promotion, he felt he was *in a rut*.

1   My boss couldn't tell me anything officially but ....
.... he told me a promotion was imminent.

2   She ....
when her neighbours played their stereo at full volume for the fourth consecutive night.

3   Having lived and worked in more than a dozen countries, he thought it was about time he ....
.... in one place.

4   The bus drivers voted to ....
.... in an attempt to break down the management's resistance to their demands.

5   You've eaten so much that ....
.... you feel sick.

6   I'd been unable to contact her for three days so .....
.... I drove the thirty miles to her house to see what was going on.

7   Paul's only just started work here, so he doesn't really .... yet.

8   This may be an expensive purchase now but ....
.... it will save us a lot of money.

9   He had to ....
to remember where he had left his spare car keys.

9b English in Use

PREPOSITIONS

9 *Look at Appendix 5 and fill in the blanks with the correct preposition.*

0 Susan's quest *for* a satisfying job was at last realised.
1 We had to queue .... before we could get into the cinema last night.
2 Heavy rain resulted .... widespread flooding.
3 I was reminded .... my childhood when I heard that nursery rhyme.
4 Green vegetables are rich .... vitamins and minerals.
5 She is quick .... doing mental arithmetic.
6 Queen Victoria reigned .... Britain and Ireland for more than sixty years.
7 The sight of the snake made him recoil .... horror.
8 His style of writing is reminiscent .... Thomas Hardy's.
9 There has been a sharp rise .... unemployment this year.
10 Please keep .... touch after you've gone back to America.
11 As she didn't have a lot of cash, she bought the fridge .... credit.
12 They live .... the outskirts of a large industrial town.
13 .... average, English students study at university for three years.
14 Mike is not really .... tune with the rest of the group.
15 The writer is very much .... favour with the public at the moment.
16 What is .... the agenda for today's meeting?
17 .... the one hand, he's a dependable worker, but he is also very slow.
18 Are you .... the mood for a walk on the beach?

IDIOMS/FIXED PHRASES 2

keep sth quiet:	keep sth secret
at close quarters:	from a short distance
cut sb to the quick:	deeply hurt sb's feelings
on the quiet:	secretly
call it quits:	give up/ stop
out of the question:	impossible
open to debate:	undecided/unsettled
sth begs the question:	makes people want to ask a particular question
be in a quandary:	be confused; undecided
an unknown quantity:	person or thing that one has no experience of

10 *Fill in the blanks with one of the idioms/fixed phrases.*

0 Although he was collecting unemployment benefit, *on the quiet*, he was also working as a hospital porter.
1 He was .... by her comment that his previous novel was infinitely better than his new one.
2 Whether the advertising campaign will increase sales is ....
3 The presidential candidate is virtually .... as almost nothing is known about him.
4 Although the antique table looked nice from across the room, ... you could see how badly damaged it was.
5 Jerry's sudden acquisition of a sports car .... where did he get the money to buy it?
6 If the gardening business doesn't pick up soon, I'm going to .... and get another job.
7 It is .... that you should drive the car without your licence.
8 She's .... over which flat to choose, so she'll probably end up staying on at her parents' house.
9 I'll tell you what's going on if you promise to ....

11 Complete the second sentence so that it has a similar meaning to the first sentence, using the word given. Do not change the word given. You must use between three and eight words, including the word given.

1 The new rules about school uniforms will apply next year.
force
The new rules ....
.... next year.

2 So many people were really delighted when the government lost the election.
jubilation
There ....
.... lost the election.

3 The Queen has ruled the country for almost fifty years.
throne
The Queen has ....
.... for almost fifty years.

4 That woman looks an awful lot like my mother.
bears
That woman ....
.... my mother.

5 You certainly could never accuse Tom of being mean.
nothing
Tom ....
.... generous.

6 I'm not going any further till I've had something to eat.
far
This ....
.... I've had something to eat.

7 It's entirely your own fault that you failed the exam.
blame
You have no one ....
.... the exam.

8 Bobby ate two ice creams one after the other after lunch.
row
Bobby ....
.... after lunch.

9 Was your mother any better when you visited her?
improvement
Was there ....
.... when you visited her?

10 The workforce reluctantly agreed to a cut in pay.
reluctance
It ....
.... to a cut in pay.

11 I put the cheque in the envelope without signing it.
neglected
I ....
.... in the envelope.

12 Freddy was always quarrelling with his sister.
row
Freddy ....
.... with his sister.

13 My grandmother surprised us by announcing she was going on a world cruise.
surprise
Much ....
.... she was going on a world cruise.

14 You must remember to lock the drawer, whatever you do.
account
On ....
.... the drawer.

15 No one is quite sure if the player will perform well at his new football club.
seen
It ....
.... will perform at his new football club.

16 The government will cease subsidising the project from the end of the month.
receive
The ....
....
from the end of the month.

17 Brian is a strong contender for the position.
list
Brian ....
.... for the position.

18 She blushed with embarrassment at having made such a stupid mistake.
shamefaced
She ....
.... a stupid mistake.

19 Your outrageous behaviour has caused problems for the club.
embarrassment.
Your outrageous behaviour ....
.... the club.

9b English in Use

FIXED PHRASES

make do with sth:	use/have sth not as acceptable as original
give sb their marching orders (inf):	dismiss sb
meet one's match:	compete with sb as good as/better than you
mean well:	try to be kind/helpful
living beyond one's means:	spending more than you can afford
on the mend (inf):	recover from (illness/injury)
mend one's way:	begin to behave well
to put it mildly:	to understate sth in an ironic way
miles away (inf):	deep in thought
mint condition:	perfect condition
give sth a miss (inf):	decide not to do sth or go to a place
sb gets their money's worth:	sb gets sth which is worth its price/the effort put in it
name names:	identify sb who has done sth (usually immoral or illegal)
name of the game:	the most important aspect
come naturally to sb:	be very easy for sb to do
nearest and dearest:	close relatives/friends
risk one's neck:	put oneself in danger (physically or metaphorically)
touch a nerve:	mention a sensitive subject
nest egg (inf):	sum of money saved for a particular purpose
slip through the net:	avoid being caught by a system/trap set up to catch sb
none the wiser:	know nothing more than before
poke one's nose into sth (inf):	try to interfere in sth
hand/give in one's notice:	resign

12 *Complete the sentences using the fixed phrases in an appropriate form.*

1 Having found a better job, Reg .... immediately.
2 I can't afford a new car, so I'll have to .... the old one.
3 When the challenger answered every question correctly, the current champion knew he .... in the general knowledge quiz.
4 I'm sorry if my advice upset you, but I ...., you know.
5 The .... in this sport is to be fast and accurate.
6 The minister refused to .... in the financial scandal.
7 Many tax evaders .... due to the inadequacy of the system.
8 Our next door neighbour is extremely curious and always .... other people's business.
9 Geoffrey's row with the boss led to his being .... the same day.

13 *Choose the correct item.*

1 I think you .... a nerve when you mentioned Ralph's forthcoming retirement.
 A drilled   C touched
 B had   D hit
2 Yes, I saw the last episode of the series, but I'm none the .... about what really happened.
 A better   C cleverer
 B wiser   D surer
3 Some people like to .... their neck doing dangerous sports.
 A risk   C twist
 B break   D endanger
4 The professor looked as if he were .... away in a world of his own.
 A yards   C miles
 B kilometres   D streets
5 For stamps and coins to be of value, they need to be in mint ....
 A state   C situation
 B condition   D appearance

186

6 After six months of convalescence in a nursing home, Simon is finally on the ....

A run   C go

B top   D mend

7 Dave gave the office party a .... that year.

A miss   C chance

B hit   D break

14 *Find the mistake and correct it.*

0 Nobody ~~have~~ influenced my decision.   *has*

1 She speaks English most fluently than her sister. ....

2 He disguised himself so that nobody wouldn't recognise him. ....

3 He entered into the house without making a noise. ....

4 No sooner he had arrived than he left again. ....

5 She wrote him a note saying him where she had gone. ....

6 Not only he win the race but he broke the world record as well. ....

7 The number of fatal car accidents are increasing at an alarming rate. ....

8 The details of the plan are still being working out. ....

9 The accident took place at the crossroads near my house. ....

10 Your interview will occur at 10 am on Tuesday. ....

11 It's no use try to sleep with all that noise going on. ....

12 We went by the seaside yesterday. ....

13 Passengers needn't cross the railway lines. ....

14 She wasn't influenced with his speech. ....

WORD USAGE

15 *Read the text below. Use the word given in capitals at the end of some of the lines to form a word that fits in the space in the same line.*

A TIME OF CHANGE

What we mean by the Renaissance is the rich **(0)** *cultural* development that   CULTURE

began in the late fourteenth century. It **(1)** .... in   ORIGIN

northern Italy and spread northwards during the subsequent two centuries.

Literally meaning rebirth, this age was **(2)** .... by a   CHARACTER

(3) .... interest in classical learning and values. Three discoveries,   NEW

the compass, firearms and the printing press were essential conditions for the

new epoch. The first of these, the compass, made **(4)** ....   NAVIGATE

possible and became the basis for great voyages of discovery. The second,

firearms, gave the Europeans military **(5)** .... over the   SUPERIOR

American and Asiatic cultures. Finally, printing played a vital role in

disseminating the new ideas of the Renaissance. The spirit of the Renaissance

ultimately took many forms. It was expressed at first by the intellectual movement

called **(6)** .... This philosophy can be best understood as a   HUMAN

reaction against the seemingly **(7)** .... dark ages in which   TERMINATE

every aspect of life was seen through divine light. It brought with it a new

confidence in man's worth, in striking contrast to the biased mediaeval emphasis

on the **(8)** .... nature of man. The humanists of the   PERFECT

Renaissance took as their frame of **(9)** .... man himself. For perhaps   REFER

the first time in western history, man's potential seemed **(10)** ....   LIMIT

There was so much to be done, for the restless men of this new age.

16 *Read the text below and decide which answer (A, B, C or D) best fits each gap.*

OWNING A PET

The joys and tribulations of being a pet owner! During our lifetime most of us have some experience of either owning a pet or being in (0) .... contact with someone who does. Is there such a thing as "the ideal pet"? If so, what characterises the ideal pet? Various (1) .... influence one's choice of pet, from your reasons for getting a pet to your lifestyle. For example, although quite a few pets are relatively cheap to buy, the cost of (2) .... can be considerable. Everything must be (3) .... into account, from food and bedding, to vaccinations and veterinary bills. You must be prepared to (4) .... time on your pet, which involves shopping for it, cleaning and feeding it. Pets can be demanding and a big responsibility. Are you prepared to exercise and (5) .... an animal or do you prefer a more independent pet? How much spare room do you have? Is it right to lock an energetic animal into a (6) .... space? Do you live near a busy road which may threaten the life of your pet? Pets (7) .... as turtles and goldfish can be cheap and convenient, but if you prefer affectionate pets, a friendly cat or dog would be more (8) .... People get pets for a number of reasons, for company, security or to teach responsibility to children. Pets can be affectionate and loyal and an excellent source of company as long as you know what pet (9) .... you and your lifestyle.

	A	B	C	D
0	near	(B) close	narrow	tight
1	facets	elements	factors	points
2	upkeep	maintenance	upbringing	raising
3	considering	held	taken	kept
4	take	waste	occupy	spend
5	household	housetrain	housekeep	housework
6	confined	detained	reduced	closed
7	so	for	much	such
8	suited	appropriate	likely	good
9	fits	matches	suits	goes with

17 *Choose the correct item.*

0 The cup is full to the .... so be careful when you carry it.
A border C verge
B boundary (D) brim

1 Young children are often .... to illnesses such as measles.
A liable C apt
B sensitive D susceptible

2 Thousands of refugees are camping at the .... between the two countries, hoping to find asylum.
A boundary C brim
B border D rim

3 After losing my job, I was on the .... of a nervous breakdown.
A border C bounds
B brim D verge

4 The school playing fields are out of .... while equipment is being set up for the cricket match.
A bounds C verge
B brim D border

5 Children should keep away from the river .... in case they fall in.
A bounds C bank
B brim D border

6 We're spending our holidays on the .... this summer.
A bank C cast
B beach D shore

7 The old lady .... her bag for fear she might lose it.
A seized C grasped
B grabbed D clutched

COLLOCATIONS

18 Fill in **squeaking, creaking, whining**.

1 .... floorboards

2 .... children

3 .... mice

4 .... rusty hinges

5 .... new shoes

6 .... old beds

7 .... electric saw

8 .... joints

19 Collocate the expressions with words given from the list.

- value • spoil • prophesy • decline • restore
- manage • amaze • breed • maintain • exhibit
- revive

0 *breed* horses

1 .... of doom

2 .... a painting

3 .... sb's contribution

4 .... an invitation

5 .... sb with your singing

6 .... good relations

7 .... a company

8 .... children

9 .... a play

10 .... diplomatic relations

20 Collocate the expressions with words from the given list.

- stroke • discharge • desert • abdicate • pat
- evict • gape • wind • rinse • whisper

1 .... the dog

2 .... the cat

3 .... sweet nothings

4 .... the plates

5 .... a tenant

6 .... a patient

7 .... in surprise

8 .... the clock

9 .... your family

10 .... from the throne

21 Think of one word only which can be used appropriately in all three sentences.

1
- I finally .... him after getting his home number from his wife.
- After hours of negotiation and lengthy disagreements, they finally .... a compromise.
- Her hair was so long it .... to her waist.

2
- When Laurence spilled the blackcurrant juice, it .... the new white sofa.
- Since time was of the essence, the teacher .... the tests quickly and efficiently.
- They .... the occasion of their silver wedding anniversary by hosting a large party in the grounds of the estate.

3
- The dog would greet his .... enthusiastically at the door every evening.
- Be very alert to his manipulations; he is a .... at getting his own way.
- Tim is fiercely independent and certainly his own ....; nobody tells him what to do.

4
- The conspirators were .... to secrecy.
- Although unemployed, Dudley thought that something was .... to turn up.
- The parcel was roughly .... with string.

5
- It's a strange .... whose origin is unknown.
- Pearl just stood there with a blank .... on her face.
- The .... of public opinion by demonstrations and strikes is a right of democratic societies.

6
- There was much controversy about the new education ....
- A hummingbird is a tiny multi-coloured bird which sucks the nectar from flowers with its long curved ....
- There was a reminder from the electricity company because we forgot to pay last month's ....

PREPARING FOR PART 5

MEANING AND USAGE II

22 *Read the passages and explain the words, phrases, or sentences in bold. One item has been done for you.*

> Train driver Graham Robertson, 49, told police that the train continued to race along the lines for almost 500 metres after hitting the animal. However, he was unable to control the train's speed, and it came off the lines at the bend just before Oxenholme station. Eight passengers were treated for minor injuries at the Barrow-in-Furness Royal Infirmary. "It was the most **(0) hair-raising** twenty seconds I've ever experienced," says Robertson. A police inquiry continues.

(0) *frightening/horrifying* ....

> **(1) The beauty of orbit-calculating computer software** is that it not only tells you where an asteroid is going but also where it has been. This can guide us in the re-examination of old space photographs, where an asteroid is visible but hasn't been noticed. With dates going back a few years instead of a few months, computers are able to **(2) spit out** much more accurate predictions concerning the orbit of comets and asteroids.

(1) ....
(2) ....

> I am a junior doctor, that's all. Full stop. I work 18 hours a day, get paid virtually nothing, get extremely stressed while trying to convince administration to find someone to replace me while I get some sleep, occasionally change my clothes, **(3) and ever so occasionally eat. (4) I am a junior doctor. That's all I am, twenty-four hours a day, every day.**

(3) ....
(4) ....

> With the death of actors Walter Matthau and Jack Lemmon being so recent, **(5) raving about someone else's performance in Neil Simon's classic The Odd Couple might be considered something of a sin.** On the other hand, not to praise Jack Sherwood and Peter Snowgood for their interpretation of this hilarious play would certainly be unfair. With respect to Matthau and Lemmon, one might even suggest that Sherwood and Snowgood are, at times, better than the two recently deceased masters **(6) whom the stage is going to sorely miss.**

(5) ....
....
(6) ....

> Ronan O'Gara's badly bruised and swollen left eye, **(7) tangible proof to a brutal night of rugby** between England and Australia in Sydney, has left the England management in a state of diplomatic outrage. After a game that saw five yellow cards, England manager Graham Henry spoke of a "black night for rugby", and insisted that there was "an agenda to create a bad impression about the England team" in the minds of fans and referees. **(8) In terms of peacemaking, it was less of a case of proffering an olive branch than of chopping down the entire grove for extra firewood.**

(7) ....
(8) ....

23 *Read the passages and explain what the purpose of each writer is when using the bold words, sentences or phrases. One item has been done for you.*

It is always better to judge something for yourself. That's why we're inviting you to come and take a look at the performance of the new S-Vision NE Strike 64 graphics card at any Dixon's branch on 15 and 16 June. Once you've found out about the unparalleled capabilities of the NE Strike, you'll never look at a computer the same way again. **(0) But, then again, maybe we're prejudiced.**

(0) *The writer is encouraging his readers to go and test the product themselves.* ....

Dear Mr. Fielding,
I am writing to inform you that your account is overdrawn by £194.22, which exceeds your agreed overdraft limit. **(1) I understand that this may be a simple miscalculation on your part** and trust that you will redress the balance as soon as possible.
Yours sincerely
Murray E. Banks
Branch Manager

(1) ....

Apart from some half-hearted efforts, the government have not yet made a serious attempt to effectively address the Scottish fisheries issue. **(2) Fishing is the livelihood of over 12,000 families in the north of Scotland, and over 150,000 tons of fish caught off Scotland's coast is exported annually.** Action must be taken before the problems of Scottish fishermen grow out of control, something which is much nearer than many government officials think.

(2) ....
....

All students taking Biology B625 and B695 are invited to "Researching Amphibians: Methodological Advances in the 1990s" by Professor Angela Smith of the University of Arkansas, USA, at the Proudfoot Lecture Theatre on Tuesday, 11th May, 6 p.m. Attendance will not be recorded, but students taking the above-mentioned courses are strongly encouraged to attend, **(3) since Professor Smith will examine the issues which are highly relevant to the material taught in B625 and B695.**

(3) ....

Remember the days when vegetables were sold by grocers, newspapers were sold by newsagents and hair was cut by barbers? That's all gone now. Have you noticed how your local supermarket is stocking more and more items which you wouldn't expect to find there? Clothes, perfume, jewellery, computer games, mobile phones, for goodness sake! Of course you have. **(4) Have you also noticed that the little shop on the corner is not there anymore?**

(4) ....

Last year, fewer people bought key rings and noddy dogs over the Internet than the year before. As a result, some have expressed the view that e-commerce is dying.
They couldn't be farther from the truth. Not only is e-commerce actively soaring, but the very concept of e-commerce is developing into something of a world-size applicable trade philosophy. Rather than squint over dry statistics, one should look at the types of business services now available on the net. Web-based banking, insurance and learning are all fast-developing industries, bound to transform the world of international trade in the next couple of decades. **(5) Even if you had to buy your noddy dog from your local Halford's.**

(5) ....
....

9c Practice Test Nine

Paper 3 Use of English

Time: 1 hour 30 minutes

PART 1

Read the text below and think of the word which best fits each space. Use only one word in each space.

A DYING ART

"Read a book? **(0)** *There* must be something better to do." This phrase is heard more and more frequently **(1)** .... not only the desire but also the incentive to read declines. Young people nowadays are provided **(2)** .... too many alternatives **(3)** .... reading for them to find a justification for actually sitting down and opening a book, let **(4)** .... curling up in a chair for the afternoon to enjoy a good long read for the pure pleasure of it. Even in schools, where books have been the standard **(5)** .... of storing and transmitting all types of knowledge for centuries, they are **(6)** .... supplanted by the tools of the video and computer revolution. **(7)** .... bother to turn a page when by tapping a button or touching a screen the **(8)** .... information can be flashed before your eyes within seconds? Even the act of reading **(9)** .... is being "revolutionised" by the advent of portable walkman-like devices which **(10)** .... store and display the texts **(11)** .... innumerable books without the reader **(12)** .... to turn a page. One wonders **(13)** .... future generations will ever know the actual, physical pleasures of reading: the sturdy weight of the book itself, the rough **(14)** .... smooth texture of the paper, the soothing rustle of the pages, and the indescribable scent of old paper and ink which is much **(15)** .... a perfume to the dedicated reader.

PART 2

Read the text below. Use the word given in capitals at the end of some of the lines to form a word that fits in the space in the same line.

POISONOUS SEALIFE

One of the most lethal poisons on Earth, ten thousand times more **(0)** *deadly* than cyanide,   **DEAD**
is tetrodotoxin, more concisely known as TTX. Its potency is well known in East Asia, where
it regularly kills **(16)** .... who have braved the capricious   **DINE**
(17) .... known as fugo or puffer fish.   **DELICATE**
This toxin has a **(18)** .... method of operation: twenty-five minutes after   **TERROR**
(19) ...., it begins to paralyse its victims, leaving the victim fully aware   **EXPOSE**
of what is happening. Death usually results, within hours, from suffocation or heart failure.
There is no known antidote. If lucky patients can **(20)** .... the symptoms   **STAND**
for twenty-four hours, they usually recover without further **(21)** ....   **COMPLICATE**
It is no ordinary poison. What is strange about its **(22)** .... is that it   **OCCUR**
is found in such a wide range of creatures, from algae to angelfish spanning entire
kingdoms of life. It is rather unlikely that such an unusual toxin evolved
(23) .... in so many unrelated animals.   **DEPEND**
Marine biologists have discovered that the poison is produced by bacteria living in the gut
of its host. The best explanation is that a symbiotic relationship exists between host and
the not **(24)** .... guest, where microbes exchange poison for   **WELCOME**
nutrients, providing a valuable **(25)** .... weapon for its host.   **DEFEND**

PART 3

Think of one word only which can be used appropriately in all three sentences.

0 • One doesn't need to be an expert to *appreciate* the beauty of classical music.
  • He seems confident that houses in this area will *appreciate* in value in the next few years.
  • I'll always *appreciate* your help and support.

26 • Vinnie successfully .... his father's business before joining the army.
  • The magazine editors have been heavily criticised because they .... an article on exam-cheating techniques last month.
  • We .... a wire from the ground floor to the basement so that everyone could get access to the Internet.

27 • While I understand his frustration, I think there was no .... for such rudeness.
  • The referee made a particularly dubious .... towards the end of the match.
  • The manager had to leave the meeting due to the urgent .... from the chairman.

28 • Most people regard Einstein as the cleverest man that ever lived, but he had himself rejected this .... during his life.
  • The book's .... had to be changed as it was decided it was too controversial.
  • Two of the world's best teams will be battling it out in Rome tonight for the European ....

29 • When the tenant broke the .... of the lease, the landlord took him to court.
  • As he has a low salary, we were surprised he lived in such comfortable ....
  • Skin .... such as eczema can be triggered by anxiety.

30 • The two .... contenders in the forthcoming election were female.
  • The .... difference between African and Indian elephants is the size of their ears.
  • His imaginative .... course won him the cookery competition.

31 • There is no .... way to edit a four-hour film.
  • The unrelenting problems of his life gradually removed that .... smile from his face.
  • Harold sat in the .... chair to watch TV.

PART 4

Complete the second sentence so that it has a similar meaning to the first sentence, using the word given. Do not change the word given. You must use between three and eight words, including the word given.

0 Nobody spoke when the teacher asked who the culprit was.
  remained
  Everyone *remained silent when the teacher asked* who the culprit was.

32 The staff hated Frank's new policies intensely and so went on strike.
  hatred
  So .... that the staff went on strike

33 We want to breathe new life into this project.
  rejuvenate
  We .... project.

34 My grandfather died in the early hours.
  passed
  My grandfather .... night.

35 That football team has won every match this season.
  unbeatable
  That .... this season.

36 People should be careful when walking alone at night.
  best
  It .... walking alone at night.

37 They seldom stay up late.
  rare
  It .... late.

38 Even though Simon rarely has a lot of money, he always buys his mum a birthday present.
  short
  However .... his mum a birthday present.

39 The climbers will try to reach the summit again in the morning.
  another
  The climbers will .... in the morning.

193

PART 5

*For questions **40 - 44**, read the following texts. For questions **40 - 43**, answer with a word or short phrase. You do not need to write complete sentences. For question **44**, write a summary according to the instructions given.*

With about 40 million amateur players, soccer is the most popular sport worldwide. It is also a sport associated with a fairly high rate of injury.

For players under 12 years old, the injury rate in soccer is very low – less than 1 percent – but the injury rate rises with age. Nearly 8 percent of high school soccer players are injured in a season, and among local leagues, nearly 9 percent of players 19 years old and younger sustain injuries. Older participants sustain more frequent and severe injuries than younger players, and girls are injured more often than boys. Most injuries are caused by illegal moves, poor pitch conditions, or heading the ball awkwardly.

Injuries in soccer are usually mild sprains, strains, and contusions (bruises) and mostly affect the lower extremities. The most common site of injury is the ankle, followed closely by the knee. Acute head damage rarely happens, accounting for less than 5 percent of injuries.

Injuries can be prevented if players wear shin guards, warm up before play, and follow the rules of the game. Modern equipment can also greatly enhance injury prevention efforts. Most notably, the addition of padding to goal posts can reduce the number and severity of head injuries. Laboratory testing has shown that padding reduces the force of hitting the post by 31 to 63 percent. Anchoring movable goal posts to the ground at all times, even when not in use, can also greatly reduce some of the most serious injuries.

40 Which part of the body is most vulnerable when playing soccer?

....

....

41 Why is padding goal posts recommended?

....

....

Hockey players of the past wore remarkably little and quite rudimentary protective gear. The first goalkeeper shin pads, for example, had originally been designed for cricket, and protective gloves were only introduced in the mid 50s. Proper shin guards eventually came into being, but they were often too thin to soften the impact of the puck on the leg, and players were known to use newspaper or magazines behind them for extra protection.

lines 5

Amazingly, goalkeepers played without masks until 1959, when Jacques Plante wore face protection at a game in the old Madison Square Garden after he had taken a puck in the cheekbone from Andy Bathhouse. Plante's coach, Joe Blake, pressured him to shed the mask later on, and he did for a while. But he started wearing a mask again the following spring, and other goalkeepers eventually followed suit. However, it wasn't until 1973 that a NHL goalkeeper (Andy Brown) appeared in a game without a mask for the last time.

It may also surprise one (especially with the known number of head injuries hockey players suffer) to think that players did not begin wearing helmets with any sort of regularity until the early 1970s. Prior to that, the only people who wore them did so mostly because they were recovering from a head injury, or, as was the case of one former Chicago Blackhawk forward, because they were embarrassed about being bald.

42 Why did players use "newspaper or magazines … for extra protection"? (lines 5-6)

....

....

43 Why was the first goalkeeper mask worn?

....

....

44 In a paragraph of between 50 and 70 words, summarise the functions of each piece of protective equipment discussed in the two passages.

....

....

....

....

....

....

....

....

UNIT 10a Grammar: Nouns

Nouns are parts of speech which refer to: people *(Ann)*, actions *(reading)*, objects *(apple)*, qualities *(virtue)*, places *(Athens)*, jobs *(teacher)*.

There are four kinds of nouns in English. These are:
abstract nouns *(love, freedom, thought)*
common/concrete nouns *(book, table)*
collective nouns *(family, clergy, herd)*
proper nouns *(Greg, London)*

Nouns can be used as the:
a) **subject of a verb**   *The **boat** left.*
b) **object of a verb**   *I met **Chris**.*
c) **object of a preposition**   *I met him at the **library**.*
d) **complement of *be, become, seem***   *Janet is my **friend**.*

GENDER

masculine:	men and boys (he)
feminine:	women, girls, cars, ships, countries (she)
neuter:	babies, animals, things (it)

Notes

- Babies and animals are referred to as male or female when we know their sex.
  *The Browns have got a lovely baby. **She** is so cute.*

- Cars, ships and countries are sometimes referred to as female but the neuter is more common in modern English.
  *"Do you like my new car?" "Yes, **she's** terrific."/"Yes, **it's** terrific."*

Most common nouns referring to people have the same form whether male or female.
teacher (man or woman), doctor, etc

Some common nouns referring to people have different forms for male and female.

actor - actress	emperor - empress	host - hostess	son - daughter
barman - barmaid	father - mother	monk - nun	uncle - aunt
bachelor - spinster	gentleman - lady	nephew - niece	widower - widow
boy - girl	heir - heiress	prince - princess	waiter - waitress
bridegroom - bride	husband - wife	policeman - policewoman	
duke - duchess	hero - heroine	steward - stewardess	

Some common nouns referring to animals have different forms for male and female.

bull - cow	cock - hen	tiger - tigress	
drake - duck	gander - goose	stag - doe	
dog - bitch	lion - lioness	stallion - mare	

THE PLURAL OF NOUNS

- Nouns are made plural by adding:

a) - **s**   pencil - pencils
b) - **es** to nouns ending in - o, - s, - x, - z, - ch, - sh, - ss   bus - bus**es**
c) - **ies** to nouns ending in *consonant + y*   lady - la**dies**
d) - **s** to nouns ending in *vowel + y*   toy - toys
e) - **ves** to nouns ending in *f/fe*   leaf - lea**ves**

    but   chiefs, proofs, roofs, cliffs, handkerchiefs

Note

dwarf - dwarves/dwarfs
hoof - hooves/hoofs
scarf - scarves/scarfs

- Some nouns form their plural irregularly.

child - children	goose - geese	mouse - mice	ox - oxen	tooth - teeth
foot - feet	louse - lice	man - men	person - people	woman - women

- Some nouns remain unchanged in the plural.

craft - craft	fish - fish	plaice - plaice	squid - squid	spacecraft - spacecraft
cod - cod	Japanese - Japanese	salmon - salmon	species - species	trout - trout
deer - deer	means - means	sheep - sheep	series - series	

- Some nouns are only plural. These are:

a) arms (weapons), belongings, cattle, clothes, congratulations, earnings, goods, groceries, greens (vegetables), lodgings, oats, odds (chances), outskirts, people, police, premises (building), regards, remains, riches, savings, surroundings, thanks, etc
b) garments, tools and instruments consisting of two parts: binoculars, compasses, glasses, jeans, pants, pliers, pyjamas, scales, scissors, spectacles, trousers, etc

- Collective nouns can take either a singular or plural verb, according to the meaning.

The staff were not in agreement with the new rules. (We refer to the individual members)
The staff of the school consists of fifty people. (We refer to the group as a unit)

Some collective nouns are:
audience, choir, class, clergy, club, committee, company, crew, crowd, family, firm, government, jury, orchestra, public, staff, team, union, youth, etc

- Some nouns have different meanings when turned into plural. These are:

air (atmosphere)
airs (behaviour)
cloth (a piece of material)
clothes (garments)
compass (a magnetic compass)
compasses (an instrument for drawing circles)
content (what is written or spoken about in a piece of writing, speech, etc)
contents (the things contained in a box, place, etc)
custom (a traditional event)
customs (the government department which collects taxes on imported goods)
damage (harm done to something)
damages (monetary compensation)

experience (gaining knowledge or skill over a period)
experiences (activities/events one has done/lived through)
fund (a sum of money saved for a purpose)
funds (money)
glass (a drinking receptacle)
glasses (spectacles)
hair (the hairy part of the head)
hairs (fine strands growing from the skin)
look (a style; an expression)
looks (a person's appearance)
manner (a way in which something is done)
manners (social behaviour; customs)
minute (60 seconds)
minutes (notes taken as a record of a meeting)

relation (a connection between two or more things)
relations (members of the same family) – same meaning in the singular
scale (the relative size, extent, etc of something)
scales (an instrument for weighing)
spectacle (an impressive sight; an object of attention)
spectacles (glasses; also: specs)

*Could I have a **glass** of water please?*

spirit (a person's soul or mind; a magical creature)
spirits (a person's feelings; a strong alcoholic drink)
wood (the hard material trees are made of)
woods (small forest) - same meaning in the singular
work (employment)
works (the moving parts of a machine; a place of manufacturing process)

*I can't read without **glasses**.*

Note

Some of the above nouns have their own regular plurals.
*I'll take five **minutes** to finish it. (more than one minute)*
*Jonathan was the one who kept the **minutes** of the meeting. (notes)*

- Compound nouns form their plural by adding - s/- es:

a to the noun if the compound has only one noun.
   passer-by - passers-by   *hanger-on - hangers-on*   *frying pan - frying pans*
b to the second noun if the compound consists of two nouns.
   cupboard - cupboards
c to the first noun if the compound consists of two nouns connected with a preposition.
   mother-in-law - mothers-in-law
d at the end of the compound if it does not contain any nouns.
   breakdown - breakdowns

COUNTABLE/UNCOUNTABLE NOUNS

A **Countable** nouns are those which can be counted.
   1 book, 2 books, 3 books, etc

B **Uncountable** nouns are those which cannot be counted; that is, you cannot say there are 2, 3 or 4 of them. **Uncountable nouns** take a **singular** verb and are not used with **a/an**. The words **some, any, no, (a) little, much, plenty of**, etc can be used with uncountable nouns.

   *Is there **any chocolate** left?*
   *There's **little** hope of their finding the boy.*

Uncountable nouns are:

- nouns of substance or quantity (mass nouns)   oil, water, juice, rice, etc
- nouns ending in - ics   politics*, physics, athletics, statistics*, etc
- some abstract nouns   courage, information, etc
- games ending in - s   billiards, darts, bowls, dominoes, etc
- diseases ending in - s   mumps, rickets, etc

* *politics* and *statistics* can also have plural forms.
   *What **are** your politics?*
   *The statistics **are** annoying.*

The most common uncountable nouns are:

accommodation, advice, anger, applause, assistance, baggage, behaviour, beer, bread, blood, business, chaos, chess, chewing gum, china, coal, conduct, cookery, countryside, courage, crockery, cutlery, damage, difficulty, dirt, education, equipment, evidence, excitement, food, fruit, fun, furniture, garbage, gold, gossip, grass, hair, happiness, harm, health, help, homework, hospitality, housework, information, jealousy, jewellery, knowledge, laughter, leisure, lightning, linen, luck, luggage, machinery, measles, meat, money, moonlight, mud, music, news, nonsense, patience, permission, poetry, progress, publicity, research, rubbish, safety, scaffolding, scenery, seaside, shopping, soap, spaghetti, steam, strength, stuff, stupidity, sunshine, thunder, timber, traffic, transport, travel, trouble, understanding, underwear, violence, wealth, weather, wine, work, writing.

Many uncountable nouns can be made countable by means of partitives.

a **piece** of cake/information/baggage/advice/furniture/work/equipment; a **glass** of water/beer/wine; a **jar** of jam; a **sheet** of paper; an **item** of news; a **drop** of water/oil; a **box** of chocolates; a **metre** of cloth; a **packet** of biscuits/tea; a **slice** of bread; a **loaf** of bread; a **pot** of tea; a **cup** of tea; a **ball** of string; a **lump** of sugar; an ice **cube**; a **game** of football/chess; a **kilo** of meat; a **bottle** of wine/beer/whisky; a **tube** of toothpaste; a **bar** of soap/chocolate; a **blade** of grass; a **flash** of lightning; a **clap/peal/rumble** of thunder, etc

1 *Underline the correct form of the verb. Sometimes both forms are possible.*

0 The landscape **is**/are spectacular here.
1 Inaccurate weights occurred because the scales **was/were** unbalanced.
2 Detectives agree that the evidence **is/are** overwhelming.
3 Mounting hostilities in the province **was/were** worrying.
4 Rubbish **is/are** accumulating outside the entrance to the shop.
5 The management **was/were** considering implementing the new strategy.
6 Athletics **was/were** well represented in the magazine's sports section.
7 The audience **was/were** applauding loudly.
8 Good advice **was/were** hard to come by among competitive colleagues.
9 The sewage works **is/are** where waste is treated to make it safe.
10 Work **is/are** underway to complete the new motorway.
11 The government **was/were** debating the new bill for three days.
12 A meeting is a waste of time if the minutes **is/are** lost.
13 The woods **is/are** home to hundreds of plant species.
14 **Is/Are** the designer spectacles really worth getting? I could just buy these, instead.
15 A crowd of hangers-on **was/were** pursuing the Princess.

16 The stairs **is/are** due to be replaced by a lift.
17 The premises **was/were** declared unsafe after the earthquake.
18 Argument **is/are** widespread on the global warming issue.
19 Your theory is sound but your calculations **is/are** wrong.
20 The information **were/was** passed on to another department.

2 *Underline the correct item.*

1 He has a lot of **works/work** to complete before leaving.
2 The stylist was trimming her customer's **hairs/hair**.
3 We were all impressed with the **content/contents** of his speech.
4 The magazine lost the court case and was ordered to pay **damage/damages** to the television celebrity.
5 The group doesn't have sufficient **funds/fund** to finance the expedition.
6 The **custom/customs** officer stopped us and asked if he could inspect our luggage.
7 The cook weighed out the necessary ingredients on the **scale/scales**.
8 They follow the **custom/customs** of exchanging chocolate eggs at Easter.
9 Hopkins proved popular but the man of the **minute/minutes** was De Niro.
10 The timber company received a consignment of **wood/woods**.

199

10b English in Use

3 *Read the text below and think of the word which best fits each space. Use only one word for each space.*

SAVING THE WHALE

As part **(0)** *of* Project Pelagos, a marine reserve covering the same area **(1)** .... Switzerland and located in the Ligurian Sea is being planned. The programme was devised by environmentalists from the University of Genoa **(2)** .... response to growing concern about the number of whales and dolphins **(3)** .... harmed in those waters.

Every year large numbers of dolphins, rorquals and finback whales migrate to this area from Atlantic waters in search of food. **(4)** ...., studies estimate that correspondingly large numbers never return **(5)** .... mate in native waters. The deaths are being caused by the presence of DDT, a pernicious insecticide voluntarily banned in Britain, in the seas off the Ligurian coast. **(6)** .... effect on marine animals is cumulative rather **(7)** .... instantaneous, so whales returning to the same area year **(8)** .... year are particularly vulnerable. The other major problem is the use of large fishing nets to trap dolphins and whales. Very recent laws prohibit Italy's fishing boats, some of **(9)** .... have drag nets up to 10 kilometres in length, from entering the area, but as **(10)** .... there is nothing to prevent foreign boats from fishing **(11)** ....

The nets are a particular problem and it has been estimated that approximately 400 dolphins perish in **(12)** .... each year.

The project aims to develop a safe area for these animals, but the administrators admit that funding is a problem. To remedy **(13)** ...., they have set up an adoption scheme **(14)** .... which there is a fixed registration fee. Donations have been averaging £25 and for this participants receive certification of their involvement in the scheme, an information pack about their dolphin or whale, plus regular updates. In **(15)** ...., there are plans afoot to allow some volunteers to accompany scientists going out on observation trips.

PHRASAL VERBS 1

4 *Look at Appendix 1 and fill in one of the prepositions or adverbs below, then give a synonym for each phrasal verb.*

- down • in • aside • ~~behind~~ • in for • off
- down to • about • up with • up • out
- forward • on • back • through • across

0 He had a bad time in the army but he has put it *behind* him now.

1 It is being put .... that the vice-president is involved in the scandal but as yet there seems to be no real evidence.

2 Just put .... your name and address on this card.

3 The lecturer had difficulty in putting .... his ideas.

4 He put his failure in the exam .... bad luck.

5 The drought in Africa has put .... development in the area by decades.

6 Why don't you put .... that new position at the university?

7 Make sure you put .... the fire before going to bed.

8 Could you put me .... to Mr Jones, please?

9 If you can't afford a hotel, we'll put you .... for the night.

10 He put .... an insurance claim after the accident but he got nothing.

11 How can you put .... the noise in this house? I'd go mad.

12 Don't be put .... by his manner. He always acts that way.

13 They're putting .... a dance performance in the town hall tonight.

14 We put .... a sum of money each month for our summer holidays.

15 Mr Jones has put .... the proposal that all members of staff should make a contribution to the earthquake relief fund.

PHRASAL VERBS 2

5 *Look at Appendix 1 and fill in one of the prepositions or adverbs below, then give a synonym for each phrasal verb.*

• on • through • with • out • together • down
• up to • over • on to

0 His proposal met *with* total opposition from the committee.

1 I'm afraid you'll have to learn to live .... this problem for the rest of your life.

2 We'd better move .... the housing problem before time runs out.

3 Please note .... these figures so we can go over them later.

4 She asked him to hand the document .... to her.

5 We can narrow our options .... to two or three at the most.

6 If you think you can live .... charity for ever, you're sadly mistaken.

7 You ought to try and live .... your parents' expectations.

8 I think you've missed .... John and Sally from the invitation list.

9 The detective tried to piece .... the events from the few clues he had.

10 He's used to hardships because he's lived .... two wars.

11 Tom has been passed .... for promotion in favour of a younger man.

12 New automated machinery in factories has led to the phasing .... of old production methods.

0 *had as a reaction*
1 ....
2 ....
3 ....
4 ....
5 ....
6 ....
7 ....
8 ....
9 ....
10 ....
11 ....
12 ....

IDIOMS/FIXED PHRASES 1

be in the same boat:	be in the same (usu bad) situation
go without saying:	be a foregone conclusion
behind the scenes:	in secret
be all at sea:	be in a state of confusion
be/have a close shave:	barely avoid an accident/a bad situation
be in sb's shoes:	be in sb's position
go for a song:	be sold very cheaply
smell a rat:	suspect that sth is wrong
be/get soaked to the skin:	be/get very wet
live out of a suitcase:	travel often/not have a permanent home
pull one's socks up:	make a greater effort
on a shoe-string:	on a very small budget

6 *Fill in the blanks with one of the idioms/fixed phrases.*

0 Almost everything sold at the auction *went for a song*; I've never seen so many bargains.

1 People who are involved in international business tend to .... most of the time.

2 As far as her future goes, Olivia ....; .... she hasn't got a clue what career to follow.

3 He told his son that he ought to .... or he'd never make a success of himself.

4 It .... that he'll get the role in the play; after all, he's perfect for it.

5 It would be interesting to know what goes on .... in a political campaign.

6 She .... when her husband started coming home late but he was only working overtime.

7 As far as jobs go, we're both .... I haven't worked for months either.

8 I went out in the downpour without my umbrella and got ....

9 It .... when a tile fell off the roof and nearly hit her on the head.

10 My brother travelled around the States .... I don't know how he survived on so little money.

IDIOMS/FIXED PHRASES 2

7 *Read the following sentences and explain the idioms/fixed phrases in bold.*

1 He tends to exaggerate, so **take** everything he says **with a pinch of salt**.
2 He's so **thick-skinned** that I don't think he'd notice if you insulted him.
3 **Did it show** that I was bored during the meeting? I tried to act as if I was interested.
4 Her father **made quite a scene** when she came home two hours later than she was supposed to.
5 Unless they let their daughter play with other children more often, I don't think she'll ever **come out of her shell**.
6 I'll **sleep on it** and give you my decision tomorrow.
7 After having a terrible day at work, it was **the last straw** when her car broke down on the way home.
8 The man who **gave** the police **the slip** wasn't apprehended until a week later.
9 Paul **is the spitting image of** his father - even his mannerisms are the same.
10 Could you tell me your surname one more time? I'm afraid I've got **a memory like a sieve**.
11 Laura's parents assured her that they would not **stand in her way** if she wanted to become a pilot, and would in fact help her.
12 Arresting that woman was **a long shot** as there was so little evidence against her, but in the end she turned out to be the ringleader of the gang.
13 By **pulling a few strings**, friends who work at the airline managed to get us a ticket on the next flight.
14 I can't stay awake a moment longer - I'm going **to hit the sack**.
15 Although her friend asked her not to tell anyone about her secret wedding plans, she **spilled the beans** and soon everyone knew.

PREPOSITIONS

8 *Look at Appendix 5 and fill in the blanks with the correct preposition.*

0 Mark was saved *from* drowning by the heroic action of his brother.

1 He has an excellent lawyer acting .... him and is bound to win the case.
2 The board of directors is meeting today to appoint a replacement .... the retiring chairman.
3 He was very solicitous .... our comfort and made every effort to ensure we had a pleasant journey.
4 We'd better go out for dinner; the food we have in the house isn't sufficient .... the six of us.
5 When the dam broke, a surge .... water rushed down the mountain.
6 As soon as they met Joe and Elizabeth were smitten .... each other.
7 I can't pay the electricity bill .... next week as money is short right now.
8 The manager was sympathetic .... their request for a non-smoking area.
9 Her colleagues intend to support her .... her fight against discrimination in the workplace.
10 They're bringing out a sequel .... this television series next summer.
11 I acted .... impulse and bought my wife a large bunch of flowers.
12 He's not only a comedian, but also an expert .... ventriloquism.
13 We agreed .... his plan and started making preparations immediately.
14 None of us could agree .... what to buy our teacher as a present.
15 Sam's views are often so outrageous that people rarely agree .... him.
16 The secretary's argument .... her boss led to her being fired.
17 There are strong arguments .... banning the use of aerosol sprays.
18 On our honeymoon we argued .... everything; from the food to the weather!
19 The explorer arrived .... the conclusion that he was the first person to reach the ancient site.
20 You must show your passport as soon as you arrive .... a new country.
21 Jackie is hopeless .... mathematics.

9 *Complete the second sentence so that it has a similar meaning to the first sentence, using the word given. Do not change the word given. You must use between three and eight words, including the word given.*

1 She said she was in no way responsible for the damage.
disclaimed
She ....
.... damage.

2 The new employee still hadn't appeared by 10 o'clock.
sign
There ....
.... by 10 o'clock.

3 You can dissolve these tablets in water.
soluble
These ....
.... water.

4 I can't bear your complaints any longer.
enough
I ....
.... complaints.

5 No one pities her after what she has done.
sympathy
No one ....
.... she has done.

6 They accused John of breaking the window.
put
They ....
.... the window.

7 The BBC produces programmes to interest all sorts of people.
catered
All sorts ....
.... the BBC.

8 We were reluctant to leave our old home.
with
It was ....
.... our old home.

9 Only by using a helicopter could the rescuers reach the injured climber.
means
Only ....
.... the rescuers reach the injured climber.

10 The art gallery has had at least 120,000 visitors since it opened.
fewer
No ....
.... the art gallery since it opened.

11 I eventually persuaded her not to hand in her resignation.
talked
I eventually ....
.... her resignation.

12 It was only because he persisted that he managed to get the job.
for
If ....
.... he wouldn't have got the job.

13 Flying is the form of transport I like least.
no
There ....
.... than flying.

14 Their house is now worth more than when they bought it.
increased
The ....
.... they bought it.

15 If you adjust the mirror a little, you'll be able to see more clearly.
slight
With ....
.... you'll be able to see more clearly.

16 The letter arrived completely unexpectedly this morning.
blue
The letter ....
.... this morning.

17 Although he repeatedly called the company, he couldn't get through.
after
Despite ....
............................., he couldn't get through.

18 The rainfall has been below average this month.
rained
It ....
.... this month.

19 The editor delayed publishing the article until he had checked all the facts.
did
Only ....
.... the editor publish the article.

FIXED PHRASES

have occasion to do sth:	it is necessary to do sth
rise to the occasion:	overcome a difficult situation by doing everything necessary to succeed
a drop in the ocean:	so minimal or trivial as to have little effect
on the offchance:	just in case
every so often:	occasionally
not on (inf):	unacceptable (of behaviour)
only too (+ adj):	more than (used for emphasis)
opt out:	withdraw from sth
in good order:	in good condition
made to order:	specially made, not from stock
at/from the outset:	from the very beginning
over and above:	more than or in addition to an amount
over to:	passing on to when introducing another speaker on the air
go overboard (inf):	overdo sth; go to extremes
to overflowing:	to capacity and beyond
overstep the mark:	behave in an unacceptable way
own up:	admit/confess
get your own back (inf):	get/take revenge

10 *Complete the sentences using one of the fixed phrases in an appropriate form.*

1 Angry and humiliated, he shook his fist at them and vowed he would .... on them.
2 I called ....
that you were free to go out this evening.
3 It's just ....
for you to speak to your parents in such a rude way.
4 Sylvia checked to see if the contents of the box were
.... after delivery.

5 Martin's financial needs were so pressing that his part-time earnings were ....
.............................., as far as he was concerned.
6 As he had never ....
speak in public before, he was understandably nervous.
7 The company is doing well, with sales figures that are already ....
those of last year.

11 *Choose the correct item.*

1 Isn't packing three suitcases for a weekend away going a bit ....?
   A overboard   C overload
   B overhead   D overskill

2 In spite of his stammer, Gerald rose to the .... and delivered a fascinating speech.
   A top   C bait
   B occasion   D situation

3 "How often do you visit your parents?"
   "......... so often, even though they live some distance away."
   A Even   C Never
   B Ever   D Every

4 "Do you think I should ask Andy?"
   "I'm sure he'll be only .... willing to help you with the project."
   A just   C too
   B that   D so

5 It is possible to .... out of the pension scheme if you do not wish to participate.
   A back   C charge
   B opt   D break

6 You say you need new clothes but your wardrobe is full to .... with dresses.
   A overflowing   C overlaying
   B overfilling   D overstepping

7 Frank was informed at the .... that the assignment would be no easy matter.
   A offset   C outset
   B upset   D reset

8 It will be overstepping the .... if you address the managing director by his first name.
   A line   C grade
   B mark   D limit

12 *Find the mistake and correct it.*

1 These glasses aren't mine. They're of father.   ....
2 The cabinet is made from mahogany.   ....
3 They are both colleagues of him.   ....
4 His case comes into the court on 27th February.   ....
5 She lit the candles in the birthday cake.   ....
6 They have a ten-years-old daughter.   ....
7 One of the committee members have resigned.   ....
8 I have forgotten my bag in the office.   ....
9 Please open the air-conditioning.   ....
10 On holiday I used to go to the beach or stayed by the hotel pool.   ....
11 I must extend my passport; I've just realised that it has expired. ....
12 That old pair have been happily married for sixty years.   ....
13 She had to pardon herself from the meeting for a few minutes.   ....
14 The meeting will be made in the conference room.   ....
15 I am going to pass my driving test on Friday.   ....
16 Times flies! This year has past so quickly.   ....
17 I wish you will be successful in your new job.   ....
18 The bus went straight passed me without stopping.   ....
19 All orders must be payed for in advance.   ....
20 If I weren't late, I wouldn't have been fired.   ....

13 *Read the text below and decide which answer (A, B, C or D) best fits each gap.*

A BLACK DAY FOR SPORT

Appeals were being made last night for Corsicans to come **(0)** .... and donate blood following the collapse of the football stadium in Bastia. The tragedy **(1)** .... 26 fans dead; the number of injured has been put at 700.

(2) .... to eyewitnesses, workers were still tightening bolts on the temporary scaffolding only an hour and a half **(3)** .... the match was **(4)** .... to begin, and as fans passed into the stadium, the structure, which holds up to 10,000, swayed violently and **(5)** .... collapsed.

Many of the **(6)** .... were given emergency treatment on the pitch while more serious cases were **(7)** .... to hospitals on the mainland.

A spokesman from the firm responsible for the stand's construction could only **(8)** .... horrified disbelief. According to him, although some of the bars had collapsed, others should have **(9)** .... the structure, thus preventing it from falling down.

0 A across	B over	C up to	(D) forward
1 A did	B left	C made	D remained
2 A With a view	B As far as	C According	D Referring
3 A before	B until	C since	D after
4 A up	B about	C bound	D due
5 A gradually	B actually	C eventually	D definitely
6 A injured	B wounded	C damaged	D wrecked
7 A delivered	B trafficked	C travelled	D transferred
8 A speak	B express	C say	D tell
9 A supported	B held	C defended	D carried

14 *Match the phrases, then explain the proverbs.*

Column A	Column B	Answers
1 One good turn	a make light work	1 ....
2 Least said	b is a friend indeed	2 ....
3 The end	c deserves another	3 ....
4 Many hands	d twice shy	4 ....
5 All work and no play	e don't make a right	5 ....
6 Spare the rod	f soonest mended	6 ....
7 A friend in need	g makes Jack a dull boy	7 ....
8 There's no smoke	h and spoil the child	8 ....
9 Two wrongs	i without fire	9 ....
10 Once bitten	j justifies the means	10 ....

WORD USAGE

15 *Read the text below. Use the word given in capitals at the end of some of the lines to form a word that fits in the space in the same line.*

A HAZARDOUS HISTORY

(0) *Occupational* disease is any illness associated with a particular occupation **OCCUPY**
or industry. (1) ...., the study of such diseases can **HISTORY**
be traced to the 16th century writings of the metallurgist Georgius Agricola
on the problems of (2) .... ventilated mines in **PROPER**
Saxony. His contemporary, the physician Paracelsus, reported in 1567 that
the so-called miners' disease was not, as was commonly believed, a
(3) .... for sins but rather a malady caused by the **PUNISH**
(4) .... of metal vapours. **INHALE**

During the 19th century the Industrial Revolution provoked the first serious
(5) .... of diseases associated with the workplace. **AWARE**
Long working hours, dim light, and potentially dangerous machinery took
their toll in physical injuries and decreased (6) .... to **RESIST**
such diseases as tuberculosis. The arrival into the industrial work force of
women and children (7) .... society's realisations of **HEIGHT**
the health hazards faced by all workers. In the late 18th and early 19th
centuries, (8) .... began to associate certain diseases **OBSERVE**
with specific occupations. Lung disease among textile workers was among the
first such cause-and-effect relationships to be (9) .... **CONVINCE**
established.

In the 20th century emotional and (10) .... stresses **PSYCHE**
associated with work, and their medical consequences, have taken their place
in the growing list of diseases labelled as occupational.

16 Choose the correct item.

1 Hundreds of workers have been .... due to financial problems at the factory.
A sacked   C resigned
B made redundant D retired

2 I was .... due to a personality clash with my boss.
A resigned C sacked
B retired   D made redundant

3 The .... of the failure of the bank resulted in many people losing their life-savings.
A cause   C trouble
B problem D catastrophe

4 The play was such a .... that it came off after only two nights.
A cataclysm C disaster
B calamity   D catastrophe

5 My puppy was very expensive because he's a special ....
A sect   C tribe
B breed D caste

6 The .... system in India resembles the class structure in Britain.
A breed C caste
B tribe D sect

7 Anthropologists have spent years studying the social system of this ....
A breed C caste
B tribe D sect

8 Countries often become .... to promote trade and industry between them.
A acquaintances C allies
B colleagues   D accomplices

9 Most people have few friends but many .... who they only see from time to time.
A allies   C associates
B accomplices D acquaintances

10 The foreman came to the building site to pay the workmen's ....
A fees   C salaries
B allowance D wages

COLLOCATIONS

17 a) Fill in sensible, sensitive.

1 .... attitude	5 .... shoes
2 .... clothes	6 .... idea
3 .... skin	7 .... issue
4 .... report	8 .... advice

b) Fill in gracious, graceful.

1 .... invitation	5 .... speech
2 .... ballerina	6 .... smile
3 .... walk	7 .... reply
4 .... manner	8 .... movement

18 Think of one word only which can be used appropriately in all three sentences.

1 • The skyscrapers, ... up on the horizon made an awesome sight.
• It must be an exhausting life for her, ... triplets.
• The wild horse was neighing and ...., unable to be ridden.

2 • Alice was sitting with her .... in her hands learning her ABC.
• Look first at the title at the .... of the page to get a general idea of the subject.
• At the age of 33, he was appointed .... of Italian at Manchester University.

3 • She received a(n) .... prior to submitting the first chapter of her article.
• The obstacles are intended to block the .... of offensive weaponry.
• A computerised booking system will be a(n) .... on the current situation.

4 • Everyone always said that Angela had a gentle .... about her.
• They travelled by .... as it's a faster means of transport.
• The foul smell of the polluted sea .... could be noticed for kilometres.

5 • After a month of hard work, I deserved to be .... better.
• The delicate statuette had to be .... with care.
• The disease was .... with experimental medicine.

19 *Read the following extracts and, in the spaces provided, write what each word in bold refers to. Two items have been done for you.*

0 The Jones family always shopped at the local U-Save supermarket. As valued customers, **(1) they** were offered a year's supply of breakfast cereal. Then they phoned all of their friends to tell them about **(2) it.**

1 *The Jones family.*
2 *Being offered a year's supply of cereal...*

1 Galloway Building Society are proud to present their new Home-Sweet-Home Insurance Service – a clever and flexible way to protect your home. From as little as £12 a month, **(1) you** can make sure **(2) your most valued asset** is safe. No small print, no strings attached, no hidden costs – just comprehensive home insurance. Call **(3) us** now for a free consultation.

1 ....
2 ....
3 ....

2 Piracy at sea has always existed, but modern naval policing resulted in its decline in the twentieth century. Yet, increased anti-government activity has added a new dimension to **(1) the offence**, forcing several to dictate that cargo ships have on-board security staff. **(2) This** increased the cost of shipping, and **(3) its** effect on the prices of exports and imports has not been negligible.

1 ....
2 ....
3 ....

3 At the end of World War II, London suffered from bomb damage, congestion and rapid urbanisation. The Greater London Plan was drawn up to solve **(1) these problems**. The answer was to build eight New Towns which would be separated from London by a green belt. The New Towns Act of 1946 allowed the Government to purchase land to build **(2) these settlements**. It was hoped that **(3) they** would encourage both people and industry to move out of **(4) the city**.

1 ....
2 ....
3 ....
4 ....

4 Professionals know that if you want quality results, it pays to start with quality tools and materials. Home owners can benefit from **(1) their** example. It's always a smart choice to buy the best tools you can afford, especially if you plan to use **(2) them** time and time again.

1 ....
2 ....

5 Gigantic monsters such as the mosasaur inhabited the seas during the Cretaceous period, **(1) which** lasted until about 65 million years ago. **(2) Such saurians** gave origin to our mythical notions of sea serpents. **(3) Their** scales and skin (found perfectly preserved) do not differ materially from animals of **(4) this family** existing today.

1 ....
2 ....
3 ....
4 ....

6 I have vivid recollections of myself as a child, sitting mesmerised in front of the TV, immersed in the unfolding adventures of Tarzan and his many animal companions. Often, **(1) the man of the hour** would be assisted in his heroic exploits by certain tribes that inhabited the great jungle. My imagination would inevitably be captured by the strange ways and unusual apparel of **(2) these diverse peoples**. For me, the most memorable of these tribes was **(3) one** which was made up of miniature humans known as pygmies, who could miraculously appear out of the seemingly impenetrable undergrowth.

1 ....
2 ....
3 ....

7 Here, at the internationally acclaimed Centre for Advanced Technology, our catch phrase is "safety first, profits second". At centre stage is our dedication to increasing personal safety in the work place, where the possibilities for making mistakes and the likelihood of accidents occurring are at **(1) their** greatest. **(2) This** is what drives us forward in our search for means of spotting and preventing on-the-job mishaps before **(3) they** happen.

1 ....
....
2 ....
....
3 ....

8 Puerto Rico was Spanish until 1898 and one of the oldest musical traditions on **(1) the island** is **(2) that** of the 19th-century Danza, associated particularly with the name of Juan Morel Campos and his phenomenal output of 549 compositions. **(3) This** is European-derived salon music for ballroom dancing, slow, romantic and sentimental. The peasants of the interior, the Jibaros, sing and dance the Seis in **(4) its** many varied forms, **(5) such** as the Seis Chorreao, Seis Zapateao, Seis Corrido and Seis Bombeao. Other variants are named after places, like the Seis Cagueno and Seis Fajardeno.

1 ....
2 ....
3 ....
4 ....
5 ....

9 The most common method for irradiating food uses radioactive cobalt-60 packaged into thin rods of about 18 inches long. **(1) They** are stored in a deep pool of water that is surrounded by thick concrete walls. Linear accelerators that shoot electrons down a tube can also generate radiation. **(2) These machines** do not require any radioactive material, but the beams do not penetrate deep enough to treat bulk foods.

1 ....
2 ....

10 Internet greetings are e-mail messages of special format. **(1) This** can be card-shaped frames of drawings, photographs, pieces of audio or video and, of course, customised text. Most Internet companies that offer greeting card services are charitable organisations, although portals like Yahoo and MSN also carry **(2) this feature** as a free service to **(3) their** users. More than 30,000 Internet cards were sent every day during the last couple of years of the nineties, but security issues (viruses hidden in subject lines or attached content) have led to a decline in **(4) their** popularity. Aware of the risks, most users delete them from **(5) their** mailbox without opening them nowadays.

1 ....
2 ....
3 ....
4 ....
5 ....

11 When fire alarms woke the Trimms, Steve's first concern was his family's safety. Next came the safety of his company, Innova Associates, based in **(1) the very home** which was burning to the ground. However, with his Jaz drive and **(2) its** sustained transfer rate of up to 6.62 MB per second, days earlier, he had backed up his whole company (as much as 1 whole gigabyte in as little as 10 minutes) on a single Jaz disk. While rebuilding **(3) their** lives remains a major task, Steve rebuilt his business with the click of a button.

1 ....
2 ....
3 ....

10c Practice Test Ten

Paper 3 Use of English   Time: 1 hour 30 minutes

Read the text below and think of the word which best fits each space. Use only one word in each space.

CHOOSING A LIFESTYLE

Alternative lifestyles have existed **(0)** *in* a variety of forms since the beginning of organised society. **(1)** .... have always been, and probably always will be, people who feel a need to escape from the mainstream of society and find a **(2)** .... to live that conforms more closely **(3)** .... their individual tastes and needs. The term "alternative lifestyle" **(4)** .... is a by-product of the social revolution of the 1960s and 70s, **(5)** .... the "Hippie movement" and **(6)** .... various back-to-nature and cultist offshoo... were in **(7)** .... prime, but the concept must be as old as mankind itself. **(8)** .... seems evident that in every society there must have been a **(9)** .... people who found themselves unable or unwilling to accept the status quo, who felt compelled to seek a better – or at **(10)** .... different – life out of reach of the restrictions and standards that any society must impose **(11)** .... its members. The monk in his monastery, the hermit in his cave, the solitary "witch-woman" living **(12)** .... isolation in the forest, must also have been seeking an alternative **(13)** .... the current standards of acceptability prevalent in their own societies. In our times the punks, gang-members and followers of cult-leaders are seeking, in their **(14)** .... ways, to find a life **(15)** .... suited to their individual needs, desires and dreams irrespective of the criticism they might draw.

Read the text below. Use the word given in capitals at the end of some of the lines to form a word that fits in the space in the same line.

ALLOWED ACTION

In law, nuisance is a human activity or a physical condition that is **(0)** *harmful* or	HARM
offensive to others and gives rise to a cause of action. A public nuisance created	
in a public place or public land, or affecting the morals, **(16)**	SAFE
or health of the community, is considered an **(17)** .... against	OFFEND
the state. Such activities as obstructing a public road, polluting air, and keeping	
(18) .... are public nuisances. A private nuisance is an activity or	EXPLODE
condition that interferes with the enjoyment and use of **(19)**	NEIGHBOUR
privately owned lands, without, however, constituting an actual **(20)**	INVADE
of the property. Thus, **(21)** .... noise, noxious vapours, as well	EXCEED
as disagreeable odours and vibrations, may constitute a private nuisance to the	
local landowner, although there has been no physical trespass on their lands.	
While a public nuisance, as such, is **(22)** .... only by the state,	ACTION
through criminal **(23)** ...., injunction, or physical abatement,	PROCEED
the same activity or conduct may also create a private nuisance to nearby	
landowners and thus result in a civil **(24)** .... The legal remedies	LAW
available in the case of a private nuisance are actions to prohibit the operation or	
(25) .... of the activity or condition, or to collect money damages.	CONTINUE

PART 3

Think of one word only which can be used appropriately in all three sentences.

0 • One doesn't need to be an expert to *appreciate* the beauty of classical music.
  • He seems confident that houses in this area will *appreciate* in value in the next few years.
  • I'll always *appreciate* your help and support.

26 • The instructions should be concise, but also easy for the user to ....
  • Free-range farms allow poultry to .... their natural behaviour patterns.
  • He wants to be a policeman, although his father would like him to .... in his steps and become a doctor.

27 • Many people, through lack of opportunity, are not able to .... their full potential.
  • Greg woke with a start only to .... that it had been just a dream.
  • Sanders became a rich man when he was able to .... a lot of money on his old properties.

28 • They added up the cost of the cruise and the .... total came to £10,000.
  • A trip to the seaside can be a .... day out.
  • Petula has always had .... plans for the future.

29 • To everyone's annoyance, Reg barged in and stood at the .... of the queue.
  • All complaints should be addressed to the .... of the department.
  • Whilst hammering, Dominic hit his thumb instead of the .... of the nail.

30 • If the good weather ...., we'll have the picnic.
  • In the long run, gold .... its value.
  • The state .... a celebration every year in honour of its struggle for independence.

31 • An .... was passed by the government to protect wildlife.
  • Throughout the first ...., she kept forgetting her lines.
  • The juggling .... was a great success with the youngsters.

PART 4

Complete the second sentence so that it has a similar meaning to the first sentence, using the word given. Do not change the word given. You must use between three and eight words, including the word given.

0 Nobody spoke when the teacher asked who the culprit was.
remained
Everyone *remained silent when the teacher asked* who the culprit was.

32 Mr Lurie will have to cancel his appointment.
keep
Mr Lurie ....
.... his appointment.

33 It is incredible how he managed to survive.
beyond
It's ....
.... to survive.

34 She speaks French quite well.
command
She ....
.... French.

35 He lent James £3,000 to buy that car.
owes
James ....
.... that car.

36 When he speaks, he gives you the impression that he is a really hard-working student.
think
To ....
.... a very hard-working student.

37 Vanessa practises the violin nearly every day.
by
Scarcely ....
.... the violin.

38 He realised how much he cared for her only when she had been away for a long time.
made
Her ....
.... how much he cared for her.

39 It would have taken a miracle to save the paintings from the fire.
of
Nothing ....
.... the paintings from the fire.

PART 5

For questions **40-44**, read the following texts. For questions **40 - 43**, answer with a word or short phrase. You do not need to write complete sentences. For question **44**, write a summary according to the instructions given.

The most common defensive structure in the mediaeval period was the castle. Built initially to defend a ruling minority from the subjugated population, later castles also took on a role within national defence.

Apart from one or two very untypical examples, castles did not exist before the Norman conquest. This was not so much because people were unable to build them, but because Saxon society did not need places of refuge for an alien, ruling minority. Norman nobility, on the other hand, found its true reflection in this form of architecture, almost a permanent expression of conflict between a small governing class and a subject people.

line 10 —— This symbolism, inherent in Norman castles, can firstly be seen from where they were built, as pre-existing buildings were often destroyed to make way for the castle. Secondly, from the architecture; the keep was built to protect a few defenders and not the community. Finally, the materials used. Good quality worked stone was reserved for use in churches and castles, the twin bastions of Norman control.

40 Why did castles not exist in Britain before the Norman Conquest?

....

....

41 What does the phrase "This symbolism" refer to in line 10?

....

....

line 2 —— Join the Kingmaker's household as the Earl's noblemen prepare for battle. Extra places are set in the Castle's undercroft, where new supporters of the Earl's great army are welcomed. Groups and individuals can enjoy an evening of feasting, music and revelry.

Your magical evening begins as you are led through the Castle by lamplight into "Kingmaker – a preparation for battle" in which the Kingmaker and his household are preoccupied with last-minute arrangements for tomorrow's long march. Here the everyday

line 7 —— life and smells of a mediaeval lifestyle prepare you for the bittersweet mood of the feast.

Beneath the vaulted ceiling of the 14th century undercroft, the festivities begin. The drinks begin to flow, impish tales and gossip flit from table to table, and tomorrow's engagement fades to the back of your mind.

Sumptuous food and tales of heroic deeds intermingle with lively music and revelry from the household, who amuse you through the night. But remember – this is a night of decision; will you march for glory with the Earl, or will you elect to let others decide the fate of your country and crown?

The feast for 2001 is priced at £ 38.00 per person. The Kingmaker's feast includes a tour of our mediaeval attraction "Kingmaker – a preparation for battle", sumptuous five-course feast and a full evening of mediaeval entertainment. The Kingmaker's feast is held most Friday and Saturday evenings and most evenings throughout December. For bookings and further information, please contact the sales office.

42 Who are the "new supporters of the Earl's great army", mentioned in line 2?

....

....

43 Why is the mood of the feast "bittersweet" (line 7)?

....

....

44 In a paragraph of between 50 and 70 words, summarise what the two passages tell us about the people who lived in the castles of Britain.

....

....

....

....

....

....

....

....

The Definite Article *the*

is used before a noun which is defined (singular or plural nouns countable or uncountable ones). It is omitted before nouns in the plural, uncountable or abstract nouns, when we talk about them in general.
The man standing over there is my friend.   *Money doesn't bring happiness.*

the is used before:	*the* is omitted before:
• names of objects considered *unique*. *the earth, the Eiffel Tower, the equator*	• **proper nouns.** *Nick; Smith*
• names of: **cinemas** and **theatres:** *the Rex;* **ships:** *the Titanic;* **hotels:** *the Hilton;* **institutions:** *the RSPCA;* **documents:** *the constitution;* **public bodies:** *the government;* **newspapers:** *The Times;* **historical events:** *the Second World War;* **museums:** *the British Museum;* **some jobs:** *the dentist;* **group nouns:** *the public;* **collective plural nouns:** *the police, the audience*	• names of **meals.** *Dinner is served.* but *The dinner we had was excellent. (It's a specific dinner)*
	• names of **substances.** *Oil is produced in Alaska.*
Note Restaurants, cafés, shops, banks or hotels which have the name of their founder and end in **s** or **'s** do not take *the*.	• names of: **countries:** *Greece;* **cities:** *Barcelona;* **streets:** *Oxford Street;* **parks:** *Hyde Park;* **addresses:** *3 McMillan St;* **buildings:** *Westminster Abbey;* **continents:** *Europe;* **mountains:** *Everest;* **islands:** *Cyprus;* **lakes:** *Lake Geneva*
• names of: **seas:** *the Black Sea;* **rivers:** *the Nile;* **groups of islands:** *the Dodecanese;* **mountain ranges:** *the Alps;* **groups of states:** *the USA;* **gulfs:** *the Persian Gulf;* **oceans:** *the Pacific;* **canals:** *the Panama Canal*	**Notes**
	• When the first word of a two-word noun is the name of a person or place, *the* is not used: *Westminster Abbey* but *the* is used with names with of-phrases or with an adjective or a noun modifier. *the Tower of London, the Science Museum*
• names of **people/families in the plural and nationality/ethnic nouns.** *the Browns; the Americans; the Zulus*	• Places whose name contains a common noun take *the* *the Czech Republic; the United Kingdom* **Also:** *the Netherlands; the Hague*
• **adjectives** used as nouns to describe groups of people. *the rich; the poor; the unemployed; the young; the handicapped*	• **bed, school, college, university, church, hospital, prison, market, sea, court,** when referring to them for the reason they exist. *Tom goes to **school** every weekday.* **but:** *His mother went to **the school** to get his marks.*
• **adjectives** denoting an abstract quality (singular), *the absurd = that which is absurd* *Some people enjoy **the mystical** and **the supernatural** in literature.*	• **work** when it means *place of work* *He's at **work**.*
• **titles without names.** *the Queen; the President*	• **home** when it means *place of living* *She isn't at **home**.* but: *Paris is **the home** of fashion!*
• **musical instruments.** *He plays **the piano** well.*	• **titles with proper names.** *Queen Elizabeth* but *the Prince of Wales*
• **inventions.** *the wheel; the word processor*	• **Mother/Father** when we refer to our mother/father. *Father is at work.*
• the **superlative degree** of adjectives/adverbs. *the richest; the fastest*	• names of **sports, activities** and **colours.** *He likes playing **tennis**; She hates **black**.*
• **only, last, first** (used as adjectives). *the only person*	• names of **days, months, seasons.** *We'll meet on **Monday**.*
	• **parallel phrases.** *They met **face to face**.* but *He punched him in **the face**.*

Notes

- Normally, the names of illnesses do not take *the*.
pneumonia; appendicitis; toothache;

- Some common illnesses though, can take *the*.
the measles; the flu; the mumps.

  Also: *a cold; a headache*

Notes

- When we use a noun in the singular number to represent a class of things/animals, *the* or *a/an* must be used.
The whale is a mammal.
A whale is a mammal.

- For generalisations we can also use the plural.
Elephants are in danger of becoming extinct.

The Indefinite Article *a/an*:

can be used only with singular countable nouns, when we do not define *which one* we talk about. **Some + plural or uncountable noun** is equivalent to *a/an + singular noun*.
There are some documents on the desk. (*some* documents = a number of documents)
There's some sugar in the jar. (*some* sugar = an amount of sugar)

a/an can also be used with:

money: *a/one dollar*, **fractions:** *a/one quarter*, **measurements:** *a/one foot*, **weight:** *a/one kilo*, **whole numbers:** *a/one thousand*, **price/weight:** *90 p a kilo*, **frequency/fuel:** *three times a day*, **distance/fuel:** *40 kilometres a litre*, **distance/speed:** *60 km an hour*, **illnesses:** *a headache*

Notes

a/an + noun (any one)
I'd like a coffee, please.

one + noun (when counting)
I ordered one coffee, not two.

1 *Put a, an or the where necessary.*

0 The window alcove measures exactly *a* metre across.

1 When you go to .... Athens, don't forget to visit .... Acropolis and .... Ancient Agora.

2 .... famous actress wanted to be married in .... British castle.

3 My new BMW motor cycle can reach speeds of over 300 kilometres .... hour.

4 The community managed to raise quite .... large sum of money for the building of the new school.

5 Many people are attracted by .... unknown and .... unexplained in .... nature.

6 During .... Napoleonic Wars, the army tried to defeat .... Russia.

7 This government doesn't care about .... jobless.

8 .... Indian Ocean lies between .... West coast of Australia and .... country from which it was named: .... India.

9 Did you know that .... gold was discovered in .... Australia in .... 1850s?

10 Imogen always wanted to have .... pony as .... child.

11 Hikers in .... Loch Ness reported seeing .... large moving mass at .... dawn.

12 I've got two tickets for .... Opera House.

13 Timothy had to go to .... hospital to have .... x-ray.

14 Nancy's got .... migraine; she really should go .... home.

15 .... reigning monarch stayed at .... plush five-star hotel in .... city centre.

16 Let's meet outside .... Palace of Congresses.

17 .... director will chair .... meeting tomorrow so everybody should come prepared.

18 Patrick is in .... hardware shop buying .... paint.

19 .... Bermuda Triangle has received .... notoriety as .... area of misfortune because .... number of vessels have disappeared there.

20 My mother cleaned the house from .... top to .... bottom.

21 They are .... husband and .... wife.

2 *Read the text below and think of the word which best fits each space. Use only one word in each space.*

LIVING IN THE SHADOWS

Hands up all those **(0)** *of* you who are shy. Well, you are **(1)** .... not going to tell me, but you are in good, or at least numerous, company. Recent research indicates that up to 40% of the U.S. population suffers from shyness to **(2)** .... extent and a similar proportion could be affected in Britain. It is **(3)** .... thing to pinpoint a figure, **(4)** ...., and another thing entirely to quantify the cost, to the individual, of shyness. But at what cost? A recent study presented at a British Psychological Society conference indicated that children **(5)** .... were recognised by their teachers as shy, performed less well in tests than **(6)** .... more self-assured peers. The study, **(7)** .... 320 children, showed that, although shy children do as **(8)** .... as other children at the age of five, by the age of ten, when they are old **(9)** .... to realise that they are being evaluated, they fare worse in their school work. Keeping a low profile and **(10)** .... no trouble at school **(11)** .... constantly underachieving, a shy child will grow **(12)** .... a shy adult. Then their career, social life and close relationships will all suffer from that paralysing inability to push **(13)** .... forward self-confidently, so that they become unable to cope **(14)** .... promotions involving increased responsibility, unwilling to climb the career ladder or entirely depend on a partner for friendship and intimacy. **(15)** .... not always taken seriously, their shyness is, as we have seen, debilitating.

PHRASAL VERBS 1

3 a) *Look at Appendix 1 and fill in the blanks with the correct preposition or adverb from the box below, then give a synonym for each phrasal verb.*

- behind • after • up • away with
- up against • down • out of • in • off
- into • through • across • away

0 He's always running *down* his boss although she actually treats him well.

1 The secretary was asked to run .... copies of the report for the employees.

2 We ran .... Sally at the shops yesterday; I hadn't seen her for months.

3 He ran .... the boy, but didn't manage to catch him.

4 We've run .... coffee. Could you go and buy some?

5 He ran .... debts amounting to millions of dollars last year.

6 Let's run .... that scene again; then you can all go home.

7 Their son ran .... at the age of 12 and didn't contact them for four years.

8 The old woman was run .... by a taxi.

9 You'd better run .... your new car before you drive it on the motorway.

10 We ran .... some valuable old books while we were clearing out the attic.

11 Don't run .... the idea that you can come home at whatever time you like!

12 Everything was going smoothly until we ran .... the problem of lack of funding.

13 My father fell asleep at the steering wheel and ran .... a lamp post.

14 I'm running .... schedule as my meeting lasted longer than I'd expected.

b) *Explain the meaning of the words in bold italics.*

1 The *runaway* horse created chaos as it galloped through the busy streets. ....

2 The financial analyst was given a *run-down* of the company's situation. ....

3 Since the recession, more and more towns have become *run-down*. ....

PHRASAL VERBS 2

see about:	make arrangements for
see off:	accompany a traveller to his/her train etc.
see out:	accompany sb to an exit
see over:	inspect property
see through:	1) not be deceived
	2) support sb through a difficult time
see to:	take care of
settle down:	live a more permanent lifestyle
settle in:	become used to a new house or job
settle on:	decide on
settle for:	accept sth (less than expected)
settle up:	pay (a debt, a bill etc)

4 *Fill in the missing preposition or adverb.*

0 He was hoping to sell his car for £1,000 but he had to settle *for* £800.

1 Once we've settled ...., we'll invite you for a long weekend.

2 Could you please see .... getting the sofa re-covered?

3 They settled .... the Ritz as the best place for the reception.

4 We made an appointment to see .... the cottage before we decided to buy it.

5 The children were seen .... at the station by the entire family.

6 Could you see .... those messages while I read through this report?

7 He said he would make me a rich man, but I saw .... him immediately.

8 After wandering for years, they settled .... in a small village in Wales.

9 He saw his best friend .... his divorce.

10 I'll see you ....; you may not be able to find your way to the lift.

11 Let's settle .... with the waiter and go home. I'm feeling tired.

IDIOMS/FIXED PHRASES 1

be (as) thick (as a brick):	be stupid
on second thoughts:	having changed one's mind
lay the table:	prepare/set the table for a meal
play truant:	stay away from school without permission
red tape:	unnecessary bureaucracy
touch and go:	with uncertain result
put two and two together:	arrive at the truth by looking at the facts
in a tick:	shortly, soon
through thick and thin:	whatever happens
out of turn:	not in the correct order/time

5 *Fill in the blanks with one of the idioms/fixed phrases.*

0 "Are you coming?" shouted Tim's father. "Yes, I'll be ready *in a tick*", replied Tim.

1 That man .... He can't even add up two and two without making a mistake.

2 "Dinner is ready. Will someone .... please?" mother said.

3 "Will he live?" asked the nurse. "Well, it's .... whether he will or not."

4 Although she didn't say anything directly, we .... and realised that she was about to resign from her job.

5 "Don't ever leave me", pleaded Sally. "Don't worry, we'll be together ....," answered Jim.

6 With so much .... involved, the government have made it very difficult for foreigners to obtain a work permit.

7 "Write this essay for homework," the teacher said. "No, ..., do it now", he added.

8 When he was at school he always .... on Mondays, to go to the cinema.

9 The debate became unmanageable when everyone started speaking ....

IDIOMS/FIXED PHRASES 2

(by) trial and error:	learning from one's mistakes
not be one's cup of tea:	not suit one's taste
be ahead of one's time:	have progressive ideas (opp.: be behind the times)
for the time being:	temporarily
in the nick of time:	just in time
kill time:	pass time while waiting for sb/sth
come to terms with:	accept a difficult situation
be tickled pink:	be really pleased
paint the town red:	have a great time
take one's time:	not hurry

6 *Fill in the blanks with one of the idioms/fixed phrases.*

0 They went for a walk to *kill time* while they waited for the ferry.

1 The inventor was .... when he invented a space rocket in the last century.

2 John and several of his friends went out to .... on his stag night.

3 The ambulance men arrived ....
.... to resuscitate the heart attack victim.
4 After six years, she still cannot ....
.... the fact that her husband left her.
5 Don't eat your food so quickly; ....
.... and enjoy it.
6 My grandmother ....
when she won at bingo last week.
7 You can use my spare room ....
.... but you must look for a flat of your own.
8 The chef often comes up with his best recipes after
a tedious process of ....
9 Opera isn't ....;
I prefer rock music.

PREPOSITIONS

7 *Look at Appendix 5 and fill in the blanks with the correct preposition.*

0 While running to answer the telephone, I tripped *over* my brother's briefcase.
1 Being new .... the neighbourhood, they were unable to find where the greengrocer's was.
2 That's typical .... Peter to refuse to help!
3 I'm having trouble .... my car; it keeps stalling.
4 Jenny is terrified .... flying.
5 Our neighbours are very tolerant ....
the noise we make.
6 My father is fascinated with cars. In fact, he's in the garage tinkering .... the old Ford right now.
7 Tuck your shirt .... your trousers!
8 The river was teeming .... trout.
9 She is so thirsty .... success that she would do anything.
10 He triumphed .... his competitors by flooding the market place with advertising.
11 She's patient .... children and so is a very good teacher.

8 *Look at Appendix 5 and fill in the blanks with the correct preposition.*

0 The neighbours are very anxious *for* their missing daughter to phone home.
1 Don't tell me you like his taste ....
clothes! He looks terrible!

2 Working flexitime has many advantages .... regular working hours.
3 This summer, admission .... most cinemas is double what it was last year.
4 The customer was very angry .... the assistant's casual attitude towards him.
5 Young children are awkward .... dancing as they can't co-ordinate their movements well.
6 Her admission .... guilt shocked everyone; no one thought she was capable of fraud.
7 My husband is so awkward .... a needle and thread that I have to sew on all his shirt buttons myself.
8 I was very angry .... being woken up in the middle of the night by an alarm bell.
9 My new computer has the advantage ....
being more compact than my old one.
10 The government was anxious ....
the influx of refugees into the country.

9 *Complete the second sentence so that it has a similar meaning to the first sentence, using the word given. Do not change the word given. You must use between three and eight words, including the word given.*

1 Sheila often suffers from really bad headaches.
prone
Sheila ....
.... really bad headaches.
2 How inconsiderate he was to take your book!
thoughtless
It ....
.... your book.
3 He suggested that we should invite Tom to the party.
invited
He ....
.... to the party.
4 My grandmother was nearly 86 when she died earlier this year.
now
My grandmother, ...
.... 86.
5 The price of oranges has fallen because there are so many on the market.
such
There is ....
.... on the market that the price has fallen.

6 Very few residents came to the meeting last night.
poorly
The ....
.... attended.

7 Parking is not allowed in this street.
prohibited
It ....
.... in this street.

8 In our family, my brother is the best at cooking.
cooks
There's no-one ....
.... my brother.

9 These low-lying areas are constantly threatened by floods.
flooding
There ....
.... these low-lying areas.

10 I thought that you might like to go on holiday with us.
wondering
I ....
.... to go on holiday with us.

11 He suddenly realised that she was never coming back.
dawned
It ....
.... she was never coming back.

12 I can't possibly finish this work without your help.
depending
I ....
.... this work.

13 The new presenter certainly has plenty of confidence.
lack
The new presenter ....
.... confidence.

14 Meg wants it to be clear to people that she's fair.
seen
Meg ....
.... fair.

15 I want to go to London for our holiday but my husband won't even consider the idea.
hear
My husband ....
.... for our holiday.

16 The original plan was to complete the building by August.
due
The ....
.... August.

17 Do you think there's any chance of the socialist party winning the election this time round?
get
Do you think there's any chance ....
.... this time round?

18 Since the advertisement, we've had more applications than we can deal with.
swamped
Since the advertisement, ...
.... applications.

19 I feel it's wrong that this site is going to be redeveloped by the council.
earmarked
I feel it's wrong that ....
.... the council.

20 When Rania stood next to the basketball players, she looked very small.
dwarfed
When Rania stood next to the basketball players,
.... them.

21 Unfortunately, the rain forced the cancellation of the parade at the weekend.
rained
Unfortunately, the ....
.... at the weekend.

22 Mary was always making John the subject of her cruel jokes.
butt
John ....
.... cruel jokes.

23 Susy managed to cope with so many problems when she was declared bankrupt.
stride
Susy ....
.... when she was declared bankrupt.

24 The M.P. often had a different opinion from the accepted Party policies.
step
The M.P. ....
.... his Party's policies.

25 I's so busy at the moment that I can't take on any extra work.
plate
I ....
.... at the moment that
I can't take on any extra work.

FIXED PHRASES

at one's own pace:	at a speed which is comfortable for one
go to great pains:	try hard to do sth because it is important
feel below/under par:	feel tired and unable to work etc as well as usual
pass up:	not take a chance or opportunity
in passing:	incidentally
not put it past sb:	not be surprised if sb did sth they shouldn't
not a patch on (inf):	not nearly as good as; not comparable
bring sb down a peg or two:	reduce sb to their true status
phase in:	introduce gradually
say your piece:	give your view or opinion
pile up:	mount up
feel the pinch:	be in a difficult financial situation
play at (inf):	do sth others don't understand
take the plunge:	take a/the risk
pluck up the courage:	make an effort to be brave
plumb new depths:	be worse than ever
go to pot (inf):	deteriorate
keep sb posted:	keep sb informed
pit your wits against sb (or sth):	compete with sb (or sth) in intelligence/a test of knowledge
at a premium:	1) at a higher price than usual because it is scarce 2) wanted/needed but difficult to get/ achieve
press on/ahead:	continue determinedly

10 Complete the sentences using one of the fixed phrases in an appropriate form.

1 You are allowed to work .... in this relaxed, friendly company.

2 Houses with gardens and garages are often .... in city centres.

3 He mentioned, just ...., that he had spent some years in the navy.

4 You ...., as you feel so strongly on this matter and then I'll tell you what I think.

5 Just what did you think you were .... , going behind my back like that?

6 It is a pointless exercise .... a computer in chess tournaments.

7 I would .... Gus to leave the firm without giving notice.

8 Since I broke my leg last week the housework has just been ...., I'm afraid.

9 Many people feel that the welfare system is ...., due to lack of funding.

10 You shouldn't .... that opportunity of a once-in-a-lifetime round the world cruise.

11 Unless we .... with our effort, the project won't be completed on time.

11 Choose the correct item.

1 Victoria went to great .... to complete a high quality presentation.
A pains   C efforts
B torment   D difficulty

2 Julia's work is not a .... on Natalie's.
A spot   C scratch
B patch   D scrap

3 Somebody as conceited as Ron needs bringing down a .... or two.
A step   C peg
B notch   D rung

4 New technology is being .... in at work.
A shown   C installed
B phased   D filtered

5 Many people are feeling the .... now that there is an economic recession.
A strain   C pinch
B prod   D pain

6 I have no appetite and I am lethargic. I've been feeling under .... for ages.
A pair   C stress
B par   D threat

7 The economic situation makes many people unwilling to take the .... and open their own businesses.
A initiative   C plunge
B bull   D opportunity

8 I don't know how I can .... up the courage to tell him the awful news.
A pick   C store
B pluck   D set

9 The new soap opera on Channel 3 .... new depths in terms of tastelessness.
A plumbs   C fills
B reaches   D achieves

10 We'll keep you .... of any further changes in the examination specifications.
A noticed   C mailed
B announced   D posted

12 *For questions 1-10, read the text below and decide which answer (A, B, C or D) best fits each gap.*

A MUSICAL CITY

Strolling to the **(0)** .... of Narodni brought us to Wenceslas Square, which is really a(n) **(1)** .... boulevard, dominated at one end by a(n) **(2)** .... statue of the good king in front of the National Museum. Concerts are **(3)** .... there every evening and **(4)** ...., the audience sits on the stairs (a(n) **(5)** .... feature at other venues) of the museum's main hall. Wherever you go in central Prague, you will be **(6)** .... bits of paper **(7)** .... the virtues of various rival concerts, which are a feature of this **(8)** .... city. Most of the concerts last about an hour and revolve around the more popular classics. **(9)** .... musical evenings take place at St. Francis of Assisi at the approach to the King Charles' Bridge. These tend to be a little 'heavier', however, **(10)** .... the work of more serious composers such as Bach.

	A	B	C	D
0	finish	stop	end	extremity
1	extensive	broad	ample	immense
2	impressive	touching	inspiring	stirring
3	held	taken	retained	contained
4	traditionally	historically	conventionally	ordinarily
5	normal	public	common	usual
6	handed	passed	circulated	provided
7	commending	applauding	supporting	extolling
8	vigorous	virulent	vibrant	virile
9	Customary	Typical	Routine	Regular
10	exhibiting	featuring	exposing	showing

13 *Match the phrases, then explain the proverbs.*

Column A	Column B	
0 Better safe	a is not gold.	0 *d*
1 He who pays the piper	b is lost.	1 ....
2 All that glitters	c in for a pound.	2 ....
3 A trouble shared	d than sorry.	3 ....
4 Blood	e breeds contempt.	4 ....
5 He who hesitates	f saves nine.	5 ....
6 A stitch in time	g is thicker than water.	6 ....
7 In for a penny	h you gain on the roundabouts.	7 ....
8 What you lose on the swings	i calls the tune.	8 ....
9 Familiarity	j is a trouble halved.	9 ....

WORD USAGE

14 *Use the words given in capitals at the end of some of the lines to form a word that fits in the space on the same line.*

FINDING INFORMATION

Almost one in ten children have stopped using **(0)** *reference* books and are relying on **REFER**
electronic sources, chiefly the Internet, to get their information, according to a full study of
reading habits. All age groups of the **(1)** .... were involved in the survey from **POPULATE**
young children to the elderly. The report offers the first **(2)** .... evidence that **STATISTIC**
a new generation of children growing up in the microchip era has **(3)** .... **MARK**
different attitudes to the **(4)** .... of knowledge from those of their parents. **ACQUIRE**
After the age of five, a small **(5)** .... about 15% make use of electronic **MINOR**
sources. However, this percentage increases **(6)** .... to more than half for **DRAMA**
12-16 year olds, where **(7)** .... sources of information are used in favour **DIGIT**
of text-books. After this age, the **(8)** .... of people using technology **PERCENT**
to acquire information falls sharply and books, **(9)** .... in earlier ages, **POPULAR**
are more widely used. Evidence also reveals a **(10)** .... difference **SUBSTANCE**
in the attitude of parents and their offspring to attaining knowledge. The 180-page study
indicates that the old habit of reading books continues to flourish despite all counter
attractions, as by far the biggest cultural pastime in Britain.

15 *Choose the correct item.*

0 Relief workers .... hundreds of crates of second-hand clothing which had been donated.
  (A) unpacked   C unwrapped
  B revealed   D unveiled

1 The Queen was present at the official .... of the statue.
  A revealing   C unwrapping
  B unpacking   D unveiling

2 The hut finally fell down, unable to .... days of violent winds and rain.
  A put up with   C support
  B withstand   D afford

3 As a single parent, it's difficult for her to .... a family.
  A support   C put up with
  B afford   D withstand

4 I phoned the company, who .... me that my goods had been despatched.
  A confirmed   C assured
  B guaranteed   D reassured

5 Please send a reply to the wedding invitation in order to .... your attendance.
  A guarantee   C assure
  B confirm   D reassure

6 It was extremely .... of you to drive home in that blizzard.
   A adventurous   C impervious
   B reckless   D instinctive

7 I really admire the hero of the film. He's so ....
   A reckless   C foolhardy
   B adventurous   D instinctive

8 The weekend is over, so tomorrow morning it's back to the ....
   A grind   C drudgery
   B labour   D toil

9 Looking after a house, four children, a lazy husband and two dogs is real ....
   A labour   C toil
   B drudgery   D grind

COLLOCATIONS

16 a) Fill in polish, brush.

0 *polish* shoes   4 .... silverware
1 .... the cat   5 .... nails
2 .... hair   6 .... clothes
3 .... teeth   7 .... a speech

b) Fill in dirty, squalid.

0 *dirty* mind   4 .... lifestyle
1 .... conditions 5 .... knees
2 .... trick   6 .... town
3 .... clothes   7 .... flat

17 Collocate the expressions with words from the given list.

   • covet • entice • repel • bolt • conform
   • rejoice • avenge • harvest • sip

0 *bolt* your food.
1 .... at good news
2 .... a drink
3 .... sb's death
4 .... the corn
5 .... sb's possessions
6 .... to society's ideas
7 .... sb into wrongdoing
8 .... sb with your rudeness

18 Think of one word only which can be used appropriately in all three sentences.

0 • One doesn't need to be an expert to *appreciate* the beauty of classical music.
  • He seems confident that houses in this area will *appreciate* in value in the next few years.
  • I'll always *appreciate* your help and support.

1 • The manufacturers .... the faulty appliances from department stores nationwide.
  • After the diplomatic row between the two countries, Ruritania .... its ambassador for consultation.
  • When the old lady .... her childhood, her memories were of happy, carefree days.

2 • You've been crying; what's the ....?
  • It is not so much a .... of justice being done as of its being seen to be done.
  • I'm taking these magazines so as to have plenty of reading .... for the train journey.

3 • It was a local citizen of .... who founded the civic centre.
  • Tom found a short .... on the table telling him that his dinner was in the oven.
  • A .... of bitterness was heard in Cynthia's voice.

4 • If money were no ...., as far as I'm concerned, I would travel round the world.
  • The .... of the game is to score as many points as possible.
  • It was a curious ...., which was presumably used in Victorian kitchens.

5 • It escaped my .... that my keys were still on the table when I closed the door.
  • Gilbert handed in his .... after he had found a better job.
  • The large .... on the bench read "wet paint".

6 • During the ...., many ordinary citizens suffered.
  • Paragliding is a dangerous .... but an enjoyable way to spend time.
  • The student .... prevented lectures from taking place.

7 • A .... injury kept Gerry away from the office for a couple of days.
  • Shirley has had a few .... roles in films, but she is certainly not the star that she makes herself out to be.
  • When Francis was at university, he majored in modern languages but his .... subject was European Studies.

223

PREPARING FOR PART 5

WORKING WITH "ECHOED" IDEAS II

19 *Read the following passages and answer the questions that follow. One item has been answered for you.*

Silk is an animal fibre produced from the cocoons of silkworms. The origin of silk production is ancient, but the industry actually began in China sometime before the 3rd millennium BC. Silk was sought by countries and was traded throughout Europe. **(0) The smooth, lustrous qualities of silk** made it a highly prized commodity in the west and became identified with a particularly lavish lifestyle. After World War II, the production of synthetic fibres replaced silk. **(1) Man-made fibres were considered practical and far more convenient to maintain and use**. As a consequence, the silk industry declined in western countries.

It is becoming increasingly difficult to find garments made of natural fibres. The clothes market is full of easy-to-wash, cheap-to-wear synthetic materials. Once on your skin, the body is unable to breathe. People are forgetting the feel and look of some of nature's alternatives, such as cotton, linen or wool, which were once an essential part of one's wardrobe. **(0) Silk, for instance, is a fine, luxurious material** which is expensive but well worth the price. The quality of a silk blouse or evening dress can never be matched by any synthetic counterpart.

(0) Which sentence in the second passage echoes the idea of silk having *"smooth, lustrous qualities"* expressed in the first passage?

"Silk for instance, is a fine, luxurious material."

(1) Which sentence in the second passage echoes the idea that *"Man-made fibres were considered practical and far more convenient to maintain and use"* expressed in the first passage?

....

....

These days, neither war nor commerce forces ships to circumnavigate the globe – one reason why only three vessels of any type have beaten the challenge set for Phileas Fogg in Jules Verne's *Around the World in 80 Days*. The three vessels to attempt the journey were all sailboats vying for the trophy bearing the author's name. The record holder *Spoc-Elec* sailed around the world via Cape Horn in 71 days in 1997. This feat demonstrated the ability to maintain high speed in the open ocean, and at the same time underscored a major problem facing a powerboat trying to make the same trip: **(2) the restrictions imposed by having to use fuel**.

One of the greatest challenges faced by balloonists attempting to fly around the world is minimising the delay caused by refuelling stops. Most balloonists plan between three and six stops, with a small number of possible alternative locations should the weather not permit them to land in their first-choice destinations. In the need for speed, stopping as few times as possible is essential; however, the need for long distances to be covered between refuelling stations means that the aircraft must be equipped with a large, heavy fuel deposit. Some research has begun to take place with the intention of establishing whether more frequent stops could be more efficient: a 15% difference in aircraft weight could add up to 35% more airspeed – not to mention the added bonus of being able to refuel in dozens of alternative locations.

(2) Which two phrases in the second passage give examples of *"the restrictions imposed by having to use fuel"* discussed in the first passage?

....

....

MOLINEUX 50s STAR SAYS GOODBYE

1950s Wolves full-back William Rask died from a heart attack at his Leigh-on-Sea holiday home yesterday. He was 82 years old.

(3) Rask was influential in the team's success in the late 50s, forming the backbone of the club's defensive line-up along with George Mariner during the 1958 and 1959 seasons, when Wolves won the championship for two years in a row.

Molineux officials have organised a friendly game against Rochdale, the club at which Rask began his career, for June 25. Gate receipts will be donated to the British Heart Foundation

Although Will was a rare goal-scorer, I remember one particular goal back in '58 which practically gave Wolves the championship. With three matches to be played, we were at the top of the table, leading Arsenal by 5 points. That Saturday we played Arsenal at Highbury; we were 1-0 down with a few minutes to go, when Willy came out of his defence and equalised with a header. Only two points were awarded for a win back then, so we were champions at the final whistle.

But Willy's contribution to the team over the eight years at Molineux was too extensive to be described with isolated, concrete examples. He exhibited a team spirit which bound us all together and a highly infectious enthusiasm which gave the team maximum motivation.

(3) Which two qualities discussed in the second passage elaborate on the statement that *"Rask was influential in the team's success in the late 50s"* made in the first passage?

....

....

One of the biggest drawbacks of owning a satellite TV system is the inability to view local terrestrial channels – you need either a standard TV antenna or a subscription to cable TV as well. Now that may be changing as more satellites are becoming available for local channels.

Leading the way is Echostar, which launched a satellite for its Dish Network last October and plans another this spring. These satellites allow the company to offer local channels on a market-by-market basis. The content from both satellite and terrestrial programmes can be merged onto your on-screen output, so you can easily flick from satellite to terrestrial reception without having to switch off your decoder.

I decided to blow £25 a month on satellite TV. Not being a techno-wizard, I could not understand why I couldn't just get my TV to show the terrestrial channels after watching something on satellite. **(4) The man from the satellite TV company said that I needed to do two things: firstly, get a double antenna jack which must be installed on the back of my TV; secondly, switch off my satellite TV decoder whenever I want to view something on terrestrial.** Now, he could have someone to come over to my place and take care of the technical side of things, but that would "incur a small cost." And if I want a composite remote control which will automatically switch off my satellite system whenever I choose to view a terrestrial channel, no problem – he'd send me one for £19.95.

Do TV companies remember the word "sensitivity?"

(4) Which sentence in the first passage states that Echostar technology solves the problem with conventional satellite decoders described in the bold part of the second passage?

....

....

11c Practice Test Eleven

Paper 3 Use of English   Time: 1 hour 30 minutes

Read the text below and think of the word which best fits each space. Use only one word in each space.

AN ECONOMIC PROBLEM

Inflation is not a new phenomenon, **(0)** *but* one that has existed at various times in various places. In **(1)** .... severest form, **(2)** ...., hyperinflation can destroy a nation's economy. **(3)** .... happened in revolutionary France and Weimar Germany, **(4)** .... bundles of notes were needed to pay for a loaf of bread. But what is inflation? Briefly, it may be defined **(5)** .... a continual increase in prices affecting the economy. The rate of inflation is determined **(6)** .... changes in the price level, which is an average of all prices. When **(7)** .... prices rise while others fall, this will not necessarily affect the price level, as inflation occurs **(8)** .... if most major prices increase. The problem with inflation is that it reduces the value **(9)** .... purchasing power of money, as well as eroding people's savings. Wage increases which are below or equal **(10)** .... the level of inflation will result in a declining or static **(11)** .... of living for workers, while wage increases above the rate of inflation will merely stoke the fire for further inflation. So what can a government do to stop the process? It can increase taxes, raise interest rates, decrease the money supply, reduce government spending or set a ceiling **(12)** .... price and wage rises. **(13)** .... none of these is a popular measure is understandable, but if they reduce inflation **(14)** .... a mild two to four percent per annum, as opposed to allowing it to rise to double-digit severe inflation, it is preferable in the **(15)** .... run.

Read the text below. Use the word given in capitals at the end of some of the lines to form a word that fits in the space in the same line.

MINOAN RECREATION

The Minoans were a sport-centred society. In **(0)** *antiquity* all sports were ultimately	ANTIQUE
derived from religious rituals, but by the time the Cretans were enjoying their palace	
civilisation, sport had passed over into a **(16)** .... activity.	RECREATION
A great deal can be surmised about Cretan sports because they are a common subject of	
wall paintings and vase **(17)** .... One of the most frequently illustrated	SCULPT
(18) .... in Minoan painting and ceramics was the sport of bull jumping.	ACT
Bull jumping was a test of both courage and **(19)** .... We can imagine the	AGILE
difficulty of vaulting either onto a charging bull's back or over it in a somersault landing	
with one's feet on the other side of the bull from the eloquent depictions of this event on	
Minoan vase work.	
Successful execution of the event involved **(20)** .... seizing	PARTICIPATE
hold of the horns of a bull in full charge at the moment when it tosses its head. Completion	
of a successful somersault depended upon the **(21)** .... using	COMPETE
the **(22)** .... from the bull's violent head jerk and using it	MOMENT
(23) .... to either mount or vault along the length of the bull's body.	GRACE
The Minoan depictions of this event reveal a remarkably elegant sport **(24)**	RELY
on precise timing that seemed less about bravery and strength than about spectacle and	
fluidity and, unlike in modern-day bullfighting, the animal was **(25)**	HARM

PART 3

Think of one word only which can be used appropriately in all three sentences.

0 • One doesn't need to be an expert to *appreciate* the beauty of classical music.
  • He seems confident that houses in this area will *appreciate* in value in the next few years.
  • I'll always *appreciate* your help and support.

26 • The patient .... his gaze on the hypnotist's swinging watch.
  • Although the plumber .... the broken drainpipe, he charged a fortune for it.
  • Well, have you .... a date for the wedding?

27 • The young actress was delighted to land one of the leading .... in Blomfeld's latest film.
  • Spare .... are not always available for older domestic appliances.
  • The medicine should be diluted so that it is two .... water to one third medicine.

28 • This chair is so .... that I need a cushion.
  • Len has always found maths a .... subject to do.
  • A .... winter had destroyed all the flowers in the garden.

29 • If the weather is fine on Sunday, let's go for a .... in the country.
  • The .... for survival kept the castaway alive for weeks.
  • The new manager has plenty of .... and enthusiasm.

30 • Dennis Shepton has been .... as the greatest portraitist of his century.
  • Although she had a cultivated accent, she obviously .... from a working-class background.
  • He .... a taxi, jumped in and it sped away.

31 • The .... of this needle is so small that I can't thread it.
  • Suddenly they found themselves at the .... of the storm.
  • Joe has an .... for recognising gifted new artists.

PART 4

Complete the second sentence so that it has a similar meaning to the first sentence, using the word given. Do not change the word given. You must use between three and eight words, including the word given.

0 Nobody spoke when the teacher asked who the culprit was.
  remained
  Everyone *remained silent when the teacher asked* who the culprit was.

32 The sofa and the carpet are a good match.
  well
  The sofa ....
  .... carpet.

33 There is someone in the office twenty-four hours a day.
  staffed
  The office ....
  .... day.

34 Each new generation is given the family jewels.
  down
  The ....
  .... generation.

35 The government received many criticisms concerning their new housing policy.
  few
  The government came ....
  .... of their new housing policy.

36 He was given an honorary medal by the military.
  conferred
  An honorary medal ....
  .... by the military.

37 She claimed she handed in her resignation as a result of provocation.
  provoked
  She claimed ....
  .... her resignation.

38 Miranda's mother became very emotional when she saw her daughter in her wedding dress.
  overcome
  Miranda's mother ....
  .... in her wedding dress.

39 Is there enough ice cream for everyone, or shall I go and buy some more?
  round
  Is there ....
  ...., or shall I go and buy some more?

227

PART 5

For questions **40-44**, read the following texts. For questions **40 - 43**, answer with a word or short phrase. You do not need to write complete sentences. For question **44**, write a summary according to the instructions given.

The typical Romantics were young men, often university students, although they didn't always take their studies very seriously. They had a strong anti-middle class approach to life and would refer to the police or their landladies as "philistines", or simply as "the enemy". The first generation of Romantics were young in about 1800, and we could actually label the Romantic Movement as the first of Europe's student uprisings.

The Romantics were not very different from the hippies of the 1960s and 70s. "Idleness is the ideal of genius, and indolence the virtue of the Romantic" was their motto. It was the duty of the Romantic to experience life uniquely – to dream himself away from it. Day-to-day business could be taken care of by the "philistines".

Both Byron and Shelley were Romantic poets. Byron, moreover, provided the Romantic Age with its idol, the Byronic hero - the alien, moody, rebellious spirit – in life as well as art. Byron himself could be both wilful and passionate. Being also handsome, he was besieged by women of fashion. Public gossip attributed the romantic adventures of his verses to his own life, but, although he had numerous relationships, true love remained as elusive for him as Novalis's blue flower.

40 What does the first paragraph tell us about the way Romantics viewed various forms of authority?

....

....

41 What can be inferred from the passages about the Romantics' attitude to work?

....

....

Byron had a profound impact on European and especially French Romanticism. The influence derived mainly from a character type, the "Byronic hero", first portrayed in Cantos I and II of *Childe Harold* and thereafter developed in many

line 4 —— of his other works. This figure haunted 18th and 19th century literature. He is a man greater than others in emotion, capability and suffering. Only among wild and vast forms of nature, the ocean, the precipices and glaciers of the Alps, can he find a counterpart to his own titanic passions. No one can resist his hypnotic fascination and authority. He has committed a sin that expresses his superiority, and lesser men could not even conceive such a transgression. Against his own suffering, he brings a superhuman pride and fortitude.

Many assume that this hero was Byron's projection of how he understood his own self, although considerably exaggerated. They say that Byron lived a wanderer's life, running away from a mysterious sin he committed when young,

line 14 —— constantly looking for new challenges or even new confrontation. The remark is somewhat unfounded, since it takes the premise that Byron was a widely travelled man to mean that he was lonely, angry and unloved. It only takes a slightly more careful reading of Byron's works to realise that the writer's psychosynthesis is quite different from the sinister darkness within the Byronic hero's soul.

42 What does the writer mean by the sentence "This figure haunted 18th and 19th century literature"? (line 4)

....

....

43 What does the phrase "The remark" refer to in line 14?

....

....

44 In a paragraph of between 50 and 70 words, summarise what the two passages tell us about Lord Byron's life and personality.

....

....

....

....

....

....

....

....

UNIT 12a Grammar: Causative form

Have + object + past participle is used to suggest that we are *instructing* someone to do something for us.
I'll ask the mechanic to repair my car.
I'll have my car repaired. (not I myself but the mechanic will do the work.)

Notes

- The verb *to have* forms its question and negative with **do/does** in the Simple Present and **did** in the Simple Past.
  Don't print the files, please!
  ***Don't have** the files printed, please!*

- **Have/get + object + past participle** can also be used to replace a passive verb usually describing an accident or misfortune.
  *He **had/got** his car stolen. (= his car was stolen)*

- **Get + object + past participle** can be used to mean *finish doing something* or to replace *have* in the structure ***have something done**.*
  *I must **get my homework done** over the weekend.*
  *You should **get your trousers taken in** now that you've lost weight.*

- **Get + object + to infinitive** means *make or persuade somebody* to do something.
  *The coach **got the players to train** hard for five hours every day.*
  *See if you can **get Paul and Mary to join** us at the concert.*

- **Get + object + present participle (-ing)** is used informally to mean **make somebody/something start doing something**.
  *Once you **get her talking** about her travels, she never stops.*
  Also: get moving; get going (without an object)

- **Have + object + bare infinitive,** though not common in British English, is used for giving instructions or orders.
  *The teacher **had the pupils do** the exercises in class.*

- **Want** and **need** are also used with an object and a past participle, to indicate that you would like or need sth to be done.
  *I **want** the room **cleaned**.*
  *I **need** the reports **checked**.*

---

1 *Rewrite the following sentences without changing the meaning of the sentences printed before them.*

0 The repairman is servicing her television.
She *is having her TV serviced (by the repairman).*
....

1 Someone was setting up Jim's computer when there was an electricity black-out.
Jim ....

2 The tailor hemmed my new trousers.
I ....
....

3 Someone washed all the windows in Ruth's home.
Ruth ....
....

4 Someone is editing his thesis.
He ....

5 The dentist has whitened her teeth.
She ....

6 The insurance company is inspecting Lyn's car.
Lyn ....
....

7 The shoe repairer dyed Anna's white shoes.
Anna ....
....

8 The workman will tar the restaurant's roof for us.
We ....
....

9 The store will deliver my aunt's new refrigerator to her flat.
My aunt ....
....

CONVERSATIONAL GRAMMAR

2 *Choose the correct item.*

1 "How did the bride wear her hair?"
"She .... into a bun."
A had it styled   C has styled it
B had been styled it   D has had it styled

2 "Why doesn't Constance buy a dishwasher?"
"She can't .... because there isn't enough space in her kitchen."
A have one installed   C have one install
B have installed one   D have install one

3 "Has Paul moved back to his house?"
"Yes. He .... all the earthquake damage repaired."
A has had   C had
B has   D had been having

4 "Why are there so many workers in Zoe's garden?"
"She .... it landscaped."
A had   C will have had
B had had   D is having

5 "Your shoes look new."
"I .... by the hotel porter."
A had polished them   C have them polished
B had them polished   D have polished them

6 "What are you going to wear to dinner?"
"I don't know. I wish I .... my lace dress cleaned yesterday."
A have had   C was having
B would have   D had had

7 "We were thinking about doing our place up."
"Oh, ... the house completely renovated; just revamp it with some new furnishings."
A don't have   C not to have
B haven't   D not having

8 "When do you want this report by?"
"I'd like .... finished by 4 o'clock."
A to have the work   C have the work been
B the work to have   D having the work

9 "Why is Ron so upset?"
"He .... broken into."
A gets a house   C didn't get his house
B hasn't got a house   D has had his house

10 "Where've you been Mary?"
"Well, my tutor .... some research into post graduate studies."
A made me to do   C got me to do
B had me to do   D put me do

11 "Did the kids enjoy the circus?"
"Absolutely! The clown got them .... all the time."
A laugh   C to laugh
B to be laughing   D laughing

12 Shall we get .... ? It's getting late.
A to go   C going
B go   D gone

STRUCTURAL CONVERSION

1 *Somebody is going* to water the flowers for her.
She's going to have the flowers watered.
2 *Your hair needs* cutting.
You'll have to have your hair cut.
You should have your hair cut.
3 *I'm having* my house decorated.
My house is being decorated.
Someone is decorating my house.
4 *Is anyone* checking your answers?
Are you having your answers checked?

5 *The dentist filled* her tooth.
She had her tooth filled.
She got her tooth filled.
Her tooth **was filled**.
6 *I hate her asking* someone else to do her homework.
I hate her having her homework done by someone else.
7 *I'd love it* if someone cut the grass for me.
I'd love to have the grass cut.
8 *The hairdresser permed* my hair.
I got my hair permed at the hairdresser's.

231

3 *Complete the second sentence so that it has a similar meaning to the first sentence, using the word given. Do not change the word given. You must use between three and eight words, including the word given.*

1 All the arrangements were made by his secretary.
everything
He ....
.... by his secretary.

2 She burnt her hands during the fire.
got
She ....
.... the fire.

3 Are you going to have the roof fixed before winter?
repair
Are ....
.... before winter?

4 Our broken immersion heater must be repaired urgently.
seen
We must ....
.... urgently.

5 The windows need draught-proofing.
have
You'll ....
.... draught-proofed.

6 A famous architect designed their new home.
had
They ....
.... their new home.

7 It would be a good idea for an accountant to sort out your tax problems.
should
You ....
.... an accountant.

8 Her wedding dress is going to be made by a famous designer.
have
She ....
.... by a famous designer.

9 Joe's brother treated him to a meal.
paid
Joe ....
.... for him by his brother.

10 Henry is going to ask for professional help to upgrade his PC.
get
Henry ....
.... his PC.

11 An ophthalmic optician carried out a second operation on his eye.
perform
He ....
.... on his eye.

12 It would be a good idea for your teeth to be capped, you know.
ought
You ....
...., you know.

13 A party will be thrown for the twins when they return.
them
The twins ....
.... when they return.

14 We used to read fairytales to our children at bedtime.
them
Our children ....
.... at bedtime.

4 *Underline the correct item.*

0 Could you please have the parcel **deliver/delivered** by midday?

1 No matter what Jo said, she couldn't get him **to see/see** her point.

2 Sam **had his ankle broken/had broken his ankle** in the rugby match last night.

3 Jane had her favourite vase **smashing/smashed** by the removal men.

4 Get **to move/moving**, will you? We'll miss the train.

5 You should **have seen to this/have this seen to** as soon as possible.

6 Our teacher had us **working/to work** in pairs for this project.

7 Cassie **had her telephone reconnected/has reconnected her telephone** after she'd paid the bill.

5 *Read the text below and think of the word which best fits each space. Use only one word in each space.*

THE SIXTH SENSE

For many years scientists have been carrying **(0)** *out* research into the world of the unknown and unexplained.

One of the most fascinating categories of psychic phenomena is **(1)** .... of "precognition", the ability to foresee future events. Terms **(2)** .... as "prophecies", "auguries" and "miracles", familiar in ancient times, have been replaced by the scientific, **(3)** .... prosaic-sounding term "extrasensory perception" (ESP). This phenomenon is also commonly known as "the sixth sense", enabling a person who possesses it to know something in **(4)** .... of its happening, an experience **(5)** .... unknown by those who possess the ordinary five senses of hearing, sight, touch, taste and smell. Precognition may occur in the form of a dream or in a waking state. Many scientists have devoted their careers **(6)** .... investigating ESP phenomena. They describe their research field as "the science of parapsychology", derived **(7)** .... the word "paranormal", which ESP phenomena **(8)** .... said to be because they seem to be **(9)** .... the limits of our present understanding. Surveys have shown that belief in psychic powers remains strong all over the world, **(10)** .... a large percentage of people claiming to have actually experienced ESP. Considering the influence ESP has had **(11)** .... the history of mankind, from the time of the ancient Greeks, who often consulted the oracles in moments of crisis, it is difficult to comprehend **(12)** .... sceptics can brush all ESP phenomena aside as mere fantasy, hallucination or superstition, especially **(13)** .... the light of so many predictions having been proved to have come true.

Parapsychologists continue to study the paranormal but, as **(14)** ...., it remains unexplained. There may come a time, **(15)** ...., when ESP may become explicable in rational scientific terms.

PHRASAL VERBS 1

set about:	begin
set aside:	save for a special purpose
set back:	hinder
set sb back (inf):	cost sb a lot of money
set in:	begin (of a period, usu.bad)
set off:	1) start a reaction (inf)
	2) begin a journey (= set out)
set an animal on (sb):	cause an animal to attack sb
set out:	begin a task/job with a specific intention
set up:	1) establish (a record)
	2) start a business
	3) erect

6 *Fill in the correct preposition or adverb.*

0 We'd better have central heating installed before winter sets *in*.

1 A wedding reception for two hundred people will certainly set you .... thousands!

2 They set .... for their destination at 5 o'clock in the morning.

3 He set .... a new world record for the 100 metres race.

4 His jokes set the whole class .... laughing.

5 A fire in the factory set production .... by several weeks.

6 She set .... to become a dancer but an injury prevented her from fulfilling her ambition.

7 She decided to set .... a computer graphics firm with the money she inherited.

8 You'd better set .... some money every month if you want to buy a new car.

9 How would you set .... teaching a dog to perform tricks?

10 The town council has decided to set .... a memorial to the princess.

11 He threatened to set the dogs .... us if we didn't get off his property.

PHRASAL VERBS 2

stand by:	1) remain loyal to sb
	2) do nothing to stop a bad situation
	3) be ready for action
stand down:	resign from a position
stand for:	1) support sth
	2) mean, symbolise
	3) tolerate
	4) enter oneself for election
stand in for:	replace temporarily
stand out:	be conspicuous/obvious/better
stand up for:	defend/support
stand up to:	defend oneself against

IDIOMS/FIXED PHRASES 1

be up and about:	have recovered from an illness
be on the up and up:	improve steadily
up and coming:	likely to be successful
ups and downs:	good things alternating with bad ones
quick/slow on the uptake:	quick/slow to understand
make a flying visit:	make a quick trip
give vent to:	express sth freely
speak volumes:	be strong evidence of sb's feelings, merits etc
drive (sb) up the wall:	make sb angry/annoy sb
not hold water:	not seem reasonable or in accordance with the facts

7 *Fill in the correct preposition(s) or adverb.*

0 I'll stand *by* Ryan, no matter what people say about him.

1 His grandfather once stood .... Parliament, but he only got 56 votes.

2 Nobody would stand .... that sort of behaviour for a minute.

3 The police stood .... in case trouble broke out after the football match.

4 He's such a brilliant dancer that he stands .... from the rest of the troupe.

5 Our group stands .... equality for people of all races.

6 Could you stand .... John if he's called away?

7 You ought to stand .... your little brother when the others tease him.

8 The letters MP stand .... Member of Parliament.

9 How can you stand .... and watch him mistreat the children like that?

10 If he can't stand .... his opponent in a debate, he won't be a success in Parliament.

11 The President was forced to stand .... due to his involvement in the scandal.

8 *Fill in the blanks with one of the idioms/fixed phrases.*

0 We've had our *ups and downs* since we left London, but for the most part we're very happy living in the country.

1 In spite of the negative economic outlook, car sales .... this month.

2 The noise those builders are making is ....

3 Sarah .... her feelings of frustration and dissatisfaction when she spoke to her boss.

4 Unless you can support your argument with some statistics, I'm afraid it ....

5 In spite of the seriousness of the operation, she .... in a few days.

6 Although she said nothing about missing her husband, the expression on her face ....

7 The .... young actress had been offered a role in "The Tempest".

8 With only a few hours to spare, Sarah knew she could only .... to her old school.

9 Mike is so .... that you never have to repeat instructions twice.

IDIOMS/FIXED PHRASES 2

wet behind the ears:	inexperienced
make waves:	cause trouble
frosty welcome:	unfriendly reception
get out of bed on the wrong side:	be in a bad mood
give way to:	give in/yield
set in one's ways:	fixed in one's habits/routine
under the weather:	depressed/unwell
be all very well:	appear satisfactory but in fact not be
get wind of:	receive information about sth indirectly
no/little wonder:	not surprising

9 *Fill in the blanks with one of the idioms/fixed phrases.*

0 It's *no wonder* he's in a bad mood if it's true that his wife just left him.

1 If you always .... people's wishes, then they're bound to take advantage of you.

2 He's so .... that if you gave him tea at 4 o'clock instead of 4.30, he'd complain.

3 My boss accused me of .... when I complained about our working conditions.

4 It's .... him saying he'd replace the vase he broke but he hasn't done so yet!

5 She realised that her boss had .... when he snapped at her before she had even said good morning.

6 We got such a(n) .... when we arrived at the party that we almost wished we hadn't gone.

7 Although he's young and ...., he has such a pleasant manner that we decided to hire him.

8 I don't know how they .... our plans; I've certainly never discussed them with anyone.

9 John's been a bit .... lately, but I think he'll cheer up once we go on holiday.

PREPOSITIONS

10 *Look at Appendix 5 and fill in the blanks with the correct preposition.*

0 The food at that restaurant was labelled "unfit *for* human consumption" by the environmental health officer.

1 Your visa is valid .... one year and will subsequently need renewing.

2 She felt very uneasy .... leaving the baby with Miriam for the evening.

3 After suffering a major illness, he was very vulnerable .... minor ailments such as colds.

4 He didn't just express his aversion .... cloning but also argued .... it in a very persuasive way.

5 I can vouch .... Sandra's integrity, so I recommend we include her in our discussions.

6 The boys ran down to the garden and vaulted .... the fence at the bottom.

7 Clara is unswerving .... her determination to become a lawyer.

11 *Look at Appendix 5 and fill in the blanks with the correct preposition.*

1 Tom's absorption .... his studies means he has no social life.

2 Eating too much fat and sugar is detrimental .... your health.

3 The amount of water absorbed .... cotton wool is greater than that .... paper.

4 The bank wrote to me to advise me .... their new overdraft facilities.

5 If you need advice .... exam techniques, any of our trained staff will help you.

6 He cared .... the environment and gave an inspiring speech .... the issue.

7 At the Chinese restaurant we started .... spare ribs, then had chicken chop suey and coconut ice cream to finish.

8 The doctor advised us .... travelling to Egypt without having the proper inoculations first.

12 Complete the second sentence so that it has a similar meaning to the first sentence, using the word given. Do not change the word given. You must use between three and eight words, including the word given.

1 The government is always changing its policies on transportation.
lack
There's ....
.... policies on transportation.

2 Tom teased Alice about her new hairstyle.
poked
Tom ....
.... new hairstyle.

3 Fresh fruit is plentiful at this time of year.
shortage
There's ....
.... of year.

4 The prospect of meeting him again didn't please her.
forward
She ....
.... again.

5 The exhibition is likely to be a success.
probability
In ....
.... a success.

6 Could you tell me where the post office is?
direct
Could ....
.... post office?

7 Harvey ordered some new equipment without prior permission.
liberty
Harvey ....
.... some new equipment.

8 Naturally, you will have points deducted for misspellings.
penalised
Naturally, ...
.... misspellings.

9 Most scientists argue that it is preferable to use organic products.
averse
Most scientists ....
.... of organic products.

10 The new manager wants us to call him 'Sir'.
addressed
The new manager ....
.... 'Sir'.

11 I can't say I like it when she praises my work in front of my colleagues.
having
I can't say ....
.... in front of my colleagues.

12 You'll have to make up your minds by the weekend.
be
A ....
.... by the weekend.

13 It's just possible that we may have to introduce pay cuts.
ruled
We ....
.... pay cuts.

14 Surely he can't like it when she insults him in public.
being
Surely ....
.... in public.

15 Never forget that she hasn't had your education.
bear
You should ....
.... she hasn't had your education.

16 It's pointless going now; let's just stay in and watch TV.
well
We ....
.... and watch TV.

17 I don't think there's much chance of his coming now.
doubt
I ....
.... now.

18 I don't think they should expect that much of her.
asking
I ....
.... her.

19 Sharon has been promoted because she is capable of working under pressure.
account
Sharon has been promoted ....
.... to work under pressure.

20 Alex grimaced as he swallowed the foul-tasting medicine.
pulled
Alex ....
.... the foul-tasting medicine.

FIXED PHRASES

be/have (a) qualified success:	be partially successful
give sb no quarter:	show no mercy
a race against time:	work fast in order to do sth on time
rack one's brains:	try hard to think
lose one's rag (inf):	become angry
rain or shine:	in any circumstances
ram home sth:	make sth clear and forceful
go on the rampage:	rush about violently
raring to go:	eager to do sth or go somewhere
have/get a raw deal (inf):	be treated unfairly
take it as read:	accept sth as true without question
recharge your batteries:	take a break to renew/refresh yourself
on reflection:	after careful thought
be well rid of sb or sth:	better off without sb or sth
be taken for a ride:	be deceived/cheated
be as right as rain:	recover from an illness
hit the road (inf):	begin a journey
do a roaring trade:	sell a lot of sth
take the rough with the smooth:	accept unpleasant as well as pleasant situations
rub sth in:	insist on reminding sb of sth unpleasant or embarrassing
up and running:	operating normally

13 *Complete the sentences using one of the fixed phrases in an appropriate form.*

1 I'm going to watch the football match, ...

2 No matter how much I ...., I couldn't answer the riddle.

3 As a politician he is a forceful speaker and .... his point with great conviction.

4 The bull escaped from his pen and .... through the town, provoking panic in his wake.

5 Barry liked the idea of a fine arts course but .... he decided to go in for accountancy.

6 The job was making her so stressed and unhappy that she handed in her notice, deciding that she .... it.

7 It is a .... to find cures for many diseases of our time, including cancer and AIDS.

8 This particular interviewer .... to politicians that he interviews and insists on a direct answer to all his questions.

9 When somebody has made a mistake, it's kinder not to .... by constantly reminding them of it.

10 The doctor told Jo she'd be .... in no time as long as she took the course of antibiotics.

14 *Choose the correct item.*

1 The experimental play was only a .... success, which disappointed the playwright.
A local   C reserved
B qualified   D cautious

2 It takes time to get a financial system up and .... after the introduction of a new currency.
A walking   C running
B proceeding   D going

3 Life is so full of both good fortune and misfortunes that you have to learn to take the rough with the ....
A smooth   C calm
B ready   D tough

4 Stephen really lost his .... when his dental appointment was cancelled yet again.
A head   C calm
B voice   D rag

5 In today's competitive world, everyone needs a regular holiday to .... their batteries.
A refill   C rectify
B recast   D recharge

6 When my new motor kept breaking down, I knew I'd been taken for a .... by the second-hand car salesman.
A drive   C walk
B ride   D stroll

7 Don't take it as .... that you'll be promoted in your job; other colleagues stand a good chance too.
A fixed   C read
B standard   D word

8 Believing that the firm had given him a raw .... he took his case to an industrial tribunal.
A deal   C apple
B meal   D nerve

9 It was a hot summer day and ice cream salesmen were doing a .... trade.
A busy   C bustling
B lucrative   D roaring

15 *Find the mistake and correct it.*

0 He is used to ~~get~~ up early.   *getting*
1 He argued that he had good reason of what he had done. ....
2 I go to bed early in night. ....
3 His favourite play is "Scrabble". ....
4 The police have released a description of the asked man. ....
5 He denied to help me. ....
6 I told him that I would rather to be left alone. ....
7 I've always preferred contemporary music than classical. ....
8 There is no scientific proofs that life exists on Mars. ....
9 This law may help deter criminals commit crimes. ....
10 Civilisation seems to have done little progress in the last century. ....
11 I would prefer going now. ....

WORD USAGE

16 *Read the text below. Use the word given in capitals at the end of some of the lines to form a word that fits in the space in the same line.*

A JAPANESE TRADITION

Of the myriad of Japanese ceremonies introduced to the West, the Japanese tea ceremony would have to be the least (0) *accessible*. Like many aspects of Japanese culture, the practice of drinking tea was brought from China well over a thousand years ago. In Japan, green tea developed its own character, and the Japanese tea ceremony has evolved into a (1) .... Japanese phenomenon.
The modern tea ceremony can be traced back to the 17th century where it developed alongside another singular Japanese (2) .... of Chinese culture: the philosophy of Zen. The tea ceremony eventually became established as a recognised form of high art, where it was practised in diverse (3) ...., from a Zen temple to an ordinary home. Even today, the simplest and most secular tea ceremony still embraces the Zen aesthetic of simplicity, (4) .... and devotion.
During the ceremony strictly prescribed words of invitation and (5) .... are murmured quietly; tea maker and guests play their roles with (6) .... and respect.
A brief moment of profound tranquillity has been (7) .... created and shared. It is simultaneously an aesthetic, social and (8) .... moment.
Significantly, it is a Japanese moment, fleeting and poignant with its own (9) .... where the noise and confusion of the everyday world is temporarily suspended as a vague, (10) .... sense of the eternal pervades.

ACCESS

PECULIAR

ADAPT

LOCATE

AUSTERE
GRATEFUL
HUMBLE
COMMUNE
SPIRIT

PEACE
DEFINE

17 *Read the text below and decide which answer (A, B, C or D) best fits each gap.*

THE BBC ENGLISH DICTIONARY

The BBC, in the form of the language-teaching arm of the World Service, and Harper Collins have (0) .... forces to publish the BBC English Dictionary, "A Dictionary for the World". It is (1) .... at the 120 million listeners to the World Service who cannot find the expressions in (2) .... dictionaries. (3) .... on 70 million words broadcast at least ten times a year on the World Service, the compilers, (4) .... by Prof. John Sinclair, have included (5) .... expressions and word usage, without judging whether they are being used (6) .... Elizabeth Smith, the BBC's Controller of English Services, said: "Our language is (7) .... on statements by real people, like politicians and (8) .... which the BBC has accurately recorded. As broadcasters, we try to use a few idioms and metaphors but only to show that we (9) .... in the real world."

0	A connected	B joined	C attached	D fixed
1	A pointed	B directed	C trained	D aimed
2	A functional	B traditional	C conventional	D partial
3	A Counting	B Trying	C Drawing	D Bearing
4	A headed	B chaired	C dictated	D treated
5	A recent	B current	C nowadays	D late
6	A correctly	B truly	C sincerely	D finely
7	A designed	B made	C formed	D based
8	A so many	B thus far	C as to	D so on
9	A inhabit	B live	C stay	D be

(B) joined

0 It has been medically proven that a poor diet leads to .... growth.
A controlled
(B) stunted
C curbed
D tempered

1 My husband and I are not rich but we are ....
A wealthy
B tight
C comfortable
D hard-up

2 Bob is so short-tempered; he should try to .... his anger.
A curb
B control
C temper
D stunt

3 If you .... your demands, they may be accepted by others.
A control
B temper
C stunt
D curb

4 The teacher told us to .... the poem by the next lesson.
A remember
B recollect
C remind
D memorise

5 I don't .... her name, as we met only once.
A memorise
B reminisce
C recollect
D remind

6 Don't expect Alan to buy you a drink. He earns plenty of money but he's very ....
A hard-up
B wealthy
C tight
D comfortable

7 Could I borrow a few pounds? I'm a bit .... at the moment.
A comfortable
B wealthy
C tight
D hard-up

COLLOCATIONS

19 *Collocate the expressions with words from the given list.*

- jeopardise • elaborate • thwart • amplify
- excel • anchor • curb • supplement • dismantle
- ventilate

1 .... a car engine
2 .... a room
3 .... a ship
4 .... your future
5 .... on the facts
6 .... your temper
7 .... your diet with vitamins
8 .... the sound
9 .... in an exam
10 .... someone's plans

239

20 a) Fill in renew, restore.

1 .... a visa
2 .... order
3 .... a bus-pass
4 .... a relationship
5 .... a painting
6 .... to power
7 .... hope
8 .... a house

b) Fill in free, liberated.

1 .... spirit
2 .... feeling
3 .... gift
4 .... lifestyle
5 .... kick
6 .... of worry
7 .... woman
8 .... city

21 Collocate the expressions with words from the given list.

• mislead • represent • overhaul • pry • cheat • disregard • conspire • mix • gatecrash • compliment

1 .... eggs and flour together
2 .... sb into believing sth false
3 .... sb on a new dress
4 .... advice
5 .... into sb's private life
6 .... a party
7 .... your country in a sport
8 .... to do a deed
9 .... a system
10 .... at cards

22 a) Fill in refuse, deny.

1 .... an accusation
2 .... an invitation
3 .... the truth
4 .... help
5 .... a gift
6 .... a charge
7 .... access

b) Fill in the following collocational grid.

	with fear	hand	with horror	at the thought	voice	ground	with rage	with cold
trembling								
shuddering								
quaking								
shivering								

23 Collocate the expressions with words given from the list.

a) • seek • shield • hide • struggle • expose • exhibit • search • baffle • restrict • proclaim

1 .... a building
2 .... sb the winner
3 .... sb from harm
4 .... sb's freedom
5 .... sb with a problem
6 .... an answer
7 .... a painting
8 .... a politician's lies
9 .... your feelings
10 .... against oppression

b) • flit • outdo • prune • stroll • hire • amend • retain • flaunt • scour • accumulate

1 to .... from city to city
2 to .... dust
3 to .... a sense of perspective
4 to .... a text
5 to .... your rivals
6 to .... your wealth
7 to .... a place for clues
8 to .... a bush
9 to .... around the park
10 to .... a boat for the day

c) • challenge • scrape • lead • disclose • pledge • subscribe • show • be obsessed • release • bend

1 to .... a group of people
2 to .... to a magazine
3 to .... the rules
4 to .... someone's authority
5 to .... your loyalty to someone
6 to .... a document
7 to .... sympathy to someone
8 to .... with soap operas
9 to .... through an exam
10 to .... a secret

24 *Think of only one word which can be used appropriately in all three sentences.*

0
- One doesn't need to be an expert to **appreciate** the beauty of classical music.
- He seems confident that houses in this area will **appreciate** in value in the next few years.
- I'll always **appreciate** your help and support.

1
- After such a .... meal, the Prescotts thought it better to go for a walk.
- The .... bracelet was engraved with flowers and leaves.
- Reports have been coming in of .... traffic on all routes leading out of the city.

2
- The examiner gave the candidate no .... as to whether she had passed.
- A helpful .... is to put the mixture in the fridge for ten minutes before baking it.
- It's a delicious dish with just a .... of allspice and nutmeg.

3
- I'm living in Paris now but my permanent .... is Amsterdam.
- After buying a new computer, Glen had to find a .... for his old one.
- Being an orphan, Bobby was brought up alternately in a local authority .... and by foster parents.

4
- I feel .... after eating those mushrooms; they must have been off.
- The joke that Todd told was not very .... so nobody laughed.
- That's .... ; the car won't start, even though I had it serviced this morning.

5
- The discussion covered the same .... and still no one could find a solution to the problem.
- After the volcanic eruption, the .... in the surrounding area was much more fertile.
- The school governors made a big mistake when they sold off the playing .... opposite the school.

6
- The school had a .... of money available to subsidise class excursions.
- The Websters have dug a small ornamental .... in their garden.
- Walter was down at the leisure centre playing .... with his friends.

7
- It is difficult to hang curtains on that .... because there is a narrow pelmet hanging over it.
- I think I'd prefer to fly to Edinburgh rather than go by ....
- Maude held on firmly to the .... as she climbed slowly up the stairs.

8
- Despite lack of practice, his .... improved as the chess match progressed.
- Hunters returned empty-handed, the .... having been protected by animal rights activists.
- It was the first .... of the season and ten goals were scored.

9
- Parker .... in a brief speech that he would be leaving the company.
- It was once believed that dreams .... future events.
- The driver .... left but immediately turned right!

10
- Our local .... of Floyd's Bank has closed down, so now I have to trek all the way to the town centre to cash my cheques.
- A great-aunt of mine was a millionairess but I belong to the poorer .... of the family.
- Sid ducked just in time to avoid a large .... which fell from the old apple tree.

11
- We'll .... your lateness just this once.
- The houses .... a school playing field.
- Fred didn't .... the pains in his chest. He immediately consulted a doctor.

12
- Gavin has a .... for fast sport cars.
- I love the .... of that spicy tomato sauce.
- After a brief .... of city life, the farmer returned to the country.

13
- Deborah's lack of a higher education is a .... to her getting promotion.
- If you are going to have a shower, there's a new .... of soap in the soapdish.
- Oh look, there's a coffee .... over there; let's pop in for something to eat.

PREPARING FOR PART 5

IDENTIFYING WRITER'S TONE II

25 *Read the following extracts and decide with which of the suggested statements the writer would probably agree. Then choose an adjective which best characterises the writer's tone. An example of each kind of question has been done for you.*

Dear John,

   This is just a quick note to inform you that our negotiations with SuperCars Ltd have ceased. Mr Cowanne, their representative, seems to have changed his mind about the terms we discussed over the telephone before he visited me in London. I'm sorry I wasn't able to complete the deal for you, but believe me when I say it wasn't for lack of trying on my part.

Regards,
Ernest Merson

(0)   *Which of the following statements would the writer probably agree with?*
   A   Mr Cowanne was a hard person to do business with.   ✓
   B   Perhaps there are things I could have done to complete the deal which I didn't do.   ✗
   C   I'm not happy with Mr Cowanne's business conduct.   ✓

(00) *Which of the following adjectives best characterises the writer's tone?*
   A condescending   (B) apologetic   C implicating

   There is no business like show business, or so they say. It's a good motto to have too, if you're an aspiring actor or singer. However, when TV news presenters begin to aim to entertain rather than inform, it's bad news for the news.
   Channel Seven's very own Chris Chandler, the station's new eight-o'clock face, seems to confuse television journalism with the auditions he probably had when he was about to finish drama school. He can nod, frown, smile, gasp and, most importantly, apply over four adjectives to each noun ("crushing", "devastating" and "stupendous" comprise his favourite set). So interesting is his delivery that I miss most of the actual news because I'm trying to concentrate on his ever-transforming eyebrows. As for his million and one ways of saying hello and goodbye – what can I say? This, dear readers, is news Broadway style. Expect him to tap-dance on the desk next, when he tries to spice up the Denny by-election results next Thursday.

(1)   *Which of the following statements would the writer probably agree with?*
   A   TV news reporters must present news with calm and composure.   ....
   B   News reports should be made more interesting.   ....
   C   News reporters must behave professionally.   ....
   D   TV news should both inform and entertain, but not at the same time. ....

(2)   *Which of the following adjectives best characterises the writer's tone?*
   A caustic   B impertinent   C hostile

Tyrel Books' *Collected American Short Stories* (edited by Alan Ward, £18.95) comes at a time when the market is already busy trying to find an audience for two other such volumes, Richard Ford's *The American Short Story* and Ian McGiddy's *Exploring the American Short Story*. Looks like Tyrel Books are not worried about the competition, though, so neither am I.

As with every short story collection, Ward features some good examples of modern American writing, O'Brian's *The Things They Carried* and Robertson's *Perfect Square*, for example. Yet, unlike Ford and McGiddy, who arrange their collections so that there is a definite structure, Ward relies on the value of the individual stories alone – so the question arises, why bother putting them together in the first place?

(3) *Which of the following statements would the writer probably agree with?*
   A It is always good to see new story collections, no matter how many there are on the market. ....
   B Ward's collection is not as interesting as those by Ford and McGiddy. ....
   C A good collection is more than just a lot of good stories put together. ....

(4) *Which of the following adjectives best characterises the writer's tone?*
   A critical   B detached   C biased

The amount of debt in Inverness is continuing to spiral upwards – along with the number of people seeking help over money difficulties.

In the past year, Inverness Citizen's Advice Bureau has dealt with debt totalling more than £4 million, while the number of clients with multiple debts has soared by 30 per cent.

According to the bureau, the amount of multiple debt it handled in the year up to June came to £2.6 million – an increase of 41 per cent from the previous year. In addition, there was estimated £2 million-worth of single debts.

"These are shocking figures, and we must read them as a warning that the problem could escalate unless our society becomes less materialistic," said Bureau spokesman Andrew Watson.

(5) *Which of the following statements would Andrew Watson probably agree with?*
   A The fact that so many people get into debt is due to their materialistic lifestyle. ....
   B The figures indicate that more people will probably get into debt in the near future. ....
   C The city is spending far too much on advising people how to get out of debt. ....

(6) *Which of the following adjectives best characterises Andrew Watson's tone?*
   A fault-finding   B dejected   C concerned

Girls now outperform boys in developed countries around the world and governments want to know why. Increasingly, it is being suggested that education, the predominantly female profession (83 per cent of primary school teachers in England and Wales are women), will have to change its approach to the teaching of boys. Women teachers may point out that studies show they give three times as much attention to boys as to girls. But the same research shows that much of this attention is spent chastising boys for what is seen as inappropriate behaviour.

Could it simply be that female primary school teachers find the natural behaviour of young boys too noisy, too aggressive and too boisterous, especially among those from low-income families?

(7) *Which of the following statements would the writer probably agree with?*
   A Female teachers should teach girls and male teachers should teach boys. ....
   B Young boys who come from low-income families are more likely to annoy a female teacher. ....
   C Many female teachers treat boys unfairly. ....

(8) *Which of the following adjectives best characterises the writer's tone?*
   A anxious   B pedantic   C biased

12c Practice Test Twelve

Paper 3 Use of English

Time: 1 hour 30 minutes

PART 1

Read the text below and think of the word which best fits each space. Use only one word in each space.

MASKS

Simply defined, a mask is a form **(0)** *of* disguise. It is an object that is frequently worn **(1)** .... or in front of the face to hide the identity of a person and, with **(2)** .... own features, to establish **(3)** .... being. This essential characteristic concealing and revealing personalities or moods is common **(4)** .... all masks. **(5)** .... cultural objects, they have been used **(6)** .... the world in all periods **(7)** .... the Stone Age and have been as varied in appearance as in **(8)** .... use and symbolism.

Masks have been designed in innumerable varieties, **(9)** .... the simplest of crude "false faces" held by a handle to complete head coverings with ingenious movable parts. Mask makers **(10)** .... shown great resourcefulness **(11)** .... selecting and combining available materials. Among the items used **(12)** .... woods, metals, shells, clay, feathers, paper and cloth. The artist is usually sought **(13)** .... as a maker of masks **(14)** .... of his known ability to give a visually expressive **(15)** .... an aesthetically pleasing presentation of the required image.

PART 2

Read the text below. Use the word given in capitals at the end of some of the lines to form a word that fits in the space in the same line.

THE FASCINATION WITH MARS

(0) *Historically*, Mars was thought to be the most likely planet to harbour life. There	HISTORY
is a reflection of such **(16)** .... in popular culture as expressed	BELIEVE
in literature, radio and film.	
Public fascination with Martians began in the late 19th century when, in 1877,	
astronomer Giovanni Sciaparelli reported **(17)** .... of	OBSERVE
large channels on Mars. In 1897, H. G. Wells' *The War of the Worlds* was the first	
major work to explore the **(18)** .... of the "extraterrestrial	CONCEIVE
invader" and exerted a substantial influence on the public psyche. A few years later,	
even **(19)** .... astronomers such as Percival Lowell seriously	KNOWLEDGE
advocated the possibility of life forms as described in his book *Mars as the Abode of*	
Life (1910). **(20)** ...., Mars began to take a special place in	CONSEQUENCE
popular culture around the turn of the 20th century, continuing until today.	
However, this does not **(21)** .... the unique role of Mars in the history	LITTLE
of science. Specifically the **(22)** .... of the movement of	DOCUMENT
Mars, by Johannes Kepler (1571-1630), led to the formulation of his three laws of	
(23) .... motion which shattered mediaeval anthropocentric	PLANET
notions of astronomy and laid the foundations for the **(24)**	DISCOVER
of Isaac Newton (1643-1727). Like no other planet, Mars has left a(n)	
(25) .... mark on human imagination and thought.	REPLACE

PART 3

Think of one word only which can be used appropriately in all three sentences.

0 • One doesn't need to be an expert to *appreciate* the beauty of classical music.

• He seems confident that houses in this area will *appreciate* in value in the next few years.

• I'll always *appreciate* your help and support.

26 • The problems of global warming are .... the minds of scientists.

• During the summit meeting, protesters were .... the right of free speech.

• By playing tennis, you are in fact .... nearly every muscle in your body.

27 • Stephen's father is a famous doctor in the .... of medicine.

• We walked through the .... as the summer sun shone down on us.

• The sports .... is flooded and it must be drained before the next match.

28 • The sun was setting as the ferry .... to the opposite shore of the river.

• He .... his arms over his chest and waited to hear his son's excuse.

• Anastasia's name was .... off the list of guests as she couldn't attend the event.

29 • Miss Staples reads the newspaper's social ...., hoping to see her name.

• The thin .... gave way under the pressure of the heavy ceiling.

• The accountant added the .... of figures, trying not to make a mistake.

30 • Heat the vegetable mixture and serve it on a .... of rice.

• After an eventful day, he was glad to lie down on his .... for a few minutes.

• Gardeners prepared the flower .... with the appropriate soil for roses.

31 • The room was .... except for a rocking chair in the corner.

• After years of experience, I finally realised he made nothing but .... promises.

• Being separated from his young son left Eric feeling ....

PART 4

Complete the second sentence so that it has a similar meaning to the first sentence, using the word given. Do not change the word given. You must use between three and eight words, including the word given.

0 Nobody spoke when the teacher asked who the culprit was.
remained
Everyone *remained silent when the teacher asked* who the culprit was.

32 She was an excellent playwright whose work didn't get the recognition it deserved.
renown
She was an excellent playwright ....
.... her work.

33 I knew the project would not succeed from the start.
doomed
I knew the project ....
.... from the start.

34 That man reminds me a lot of my father.
bears
That man ....
.... father.

35 Laurence's car became his most prized possession when he first bought it.
joy
Laurence's car became ....
.... he first bought it.

36 Most people are indifferent to the mistreatment of animals.
show
Most ....
.... of animals.

37 It's quite likely that they will consider our offer too low.
well
They ....
.... too low.

38 Those of us at the back couldn't hear most of the play.
to
Most of the play ....
.... those of us at the back.

39 The exam results will determine her choice of university.
dependent
Her choice of university ....
.... the exam results.

245

PART 5

*For questions **40-44** read the following texts. For questions **40 - 43** answer with a word or short phrase. You do not need to write complete sentences. For question **44**, write a summary according to the instruction given.*

Orson Welles' 1948 production of Shakespeare's Macbeth is a fairly faithful rendition of Shakespeare's play. The video package calls it "... one of the greatest experimental films ever made under the Hollywood studio system." But that, of course, is saying very little. Although as a film this work is distinguished only by its atmospherics as far as cinematography is concerned, as a stage production it has much to recommend it.

This film's greatest attribute is its cast. Welles himself plays Macbeth and he excels in the role. He very convincingly portrays the combination of ambition and remorse that provides the key to the actions of Macbeth throughout the play. Many productions of the play make Lady Macbeth the sole source of the couple's avarice for power, but Welles embodies a Macbeth who accepts the larger chunk of the blame.

Lady Macbeth is played by Jeanette Nolan and she, too, gives a superb performance. Her Lady Macbeth exhibits a sharpened passion that motivates both her all-consuming ambition and, later, her all-devouring guilt. This provides great depth to a character who is all too often played as a two-dimensional cartoon.

Recently restored to its original, full-length version, Welles' *Macbeth* brings to the viewer a powerful interpretation of Shakespeare's writing, in a setting reminiscent of the *film noir* genre, whose popularity was soaring in the late forties.

40 What, according to the writer, explains Macbeth's behaviour?

....
....

41 What does the writer say about the way in which most productions portray Lady Macbeth?

....
....

Director Terry Hands has taken an unexpected approach to his production of Macbeth, which opened last night at the Music Box Theatre. *Macbeth* is one of Shakespeare's bloodiest plays, in every sense of the word, full of grand, all-consuming emotions, begging to be played with a lusty arrogance and a snarl. Here we are given a cold, distanced, intellectual production that dispenses with overt theatricality in favour of a brutal and unforgiving look at a mind ravaged by ambition and guilt.

As Macbeth, Kelsey Grammer gives a simple and straightforward performance, making the character easily accessible to a young audience. Mr. Grammer's great strength as an actor, particularly notable in a live performance, is an ability to let the audience "see" his thoughts, let them in on what his character is thinking at any given moment. His performance is the overriding pleasure of the evening.

Terry Hands has taken note of Grammer's performance style and has assembled a worthy cast around it. The prevailing tone is one of restraint and underplaying, and the supporting actors, led by the calculating Lady Macbeth of Diane Verona, give this production a rare and rewarding unity, focus, and strength. Pointing out individual performers in such a well integrated cast seems almost unfair, but pay particular attention to Verona, Kate Forbes' Lady Macduff, and Peter Michael Goetz's Duncan.

line 4
line 17
line 18

42 What does the writer mean when he says that *Macbeth* is a play "...begging to be played ...with a lusty arrogance and a snarl" (line 4)?

....
....

43 Why does the writer say that "pointing out individual performers... is almost unfair"? (lines 17-18)

....
....

44 In a paragraph of between 50 and 70 words, summarise the two reviewers' comments on the performances of Orson Welles and Kelsey Grammer.

....
....
....
....
....
....
....
....

247

UNIT 13a Grammar: Clauses

Subordinate clauses complete or add to a main clause. They may function grammatically as subject, object, complement or adverbial in a main clause. They can be:

a) **noun clauses**
    He told me **(that) the film was interesting**.

b) **relative clauses**
    Tom, **who is a teacher**, left early.

c) **adverbial clauses** i.e. time clauses, clauses of **manner/place/reason/purpose/result/comparison/concession/condition**
    He is taller **than his sister**.

TIME CLAUSES

Time Clauses are introduced with time conjunctions or expressions such as: **after, as, as soon as, before, by, by the time, hardly... when, immediately, no sooner... than, now that, once, (ever) since, the minute (that), the moment (that), then, the sooner... the sooner, till/until, on/upon, when, whenever, while.**
He waited for an hour **before** he was interviewed by the manager.

Time Clauses follow the rule of the sequence of tenses; that is, when the verb of the main clause is in a present or future tense, the verb in the subordinate clause must be in a present or future tense too, and when the verb of the main clause is in a past tense, the verb in the subordinate clause must be in a past tense too.
I'll **watch** TV after I **have finished** doing my homework.
She **left** before he **came**.

We never use a future tense in a future time clause; instead, we use a present tense.
They will leave in an hour. I'll do the washing up then.
I'll do the washing up **when/after** they **leave/have left**. (not ~~will leave~~ or ~~will have left~~)

Compare:

when (time conjunction) **+ present tense**
When I find it, I'll tell you.

when (question word) **+ present tense + future**
When will John **get** back from Austria?

CONVERSATIONAL GRAMMAR

1 *Choose the correct item.*

0 "Can I come without any notice? Are you sure?"
    "Definitely. Whenever you .... in the area."
    A will be   C have been
    Ⓑ are   D will have been

1 "How did Harry suspect the new franchising company might be a fiasco?"
    "As soon as he .... some tricky terms in the contract, he knew there was something wrong."
    A has spotted   C would spot
    B spotted   D spots

2 "Whenever I .... Jane, she talks about the new house she's having built."
    "Well, I think she's really obsessed with the matter."
    A am meeting   C meet
    B met   D have been meeting

3 "Are you sure it was Pete?"
    "Yes. The moment I saw him he .... the building."
    A was entering   C has entered
    B would enter   D had been entering

4 "I'm afraid Jenny Jones has been consistently late all this week, Mr Taylor."
"When Miss Jones .... in, tell her I'd like to have a word with her."
   A is coming   C will have come
   B comes   D came

5 "How about joining me on a skiing trip this weekend?"
"Well, I really can't take a holiday until I .... my thesis."
   A have finished   C will have finished
   B finished   D am finished

6 While she .... for her friend to pick her up, her mother arrived.
   A has been waiting   C had been waiting
   B was waiting   D is waiting

7 "......... had we arrived at the beach when it started pouring with rain."
   A No sooner   C As soon as
   B The minute   D Hardly

8 "Why was Jane upset?"
"The minute she .... into the party, she saw someone wearing the same dress."
   A had walked   C walking
   B was walking   D walked

9 "It was unwise of David to make light of such a sensitive issue."
"Exactly. No sooner .... the joke than everyone got up and left!"
   A has he told   C had he told
   B he told   D having told

10 "You must have been worried knowing she was alone so late at night."
"Well, once I .... her come in, I began to relax."
   A have heard   C heard
   B hear   D am hearing

11 "Where is Emma's report?"
"I think she put it on your desk before she ...."
   A left   C has left
   B had left   D was leaving

2 *Complete the second sentence so that it has a similar meaning to the first sentence, using the word given. Do not change the word given. You must use between three and eight words, including the word given.*

1 Sean did all the illustrations for the book but no one acknowledged his work.
credit
Sean wasn't ....
.... all the illustrations in the book.

2 Having finished your studies, you must decide what to do next.
future
You must ....
.... finished your studies.

3 As soon as they received the information, it was sent to the editor.
minute
The information was ....
.... they received it.

4 The rain ended and immediately the sun came out.
barely
It ....
.... the sun came out.

5 Russ's opinions on the new management policies were very different from those of his fellow workers.
odds
Russ ....
.... the new management policies.

6 The way many sportsmen behave in public influences their young fans.
impression
The way many sportsmen behave in public ....
.... their young fans.

7 Not until they leave will she begin cleaning the house.
start
She will only ....
.... they have left.

8 Could you give me a shout the minute dinner is ready?
know
Could you ....
.... is ready?

CLAUSES OF PURPOSE

Full infinitive is commonly used to express purpose. We can also use **in order to** and **so as to**. In order to and so as to are more emphatic and also more formal.
*He left early **(in order/so as) to avoid** the heavy traffic.*

Note:

We cannot use the full infinitive with a subject different from that of the main verb. Instead we can use **so that/in order that**.

Clauses of purpose are introduced with **so that/in order that** in the following way:
so that   + will/can/present tense (reference to the present)
in order that + would/could/past tense (reference to the past)   } (common structure)
*Wake him up early **so that** he **catches/'ll catch** the first bus.*
*We bought more food **so that** we **would have** enough for the extra guests.*

so that   + may/might
in order that + shall/should   } + infinitive (formal structure)
*The President left early **so that** he **should** not be late for his next meeting.*

Note:

We use **so that** rather than the to-infinitive structure when the main and the subordinate clause have different subjects.
*Kate left some salad **so that James** could eat it later.*

Negative purpose can be expressed with:

- **so as not to + infinitive** (only when the subject of the verb is also the subject of the infinitive)
  *We are staying in this weekend **so as not to spend** any money.*

- **so that + won't/can't/present tense** (present reference)
  so that + wouldn't/couldn't (past reference)
  *They've locked the gate **so that** we **can't/don't** get in.*
  *He left an hour ago **so that** we **wouldn't** be caught in the traffic.*

- **for fear (that) + might/should/would** (very formal)
  for fear of sth/doing sth
  lest + (might/should) + infinitive (formal subjunctive) (very formal)
  *They asked their neighbours to keep an eye on the house **for fear (that)** burglars **might** break in.*
  *She didn't make a noise **for fear of waking** her parents.*
  *She banned smoking **lest** the house **should catch** fire.*

- **for + noun** (to express the purpose of an action)
  *We went out **for** some fresh **air**.*
  for + gerund (to express the general purpose of a thing)
  *A saw is a tool **for cutting** wood.*

- **in case + Present Simple/should** (refers to the present/future)
  in case + Past Simple/should (refers to the past)
  *Take an umbrella **in case** it **rains/should rain**.*
  *They left early **in case** the traffic **was/should** be heavy.*

Note:

Will/would are never used with **in case**.
*Take your coat **in case** it **gets** cold.*
NOT *Take your coat in case it ~~will get~~ cold.*
- **prevent + noun/pronoun + (from) gerund**
  *It's impossible to **prevent** cats **(from) scratching** furniture.*

- avoid + gerund
  You should **avoid carrying** heavy bags if you have a bad back.

Clauses of Purpose follow the rule of the sequence of tenses.
I'll **leave** early so that I'll **be**/I'm home before they come.
He **avoided** mentioning it so that he **wouldn't offend** her.

CONVERSATIONAL GRAMMAR

3 *Choose the correct item.*

0 "What's in all the boxes?"
"Some extra refreshments .... we run out."
Ⓐ in case   C so that
B to prevent   D for fear

1 "Did you go around to see Janet's newborn son?"
"I had the flu so I didn't go for fear .... infecting the baby."
A for   C that
B of   D lest

2 "Why is everyone so busy?"
"They're tidying the show room in case the managing director .... in."
A drops   C will drop
B dropped   D would drop

3 "Why didn't you go to the party on Saturday night?"
"I wanted to avoid .... Josh."
A see   C seeing
B that I see   D to see

4 "The baby's not screaming any more."
"He's teething and I gave him an aspirin so that he .... down."
A are calming   C should calm
B would calm   D calmed

5 "What are you doing over the summer?"
"I've got a temporary job .... I can save some money."
A so that   C so as to
B in case   D in order

6 "I'm not sure what to say to Paul."
"You could always tell a white lie to .... hurting his feelings."
A avoid   C prevent
B prevent from   D avoid to

7 "What's the use of this object?"
"It's a device .... screwing bolts into nuts."
A of   C so that
B for   D so as to

STRUCTURAL CONVERSION

1 He put on a mask to avoid *being recognised by his wife.*
He put on a mask to prevent *his wife (from) recognising him.*
He put on a mask for fear *his wife might recognise him.*
He put on a mask so that *his wife wouldn't recognise him.*
He put on a mask in case *his wife recognised/should recognise him.*
He put on a mask because *he didn't want his wife to recognise him.*

2 I didn't go out because *I didn't want to catch cold.*
I didn't go out so that *I wouldn't catch cold.*
I didn't go out to avoid *catching cold.*
I didn't go out in case *I caught/should catch cold.*

3 I'd better wait because *it's possible he'll come back.*
I'd better wait in case *he comes back.*

4 I daren't make a noise because *John might hear me.*
I daren't make a noise for fear *(that) John might/should hear me.*

4 Complete the second sentence so that it has a similar meaning to the first sentence, using the word given. Do not change the word given. You must use between three and eight words, including the word given.

1 They tied the dog up for fear it might escape.
case
The ....

.... escaped.

2 We didn't phone you in case we woke you up.
so
We didn't ....

.... you up.

3 She opened the door quietly because she didn't want to wake the baby.
to
She ....

.... the baby.

4 He did the exercise carefully because he didn't want to have to do it again.
as
He did ....

.... to redo it.

5 They were reluctant to announce the news because they didn't want to worry the public.
fear
They were reluctant to announce ....

.... the public.

6 He hid the package in case his mother found it.
from
He hid the package ....

.... it.

7 He turned down the music for fear of upsetting the neighbours.
would
So ....

.... he turned down the music.

8 She carried an umbrella so she wouldn't be wet.
getting
She carried an umbrella ....

.... wet.

CLAUSES OF RESULT

Clauses of Result are introduced with **such (a) ... that, so ... that, so ... as to, (and) so**, and are used as follows:
*Would you be **so kind as to** open the door for me?*
*They missed the last train, **(and) so** they had to walk home.*

such a(n) + adjective + singular countable noun
*It was **such a thrilling novel that** I couldn't put it down.*

such + adjective + uncountable or plural noun
*He played **such moving music that** many people in the audience felt close to tears.*

such + a lot of + noun
*There was **such a lot of noise that** the children couldn't hear what the teacher was saying.*

so + adjective/adverb
*We were **so pleased** with their present **that** we rang them immediately.*

so + much/many/little/few + noun
*We had **so little time that** we didn't manage to visit all our friends.*

so + adjective + a(n) + singular noun (not usual)
***So beautiful a girl** was she **that** the prince fell in love with her at first sight.*

Note:

Clauses of Result follow the rule of the sequence of tenses.
*He **is** so tall that he **can reach** the top shelf.*
*She **was** such a good actress that everyone **admired** her.*

── STRUCTURAL CONVERSION ◄─────────────────────

1 The trousers were *so tight* that he couldn't put them on.
  The trousers were *too* tight for him to put on.
  So tight were the trousers that he couldn't put them on.
2 The snow was *so deep* that they couldn't leave the house.
  It was *such deep snow that* they couldn't leave the house.
  So deep was the snow that they couldn't leave the house.
3 The exercise was *so hard* that I couldn't do it.
  It was *such a hard exercise* that I couldn't do it.
  The exercise was *too hard* for me to do.
4 It was *such an expensive* dress that I couldn't buy it.
  The dress was *too expensive* for me to buy.
  The dress wasn't *cheap enough* for me to buy.

5 He was *so tired that* he couldn't work any more.
  He was *too tired* to work any more.
  So tired was he that he couldn't work any more.
6 His fear was *such that* he almost fainted.
  Such was his fear that he almost fainted.
  He was *so afraid* that he almost fainted.
7 There was *so much dirt* in the room that she couldn't clean it.
  The room was *so dirty* that she couldn't clean it.
  So dirty was the room that she couldn't clean it.
  It was *such a dirty room* that she couldn't clean it.

5 *Complete the second sentence so that it has a similar meaning to the first sentence, using the word given. Do not change the word given. You must use between three and eight words, including the word given.*

1 The day was so beautiful that we went for a walk.
  such
  It ....
  .... we went for a walk.
2 It was such an impressive painting that I had an irresistible urge to buy it.
  so
  It ....
  .... I had an irresistible urge to buy it.
3 He ate so many chocolates that he felt sick.
  lot
  He ....
  .... he felt sick.
4 The weather was so nice that we were able to sit outside.
  pleasant
  It ....
  .... we were able to sit outside.
5 It was such a beautiful cake that she didn't want to cut it.
  reluctant
  The ....
  .... to cut it.
6 She considered climbing the stairs, but decided she was too tired.
  exhausted
  She ....
  .... not to climb the stairs.

7 Genetic scientists are advanced enough to artificially produce even endangered species like elephants and tigers.
  clone
  Genetic scientists are so ....
  .... endangered
  species like elephants and tigers.
8 The house is considered to be too small for the family to live in.
  expected
  The family ....
  .... a small house.
9 Her dog was too badly behaved for her to control.
  disobedient
  Her dog ....
  .... couldn't control him.
10 The water was too shallow for us to swim in.
  enough
  The water was ....
  .... to swim in.
11 He was too lazy to answer the door.
  bothered
  He ....
  .... the door.
12 David was so enthusiastic about the proposal that he accepted immediately.
  was
  Such ....
  .... that he accepted immediately.

253

CLAUSES OF CONCESSION

Clauses of Concession are introduced with: as, although, though, even though, even so, even if, while, whereas, much as*, in spite of, despite, nevertheless, but, however, yet, still, for all.

* used with verbs such as (dis)like, admire, enjoy, etc

Clauses of Concession follow the rule of the sequence of tenses.
Much as I like her, **I disapprove** of her teaching methods.
Sensible **as/though** he usually **is**, he **has acted** foolishly in this case.
Even though he **studied**, he **failed** his tests.

- **in spite of/despite + noun/gerund/the fact that + clause**
  In spite of/Despite her ill health, she still takes care of the house and children.
  In spite of/Despite being ill, she went to work.

- **however/no matter how + adjective/adverb + subject + may + verb**
  No matter how hard I try, I can never solve crosswords.
  However hard he may try, he won't succeed.

- **whatever/no matter what + clause**
  No matter what the time is, ring me when you arrive at the station.

- **even if + should + infinitive** (unlikely to happen)
  Even if it should rain, I'm still going swimming.

- **adjective/adverb + though + subject + (may) verb**
  Rich though he is/may be, he is not happy.
  Late though he stayed, he didn't finish the work.

- **adjective/adverb + as + subject + verb**
  Tall as he is, he couldn't reach the branch of the tree.
  Fast as he ran, he didn't catch the bus.

- **infinitive form + as + subject + may/might**
  Try as you may/might, you won't solve the riddle.

- **for all + noun**
  For all their poverty, they managed to live happily.

6 Complete the second sentence so that it has a similar meaning to the first sentence, using the word given. Do not change the word given. You must use between three and eight words, including the word given.

1 Even if she comes late, ring me when she arrives.
how
Give me a ring when ....
.... late she is.

2 Talented though he is, he can't find a job.
fact
He can't ....
.... he's talented.

3 In spite of the train strike, she still managed to get to work on time.
succeeded
She ....
.... there was a train strike.

4 Whatever you say in protest, you can do nothing to change the situation.
much
You cannot ....
.... you protest.

5 Although it's cold at night, it's warm in the daytime.
nights
Cold ....
.... the days are warm.

6 Even though she has rich parents, she has little money herself.
having
She has ....
.... parents.

7 Despite the fact that he's never been to China, he loves Chinese food.
even
He loves ....
.... never been to China.

CONVERSATIONAL GRAMMAR

7 Choose the correct item.

0 "Has Bob passed his IELTS exams?"
"Even .... he studied hard, he didn't make it."
A although   C no matter
(B) though   D despite

1 "The project was a failure .... the huge sums spent on it."
"I call it a terrible waste of tax-payers' money."
A however   C though
B yet   D in spite of

2 "........ I dislike Winston, I have to admit that he came up with some brilliant suggestions at the management meeting."
"That's true. I particularly liked his introduction to the 'Research & Development' project."
A Much as   C However
B No matter   D For all

3 "Cathy looked rather plump in that new dress."
"Yes, ... being on a diet for weeks, she's hardly lost any weight."
A in spite   C though
B despite   D while

4 "I'm astounded by your grandmother's energy and enthusiasm for life."
"Yes. She's still very active, ... she is in her eighties."
A even though   C whereas
B while   D even so

5 "It was such a bargain; I wish it hadn't fallen to bits."
"It was a waste of money, ... cheap it was!"
A yet   C however
B still   D but

6 "Have you heard, Nick has just been awarded his PhD?"
"Yes, but intelligent .... he is, he has no basic common sense."
A although   C however
B while   D though

STRUCTURAL CONVERSION

1 She wasn't fat; *nevertheless*, she went on a diet.
She went on a diet. She *wasn't fat*, **though**.
Even though she wasn't fat, she went on a diet.
Although she wasn't fat, she went on a diet.
In spite of not being fat, she went on a diet.

2 **Despite the fact that he was afraid**, he climbed the mountain.
He was afraid. He climbed the mountain, **though**.
Even though he was afraid, he climbed the mountain.
In spite of (his) being afraid, he climbed the mountain.
Although he was afraid, he climbed the mountain.

3 *Although he spoke loudly*, he could not make himself heard.
Loudly as/though he spoke, he could not make himself heard.

4 *Apart from Paul*, we all have cars.
We all have cars, **with** the exception of Paul.
We all have cars except (for) Paul.

5 *Although she is talented*, she is too shy to perform in public.
Even though she is talented, she is too shy to perform in public.
In spite of her talent, she is too shy to perform in public.
She is talented. She is too shy to perform in public, **though**.
She is talented, **though** too shy to perform in public.

6 **Whatever they do**, they do it well.
No matter what they do, they do it well.

7 *No matter how carefully you do it*, it's bound to be difficult.
However carefully you do it, it's bound to be difficult.
It's *bound* to be difficult, **however carefully** you do it.

8 The film was awful but we went on watching it.
Despite the film being awful, we went on watching it.

9 *Although it seemed to be harmless*, the dog was in fact dangerous.
Although it seemed to be harmless, on the contrary, the dog was dangerous.

8 *Complete the second sentence so that it has a similar meaning to the first sentence, using the word given. Do not change the word given. You must use between three and eight words, including the word given.*

1 Although we warned her of the potential danger, she swam there anyway.
   determined
   She ....
   .... the fact that we'd warned her not to.

2 In spite of his being wealthy, he's terribly mean.
   renowned
   Rich ....
   .... for his generosity.

3 No matter what he says, he intends to retire early.
   say
   Whatever ....
   .... retiring early.

4 However you speak to her, she always takes offence.
   matter
   She ....
   .... you speak to her.

5 Apart from geography, she enjoys all her lessons.
   with
   She enjoys all her lessons, ...
   .... geography.

6 She isn't experienced; nevertheless, she was hired by a multi-national company.
   for
   She was hired by a multi-national company, ...
   .... experience.

7 No matter how attractive a salary you offer him, he won't accept the job.
   down
   He'll ....
   .... him a really attractive salary.

8 Slow as he is, he ran the race faster than I did.
   before
   He finished the race ....
   .... he's slow.

9 Despite the fact that she practises regularly, she doesn't play tennis well.
   competent
   She ....
   .... she practises regularly.

10 They are not wealthy; nevertheless, they seem to spend a lot of money.
   off
   They aren't ....
   .... that they seem to spend a lot of money.

11 However hard she tries, she'll never get an answer out of him.
   how
   She'll never get ....
   .... she tries.

EXCLAMATIONS

An exclamation is a type of sentence used to express the speaker's feeling or attitude. Exclamations are not subordinate clauses. We do not alter the order of subject and verb. They are introduced with **what** and **how** as follows:

What + (a/an) (adjective) + noun
What an interesting lecture!
What awful furniture!

How + adjective/adverb/verb
How beautiful she is!
How slowly he walks!
How I loved him!

Exclamatory sentences can also be expressed:
- with **such + a/an + adjective + noun** or **so + adjective / adverb.**
  She is such a beautiful girl!
  She is so beautiful!

- with an **interrogative - negative** form at the beginning of the sentence.
Isn't she sweet!
Doesn't he eat a lot!

- by beginning the sentence with an **adverb** or an **adverbial particle** (away, up, out, etc) followed by a **verb of movement + noun**, or **pronoun + verb of movement**.
Off went the boys!
Out they went!

CONVERSATIONAL GRAMMAR

9 *Choose the correct item.*

0 "Did you see Sharon's place?"
"......... untidy that flat was!"
A How   C How an
B What an   D What

1 "I fell asleep during the economics lecture!"
"......... boring presentation!"
A Was it   C Such
B What a   D How

2 "I really like Gerald."
"......... friendly smile he has!"
A How a   C What
B How   D What a

3 "I feel sorry for Patricia and John."
"......... they have a rough time!"
A Can't   C Didn't
B Aren't   D Wouldn't

4 "We've just been to see 'Dracula'."
"......... it a scary movie!"
A Was   C What
B Wasn't   D How

5 "Harriet is always so considerate."
"......... she a kind person!"
A Isn't   C How is
B Such is   D Doesn't

6 "What do you think of your new English teacher?"
"She speaks .... fast!"
A such   C how
B so   D what

7 "Have you seen my grandmother's hand-embroidered quilt?"
"......... meticulous piece of work!"
A How   C Such
B What a   D So a

8 "Are you going to take the new job?"
"Oh yes. It is .... exciting opportunity!"
A so   C such
B so an   D such an

9 "Robert concluded by pointing out that we cannot increase productivity with this poor machinery."
"......... an apt remark!"
A How   C Wasn't it
B So   D Was it

CLAUSES OF REASON

Clauses of Reason are introduced with **as, since, because, for,** and follow the rule of the sequence of tenses.
*Since she **hasn't got** any money, she **can't go** shopping.*
*He **failed** his test **because** he **wasn't** well prepared.*

- **Because** and **for** can both be used to introduce a clause of reason. However, **for** can't be used at the beginning of a sentence, or as an answer to a why-question. If used, there is always a comma before it in written speech, or a pause in oral speech.
***Because** I didn't know how, I didn't do it.*
*I didn't do it **because** I didn't know how.*
*I didn't do it, **for** I didn't know how.*

Also: **because of + noun/gerund = owing to/due to + noun**
Because of/Due to the rain, the match was cancelled.

- We can also use the preposition **in view of** or a finite clause (a clause based on a verb tense) after **in view of the fact that**.
  The scheme was abandoned **in view of the fact that** it was proving unpopular.

- **Out of** + noun can also express a motive for an action.
  I had a look just **out of** curiosity.

- A **participle clause** (with a present or perfect participle) can also express reason.
  Lots of fans were waiting at the airport, **hoping** to see Ricky Martin arrive. (= because they were hoping to see him arrive)
  Having lost my I.D., I have to apply for a new one. (= because I have lost my I.D.)

- **Considering/Seeing that** can introduce clauses of reason.
  Considering (that) she's sixty, Margaret is remarkably fit.

STRUCTURAL CONVERSION ◄

1 *"I'm sorry I didn't buy you a birthday present,"* he said.
   He apologised for not buying/having bought me a birthday present.
   He said he was sorry for not buying/having bought me a birthday present.
2 **What reason** did he give for acting that way?
   What reason did he give for his actions?
   Did he give any reason why he acted that way?
   Was there any reason given why he acted that way?
3 **They thought** it was going to be hot, so they went to the beach.
   They went to the beach because they thought it was going to be hot.
   If they hadn't thought it was going to be hot, they wouldn't have gone to the beach.
4 **Being** unable to fix the tap, I was forced to call a plumber.
   As I didn't know how to fix the tap, I was forced to call a plumber.
   Not being able to fix the tap, I was forced to call a plumber.
   I was forced to call a plumber because I couldn't fix the tap.
5 **Didn't he say why** he hadn't turned up at the meeting?
   Didn't he give any reason for not turning up at the meeting?
   Did he give any reason why he hadn't turned up at the meeting?
6 **He's ill so** he won't be coming to the party.
   He won't be coming to the party because he's ill.

CONVERSATIONAL GRAMMAR

10 Choose the correct item.

1 "Why was Danny given a month off?"
   "I think it's .... he's worked so hard lately."
   A due to the fact that   C seeing that
   B because of   D owing to

2 "Should I take the dog for a walk?"
   "......... it's raining right now, wait until it stops."
   A Because of   C Due to
   B Seeing that   D Owing to

3 "You didn't come to the football match last night."
   "......... I had so much homework to do, I didn't have a choice."
   A For   C Due to
   B Owing to   D As

4 "Is Dennis buying a house?"
   "Yes. .... he's earning more money now, he can afford one."
   A For   C Since
   B Due to   D Because of

5 "Why aren't you going away for your holidays?"
   "......... my daughter's wedding in September, we've many expenses coming up."
   A Because of   C Seeing that
   B Because   D For

6 "Were the necessary contracts signed yesterday?"
   "No, ... one member of the board was absent."
   A due to   C because
   B because of   D owing to

11 Complete the second sentence so that it has a similar meaning to the first sentence, using the word given. Do not change the word given. You must use between three and eight words, including the word given.

1 "I'm sorry that I didn't phone yesterday", said Gary.
for
Gary .... the previous day.

2 Did he explain why he looked so miserable?
reason
Did he .... so miserable?

3 If it hadn't been for Mr Copley's efforts, the campaign wouldn't be so successful.
due
The success .... Mr Copley's efforts.

4 We were forced to go by bus because we didn't have enough money for a taxi.
afford
Not ...., we had to go by bus.

5 If they hadn't trusted him, they wouldn't have followed his advice.
took
They ....him.

6 Sandra quit her job because she found the work very dull.
uninspiring
Sandra found .... she left her job.

CLAUSES OF PLACE

Clauses of Place are introduced with **where, wherever, as far as, as high as, as low as, as near as**, etc as follows:

where wherever as high as as low as as far as as near as	+ present tense/may	present/future reference	*No matter where I go, I always bump into someone I know.*
	+ past tense/might	past reference	*The dog went wherever I went/did.*

Note:
Simple Future is not normally used in clauses of place. *He'll go **wherever I go**.*

CONVERSATIONAL GRAMMAR

12 Choose the correct item.

1 "I hear little Isabella is walking now."
"Well, she can walk .... that chair before falling."
A where   C wherever
B as far as   D as high as

2 "Are you going away for Christmas?"
"Yes, I'll be going to Hull, which is .... my family lives."
A wherever   C as near as
B as far as   D where

3 "Does Joanna walk to work?"
"No. .... it is, she always takes the car."
A Where   C As near as
B Wherever   D As far as

4 "Does Peter enjoy going away on business?"
"He does; .... he goes, he always manages to enjoy himself."
A as far as   C where
B as near as   D wherever

13b English in Use

13 *Read the text below and think of the word which best fits each space. Use only one word in each space.*

CABBIES FAR AND WIDE

The study of taxi drivers is a study **(0)** *of* contrasts. Within this group we find the two extremes of human nature – the polite and sociable, and the downright rude. **(1)** .... is not to say that taxi drivers can't fall into that broad spectrum that lies in between, but it is the extremes that **(2)** .... to be the most common (or at least the most memorable). We have all **(3)** .... a ride with the driver who acknowledges our presence with a cursory nod and a flick of the meter switch and who responds **(4)** .... our timid questions with nothing **(5)** .... grunts. The really unlucky passengers find **(6)** .... travelling round and round in acute embarrassment **(7)** .... been told in no uncertain terms that it is their fault that the driver has no clue where they are going. Of course, these people are **(8)** .... to feel suitably guilty despite never having **(9)** .... foot in the city before.

On the other hand, we have the non-stop friendly talker who assails you with irrelevant chit-chat before you have **(10)** .... managed to close the door. The conversation includes every topic **(11)** .... the sun and by the end of the journey, you are suitably prepared to write the next edition of the "Encyclopaedia Britannica". **(12)** .... drivers succeed in telling you all about their family life **(13)** .... trying to learn your entire life history at the same time.

Whichever type of taxi driver you find yourself with, there is **(14)** .... doubt that you will reach your destination emotionally exhausted – but can you think of a **(15)** .... interesting way to travel?

PHRASAL VERBS 1

take aback:	surprise
take after:	look/be like a relative
take against:	dislike sb
take away:	remove
take back:	withdraw a statement or comment
take down:	1) write down 2) remove sth from a high place
take sb for:	mistake sb/sth for sb/sth else
take in:	1) deceive 2) allow sb to stay in one's home 3) understand 4) make clothes smaller
take up:	1) begin a hobby, sport etc. 2) occupy space

14 *Fill in the correct preposition or adverb.*

0 She takes *after* her father: she has the same gestures and mannerisms.

1 His lecture was so complicated that I only took .... a few words of what he said.

2 These magazines must be read in the library. You can't take them ....

3 The secretary took .... the list of titles as her boss read them out.

4 We were so taken .... by his decision to resign that we didn't know what to say.

5 I'll never forgive you if you don't take .... what you said about me.

6 Since his retirement, he has taken .... painting to fill up some of his spare time.

7 She seems to have taken .... me, as if I had offended her somehow.

8 Nobody was taken .... by his story, although it seemed convincing at first.

9 You have to take .... these curtains. They look very dirty.

10 If you take this skirt .... a little, it should fit you perfectly. It's too big for you now.

11 She is always being taken .... Elizabeth Taylor, even though she doesn't look that much like her.

12 When they discovered that the child was an orphan, they offered to take him ....

13 That desk is so big that it takes .... most of his office.

PHRASAL VERBS 2

take off:	1) remove (clothing)
	2) leave the ground (of aeroplanes etc)
	3) imitate sb in a comic way
	4) begin to succeed (of plans, ideas, etc)
take on:	1) undertake sth
	2) employ staff
	3) accept sb as an opponent
take out:	1) extract, remove
	2) accompany sb to a theatre, etc
take over:	take control of sth esp in place of sb else
take to:	1) find agreeable/like
	2) begin a habit
	3) escape to/hide in
take up with:	become involved in (usu derog)

IDIOMS/FIXED PHRASES 1

go back on one's word:	not fulfil a promise (opp. keep one's word)
have words with sb:	have an argument
make one's day:	make sb very happy
in deep water:	in trouble/difficulty
an old wives' tale:	false belief (usu about health)
have/keep one's wits about one:	be alert and able to deal with difficulties
the year dot:	a long time ago
be born yesterday:	be easily deceived/naive
not have it both ways:	refuse to make a decision between two pleasant things (usu in expression "You can't have it both ways!")

15 *Fill in the correct preposition(s) or adverb.*

0 She took the cover *off* the sofa and had it cleaned.
1 The amateur boxer was apprehensive about taking .... such an experienced fighter.
2 I don't think he'll take .... the new project unless we offer him more money.
3 He has taken .... drinking cocoa at night to help him sleep.
4 You'd better take this paragraph .... as it weakens your argument.
5 Their plane was due to to take .... at 10 pm but it was delayed because of fog.
6 He's such an aggressive person that nobody really takes .... him.
7 Their daughter has taken .... a group of friends who have no intention of ever finding work.
8 Mark was sent home from school because he was seen taking .... the headmaster.
9 Mr Johnson's son is going to take .... as chairman of the board.
10 After a slow start, their new line of cosmetics has begun to take ....
11 They've decided to take .... at least twenty new sales people this year.
12 The rebels took .... the mountains after their leader had been captured.
13 He promised to take me .... for dinner on Friday evening.

16 *Fill in the correct idiom/fixed phrase.*

1 She .... when she saw the fire in the kitchen; instead of panicking, she went out and phoned the fire brigade.
2 She is forever making promises and then ....
3 Unless you can explain where you got the money, I'm afraid you'll find yourself ....
4 You can't .... - either take the well-paid job or keep the job you enjoy doing.
5 I don't believe you're a millionaire. I ...., you know.
6 I think the idea that you can cure colds by eating onions is just ....
7 My mother .... the cleaner today as she is always breaking the crockery.
8 She .... when she accepted his proposal; it was the happiest day of his life.
9 It looks as if this house hasn't been decorated since ....

It will have to be done up completely before we move in.

261

13b English in Use

IDIOMS/FIXED PHRASES 2 (COLOUR IDIOMS)

the black sheep of the family:	a disgraced family member
red herring:	sth which distracts you from sth important
green belt:	the area on the outskirts of the town adjoining the country
the pot calling the kettle black:	accusing sb of a fault one has oneself
in the red:	owe money to a bank (opp: in the black)
see red:	suddenly become angry
see/look at sth through rose-coloured spectacles:	see sth from an unrealistically positive point of view
have a yellow streak:	be a coward
pitch black:	very dark
have green fingers:	be good at gardening
until one is blue in the face:	as hard/long as one possibly can (usu without success)
black tie:	formal clothing
be green with envy:	be very jealous
green (matter/issue):	concerned with ecology

17 Fill in the correct idiom/fixed phrases.

1 She was .... when she saw Jim's new sportscar.
2 When he opened his bank statement, he saw he was .... to the tune of £5,000.
3 The plot of the novel contained so many .... that I couldn't guess how the story would end.
4 Being ...., ... he was cut out of his uncle's will.
5 It was .... as I walked home under a moonless sky.
6 You can ask .... but I still won't let you borrow the car.

7 Ecologists want to protect the .... of the town from being developed.
8 Ruth wanted to help protect the environment so she insisted on buying .... household cleaning products.
9 Brian wore his dinner jacket to the reception as it was a .... occasion.
10 It was a case of .... when Jack said I was lazy.
11 The boys accused him of having .... because he wouldn't enter the derelict house.
12 Tom must have .... as his tomatoes always win first prize in the agricultural show.
13 Stephane .... when her manager falsely accused her of being unpunctual.
14 Optimists have a tendency to .... rather than being realistic.

PREPOSITIONS

18 Look at Appendix 5 and fill in the blanks with the correct preposition.

1 I'm very wary .... riding that horse; it's been known to shy at traffic.
2 The schoolboy winced .... the sight of the cane in the headmaster's hand.
3 She yearns .... a relaxing holiday in the sun.
4 You won't solve your problems by wallowing .... self-pity.
5 The student wrestled .... the difficult mathematics problem.
6 Wind and rain have whittled away .... the old stone wall for the past three centuries.
7 Ray winked .... us to show that he wasn't being serious.
8 After six months in the countryside, Alan has a yen .... the bright lights of the city.
9 The woman yelled .... the boys when they ran through her garden.
10 She tried not to yield .... temptation and have another piece of cake.

19 *Look at Appendix 5 and fill in the blanks with the correct preposition.*

1 The spy had little choice .... the matter but to destroy the microfilm.
2 There's no point crying .... things you can't change.
3 We had to choose .... a hotel in Rome and a villa in Tuscany for our last holiday.
4 The restaurant menu offered a choice .... trout, beef or chicken.
5 Membership of the society has decreased .... number since last year.
6 The national debt has been decreased .... £10 billion this year.
7 Do you mean you still haven't decided .... your holiday yet?
8 She can't decide .... what style of wedding dress to buy.
9 If you clean the hall, we'll deal .... the kitchen together.
10 My uncle deals .... antique furniture.
11 The baby was crying .... its milk.

20 *Complete the second sentence so that it has a similar meaning to the first sentence, using the word given. Do not change the word given. You must use between three and eight words, including the word given.*

1 He was dismissed because he was inefficient.
lost
He ....
.... inefficiency.
2 Jerry feels his colleagues despise him for not having a degree.
look
Jerry ....
.... for not having a degree.
3 Only Martha survived the crash.
sole
Martha ....
.... crash.
4 If you give in to them, you'll be sorry.
stand
If ....
...................................., you'll be sorry.

5 Jack's teacher says he's particularly good at languages.
flair
Jack's teacher says ....
.... languages.
6 People often make that mistake in the beginning.
common
It ....
.... in the beginning.
7 The majority of their clientele is made up of local people.
comprise
Local people ....
.... their clientele.
8 The politician tried to find people who were willing to back his campaign to help the homeless.
drum
The politician tried to ....
.... campaign to help the homeless.
9 Karen's bad mood is totally unconnected with the matter in hand.
bearing
The ....
.... Karen's bad mood.
10 Further confusion was caused by the loss of the map.
led
The ....
.... further confusion.
11 The custom dates back to mediaeval times.
roots
The ....
.... mediaeval times.
12 It's difficult to imagine his work being improved on by anyone.
bettering
It's difficult ....
.... work.
13 To this day no one has equalled his achievements in the field of technology.
unsurpassed
To this day ....
.... in the field of technology.
14 Their rivals are still a long way behind.
streets
They ....
.... rivals.

FIXED PHRASES

(to) be on the safe side:	do sth to prevent the possibility of sth bad happening
not one's scene (inf):	not like/enjoy sth
settle a score:	take revenge
without a shadow of (a) doubt:	without any doubt
talk shop	talk about work or business
if push comes to shove (inf):	if a situation becomes really bad/difficult
get on the wrong/bad side of sb:	do sth to annoy sb
a sore point with sb:	sth that makes sb angry or embarrassed
spick and span:	clean and tidy
enter into the spirit of sth:	take part in sth with enthusiasm
in the spotlight:	receiving a great deal of public attention
be/get in a state:	be very nervous/ upset about sth
in stitches (inf):	unable to stop laughing
in store for one:	about to happen in near future
take sth by storm:	be extremely successful or popular
get into the swing of sth:	get involved/get into the rhythm
in sync (inf):	well matched/ work simultaneously as it should
	(**opp.** out of sync badly matched not simultaneous as it should)

21 Complete the sentences using one of fixed phrases in an appropriate form.

1 You don't want to .... of Roy as he makes a formidable opponent.
2 After my spring clean, the house was .... which made all my hard work worthwhile.
3 The new musical .... the town .... and people were flocking to see it.
4 The problem with the printer is that it is .... with the rest of the system.
5 Some celebrities have such a thirst to be continually .... that they seek out every opportunity for publicity.
6 .... and money is really tight, Lloyd will think about getting a second job.
7 Both teachers and pupils .... things, so the end of year concert was a great success.
8 Little did she know what was .... when she accepted the job.

22 Choose the correct item.

1 The audience were in .... as they watched the latest Aykebourne comedy.
   A stitches   C tears
   B pleats   D shreds

2 Don't mention work to Ray, as it's a sore .... with him at the moment.
   A finger   C place
   B point   D thumb

3 It's hard to get back into the .... of things after a long holiday.
   A pace   C swing
   B way   D rhythm

4 The trouble with socialising with colleagues is that they usually end up talking ....
   A sense   C back
   B shop   D rot

5 Take your mobile phone with you just to be on the .... side.
   A sunny   C straight
   B secure   D safe

6 The opposition will be elected into government at the next election, without a .... of a doubt.
A shadow   C benefit
B shade   D hue

7 Noisy parties are really not my ....
A idea   C scene
B liking   D preference

23 *Find the mistake and correct it.*

0 I live in a house ~~at~~ a lake.   *beside/by/on*
1 The church had been built in the 18th century. ....
2 Except from John and Mary, nobody wants to go to the cinema. ....
3 He wants to go home and he hasn't finished work yet. ....
4 My neighbours make enough noise to rise the dead. ....
5 Keeping a dog is fairly expensive, so I had rather keep a goldfish. ....
6 The farmer's chickens have lain ten eggs today. ....
7 Although he's been working in the bank for two years, he yet hasn't been promoted. ....
8 The streets are flooded. It can't have been raining all night. ....
9 Children under five mustn't pay to travel on public transport. ....
10 A farmer who went missing yesterday while a blizzard has been found alive and well. ....
11 I'm exhausted as I've had quite a long day at work. ....
12 My feet are killing me! I need to lay down. ....
13 Bob can't go to the cinema because he's still spent all his pocket money. ....
14 It's only 9:30. He might have arrived already. ....
15 This is a secret. You needn't tell anyone. ....
16 Unemployment was the government's main concerning. ....

WORD USAGE

24 *Read the text below. Use the word given in capitals at the end of some of the lines to form a word that fits in the space in the same line.*

MAKING AN ALTERNATIVE SCENE

An underground film is a motion picture made and distributed outside the commercial film industry, usually as a(n) **(0)** *creative* expression of its maker. Underground films display greater **(1)** .... in form, technique, and content than films directed toward a mass audience. The term came into common use in the 1950s, when the greater **(2)** .... of good-quality 16-millimetre film stock and **(3)** .... permitted an increasing number of non-professionals to engage in cinema art. The term was also **(4)** .... to earlier films that were considered too **(5)** .... for the general public. As opposed to a high-budget film maker, the underground film maker **(6)** .... uses such production methods as filming with a 16-millimetre or 8-millimetre camera, which are quite **(7)** .... The films vary **(8)** .... in length. Robert Breer's *A Miracle* (1954) is 14 seconds long while Andy Warhol's *Empire* (1964) lasts eight hours. During the 1920s, film making was stimulated by the Dadaist, Cubist, and Surrealist movements. Little of comparative interest was produced until the late 1950s, when a host of new cinema artists arose in the United States. Unlike their **(9)** .... , they were strongly influenced by the techniques and personal expression of anti-commercial art films by directors such as Federico Fellini. Since the 1970s, underground film continues to be explored by film makers from the **(10)** .... world.

CREATE
FREE

AVAILABLE
EQUIP
APPLY
EXPERIMENT
ORDINARY
EXPENSE
CONSIDER

RUN

ART

25 *Collocate the expressions with words from the given list.*

- bind • ponder • foresee • appreciate • assign
- shrivel • speculate • transmit • infer

0 *infer* a meaning from sb's statement

1 .... on a problem

2 .... the dangers

3 .... a book

4 .... a radio message

5 .... sb to a task

6 .... on a matter

7 .... in the heat

8 .... in value

26 *Choose the correct item.*

1 I hate the way Tony .... around looking so self-important.
   A struts   C slithers
   B scampers   D slinks

2 The dog .... under the table when I shouted at him for eating my steak.
   A slithered   C slunk
   B scampered   D strutted

3 Rosie the kitten .... playfully around with a ball.
   A slunk   C slithered
   B strutted   D scampered

4 A long, green snake .... through the grass and disappeared.
   A strutted   C slunk
   B slithered   D scampered

5 She tried to .... Tom's importance to the company in order to gain a promotion for herself.
   A diminish   C shrink
   B dwindle   D reduce

6 Due to inflation, my savings have .... gradually to practically nothing.
   A shrank   C reduced
   B dwindled   D diminished

7 My new pullover .... to half its previous size when I washed it.
   A shrank   C diminished
   B reduced   D dwindled

8 I need to .... my weight by about ten kilos for health reasons.
   A reduce   C dwindle
   B diminish   D shrink

9 I don't think you're suitably .... for this party.
   A clothed   C wearing
   B clad   D dressed

10 The mountains were .... in thick cloud.
   A clothing   C dressing
   B clothed   D wearing

COLLOCATIONS

27 *Collocate the expressions with words from the given list.*

- enunciate • dye • refute • petition • commend
- beseech • applaud • engrave • despatch
- undertake

1 .... sb for help

2 .... a claim

3 .... for sb's release

4 .... to do a job

5 .... sb very highly

6 .... a hero

7 .... a piece of jewellery

8 .... a document

9 .... your words carefully

10 .... your hair

28 *Fill in* **sound, stone, hard.**

1 .... advice
2 .... bargain
3 .... cold
4 .... conditions

5 .... deal
6 .... dead
7 .... evidence
8 .... time

29 *Think of one word only which can be used appropriately in all three sentences.*

0 • One doesn't need to be an expert to *appreciate* the beauty of classical music.
   • He seems confident that houses in this area will *appreciate* in value in the next few years.
   • I'll always *appreciate* your help and support.

1 • The journalist gave a lot of details about the case but refused to .... his source.
 • When she was a baby, Paula's parents wanted to .... her Sheba but were talked out of it.
 • If you wanted to sell that painting, you could .... your own price.

2 • The government intends to .... interest rates at a high level in order to discourage public spending.
 • Amanda continues to .... that her dismissal was unfair.
 • Their house is so big that it must cost a fortune to ....

3 • The country's .... birth rate was studied by a group of demographers.
 • The hotel staff prepared the accommodation for the coming .... season.
 • Amanda was held in .... esteem for having landed the advertising account.

4 • Jones does a wicked .... of the headmaster that is just like him.
 • From what you said I got the .... that you weren't at all that interested in going to the party.
 • From the look on their faces, it seemed that Neville's impassioned speech and vision had made no .... on his companions.

5 • Jane visited me unexpectedly last night but I managed to throw together a .... meal of omelette and salad.
 • The maths exam was so .... I passed with flying colours.
 • He was a .... child and was not capable of following the regular classes at school.

6 • The bull .... his back foot to shake off the flies which kept in landing on him.
 • BMW .... the vehicle's identification number under the bonnet on their latest model.
 • Michael .... off to his room after losing an argument with his father.

7 • We need an .... to the pressing problem.
 • Robbie wrote the best .... in the history test.
 • Without waiting for their ...., she left the room.

8 • The sudden .... of the film star at the party caused a stir.
 • The modern extension did nothing to add to the .... of the grand old house.
 • Fears are growing about a possible typhoid epidemic following the .... of quite a few cases in the village.

9 • Hours before the awards ceremony, the actress had her hair .... and styled.
 • My electricity was .... when I forgot to pay the bill.
 • Unfortunately, the government .... costs by reducing its funding for education.

10 • They considered painting the room in .... colours; oranges, pinks or yellow.
 • Put on a .... coat before you go out in the snow.
 • Their .... welcome immediately put me at ease and made me feel as if I were home.

11 • They never thought Harry would be capable of such .... behaviour.
 • He murmured "All right" in a .... voice.
 • From a .... position in the company, Hannah worked her way up to a directorship.

12 • The actor was given his big .... on television by a famous producer.
 • Fran took a short .... in Italy after her operation.
 • The chairman called for a .... in the meeting to consider the new proposals.

13 • Professor Carson is an .... on mediaeval music.
 • The local planning .... will take the final decision about the new shopping complex.
 • Without being given .... by the head of department, I cannot sanction your transfer.

14 • She has a .... figure and looks good in everything she wears.
 • Kristina keeps her house so .... and spotlessly clean.
 • Julia wore a .... checked suit on her first day at work.

267

PREPARING FOR PART 5

SUMMARY WRITING I Answering Detail Questions II

30 *Read the following passages and underline the parts where the answer to each of the following questions is contained. Then paraphrase the underlined parts to answer the questions. Answer accurately, but use as few words as possible. Item (0) has been done for you.*

Electronic mail may be one of the great conveniences of modern life, but it isn't very portable. **(0)** <u>In order to read and send e-mail, your computer and software normally must travel with you.</u> But a new breed of web-based e-mail service – many of them free – lets you check and reply to e-mail from any computer with an Internet connection.

Hotmail (www.hotmail.com), recently acquired by Microsoft, and Bigfoot (www.bigfoot.com) were two of the first "e-mail anywhere" providers. But they've been joined by popular web search services such as Yahoo and Excite. All work similarly. Yahoo Mail (mail.yahoo.com), for example, is free and lets you send or receive e-mail from any computer. You simply log on to the Yahoo website and enter a password to check your e-mail. You can also access your e-mail from other systems that use a standard "post office protocol" (called POP3, used by most office networks).

Aside from the fact that it is free, one of the best perks of web-based e-mail is that you get a permanent e-mail address you can keep even if you switch to a different Internet service provider or browser software. And the e-mail software is built into the website, so there's never any upgrading required.

0 What does the writer mean by the phrase "Electronic mail... isn't very portable"?
That you must use your own computer to send or receive messages.

1 What differences are there between the various web-mail services as far as the way in which they function is concerned?
....
....

2 What do you have to do to check your e-mail if you're using Yahoo web-mail?
....
....

3 What are the two major advantages of web-based e-mail apart from the facts that it is free and that you can access it from anywhere?
....
....

Women who eat healthy foods have a significantly reduced risk of suffering a heart attack, according to a study published this week in the Archives of Internal Medicine.

In 1984, 70,000 American women filled out a questionnaire concerning their dietary habits. The diets were then rated according to how closely they resembled a so-called "prudent diet" (defined as a diet with large amounts of fruit, vegetables, fish and poultry) or a so-called "Western diet" (defined as a diet rich in sweets, fried foods, and refined grains). The incidence of heart attacks was then documented during a 12-year follow-up period.

The researchers found that women whose diets most closely resembled the "prudent diet" were 24% less likely to suffer a heart attack than were the rest of the women in the study. Also, women whose diets most closely resembled the Western diet were 46% more likely to suffer a heart attack. Studies of this type in the past have generally focused on the effect of a particular dietary component (e.g. vegetables or sugar) on the incidence of heart disease. While the new study did not identify which particular dietary components were most important, it did show that consuming the type of diet that is widely regarded as healthy can reduce the risk of suffering a heart attack.

1 How large was the group of participants used in the research project?
   ....
   ....

2 For how long were the women who took part in the research monitored?
   ....
   ....

3 What were the findings of the research?
   ....
   ....

4 How was this study different from others of its type that had been conducted in the past?
   ....
   ....

13c Practice Test Thirteen

Paper 3 Use of English

PART 1

Read the text below and think of the word which best fits each space. Use only one word in each space.

POWERFUL EFFICIENCY

The energy crisis has been with **(0)** *us* for some time now, promoting calls for developing a better, more efficient use **(1)** .... our ever-dwindling conventional power sources and the need to develop new **(2)** .... As regards the latter, nuclear physicists haven't as **(3)** .... come up with a reliable fast breeder reactor or properly regulated nuclear fission. For solar energy, scientists need to find new **(4)** .... of gathering, concentration and storage. In **(5)** ...., new methods have to be found to recover the energy contained **(6)** .... liquid and solid wastes. In the meantime, a top priority is the development of a safe, clean transportation fuel **(7)** .... a replacement for petroleum. **(8)** .... power companies were able to produce it cheaply enough, hydrogen could replace fossil fuels. **(9)** .... fuel cells and solar cells have supplied the power for space programmes, they are **(10)** .... expensive for individual use. Conventional fossil fuels can, however, be **(11)** .... wisely used than they are at present, **(12)** .... petroleum and mining engineers developing more economical and eco-friendly methods of extracting oil, gas and coal from the earth and engineers designing more efficient transportation systems which **(13)** .... reduce levels of energy in transit as **(14)** .... as more energy effective power plants and machinery. The watchword, therefore is to develop new energy sources **(15)** .... conserving and properly managing existing ones.

PART 2

Read the text below. Use the word given in capitals at the end of some of the lines to form a word that fits in the space in the same line.

UNWANTED VISITORS

Loss of habitat poses the single greatest threat, **(0)** *endangering* indigenous species. The second largest threat to native flora and fauna would have to be the **(16)** .... of alien species into an environment other than their own. Alien species are able to cause such cataclysmic damage because they are usually more **(17)** .... in competing for food. They introduce diseases to which the local inhabitants do not possess **(18)** .... Interbreeding has caused the destruction of entire species because the first hybrid generation will eventually **(19)** .... the parent stock. Hybrid individuals tend to possess greater vigour and will therefore compete more **(20)** .... with the remaining pure stock. Their offspring may also be infertile, resulting in the **(21)** .... of an entire species because of a reduction in the number of breeding animals. The **(22)** .... of guidelines has been called on to exclude non-native wildlife, contain it where it has a foothold, and eliminate it if possible. The principles call for border controls, **(23)** .... in international trade and technical and financial **(24)** .... to help poor countries detect and combat **(25)** ....

DANGER

INTRODUCE

SUCCESS
IMMUNE

PLACE
EFFECT

POPULATE
FORM

CAUTION
ASSIST
INVADE

PART 3

Think of one word only which can be used appropriately in all three sentences.

0 • One doesn't need to be an expert to *appreciate* the beauty of classical music.
  • He seems confident that houses in this area will *appreciate* in value in the next few years.
  • I'll always *appreciate* your help and support.

26 • The family .... down the priceless antique from generation to generation.
  • She was upset because a colleague had .... comments about her new dress.
  • Parliament .... a new law regarding the regulisation of petrol prices.

27 • News of the influential diplomat's death .... international political circles.
  • As the town was still reeling from the first tremor, a second one .... it to its foundations.
  • The hammock .... gently in the afternoon breeze, and it wasn't long before James fell asleep.

28 • Diana .... her hair in a simple ponytail tied with a pretty blue ribbon.
  • Andy .... a puzzled look on his face as he read the anonymous letter.
  • She was upset by the fact that her boss told her off simply because she .... sandals for work.

29 • He was .... his jacket in his wardrobe when he saw a paint stain on the sleeve.
  • My daughter enjoys .... around my study and watching me work on the computer.
  • Against all odds, underdogs Redwood United are still .... onto the top of the league table.

30 • The young boxer .... the champion a powerful uppercut and knocked him out.
  • During his trip to Morocco, Jim .... with various African businessmen who are interested in our services.
  • Considering all his financial problems, Tom has .... with the situation well.

31 • After passing my exams, I decided to .... myself to a long holiday.
  • I'm afraid you didn't .... the issue with appropriate care.
  • The doctor decided to .... her patient's rash with antibiotics and an ointment.

PART 4

Complete the second sentence so that it has a similar meaning to the first sentence, using the word given. Do not change the word given. Use between three and eight words, including the word given.

0 Nobody spoke when the teacher asked who the culprit was.
  remained
  Everyone *remained silent when the teacher asked* who the culprit was.

32 Would you please send me your response as soon as possible?
  grateful
  I ....
  .... your response as soon as possible.

33 The reason for his resignation is still not known.
  caused
  We ....
  .... resign.

34 This essay shows a slight improvement on the last.
  marginally
  This essay ....
  .... the last.

35 Susie couldn't stop crying when her pet rabbit died.
  floods
  Susie ....
  .... her pet rabbit died.

36 He specifically stressed the need for absolute honesty.
  emphasis
  He ....
  .... absolute honesty.

37 I couldn't work out what he was trying to say, could you?
  driving
  I couldn't work out ....
  ...., could you?

38 She realised immediately that his story was made up.
  through
  She ....
  .... story.

39 There is a considerable number of choices on offer in this brochure.
  array
  This ....
  .... choices.

PART 5

*For questions **40 - 44**, read the following texts. For questions **40 - 43**, answer with a word or short phrase. You do not need to write complete sentences. For question **44**, write a summary according to the instructions given.*

In the first few months following a child's birth, most women become particularly attuned to the needs of their newborn. In fact, in some situations the mother-child bond is so strong that some women perceive themselves and the infant as a single, inseparable entity.

Where does this most special of relationships come from? Perhaps its basis lies in the fact that for the preceding nine months mother and child were indeed one. On the other hand, there could be a more practical reason for the bonding which occurs between a woman and her child. Being the main care-giver, women tend to develop an ability to anticipate what their child wants or needs. In a sense, it is the woman's job to be perfectly attuned to what is going on with her child.

line 11 —— If this is the case, what is the father's function in the life of the child? Because the father is neither as psychologically nor physically linked to the infant as the mother is, the father views the child in a different light. He is able to stand back and see the child as an individual in its own right and not only one part of the mother-child pair. It is the male's job to keep this separateness in mind even if the mother loses sight of it from time to time.

While this paternal task may appear secondary to the maternal role, it actually has an incredible influence on the child's growing sense of self-awareness. When a child is treated as a separate individual, he begins to understand that he has a life apart from his mother and that he exists even when she is absent.

40 Which factors determine the uniqueness of the relationship between mother and child?

....

....

41 What does the word "this" represent in the phrase "If this is the case..." in line 11?

....

....

One of the greatest things about being a dad in the 90s has been the ease with which I can do things with my children that used to be considered, well, "mummy's work". Right from the very beginning, I have been closely involved — line 3 — with each of my daughters. Short of actually giving birth to them, there was nothing I couldn't do. Because of this attitude, it came as quite a shock to me when I inadvertently discovered that my wife and I were not as interchangeable — line 6 — as I had believed.

My wife and I had developed very personal ways of wishing our girls good night. Without these special bedtime rituals, both children found it very difficult to drift off to sleep. I can even remember one time when we had both had to be away for a week, so we had each recorded our good night ceremonials.

When it happened that my wife was called out one evening, it fell to me to get the girls safely tucked in. I assumed that I would simply say my good night to them and tell them that mummy would do the same the next night. My younger daughter insisted that I sing her favourite bedtime song just as her mother routinely did. I was abashed when, because of my not knowing the words, my little girl burst into tears. Time has eased the pain and I have learned to deal with the inevitable fact that mothers and fathers play very particular roles in their children's lives. Mummy is Mummy and Daddy is Daddy, and I guess that's that.

42 Why does the writer place the term "mummy's work" in quotation marks? (line 3)

....

....

43 Explain the phrase "my wife and I were not as interchangeable as I had believed" (lines 6-7).

....

....

44 In a paragraph of between 50 and 70 words, summarise the arguments found in the two passages which claim that fathers and mothers have separate roles.

....

....

....

....

....

....

....

....

....

....

UNIT 14a Grammar: Inversion

Inversion means putting the verb before the subject in a sentence. It is used after certain expressions which are placed first in the sentence in order to give emphasis.

Inversion Type 1 with auxiliary verb

- **negative, restrictive or emphatic expressions:** Not only, Little, No sooner ... than etc
  No sooner had he got into the bath than the phone rang.

- **clauses or result:** Such/So, To such a degree ...
  Such a brilliant pianist was he that he carried off all the prizes.

- **inversion in the main clause:** Only after, Only by, Only if, Only when, Not only/till, Not since
  Only by keeping a signal-fire burning did the woman manage to alert her rescuers.

- **conditionals:** Should I ... (Type 1), Were I ... (Type 2), Had I ... (Type 3)
  Were you a brighter fellow, you'd have gone along with the scheme.

Inversion Type 2 without auxiliary verb

- **after adverbs and adverbial expressions**
  "There goes Tom!" BUT "There he goes!"
  "Up went the balloon!" BUT "Up it went."

- **after the quoted words of direct speech**
  "I've just finished", said Tom. BUT ... he said.

There are adverbs and adverbial expressions with a negative, restrictive or emphatic meaning, which are followed by inversion when placed first in a sentence. The most common adverbs and adverbial expressions with negative, restrictive or emphatic meaning that are followed by inversion are: Seldom, Rarely, Little, Nowhere, Not even once, In no way, Scarcely ... when, Hardly ... when, Barely ... when, No sooner ... than, Not only ... but (also), On no occasion/account/condition, In/Under no circumstances, Only after, Only in this way, Only by, Only then, Only when, Only if, Not till/until, Never, Never before, Not since, Neither/Nor/So, Well (formal) etc
"I like chicken". "So do I".
Well did he remember the night the earthquake struck.
On no occasion was the girl allowed to stay out late.
Never had he had such a terrifying experience.
Little did he know what his decision would lead to.

Notes

Only after, only by, only if, only when, not until/till when placed at the beginning of the sentence for emphasis, require the inversion of the subject and the auxiliary verb in the main clause.
Only after all her guests had left did she wash the dishes.
Only by standing on a chair could he reach the shelf.
Not till the last guest had left were we able to relax.

-- STRUCTURAL CONVERSION ◄- -

1 *All* the food had been prepared and the table had been laid as well.
   Not only had all the food been prepared but also the table had been laid.

2 *As soon as* he was promoted, he started behaving arrogantly.
   No sooner had he been promoted than he started behaving arrogantly.
   Hardly/Scarcely had he been promoted when he started behaving arrogantly.

3 *He had no* idea that the treasure had been hidden in his garden.
   Little did he know that the treasure had been hidden in his garden.

4 *She danced so much* that she couldn't walk afterwards.
   So much did she dance that she couldn't walk afterwards.

5 *It was such* a nice day that we went on an excursion.
   Such a nice day was it that we went on an excursion.

6 *They finished* painting and then they moved into their new house.
   Only after they had finished painting did they move into their new house.

7 *If I were* you, I would accept his offer.
   Were I you, I would accept his offer.

8 *If I had* been told earlier, I would have reacted differently.
   Had I been told earlier, I would have reacted differently.

9 *If I (should)* change my mind, I'll let you know.
   Should I change my mind, I'll let you know.

10 *She didn't phone me;* she didn't drop me a line either.
   She didn't phone me nor did she drop me a line.
   She neither phoned me, nor did she drop me a line.

11 *She won't* tell lies for any reason.
   On no account will she tell lies.

12 *The boy* ran away.
   Away ran the boy!

(CONVERSATIONAL GRAMMAR)

1 *Choose the correct item.*

1 "I'm going out now."
   "......... you happen to pass a chemist's, would you get me some aspirins?"
   A Had   C Would
   B Did   D Should

2 "Did you know the Queen was in town yesterday?"
   "Yes. .... I gone shopping, I would have seen her."
   A Were   C Had
   B Was   D Should

3 "I can't understand our new French teacher's accent."
   "........."
   A Nor can I   C Neither do I
   B Nor do I   D Neither will I

4 "So, how was the film?"
   "It was great! .... you come, you would have enjoyed yourself."
   A Should   C Were
   B Had   D Would

5 "Jane bought a new dress this morning."
   "What a coincidence! ...."
   A So have I   C Nor did I
   B So did I   D Nor have I

2 *Complete the second sentence so that it has a similar meaning to the first sentence, using the word given. Do not change the word given. You must use between three and eight words, including the word given.*

1 You must never mention this to him.
   circumstances
   Under ....
   .... this to him.

2 They could only get to the island if they hired a single-engine aircraft.
   by
   Only ....
   .... get to the island.

3 He talks so much that he drives everyone mad.
   does
   So much ....
   .... everyone mad.

4 You must not leave the iron switched on for a long time.
   account
   On ....
   .... switched on for a long time.

5 I hardly ever travelled abroad when I was a student.
   travel
   Rarely ....
   .... I was a student.

3 Read the text below and think of the word which best fits each space.

LIGHT YEARS AWAY

The sun **(0)** *is* the brightest object in our solar system, the centre around **(1)** .... we revolve and **(2)** .... which life on Earth could not exist. At **(3)** .... time, people believed that the sun orbited round the Earth; our knowledge has increased considerably since then, **(4)** .... to sophisticated equipment. The sun is in fact a star **(5)** .... the type known as "yellow dwarfs" and has a volume more than a million times **(6)** .... than that of our planet. Although **(7)** .... the naked eye the sun and moon appear to be of the same size (most noticeable **(8)** .... eclipses), the sun is in fact about 400 times more distant from us than the moon. In 1922 the International Astronomical Union calculated **(9)** .... average distance from Earth **(10)** .... 92,897,000 miles, but this figure is **(11)** .... to change as modern technology enables us to **(12)** .... more precise calculations. Light emitted **(13)** .... the sun takes approximately eight minutes to reach us; if it **(14)** .... to suddenly go out, it would take **(15)** .... long until we realised what had happened!

PHRASAL VERBS 1

talk about	1) gossip about sb 2) consider
talk at:	speak to sb without listening to their replies
talk back:	reply rudely
talk down to:	speak to sb as if they were less clever than oneself
talk into:	persuade sb to do sth
talk out:	settle a problem by talking
talk out of:	persuade sb not to do sth
talk round:	persuade sb to agree to sth
tell against:	spoil chances of success
tell apart:	distinguish
tell off:	scold/reprimand
think of:	take sth into account
think out:	prepare (plan) carefully
think over:	reflect upon sth before making a decision
think up:	invent or devise sth

4 Fill in the correct preposition(s) or adverb.

0 He was against the plan at first, but they managed to talk him *round*.

1 Jane was so determined to become a model that her parents couldn't talk her .... it.

2 Ann was told .... by her father for coming home late.

3 You can't talk me .... giving you more money. I've given you enough already.

4 His lack of a convincing alibi will tell .... him at the trial.

5 Our boss talks .... us as if we were childrer

6 He insisted that children who talk .... ought to be punished.

7 If you can't talk .... your differences with your fiancé, you'd better break up.

8 Stop behaving like that or the neighbours will start to talk .... you.

9 The only way one can tell the twins .... is by their haircuts.

10 He keeps talking .... moving to another city, but I doubt if he will.

11 I've never had a real conversation with Peter; he just talks .... you.

12 My parents advised me to think things .... before accepting the job.

13 Racing drivers rarely think .... the dangers involved in their profession.

14 She thought her ideas .... carefully before putting them down on paper.

15 We need to think .... an exciting advertising campaign for our new product.

PHRASAL VERBS 2

5 Look at Appendix 1 and fill in one of the prepositions or adverbs below, then give a synonym for each phrasal verb.

• away • in • on • out • off • up • down • over • into • to

0 I'd better turn *in* early. I didn't sleep well last night.

1 The woman turned the escaped prisoner .... to the police.

2 They want to turn that basement room .... a play room.

3 Hundreds of people turned .... to welcome the royal family back to London.

4 After being offered the post Simon turned it .... in his mind carefully before accepting.

5 When her business failed, she turned .... her parents for financial help.

6 Although Mark said he'd be there at 8.00, he didn't turn .... until 10.30.

7 Could you turn .... the light? I can't see well enough to read my book.

8 I offered to help him but he turned me ....

9 We were turned .... at the door of the club for being improperly dressed.

10 You ought to turn .... the heat before the sauce burns.

11 That factory turns .... hundreds of small appliances every day.

12 The lorry turned .... in the middle of the motorway, causing an enormous pile-up.

13 He turned .... to be a liar and a cheat.

14 I have a feeling I forgot to turn .... the cooker before we left.

15 Could you please turn .... the volume a bit? I can't hear it very well.

IDIOMS/FIXED PHRASES 1

6 Look at Appendix 2 and explain the following idioms in bold.

1 Any mention of animal abuse to Tony is like **a red rag to a bull**.

2 The politician **put the cat among pigeons** by revealing details of the national scandal.

3 Those two have **fought like cat and dog** since the day they got married.

4 You can ask me **until the cows come home** but I'll never agree to your proposal.

5 Even though Betty was sixty years old, she dressed like a teenager. She looked like **mutton dressed as lamb**.

6 London to Birmingham is about 180 miles **as the crow flies**.

7 I can't believe that Jane doesn't like your car; that's just **sour grapes** because she doesn't have one.

8 Susan can't resist chocolate; She's got **a sweet tooth**.

9 Something must have made John really angry; he's been **like a bear with a sore head** all day.

10 We don't need any more furniture – there's **no room to swing a cat** in here as it is!

11 I managed to **kill two birds with one stone** by inviting the boss to dinner; I made a good impression and got some useful information.

12 You've been working on this essay for hours and you haven't even written the introduction; **you're getting nowhere fast**.

13 Sharon's budget is really tight; I don't know how she'll manage **to pay her way**.

14 It is **raining cats and dogs**; we'll have to cancel the fête.

15 After working in a factory for years, Ted decided to better himself and get a **white-collar job**.

16 The man broke a vase and knocked over two chairs; he was **like a bull in a china shop**.

17 Kate has been **as busy as a bee/a busy bee** getting everything ready for tonight's party.

18 He was so tired of **the rat race** that he gave up his job in the city and moved to an island.

19 I accidentally **let the cat out of the bag** when I mentioned that I'd seen Jim and Mandy together.

IDIOMS/FIXED PHRASES 2

7 Look at Appendix 2 and explain the following idioms in bold.

1 Some people think this country has been **going to the dogs** since the 1990s.

2 The old man felt like **a fish out of water** at the party.

3 Seeing life as a case of **dog eat dog**, he treated people ruthlessly for his own benefit.

4 Ronald was so thick-skinned that all his boss's criticisms were **like water off a duck's back**.

5 I'm not lending him any more books; they always come back **dog-eared**.

6 The hairdresser made such **a dog's dinner** of my hair that I had to have it done again.

7 What you're talking about is **a different kettle of fish**; let's keep to the point.

8 If I don't remember her birthday, I'll **be in the doghouse**.

9 Our business rivals **cooked our goose** by making a higher bid for the company.

10 Steve was fed up with doing **the donkey work** while his colleagues were given interesting jobs.

11 It would be fascinating to be **a fly on the wall** when the managers have their meeting to discuss the annual pay rise.

12 Richard could **talk the hind legs off a donkey** with stories of his school days.

13 The inability to make a decision is David's **Achilles heel**.

14 My nephew was brought up near the sea and could **swim like a fish** from the age of four.

15 I'm so tired of Chris's persistent lies that I am **washing my hands of him**.

16 Being in the army was a real **dog's life**; up at 6 a.m. every day, no money and occasional leave.

PREPOSITIONS

8 *Look at Appendix 5 and fill in the blanks with the correct preposition, then make sentences using them.*

0 to have no intention *of* helping sb
1 to fail .... an attempt
2 to bestow gifts .... someone
3 to result .... an accident
4 a visitor .... the city
5 to sigh .... pleasure
6 a sequel .... a film
7 to stay .... good
8 fruits .... season
9 to resign .... your job
10 the matter .... hand
11 death .... drowning
12 to struggle .... your rights
13 to feature .... the cinema
14 to have a talent .... acting
15 entry .... the EU
16 to keep sth secret .... a friend
17 to take a shot .... the enemy
18 to buy sth .... a discount
19 bags .... shopping
20 to be satisfied .... the results
21 a choice .... dishes
22 to trip .... a stone
23 a doctor .... profession
24 freedom .... speech
25 to be valid .... five years
26 to fall in love .... first sight
27 the bearer .... good news
28 a decline .... standards
29 a bus crowded .... tourists
30 the bottom .... the sea

31 to admit .... a fault
32 to be full .... life
33 to be .... trouble with the law
34 to live .... the suburbs
35 on top .... the world
36 to fall .... despair
37 a series .... disasters
38 to dance .... the dance floor
39 to sing .... the top of one's voice
40 to have your heart .... your mouth
41 to live .... the outskirts
42 to stand .... president

9 *Look at Appendix 5 and fill in the blanks with the correct preposition.*

0 Having always been good *at* maths, he decided to study it at university.
1 He doesn't seem to be very happy .... his new job; he always looks rather worried and depressed these days.
2 As she handed over the gift, she said that she hoped we would be very happy .... our new home.
3 It will be good .... Thomas to have a strict teacher; he's never had any discipline at home.
4 The dispute occurred because the manager is so hopeless .... people; he has absolutely no idea of how to handle his workforce.
5 We've just heard .... his unexpected promotion.
6 Nervous about facing an interview panel, she hesitated .... the door and took a deep breath before entering the room.
7 A strong draught blew into the room through the gap .... the door.
8 Ruth was a genius .... mathematics and was awarded a scholarship to Cambridge when she was only fourteen years old.
9 Have you heard .... the lake "Loch Ness" in Scotland?
10 He's a genius .... a pencil and can capture a likeness in a few deft strokes.
11 His new stereo system was expensive but it's guaranteed .... fifteen years so it was worthwhile paying more.
12 My friend is worried because she hasn't heard .... her sister for days.
13 She has a real genius .... languages and has already mastered the rudiments of Greek!

14 There is a popular superstition which says that anyone who has a gap .... their two front teeth will be lucky throughout their life.

15 She hesitated .... taking any action, hoping that there was no real cause for alarm.

16 I can't honestly say that I'm happy .... your decision to emigrate to France.

17 She's very good .... animals and takes food out to the stray dogs in the street every morning.

18 The new wonder watch from Seiko is guaranteed .... any type of breakage, including water damage and accident.

10 *Complete the second sentence so that it has a similar meaning to the first sentence, using the word given. Do not change the word given. You must use between three and eight words, including the word given.*

1 She is well known for her vast knowledge of Renaissance painting.
authority
She ....
.... Renaissance painting.

2 I don't think I'll ever be able to buy my own house.
despair
I ....
.... my own house.

3 The members of the government have failed to agree on the new budget.
reached
The members ....
.... on the new budget.

4 We liked the new teacher right away.
took
We ....
.... right away.

5 The novel didn't come up to my expectations.
short
The novel ....
.... expectations.

6 Zoe always makes spontaneous decisions concerning her travel plans.
acts
Zoe always ....
.... her travel plans.

7 Jim knew he would have to go on the business trip at a moment's notice.
poised
Jim ....
.... the business trip at a moment's notice.

8 His latest theory is in complete opposition to mainstream thinking.
flies
His latest theory ....
.... mainstream thinking.

9 His interpretation of the novel was far too complex for me to grasp, I'm afraid.
head
His interpretation of the novel ....
............................, I'm afraid.

10 Julie always listens to my complaints about work.
ear
Julie always ....
.... my complaints about work.

11 I wish you would come straight to the point if you have something to say.
beat
I wish ....
.... if you have something to say.

12 Thankfully she wasn't hurt at all in the accident.
emerged
She ....
.... accident.

13 The waiters in the new restaurant were very inefficient.
shoddy
We received ....
.... in the new restaurant.

14 My grandmother is extremely proud that she can remember all her grandchildren's birthdays.
prides
My grandmother ....
.... all her grandchildren's birthdays.

15 I couldn't face telling her what I'd heard.
bring
I couldn't ....
.... what I'd heard.

16 She lost all self-control when she found out what he'd done.
contain
She ....
.... what he'd done.

17 The singer said he wanted nothing to do with the other members of the band.
distanced
The singer ....
.... of the band.

18 There was hardly any movement in the traffic in front of us.
inched
The traffic ....
.... us.

FIXED PHRASES

turn tail:	turn and run away
in tandem with:	together with, simultaneously
go off at a tangent:	suddenly change subject or course of action
(be) on target:	make good progress
in bad/poor taste:	offensive/insulting
cup of tea:	sth one likes
get one's teeth into sth (inf):	throw oneself into sth because it is interesting, complex and makes you think hard
put sth to the test:	gauge how effective sth is by putting it into practice
thick and fast:	happening quickly in large numbers
under one's thumb:	under sb's control
toe the line:	obey the rules
keep sb on their toes:	make/keep sb alert
lower the tone of sth:	make a place or event seem less respectable
tongue in cheek:	not serious, in fun
to down tools:	to stop working
be on top of the world:	be happy
(sth) gets on top of sb:	sth depresses sb/is too much to cope with
travel light:	travel without much luggage
tread water:	be in a position where no progress is being made
a trifle:	slightly/to a small extent

11 *Complete the sentences using one of the phrase in an appropriate form.*

1 Geoffrey's remark about certain members of the department were thought to be ....
.... by everybody present.

2 The secretary had allowed the backlog of paperwork .... her.

3 When I go on holiday I prefer to ....
.... with just one small suitcase.

4 Opening your own business may be preferable to
.... as an accounts employee for year after year.

5 With a full-time job, three children and a home to run, Vera is certainly ....
.... all the time.

6 Roger .... his survival skills ....
.... when he went mountaineering.

7 Seeing the broken window, Patric ....
... and fled in the direction of the railway station.

8 The mark for your composition was lower than you had expected because you ....
.... instead of keeping to the point.

12 *Choose the correct item.*

1 The headmaster at my last school was a stern disciplinarian and made sure we .... the line.
A drew   C touched
B faced   D toed

2 You never know whether to take Vic seriously or whether his remarks are tongue in ....
A cheek   C tooth
B mouth   D face

3 Applications for the course are coming in thick and......... .
A thin   C fast
B quick   D skin

4 Mike .... the tone of the formal dinner by appearing in a pair of ripped jeans and an old T shirt.
A set   C degraded
B lowered   D put

5 The exercise routine works in .... with the diet.
A tandem   C hand
B league   D co-operation

6 We are on .... for a significant increase in production this year.

  A form   C line
  B track   D target

7 Martin just loves to .... his teeth into a really challenging crossword.

  A grind   C get
  B put   D sink

8 The pudding was a .... too sweet for my liking.

  A hint   C trifle
  B drop   D tinge

9 Bungee jumping is not my .... of tea.

  A mug   C glass
  B pot   D cup

10 The labourers decided to down .... in support of their sacked workmate.

  A equipment   C apparatus
  B tools   D instruments

11 Jenny was so unhappy as she was under the .... of her husband.

  A finger   C skin
  B nose   D thumb

12 Kristina felt on top of the .... when she won the beauty pageant.

  A world   C sky
  B earth   D universe

13 *In most lines of the following text there is a spelling or punctuation error. Read the numbered lines 1-16 and then write the correct form of the word in the spaces provided for your answers. Some lines are correct. Indicate these lines with a tick (✓). The first one has been done for you.*

DINOSAUR: A SORE DINER

0 We know that herbivourous dinosaurs with long necks fed from the treetops.   herbivorous

1 We've seen them doing exactly that in "Jurassic Park", reaching up to browse   ....

2 among the leaves, haven't we? According, however, to recent studies published   ....

3 by an australian expert on the subject of dinosaurs, this was not the case.   ....

4 Dr. Roger Seymour of the University of Adelaide's Departement of Environmental   ....

5 Biology claims that the dinosaurs which we classify collectivelly as sauropods   ....

6 had, in fact to maintain their heads in a horizontal position in order to survive, ...

7 however uncomfortable this may sound for the creature. Dr Seymour gives sound   ....

8 anatomical reasons for these views. To rise its head to the treetops, the animal would   ....

9 apparently have had to possess a heart that would be too big for it's body. In   ....

10 addition to that the heart would have consumed more energy than the rest   ....

11 of the body. Finally, the heart's thick walls would not have worked properly, ...

12 expending more energy contracting than in pumping blood round the body?   ....

13 There is, of course, that modern success story in treetop feeding, girraffes, ...

14 but, even they have a tough time of it, as they have to spread out their forlegs in an   ....

15 uncomfortable position if they want to eat and drink from the ground. Food for though, ...

16 perhaps, but not for the poor old dinosaurs. No wonder they died out?   ....

14 Read the text below. Use the word given in capitals at the end of some of the lines to form a word that fits in the space in the same line.

POP ART

Pop art was an **(0)** *unconventional* art style in which commonplace objects such as comic strips, soup cans and road signs were used as subject matter and were often incorporated into the work. The pop art movement was largely a British and American cultural phenomenon of the late 1950s and '60s. Art critic Lawrence Alloway, **(1)** .... to the prosaic iconography of its painting and sculpture, named the movement pop art. It represented an attempt to return to a more **(2)** .... and universally acceptable form of art after the **(3)** .... in both the United States and Europe of the highly personal abstract expressionism. The art form was iconoclastic, rejecting both the **(4)** .... of the "high art" of the past and the **(5)** .... of other contemporary avant-garde art. Pop art became a cultural institution because of its close reflection of a particular social situation and because its easily **(6)** .... images were immediately exploited by the mass media. Although the critics of pop art described it as sensational and non-aesthetic, its proponents saw it as an art that was democratic and not **(7)** ...., bringing together both connoisseurs and untrained, **(8)** .... viewers. Even though public reaction to pop art was **(9)** ...., it found critical acceptance as a form of art suited to the highly **(10)** ...., mass media-oriented society of western countries.

CONVENTION

REFER
OBJECT
DOMINATE

SUPREME
PRETEND

COMPREHEND

DISCRIMINATE
EXPERIENCE
FAVOUR
TECHNOLOGY

15 Read the text below and decide which answer (A, B, C or D) best fits each gap.

ACCESSORIES FOR SALE

Made **(0)** .... good quality cowhide, this unisex belt bag is ideal for travelling or any other energetic outdoor pursuit where it is beneficial to have both hands **(1)** .... Compact and lightweight, the bag **(2)** .... 8" x 4 1/2" and fits up to a 41" waist. The main zipped section, and a flapover compartment with pop fastening are large enough to **(3)** .... sunglasses, a passport, a small camera and more. There is also a small zipped pocket **(4)** .... for coins. Available in black, navy and brown for £15.50, **(5)** .... is included. Our slim, hideaway travel wallet is **(6)** .... to slot over a belt and sit securely in position under trousers or a skirt. Features **(7)** .... a strong stitched band, a full length zipped pocket for notes, travel cards etc, and a small zipped section which is ideal for postage stamps or a key. Measuring a compact 7" x 4", this **(8)** .... black leather wallet is available for only £5.95. Return within seven days for a **(9)** .... if not completely satisfied.

0 A off	Ⓑ of	C from	D by
1 A free	B lose	C available	D loose
2 A weighs	B measures	C counts	D rates
3 A contain	B hold	C include	D take
4 A suitable	B appropriate	C able	D enough
5 A transport	B sending	C delivery	D conveyance
6 A proposed	B planned	C designed	D aimed
7 A include	B contain	C comprise	D embrace
8 A refined	B intriguing	C neat	D subtle
9 A compensation	B refund	C repayment	D guarantee

16 *Choose the correct item.*

0 The Prime Minister has .... the controversial statement he made about nuclear arms.

(A) retracted   C pulled out
B extracted   D renounced

1 The King was forced to .... his right to the throne when he married a divorcee.

A extract   C renounce
B pull out   D retract

2 The team had to .... of the competition because of injuries.

A pull out   C renounce
B extract   D retract

3 The text was complicated and therefore very difficult to .... information from.

A extract   C retract
B renounce   D pull out

4 She .... her finger on a sharp rose thorn.

A stung   C stabbed
B bit   D pricked

5 The baby was .... by a bee whilst playing in the garden.

A bitten   C stung
B pricked   D stabbed

6 The film star categorically .... any connection with the scandal.

A refuses   C rejects
B denies   D revokes

7 Due to his reckless driving his driving licence was .... by the court.

A refused   C revoked
B denied   D rejected

8 Sue begged Tom to help her but he ....

A denied   C rejected
B refused   D revoked

COLLOCATIONS

17 *Fill in beat, win.*

1 .... your rival
2 .... a match
3 .... money
4 .... a prize
5 .... the clock
6 .... a competition
7 .... all opposition
8 .... hands down

18 *Think of one word which can be used appropriately in all three sentences.*

0 • One doesn't need to be an expert to **appreciate** the beauty of classical music.
• He seems confident that houses in this area will **appreciate** in value in the next few years.
• I'll always **appreciate** your help and support.

1 • When he fell off his bicycle, he .... his arm.
• John really .... me when he said I was a manipulative and calculating person.
• The muscles in my leg really .... after running the marathon.

2 • In sunny weather .... people are strongly advised to wear a hat.
• If the tyres of a car are ...., there is an increased risk of slipping due to the surfaces being worn down.
• The company chairman's resignation came as a .... statement during the monthly sales meeting.

3 • You must try to .... that irritating habit of biting your nails.
• When on holiday, I enjoy listening to the waves as they .... along the shore.
• After such a long, sweltering summer, I'm longing for the weather to ....

4 • The tsetse fly is a .... which spreads diseases to cattle and humans.
• The computer engineer found a .... in the software which was corrupting files.
• There has been a stomach .... going around school for weeks.

5 • Timothy .... into the room and started shouting at the others.
• During winter water pipes often .... due to the freezing temperatures.
• If the banks of the river should ...., the town will be severely flooded.

6 • I heard the .... of the tiny bird's heart as I held it in my hand.
• Many people find the jumping .... of rock music too much to bear.
• Whilst on his ...., the policeman heard strange noises coming from the disused warehouse.

PREPARING FOR PART 5

MEANING AND USAGE II

19 *a) Read the passages and explain the words, phrases or sentences in bold.*

In the lead up to the Sydney Games, there was considerable controversy about new Olympic security laws that restricted freedom of assembly and allowed military incursion into civil society. In a country that does not have a history of terrorism or civil disturbance, a nation that takes pride in its tolerance and democratic rights record, it was a shock to many people that the Olympics had brought **(0) "the problem of the world"** to their doorstep.

0   *Problems of other societies/cultures* ....
....

The great attraction of living on the moon is the promise of a completely new life, but based on traditional principles. But how do you engineer the right mix of ages and trades to create a true community? **(1) Getting the right skills aboard the spacecraft** may also be a problem. The management will employ the staff needed to run the basic moon station services, but other residents will have to **(2) bring their careers with them.**

1   ....
....
2   ....
....

Fifteen derelict properties are due to be auctioned off this month and are expected to raise more than five million pounds. Profits will go towards cutting the fifty million pounds the borough owes to various agents. "Some people have complained that we are **(3) selling off the family silver,**" said councillor Mick Stubbs, "**(4) but much of this silver is tarnished.** With a property portfolio of three billion pounds, we have more property than we know what to do with."

3   ....
....
4   ....
....

LEO
If you are feeling a little mischievous, **(5) it won't hurt to push a few romantic buttons.** Someone certainly needs livening up, and it won't do either of you any harm. But **(6) don't think you can get away with it entirely.** Remember, what goes around comes around, usually when you least expect it. It will be an interesting and pleasurable escapade.

5   ....
....
6   ....
....

It had been a pleasurable evening with my delightful companion. We'd already decided that we would **(7) go all-out,** so I wasn't at all perturbed when my fellow diner ordered the most expensive meal in the restaurant. Relaxing after the meal, I wondered where my friend had got to; **(8) it seemed quite a long time to powder her pretty nose. (9) Then it dawned on me.** She'd gone, leaving me **(10) to pick up the tab.**

7   ....
....
8   ....
....
9   ....
....
10   ....
....

b) Read the passages and explain what the purpose of each writer is when using the words, sentences or phrases in bold. One item has been done for you.

Angina is a condition in which the blood that gets to the heart is not sufficient for it to function properly. This happens because of blockages in the arteries that deliver blood to the heart. The symptoms of angina are felt mostly during exercise, when the heart needs more blood to help the body's muscles meet the demand for more power. **(0) Chest pain (usually exactly behind the breastbone), a "burning sensation" or "tightness" in the chest area and shortness of breath are some common angina symptoms.**

Once somebody stops exercising, angina symptoms disappear because the heart is again able to meet the body's demands. However, these symptoms should always be discussed with your doctor, because they indicate that an artery is, to some extent, damaged and **(1) your chest stopping hurting doesn't mean that your artery has been unblocked. (2) These chest pains may be the only warning your body can give you against a developing heart condition – or even a possible heart attack.**

0   *The writer is trying to help his readers understand what angina feels like.* ....

1   ....

2   ....

UNLESS YOU REALLY ARE JOE BLOGGS, YOU WOULDN'T WANT TO BE TREATED LIKE HIM...

(3) At the Royal Bank of York, we have been banking with people for 104 years. That's too long a time to remain inflexible, exactly because it's long enough to realise that each and every client has his own needs.

We are now proud to introduce our unique "Banking for You" scheme. We have over 55 different account handling systems already in place, and we are happy to build one especially for your banking needs. **(4) If other banks seem too rigid to be able to help you,** why not visit one of our branches and find out what the Royal Bank of York can do for you. **(5) Our banking advisors will be delighted to offer you a free consultation.** Or call 0800-499-600 to arrange for one of our consultants to visit you at home.

...BECAUSE YOUR NEEDS ARE DIFFERENT!

3   ....

4   ....

5   ....

Once the aircraft reaches 14,000 feet, the instructor will open the aircraft door. Remember your assigned queue number, and do not leave your seat before the instructor calls it; **(6) you may get in the way of others who are preparing themselves for their jump.** Once your number is called, stand up and walk to the door without hurrying. Take extra time to adjust your equipment if you need to. By now you should know the parachute-opening procedure by heart, but if you are unsure about anything do not hesitate to ask the instructor: **(7) nobody will laugh or get mad at you, and jumping from a plane without perfect knowledge of what you have to do once in the air is dangerous.** After you've jumped, arch your back, push your stomach towards the earth and let your arms and legs reach back towards the sky. **(8) This will create a centre of gravity which will pull you towards the ground and make sure that, when you pull the cord, your parachute will open pointing upwards.** This is an important manoeuvre, and you should not jump unless you fully understand it. Not following this manoeuvre might cause the parachute to open sideways or downwards and get tangled around you.

6   ....

7   ....

8   ....

14c Practice Test Fourteen

Paper 3 Use of English

Time: 1 hour 30 minutes

PART 1

Read the text below and think of the word which best fits each space. Use only one word in each space.

STILL STANDING TALL

The Highlands is an imprecise term **(0)** *for* the upland area which covers **(1)** .... northern part of mainland Scotland. This area **(2)** .... includes the northern islands and is known for **(3)** .... mountains, sea, moors, lakes and wide, exhilarating space. This is **(4)** .... of Europe's last wildernesses, beautiful as **(5)** .... as imaginative. The north and west of the Highlands, **(6)** .... the mountains and sea collide, exhaust superlatives. South of mysterious Loch Ness stand the magnificent Cairngorm Mountains, Britain's **(7)** .... land mass. The Cairngorm Summit is **(8)** .... to many bird species which are unique **(9)** .... this area. It also offers woodland and cycle routes **(10)** .... some of the last naturally regenerating pine forests **(11)** .... existing in Britain. Famous for **(12)** .... one of the most popular walks in the Highlands, and **(13)** .... particularly strenuous is the Lost Valley walk. The Lost Valley is a hidden mountain sanctuary, **(14)** .... to be haunted by the ghosts of the murdered MacDonald clan. This highly atmospheric trek **(15)** .... fails to inspire awe in its countless visitors.

PART 2

Read the text below. Use the word given in capitals at the end of some of the lines to form a word that fits in the space in the same line.

UNICEF

The United Nations Children's Fund, **(0)** *formerly* the United Nations International Children's Emergency Fund (UNICEF), is **(16)** .... a programme of the United Nations devoted to aiding national efforts to improve the health, nutrition, education, and general welfare of children. UNICEF was created in December 1946 for the **(17)** .... of relief to children in countries devastated by World War II. After 1950 the fund's efforts were directed toward general programmes for the **(18)** .... of children's welfare, particularly in **(19)** .... countries, as well as those in various emergency situations. The change in the organisation's name to the United Nations Children's Fund was a **(20)** .... of this shift in function. Much of UNICEF's effort has been in fields in which relatively small **(21)** .... could have a significant impact on the lives of children, such as the prevention and treatment of certain diseases and the distribution of surplus food. **(22)** .... activities to which UNICEF contributes include the development of health services and the training of health personnel, the construction of **(23)** .... facilities and the training of teachers, and the extension of other welfare services. Their **(24)** .... activities are financed both by government and private **(25)** .... contributions . Headquarters are in New York City.

FORMER
DENY

PROVIDE

IMPROVE
DEVELOP

REFLECT
EXPEND

ADD

EDUCATE
HUMAN
VOLUNTEER

PART 3

Think of one word only which can be used appropriately in all three sentences.

0 • One doesn't need to be an expert to **appreciate** the beauty of classical music.
  • He seems confident that houses in this area will **appreciate** in value in the next few years.
  • I'll always **appreciate** your help and support.

26 • You are strongly advised not to .... the solar eclipse without using special sunglasses.
  • Employees are required to .... the non-smoking rule, applied on the company's premises.
  • Few people today .... the spring equinox in the traditional way.

27 • She scanned the room, looking for something to .... herself with while she waited.
  • He refused to .... the possibility of his daughter going to Africa.
  • Part of the secretary's position was to .... the wives of the visiting dignitaries.

28 • Physiotherapy is recommended following an .... on your back.
  • Removing the hardened sediments from the antique vase is going to be a delicate ....
  • There were several nuclear reactors in .... at the time of the accident.

29 • They had a cunning .... to overthrow the government.
  • This room could be made so much more attractive with a different colour ....
  • Suddenly he understood he was no longer part of her .... of things.

30 • The pianist never .... the potential he'd known as a teenager.
  • Mark .... his ambition when his novel became a bestseller.
  • Helen .... she had been cheated by the shopkeeper when she checked her change.

31 • Alicia .... the on/off switch, but the machine was not responding.
  • After giving some general information about the forthcoming exam, the professor .... on with his lesson.
  • The hospitals were crammed with injured people so some schools were .... into service as makeshift infirmaries.

PART 4

Complete the second sentence so that it has a similar meaning to the first sentence, using the word given. Do not change the word given. You must use between three and eight words, including the word given.

0 Nobody spoke when the teacher asked who the culprit was.
  remained
  Everyone *remained silent when the teacher asked* .... who the culprit was.

32 Martin cannot go any higher in his career.
  pinnacle
  Martin .... his career.

33 My husband will be angry when I tell him.
  roof
  My husband will .... when I tell him.

34 Julie and Andrew like the same sort of music.
  taste
  Julie and Andrew .... music.

35 Sam was really anxious, waiting to see if he had got a place in the cricket team.
  tenterhooks
  Sam was .... if he had got a place in the cricket team.

36 The heir to the family fortune was eventually found to be an impostor.
  exposed
  The heir to the family fortune was .... an impostor.

37 He claimed my point was not relevant to the proceedings.
  dismissed
  He .... to the proceedings.

38 He said she was happy and enjoyed her new life.
  described
  He .... her new life.

39 It's difficult to know if it should be classified as a guest house or a hotel.
  categorise
  It's difficult to know .... as a guest house or a hotel.

PART 5

*For questions **40-44** read the following texts. For questions **40 - 43**, answer with a word or short phrase. You do not need to write complete sentences. For question **44**, write a summary according to the instructions given.*

Dreaming is a very complex function that people have been trying to make sense of for a long time. People as far back as the ancient Greeks believed that dreams were messages from the heavens, in some cases intended to help us with difficult decisions and in others to warn us about possible dangers.

line 5 — But in more recent years, dreaming was not seen as a subject worth analysing. The feeling was that dreams were ephemeral incidents, not something to base solid science on. More recently, however, research has linked the creation of dreams to something more tangible - chemical reactions in the brain. It has even been noted that certain chemical reactions are responsible for certain types of dreams, but scientists have a long way to go before being able to

line 11 — construct a complete chemical map of brain activity during dreams. Be that as it may, dreams are not dismissed as meaningless anymore; rather, if we manage to discover the cause of these chemical reactions, they may prove extremely valuable in our effort to reveal the secrets of the human brain.

40 Why have dreams been considered "not worth analysing"? (line 5)

....

....

41 What does the writer mean by the term "a complete chemical map of brain activity during dreams"? (line 11)

....

....

Freud's first great innovation in the field of understanding mental life was to give people suffering from neuroses the opportunity to talk freely while he listened. It was a very simple idea, but as a formal method it was quite new. This is still the basis of the psycho-analytical methods today. Using this technique, Freud began to recognise ordinary mental activities involving the use of representations or symbols of deep psychical events. Dreams, for example, could be understood as symbols for complex mental activities. These derive from current external events in the patient's life and reverberate with hidden wishes and deeper early experiences.

The physical aspects of the psycho-analytical setting have not changed much since Freud's day. The patient comes to daily sessions at pre-arranged times and lies on the couch while the analyst sits in a chair just behind the couch. The analyst does not make notes in the patient's presence as this would interfere with the analyst's capacity to give proper attention to what the patient is conveying. Notes are sometimes made after the sessions. It is the analyst's responsibility to provide a consulting room that is cosy, peaceful, and as free from interruption as possible. Every session lasts 50 minutes and the analyst starts and ends on time. The establishment of this secure setting, together with reliable and predictable adherence to it by the psychoanalyst, provides a containing structure within which the patient and analyst are able to explore and think about the patient's difficulties.

42 Why do analysts not take notes during a psychoanalysis session?

....

....

43 What should an analyst's consulting room be like?

....

....

44 In a paragraph of between 50 and 70 words, summarise the different theories about where dreams come from discussed in the two passages.

....

....

....

....

....

....

....

There are three main ways of putting clauses or sentences together: **co-ordination**, **subordination** and **adverbial links**: You can co-ordinate or subordinate clauses by using conjunctions.

Conjunctions are used to join clauses into sentences and show how their meanings are related. There are two types of conjunctions: a) **co-ordinating conjunctions**, which join parts of a sentence that are equivalent and
b) **subordinating conjunctions**, which join a subordinate clause to a main clause.

She put on her coat	**and**	left.	You can leave	**if**	you want.
main clause	conjunction	main clause	main clause	conjunction	subordinate clause

We can use simple co-ordinating, simple and compound subordinating conjunctions *(but/as, even if)* and correlative conjunctions. Correlative conjunctions consist of two linking words separated by one or more words *(both... and/as...so...as)*.

- Co-ordinating Conjunctions

simple conjunctions	correlative conjunctions	usage
and *I like apples and adore apple-pies.*	both ... and not only ... but (also) *He was both handsome and rich.*	addition
but *I saw John but I didn't see Sam.*	not ... but *It's not navy blue but black*	contrast
or *Are you English or American?*	either ... or (else) *Either stop talking or (else) leave the room.*	alternative(s)
nor *I can't help you, nor do I wish to help.*	neither ... nor *He is neither kind nor sympathetic.*	negative addition

Note

The comma is optional before a co-ordinating conjunction. However, we never put a comma when part of the first sentence is omitted in the second.

*Do you want tea (,) or would you like some coffee? You can **either** have a Coke **or a** lemonade.*

- Subordinating Conjunctions

simple and compound conjunctions	correlative conjunctions	usage
as, than, like as if, as though *He acts as if he were the boss.*	as/so ... as *He is as naughty as a monkey.*	comparison
(al)though, while, whereas, despite, even if, even though, in spite of, in contrast to, contrary to *We're friends even though we've got little in common.*	although ... yet/nevertheless *He's not running for President, yet/ nevertheless he's willing to help in the campaign.*	contrast

simple conjunctions	correlative conjunctions	usage
if, unless, given (that), so long as, provided/providing (that), as long as, in case, supposing (that), otherwise (negative condition) *We're going on an excursion **unless** it starts raining.*	if ... then *If it's sunny, **then** we'll go swimming.*	*condition*
but, except (for), apart from, despite, in spite of *Everyone came **except (for)** John.*		*exception*
as far as, so far that *The land belongs to us **as far as** the eye can see.* *We drove **so far that** we ran out of petrol.*		*extent*
where, wherever ***Wherever** he goes, he causes trouble.*		*place*
rather / sooner than ***Rather than** help, he prefers to hinder.*		*preference*
so as to, so that, in order that, now (that), seeing that, why, for, etc	the ... the as ... so ***The** more noise you make, **the** more annoyed I get. **As** he got older, **so** his performance failed.*	*proportion* *purpose*
as, because, since, on the grounds of/that, now (that), seeing (that), why, for, etc *I don't know **why** he was late. The knight refused to kill his enemy, **for** they had been friends.*		*reason*
	so/such... that *It was **such** a difficult task **that** nobody managed it.*	*result*
if, whether *Terry asked Sue **whether/if** she could come to the party.*	whether ... or *I'm going home now **whether** you like it **or** not.*	*indirect question, alternative condition*
whenever, as, while, now (that), when, before, until, as soon as, after, since, once, the moment (that)/ immediately etc *I cry **whenever** I watch a sad film. The baby cried **until** he was blue in the face.*	no sooner ... than, hardly/barely ... when ***No sooner** had she stepped into her flat **than** she fainted.* ***Hardly** had she finished cooking **when** the electricity was cut.*	*time*
what, who, whom, whose, which, that *This is the man **whose** daughter is a famous singer.*		*relative*

15a Grammar: Conjunctions/Punctuation

Note:

A comma is placed between a subordinate clause and a main clause, when the subordinate clause is at the beginning, or both clauses are rather long or complicated.

If the weather improves, we can go to the beach. **but:** *We can go to the beach if the weather improves.*

- **Adverbial links**

Adverbial links are adverbs which are used to join two or more clauses or whole sentences which themselves contain co-ordinate or subordinate clauses.

Adverbial links	usage
besides, also, furthermore, above all, what is more, in addition, moreover, anyway, on top of that, and then *I don't feel well enough to go shopping today.* **Besides,** *I don't have any money.* *I am working long hours this week.* **On top of that,** *the au-pair girl has asked for a few days' leave.* *I'm afraid I can't afford the luxury of a winter holiday.* **And then,** *there's the semester exams.*	*addition*
therefore, so, consequently, hence, thus, as a result, in consequence *Oil resources are decreasing.* **Therefore,** *we need to find alternative sources of energy.*	*result*
however, though, (and), yet, still, nevertheless, after all, even so, all the same, in contrast, instead, on the contrary, on the other hand, whereas/while *She's an intelligent student.* **However,** *she talks too much in class.* *Delius is a famous composer. Mozart is more famous,* **though.** *It was snowing.* **Nevertheless,** *the match went on as planned.* *He never read a book.* **Instead,** *he went fishing and hunting.* *They are very wealthy.* **Even so/All the same,** *they lead a modest life.*	*contrast*
namely, in other words, for instance/example, that is (to say) *He would never consent to that,* **namely,** *he wouldn't approve of that marriage.*	*exemplification*
otherwise, alternatively *If you pay in cash you are entitled to a discount.* **Alternatively,** *you buy on credit at a low interest rate.*	*alternatives*

Note:

Adverbial links are separated from the rest of the sentence with commas.
He didn't want to go. However, he eventually did.

CONVERSATIONAL GRAMMAR

1 *Choose the correct item.*

0 "I hope you didn't go out in the hot sun."
"We waited .... the sun had gone down, before we went for a walk."

A that   C until
B to   D for

1 "Tell me about France; did you like it?"
"Actually, we didn't go. We went to Italy ...."

A still   C in contrast
B on the other hand   D instead

2 "Can you come away with me for the weekend?"
"I can't as I'm decorating the kitchen. ...., my mother is ill."

A Even so   C All the same
B On top of that   D After all

3 .... reading the question carefully, Gary started writing.

A After   C Until
B While   D Since

292

4 "I hope you have enough money to take a cab home."

"I took some extra money .... I needed it."

A even if   C unless

B in case   D so that

5 "Jane is really conscientious, isn't she?"

"Absolutely. ...., she is very efficient."

A What is more   C So

B All the same   D Still

6 "Is Leona feeling alright?"

"Yes, but she had been feeling sick for over a week .... she finally called a doctor."

A after   C once

B before   D while.

7 "What do you think of the Jeffersons?"

"......... they appeared reserved at first, they are very sociable."

A However   C Although

B Despite   D On the other hand

8 "What happened to the plane?"

"It had hardly touched down .... it burst into flames."

A when   C than

B that   D sooner

9 "Peter speaks French very well."

"......... speaking French, he speaks German and Spanish."

A Furthermore   C Nevertheless

B Instead of   D As well as

10 "Why are you so nervous about this exam?"

"Because I need to get a high score. ...., I will have to resit for it."

A On top of that C All the same

B Otherwise   D Besides

11 "Did the minister approve the building plans?"

"Not really. He turned them down .... that the costs were too high."

A on the grounds C in case

B provided   D supposing

12 "Did you arrive at the station on time?"

"No, I missed the 5 o'clock train, ..., there was another one after 5 minutes."

A despite   C however

B besides   D also

13 "Peter's amazing."

"I know. .... he had a broken foot, he managed to walk 10 miles."

A Despite   C Even though

B Whereas   D Yet

2 *Complete the second sentence so that it has a similar meaning to the first sentence, using the word given. Do not change the word given. You must use between three and eight words, including the word given.*

1 The car has been voted Car of the Year. Its engine has been modified.

of

The car, ..., has been voted Car of the Year.

2 Everyone abandoned the building. Shortly afterwards we saw smoke billowing out of the upper floor windows.

evacuated

Shortly .... we saw smoke billowing out of the upper floor windows.

3 It's rather unreasonable punishing Daniel for losing his key as he's only a child.

hardly

You .... as he's only a child.

4 The reason why I was given promotion was that Laurence recommended me.

but

I wouldn't .... from Laurence.

5 You have to be more co-operative! Your colleagues won't respect you.

esteem

You will not be held .... become more co-operative.

6 At the moment I only have time to think about my university thesis.

preoccupied

At the moment .... my university thesis.

PUNCTUATION

Full Stop [.]

- to indicate the end of a grammatically complete sentence
  He usually finishes work at 7 o'clock.

- in direct speech, to indicate the end of a spoken sentence
  He said, "I'll probably be late home tonight."
  But: If a reporting expression follows a direct speech, we usually put a comma.
  "I'll try again," he said.

  Note

  In modern British English, abbreviations tend to be written without full stops. *Mr, Ltd, kg, MA, USA*

Question Mark [?]

- at the end of a direct question
  What's the time?

- at the end of question tags
  You've finished, haven't you?

  Note

  We do not use question marks after indirect questions.
  He asked what time it was.

Exclamation Mark [!]

at the end of an exclamatory sentence, to emphasise surprise, horror or delight
I can hardly believe it!

Comma [,]

- to separate items in a list of nouns, adjectives or adverbs
  She answered the question carefully, thoughtfully, accurately and appropriately.

- to separate main clauses which describe consecutive actions
  He stormed out of the room, slammed the door behind him and left the class speechless.

- after a subordinate clause which precedes the main clause
  When we first arrived in this country, we found many things strange and intimidating.
  If we see him, we'll tell him what you said.
  But: *We'll tell him what you said if we see him.*

- before and after a non-defining relative clause
  This grammar book, which was published last year, is one of the best I've ever used.
  But: *The book that I borrowed from the college library is overdue.*

- to separate an introductory word or phrase from the main part of the sentence
  To be honest, we're not sure yet of the possible results.

- after "Yes" or "No" at the beginning of a sentence
  No, I don't know where your glasses are.

- before or after introductory verbs in direct speech
  "I've got a lot of work to do", she said, "so I'd better go home now".
  The girl said, "I seem to have lost my purse".

- before question tags
  You will give me a lift, won't you?

- to keep the word order in a sentence when expressions or words interrupt its normal progression
  The distance learning University, believe it or not, has issued many fake certificates.

Colon [:]

- before words or phrases which refer back to the statement preceding the colon and give more information about the statement (which makes complete sense on its own)
  The treatment was a complete success: all traces of the disease were eradicated.
  Also: a semi-colon or a full stop can be used here, instead of a colon.

- to introduce a list of items (which might be complete sentences in themselves)
  If you go trekking in these regions, the following items are essential: a torch, a first-aid kit and a compass.
  Deposits on hired cars will be kept by the company in the following circumstances: when the car is damaged in any way, when it is returned late or when the tank has not been refilled.

- to introduce a quotation
  Whenever I go through Customs at an airport, I am always tempted to repeat Oscar Wilde's classic comment: "I have nothing to declare except my genius."

- when direct speech is introduced by a name or short phrase (as in the text of a play)
  Here's a line from Shakespeare's "Othello": "one that loved not wisely, but too well..."

- before capitals if a colon is followed by several complete sentences
  This can be done if you proceed as follows: First, you plug your guitar into the amplifier. Second, you make sure that the red lamp is on while...

Capital Letters

- for the first letter of the first word of a sentence
  People are becoming more aware of the need to protect the environment.

- for the first letter of the first word in direct speech, immediately after the opening quotation marks
  "Where have you been?" he asked.
  He asked, "Where have you been?"

- for the personal pronoun "I"
  I don't think I'll come with you.

- for the first letter of proper nouns such as the names of people, countries, towns, days of the week, months, holidays, peoples, titles
  On Saturday, Julia and Michael went to Oxford Street in London to buy some Christmas presents for the family and Mr Jones.

- for languages and adjectives of nationality
  We stayed in a Swiss town while we were doing a short summer course in French.

- for the first letter of the more important words in the titles of books, films, plays, newspapers, magazines, hotels, etc
  Our professor told us to read "The Rise and Fall of the Roman Empire" during the summer holiday.
  Two of D.H. Lawrence's most famous books are "Sons and Lovers" and "Women in Love".

- for some abbreviations
  RSPCA (Royal Society for the Prevention of Cruelty to Animals),
  NATO (North Atlantic Treaty Organisation), BBC (British Broadcasting Corporation)
  but: Mr, Mrs, Ltd

Dash [–]

- in informal English, in the same way as colons or semi-colons, i.e. to separate a word or phrase which is independent of the rest of the sentence; it may precede a comment, a definition or conclusion, emphasise the words which follow, or introduce an afterthought
  Anger, fear, frustration, disappointment – a whole array of emotions appeared on his face.
  Despite all his assets – and they were considerable – his business enterprise failed.
  We are flying on Friday morning – at least, I hope so.

- to show an interruption in speech
  "But Sarah, I thought you said –", Jane began, then stopped abruptly.

Apostrophe [']

- where letters are omitted in contracted forms: *isn't, I'm, didn't, I'll*
- to denote possession:
  a) in singular nouns, before the possessive s: *the man's car, my mother's career*
  b) in plural nouns, after the plural s: *the teachers' salaries, the nurses' demands*
  c) in irregular plurals, before the s: *men's clothing, women's voices, children's interests*
- with certain words showing time duration:
  a) in the singular: *an hour's journey, a month's salary*
  b) in the plural: *five hours' journey, two hours' wait, three weeks' work*
- in special plurals:
  a) in plural forms of words which do not usually have plurals: *The new employees were given a list of the **do's** and **don'ts***
  b) in plurals of letters: *I can't make out his **r's** and **v's**.*
  c) in numbers: *It was in the late **1980's** (or... **1980s**).*
  d) in abbreviations: *I can recommend you two very good **GP's** (or... **GPs**).*

Quotation Marks/Inverted Commas [" "]

- to indicate direct speech, at the beginning and end of the words spoken
  "I can hardly believe it."
- before and after titles of books, films, plays, newspapers and other special names
  His performance in "Hamlet" was outstanding.
  He was reading an Agatha Christie novel called "Cat Among the Pigeons" on the train.
- to indicate irony or suggest figurative use
  We walked up the "grand" staircase, which was, in fact, in a sad state of disrepair.
  The island population has recently "exploded".
- for quotations inside quotations, we use double quotation marks inside single (or single inside double)
  She said, 'It's a case of "he who laughs last, laughs longest" if you ask me.'

Notes
a A comma precedes or ends direct speech.
   She said, "We'll tell you later."
b Question marks or exclamation marks referring to the direct speech are placed inside the quotation marks.
   "What a tremendous achievement!" he exclaimed.
   "When are you leaving?" he asked.

Hyphen [-]

- in some compound nouns: *dining-room, air-conditioning*; hyphens are becoming less common in modern English and it is usually acceptable to write the two words separately: *address book, health centre* while some combinations can be written in three ways i.e. with a hyphen, a space between the words or as a single lexical item: *ski-boots, ski boots, skiboots*
- in some compound adjectives (the second part is usually a participle): *broad-shouldered, smartly-dressed, home-made, nice-looking*
- to link a prefix with a noun or adjective: *pre-war, anti-American, pro-abortion, post-Victorian*
- in numbers between tens and units: *twenty-five, two hundred and sixty-three*
- when expressions of measurement, amount or quantity are used as adjectives before a noun: *a five-pound note, a three-mile walk, a two-hour lecture, a one-year-old child*

Semi-Colon [;]

to separate long parts of a sentence, each one of which is a complete clause on its own, but whose meanings are closely connected. It shows a pause which is longer than a comma but shorter than a full-stop.
Some critics considered him the best actor of his generation; others believed he never quite lived up to his early promise.
She was badly-dressed and slovenly in her appearance; the contrast to her sister could not have been greater.

Parentheses/Brackets [( )]

to separate additional information or a comment from the rest of the sentence
The old Odeon cinema (where I saw the first Elvis Presley film) still stands on the corner of the street.
Also: commas can be used here instead of parentheses, which is preferable in formal writing.

3 *Punctuate the following items.*

1 next sunday im going to scotland to help my aunt who is a widow to move house

2 don t use the swiss cheese use the cheese which is on the top shelf of the fridge

3 i really like shakespeares play much ado about nothing because its very witty

4 we visited numerous cities in india madras delhi and agra where of course we visited the taj mahal calcutta and mysore

5 youre going to have to improve your appearance im afraid said the manager to the sales assistant we need smartly dressed well groomed people

6 we couldnt believe our eyes when we opened the front door books clothes drawers chairs all the contents of our house it seemed had been thrown around the room

7 why i often ask myself can' t they do something about the traffic problem in this city

8 the playwright arthur miller, who was at one time marilyn monroes husband wrote the play death of a salesman

9 i couldnt tell you about this last friday because i didnt know about it then

10 your children are a pleasure to be with polite thoughtful and well-behaved i hope you know how lucky you are

11 its a threehour walk to the nearest village hopefully you will only have to go there once or twice

12 he was a quiet shy reserved sort of person his brother on the other hand was the exact opposite

13 its a well-paid job so id accept it if i were you sophia advised her friend

4 *In most lines of the following text there is a spelling or punctuation error. Read the numbered lines 1-13 and then write the correct form of the word in the spaces provided for your answers. Some lines are correct. Indicate these lines with a tick (✓). The first one has been done for you.*

PREHISTORIC PLANTS

0	Everyone has seen animals in cages, even thought they may not like the idea. Then how would	*though*
1	you feel about the prospect of plants in cages? You might think it to be some stunt dreamed	....
2	up for a science-fiction film – a re-make of John Wyndham's "The Day of the Triffids,	....
3	for example. You would, however be wrong. Believe it or not, caged plants do exist. They	....
4	are the Wollemi Pine, possibly the worlds oldest plants, and have been kept for breeding	....
5	and research purposes. The Wollemi Pine, which florished in Australia before continental	....
6	drift made for a drier climate, was discovered in 1994, after having been thought to be	....
7	exstinct for between 200 and 40 million years. It had previously been found only in	....
8	fossilised form. The present specimens, discovered in the Blue Mountains of new South	....
9	Wales, have been dated to over 1,000 years old. It is hoped that the thirty eight	....
10	genetically identical plants will thrive, despite the danger of desease which would arise from	....
11	there sharing the same DNA. One thing is for sure, though; unlike the dangerous,	....
12	and havoc-wreaking triffids, the Wollemi Pines will not be able to escape from their cages,	....
13	will they?	....

15b English in Use

5 *Read the text below and think of the word which best fits each space. Use only one word in each space.*

NEW AGE VEHICLES

The motor industry says that **(0)** *there* are really no bad cars any more. Build, quality and reliability have **(1)** .... huge strides, so even small cars today will keep you alive in a bad crash, and harmful exhaust emissions are just a fraction of **(2)** .... they were. A **(3)** .... greater variety of cars is available and they are recyclable at the **(4)** .... of their life span. The industry also says that **(5)** .... to what people may think, the car of the future has already arrived: it has just sneaked up on us **(6)** .... by bit. The most obvious changes will be **(7)** .... design. Designers will be playing **(8)** .... national identities and adding personality to their cars, often **(9)** .... modern interpretations of traditional styling values. **(10)** .... will be a greater **(11)** .... of interesting mainstream cars, as well as more niche cars, that is to **(12)** .... cars tailored to fit those with specific leisure interests or physical needs, and then, although **(13)** .... will still be in the minority, alternative-technology cars. This group is set to expand quickly, but ten years won't be **(14)** .... near long enough for them to take over, for one very good reason: making alternative technology work, is easier than making **(15)** .... affordable.

PHRASAL VERBS 1

throw about/around:	scatter sth
throw away:	discard sth as useless
throw sth back at sb:	remind sb of sth bad they did in the past
throw oneself into:	begin to do sth energetically and enthusiastically
throw oneself on sb/sth:	rely on sb/sth
throw off:	escape from, get free of
throw sth out:	get rid of unwanted item
throw sb out:	force sb to leave
throw sb together:	bring people into contact with each other
throw up:	1) give up (a job etc) 2) vomit
try on:	check the fit (of clothes)
try out:	test

6 *Fill in the missing preposition(s) or adverb.*

0 He threw *up* his studies when he was offered a well-paid sales job.

1 Although Paul is having a hard time, he doesn't want to throw himself .... his friends and ask for their help.

2 When Joana lost a lot of weight, she decided to throw .... all her larger sized clothes.

3 Would you like to try .... this new electric shaver?

4 He was thrown .... of the library when he started singing.

5 It was fate that had thrown the engaged couple ....

6 During the French Revolution the people tried to throw .... the shackles of poverty.

7 She has tried .... at least twenty dresses but she can't find one she likes.

8 I wish you would throw these old magazines ....

9 She felt very sick and threw .... several times.

10 Even though I'd only lost one contract in my career I knew my manager would throw it .... me in my annual appraisal.

11 On finishing university, she threw herself .... her new editing career with great enthusiasm.

12 Joan threw books and papers .... the room whilst trying to find her passport and her cheque book.

PHRASAL VERBS 2

wear away:	become thin, damaged, weak etc by constant use
wear off:	disappear gradually (effect of sth)
wear out:	use until useless (of clothes etc)
work off:	1) overcome the effects of sth (energy, stress, anger) 2) repay by working (a debt)
work on:	be occupied with
work out:	1) find a solution by reasoning 2) turn out successfully
work up:	1) develop 2) excite 3) advance (in business)

IDIOMS/FIXED PHRASES 1

get cold feet:	lose courage to do sth
have a cheek/nerve:	act/speak boldly or impudently
have an eye for:	be a good judge of sth
not lose (any) sleep over sth:	not worry about sth
jack of all trades:	sb who is able to do a variety of jobs
turn a blind eye to sth:	ignore
lose one's head:	lose self-control

7 *Fill in the missing preposition or adverb.*

0 She is hoping to work her way *up* to a vice-presidency.

1 It took months for the shock of her parents' death to wear ....

2 He has worked .... his business from a single shop to a huge chain.

3 I'm trying to work .... how this device was put together.

4 When Sue has had a row with someone, she works it .... by going for a long walk.

5 He is working .... a new book but it will take him a couple of years to finish it.

6 The politician's speech worked the crowd .... to a frenzy.

7 He has worn .... three pairs of running shoes in two months.

8 She was doubtful about the new system of checking accounts, but it worked .... in the end.

9 The surface of the road was worn .... by severe flooding.

8 *Fill in the blanks with the correct idiom/fixed phrase.*

0 I like going shopping with Elaine as she *has an eye for* the clothes which suit me best.

1 Jim was told off about his unacceptable behaviour but he .... it.

2 David was going hang-gliding but he .... at the last minute and decided not to.

3 Dad spends his free time mending old things: he's a ....

4 When the fire broke out, the spectators .... and started fighting their way out of the stadium.

5 You .... shouting at me because I'm late. I've never been late before!

6 The traffic warden .... to the car which was parked illegally; she didn't bother to stop and give the driver a ticket.

IDIOMS/FIXED PHRASES 2

be all fingers and thumbs:	be awkward, clumsy
a storm in a teacup:	a lot of fuss about sth that is not important
give sb the cold shoulder:	ignore/shun sb
bring (sth) home to sb:	make sb understand how important or serious sth is
bite off more than you can chew:	try to do sth which is too difficult
put one's heart and soul into sth: in clover:	be devoted to sth living a luxurious and comfortable life
have a sharp tongue:	tend to say unkind or hurtful things
tooth and nail:	fiercely
a pain in the neck:	annoying person/ thing
look down one's nose at sb/sth:	feel/act superior to sb/sth
face the music:	be criticised or punished for sth you have done

9 Fill in the blanks with the correct idiom/fixed phrase.

1 The alleged scandal turned out to be ....; all that fuss about nothing.

2 I found it really hard to .... her the implications of her actions; she just wouldn't listen.

3 Sarah was such a dedicated nurse that she .... the work.

4 Gary is doing three jobs. I think he's .... as he looks exhausted.

5 Maria has become such a snob since joining the State Orchestra; she .... the rest of us in the music club.

6 I wouldn't like to be in an argument with Penny; she ....

7 Herbert has been .... ever since he won the lottery.

8 Joe is so irritating, he's a real ....

9 I guess it's time for Chris to stop avoiding his boss and .... about his mistake.

10 It was very rude of you to .... Andy ....; you should at least say hello to him.

11 The party was awful as Helen and Barbara argued .... for most of the evening.

12 When it comes to cooking, Tina ....; if she doesn't burn things, she drops them on the floor.

10 Look at Appendix 5 and fill in the blanks with the correct preposition.

0 Since passing his accountancy exams, George has had his salary increased by 10%.

1 Railway engineers joined three additional carriages .... the train to accommodate the extra passengers.

2 Classes have increased .... size since falling levels of government funding have reduced the number of teachers in the school.

3 He joined .... when he was seventeen and he's been in the army ever since.

4 Impatient .... her arrival, he kept running to the window every time a car passed.

5 The organisers tried to get everyone to join .... the games.

6 I began to get impatient .... his continual lack of punctuality.

11 Look at Appendix 5 and fill in the blanks with the correct preposition.

1 Although we were all rather irritated by the situation at the time, we laughed .... it afterwards.

2 Tom lectured his son .... the dangers of riding a motorcycle.

3 The summer dress was lined .... light cotton to make it less transparent.

4 He was listening .... the radio when he heard the news of the earthquake.

5 I'm expecting an important call; could you listen .... the telephone while I pop out to the shops?

6 He doesn't have any savings and, since being made redundant, has been living .... his family.

12 *Complete the second sentence so that it has a similar meaning to the first sentence using the word given. Do not change the word given. You must use between three and eight words, including the word given.*

1 The community spoke enthusiastically about the recently elected mayor.
sang
The community ....
.... praises.

2 Should we go ahead with the plan?
advisable
Is ....
.... with the plan?

3 We must include buying new furniture in our household budget this year.
accounted
Buying now furniture ....
.... in our household budget this year.

4 The garage is too small for the van.
room
There ....
.... for the van.

5 In my opinion Jim deserves everything he gets.
ask
If ....
.... he gets.

6 By leaving Mary alone, I'm sure she'll finish the project on time.
devices
If Mary ....
............., I'm sure she'll finish the project on time.

7 The overfishing of cod is a matter which is worrying environmentalists.
voiced
Environmentalists ....
.... the overfishing of cod.

8 The police say that the circumstances of her disappearance are suspicious.
treating
The police ....
.... suspicious.

9 Schools should make careers lessons a priority.
emphasis
Schools should ....
.... careers lessons.

10 Who told you there was going to be a rail strike?
out
How ....
.... to be a rail strike?

11 You must do something to make sure this doesn't happen again.
steps
You must ....
.... happen again.

12 The doctor is very busy; I'm afraid he can't see you today.
spare
The doctor ....
.... today.

13 I shouldn't have trusted a stranger with my savings.
better
I ....
.... trust a stranger with my savings.

14 The journalist wrote down everything she said in his notebook.
record
The journalist ....
.... in his notebook.

15 As well as her normal salary, she makes some extra money by freelancing.
supplement
She ....
.... normal income.

16 At first no one mentioned his absence.
said
At first ....
.... his absence.

17 My supervisor did not even hint to me that he was about to resign.
indication
I ....
.... that he was about to resign.

18 The subject of productivity bonuses has been mentioned at every management and workers meeting.
cropped
The subject of productivity bonuses ....
.... management and workers.

19 I can recommend you to the manager; I'm a friend of his.
word
I can ....
.... the manager; I'm a friend of his.

FIXED PHRASES

the ultimate in:	the best/most advanced
catch/take unawares:	happen when you are least expecting it
unbeknown to sb:	when sb is unaware of sth
in no uncertain terms:	clearly and unmistakably
be given to understand that:	be informed about sth but not directly
come unstuck (inf):	fail badly in sth you are trying to achieve
be up against sth:	have a difficult situation or problem to deal with
be quick on the uptake (inf):	able to understand things quickly; clever
not be up to much (inf):	of poor quality
have its uses (inf):	have advantages or benefits
to the utmost:	to the greatest extent
do sth in vain:	not succeed in sth
banging your head against a brick wall (inf):	frustrated because sb is stopping you from making progress in sth
sb or sth is driving you up the wall (inf):	sb or sth is annoying and irritating you
have a whale of a time (inf):	to enjoy oneself very much
put years on sb (inf):	make sb look or feel much older
as yet:	up until the present time
go from bad to worse:	become more unpleasant
if the worst comes to the worst:	if the situation develops in the most unfavourable way possible

13 *Complete the sentences using one of the fixed phrases in an appropriate form.*

1 He .... in his attempt to get a first-class degree.

2 Having triple by-pass surgery has .... Charles.

3 We do not .... have reliable information about casualties from the derailment.

4 I really don't think that the new T.V. series is ...., do you?

5 Even though they were .... the league champions, Rothwell Rangers played very well.

6 You can always ask, ..., for your mortgage to be repaid over a longer period of time.

7 Some people feel that they are .... when dealing with bureaucracy.

8 Although my position of office manager has its ...., it is, by and large, a satisfying job.

9 Wanting to test her courage ...., Nora took up bunjee jumping.

14 *Choose the correct item.*

1 Jack was disappointed not to be promoted as he was given to .... that the job would be his.
A know   C realise
B understand   D say

2 That loud heavy metal music from next door is .... me up the wall.
A driving   C bringing
B sending   D pushing

3 Bright children who are .... on the uptake may get bored easily if they are not stimulated enough at school.
A swift   C quick
B fast   D rapid

4 This new model of car is the .... in driving luxury.
A penultimate C finest
B ultimate   D best

5 Shiftwork does have its .... sometimes.
A purposes   C reasons
B conveniences D uses

6 My husband told me in no .... terms that I would have to economise on household expenses.
   A unsure   C vague
   B uncertain   D unclear

7 We had a .... of a time at Jason's party yesterday.
   A whale   C whole
   B period   D week

8 In .... did I knock on the huge oak door, for nobody answered.
   A vane   C vein
   B mane   D vain

9 They were planning, ... to Hilary, to throw a surprise party for her.
   A unaware   C unbeknown
   B oblivious   D unknown

10 Investors were caught .... by the sharp drop in share prices.
   A undecided   C unsuspecting
   B unawares   D unconscious

11 The economic situation in the country is going from bad to .... after the stockmarket crash.
   A better   C worse
   B best   D worst

15 *Read the text below and decide which answer (A, B, C or D) best fits each gap.*

HAIR-RAISING FACTS

Panic is rising (0) .... hair stylists in Denmark. Some of those who often colour, perm or highlight hair – 125 stylists in all – are complaining (1) .... symptoms which may indicate brain damage. Authorities have been forced to investigate, and it appears that many stylists are (2) .... from memory loss, nausea and frequent headaches. The reason is that the chemicals (3) .... produce harmful fumes. The hairdressers' unions are funding investigations into the problem. However, scientists are (4) .... because the quantity of chemicals used is not enough to be harmful. Many stylists are now worried, so Denmark has (5) .... strict regulations. Manufacturers must now list all the chemicals contained in the products. (6) .... ventilation must be provided in hairdressing salons and clients will wear a special perm-helmet, (7) .... the fumes away from the stylist. All of Europe will have to (8) .... these new regulations. At the moment, everything is still at the committee stage, but soon the revolutionary perm-helmet will be worn in all salons. Final decisions will be (9) .... when hairdressers' unions meet in Brussels to discuss the problem.

0 A in   Ⓑ among   C between   D at
1 A from   B about   C of   D because
2 A experiencing B suffering   C impaired   D injured
3 A operated   B consumed   C exploited   D used
4 A sceptical   B thoughtful   C doubtful   D scornful
5 A introduced   B launched   C passed   D initiated
6 A Abundant   B Surplus   C Ample   D Plenty
7 A guiding   B leading   C turning   D directing
8 A apply to   B comply with   C follow   D fulfil
9 A introduced   B done   C made   D given

WORD USAGE

16 *Read the text below. Use the word given in capitals at the end of some of the lines to form a word that fits in the space in the same line.*

ALTERNATIVE SOURCES OF ENERGY

In the *Search for Free Energy*, Tutt's recently released book, he quotes, "We ought to be able to obtain the energy we need without the **(0)** *consumption* of material." These are not the words of some modern-day **(1)** ...., but of Nikola Tesla, in 1890. Among his **(2)** .... was the device to generate electricity by harnessing 'coming energy'. The search for free, and **(3)** .... energy continues. **(4)** .... are looking for 'fuelless' technologies that will not pollute or run out, and they are not referring to the puny **(5)** .... of solar or wind power. The **(6)** .... establishment has so far been proven correct, there's no such thing as a free energy lunch but that hasn't stopped mad scientists trying. They've come up with **(7)** .... patents of 'over unity' contraptions, **(8)** .... giving out more energy than you put in to get them going. The story is fascinating and rarely heavy-going, although the quotes can be overlong and the diagrams are **(9)** .... displayed. Tutt admits that only a fraction of what is claimed is true. But it's also true to say we cannot afford to dismiss them out of hand, as one of these **(10)** .... investigators may just be able to save our planet from climate change.

CONSUME
ENVIRONMENT
INVENT
EXPENSE
SEARCH
CONTRIBUTE
SCIENCE

NUMBER
SUPPOSE

ADEQUATE

CONFORM

17 *Choose the correct item.*

0 Tom always tries to .... perfection in everything he does.
   A accomplish   C gain
   (B) attain   D manage

1 The charity managed to .... a great deal during its most recent project in Africa.
   A gain   C attain
   B reach   D accomplish

2 Thank you very much, but I am afraid that, due to the political situation, the President must .... your invitation to tour your country.
   A decline   C snub
   B renounce   D reject

3 Peter was heartbroken when Sue .... his offer of marriage so cruelly.
   A spurned   C denied
   B disclaimed   D renounced

4 I wasn't .... to see a queue outside the new sports centre.
   A taken aback   C amazed
   B astounded   D surprised

5 She was a little .... by this strange coincidence.
   A astounded   C flabbergasted
   B amazed   D taken aback

6 We .... to the manager about the assistant's behaviour.
   A objected   C criticised
   B nagged   D complained

7 Instead of .... to yourself, why don't you make a formal complaint?
   A grumbling   C objecting
   B whining   D complaining

8 My mother told me that, as a child, I used to .... continually for sweets.
   A whine   C complain
   B grumble   D pester

9 The latest advertising .... for facial tissues is a free gift with every purchase.
   A scam   C gimmick
   B snare   D plot

COLLOCATIONS

8 a) *Fill in* **spray, scatter.**

1 .... paper on the ground
2 .... your hair
3 .... water on plants
4 .... a crowd
5 .... leaves
6 .... paint
7 .... seed

b) *Fill in* **respectful, respectable.**

1 .... married couple
2 .... silence
3 .... area
4 .... child
5 .... salary
6 .... family
7 .... attitude

c) *Fill in* **historic, historical.**

1 .... novel
2 .... event
3 .... building
4 .... costume
5 .... research
6 .... changes
7 .... victory
8 .... context

9 *Fill in the collocational grids.*

	lick	gulp	nibble
ice cream			
cheese			
lollipop			
water			
the bait			
one's food			

20 *Think of one word only which can be used appropriately in all three sentences.*

0 • One doesn't need to be an expert to *appreciate* the beauty of classical music.
  • He seems confident that houses in this area will *appreciate* in value in the next few years.
  • I'll always *appreciate* your help and support.

1 • After working hard in the garden he needed to .... for a while.
  • He had to .... against the gate when he felt dizzy.
  • The future of the economy will .... on the number of goods the country can export.

2 • James needs to .... his mind to the task in hand.
  • The information didn't .... to them, so they were told to ignore it.
  • When the dog darted in front of the car, I had to .... the brakes rather abruptly.

3 • At long last the couple decided to arrange a .... for their wedding.
  • This particular kind of .... grows in Egypt.
  • Susan had a dinner .... so she couldn't attend the meeting.

4 • He .... money in his will to the local children's home.
  • The little girl was .... by her mother in the old house.
  • The flight to Damascus .... much later than was scheduled.

5 • David's brother is a drummer in a famous rock ....
  • A metal .... encloses the wooden strips at each end of the barrel.
  • Primary education deals with the age .... of five or six to eleven or twelve.

6 • The joiner used an electric .... to bore holes in the door.
  • The teacher liked to give the students a regular spelling ....
  • The uniforms were made of khaki .... which was very unattractive.

7 • His chronic .... affected his ability to work.
  • The house was left in total .... after the party.
  • Incidents of civil .... led to the formation of a riot squad.

8 • Her attempt at making rice pudding failed when the mixture refused to ....
  • She .... the alarm clock so it would ring at 6 a.m.
  • Far from being impractical, Tom proved that his feet were .... firmly on the ground.

305

PREPARING FOR PART 5

ANSWERING DETAIL QUESTIONS II

21 *Read the following passages and underline the parts where the answer to each of the following question*
    is contained. Then paraphrase the underlined parts to answer the questions. Give accurate answers, but
    use as few words as possible. Item (0) has been done for you.

This morning a half-kilometre wide space rock is zooming past Earth **(0)** <u>barely 12 times farther from our planet</u> <u>than the Moon</u>. In cosmic terms, it's a near miss. But scientists say not to bother reaching for your helmets as there is absolutely no danger of a collision. Instead, the close encounter will afford astronomers a welcome opportunity to study a bright near-Earth asteroid from close range.

Today's hasty cosmic visitor – known to researchers as 2000 QW7 – was discovered just last weekend on August 26, 2000, with NASA/JPL's Near Earth Asteroid Tracking system (NEAT). QW7 caught the attention of NEAT project scientists because it was fast-moving and unusually bright. At 13th magnitude, amateur astronomers can easily spot the minor astral body through 8-inch or larger telescopes.

According to NEAT principal investigator Eleanor Helin, QW7 offers an exceptional opportunity for Earthbound observers to study a near-Earth asteroid. "This is a very important object," she said. "It's so bright that amateur astronomers can track it now and through the end of this year. We should be able to obtain a precise orbit, as well as colours, a light curve and other physical properties during this discovery."

A group of astronomers led by Jean-Luc Margot of the Arecibo Observatory has already made the first radar detection of the space rock using NASA's Goldstone antenna in the Mojave desert. "An improved orbit from the radar data will help us run the orbit backwards and discover where it was before we discovered it," added Margot. "It's a bit of mystery why we haven't seen this one before."

0 How far from the Earth is QW7 passing?
   At a distance 12 times that between the Earth and the Moon.

1 Why did QW7 catch the attention of NEAT project scientists?
   ....
   ....

2 Why is QW7 so important to NEAT?
   ....
   ....

3 In what way will detailed information about the asteroid's orbit, obtained from the radar data, help scientists?
   ....
   ....

Companies are increasingly finding that supporting the community is good for their public persona, and they have a number of different ways of getting involved. Some set up charitable sponsor, some sponsor fundraising events, some introduce cause-related marketing campaigns. All these efforts help strengthen ties with the community and can reinforce a beneficial corporate image.

Employee-based humanitarian programmes are particularly effective, since they not only foster a company's community relations, but also their own industrial relations. Research repeatedly finds that employees in businesses offering these programmes feel a stronger connection and loyalty to both their companies and their communities. Businesses also have an increased incentive to support non-profit organisations and to match employee donation programmes, since charitable corporate gifts are tax-deductible up to 10 percent of a company's annual income.

New technology tools are helping modernise and extend traditional workplace charitable campaigns. Automation is providing new ways to make these programmes simpler, and more appealing. It also helps streamline the incorporation of different types of gifts into these campaigns, including giving donations by credit card, and automatic payroll deductions.

1 Why are companies becoming more involved in supporting the community?
....
....

2 How do companies become involved in charity?
....
....

3 What is the effect of employee-based humanitarian programmes on a company's employees?
....
....

4 What financial benefit can companies gain by supporting nonprofit organisations?
....
....

5 Apart from making charitable campaigns "simpler and more appealing", how does automation help such endeavours?
....
....

Paper 3 Use of English   Time: 1 hour 30 minutes

PART 1

Read the text below and think of the word which best fits each space. Use only one word in each space.

A MAN - MADE LEGEND

Phoenix-like **(0)** *from* amidst the ecological ashes comes a story of hope. At dawn, on a usually deserted beach on the Greek island of Cephalonia, crowds compete **(1)** .... journalists and television crews, gathered together to witness the arrival of something special. Four years ago, eggs **(2)** .... by the rare Loggerhead turtle were found in a nest on **(3)** .... very beach. It was judged by experts that it was too late in the season for the hatchlings to have any chance of survival in the wild, so action was **(4)** .... The British charity, Care for the Wild, decided to fly the eggs back to Southampton University and attempt to hatch them **(5)** .... special conditions, in incubators. All four eggs hatched successfully and it was decided that when they were four years old, they were **(6)** .... of surviving in the wild. They were returned **(7)** .... the remote beach, which remains untouched by the ravages of tourism, and released in front of an audience of excited well-wishers. An example, **(8)** .... might say, of positive human intervention in the process of natural selection! **(9)** ...., their fight for survival is **(10)** .... from over. The Loggerhead turtle is one of the most endangered species of all. It has inhabited the earth for approximately ninety million years and is now facing a man-made threat which has placed **(11)** .... survival in a precarious state. The turtles can live as long as one hundred years but they don't even begin to show characteristics of their gender until they reach thirty. Effectively, our four heroes will have to struggle for another quarter of a century **(12)** .... they begin to fight back and fulfil some of the hopes invested in them. In **(13)** .... time, they will be forced to resist not **(14)** .... natural threats, but also dangers imposed on them by the fishing industry and tourist development. Their chances are slim to say the **(15)** ...., but it is hoped that their story might raise awareness of the plight of the turtles.

PART 2

Read the text below. Use the word given in capitals at the end of some of the lines to form a word that fits in the space in the same line.

AN ADOPTED ENGLISHMAN

Joseph Conrad (1857 - 1924) was a Polish-born English **(0)** *novelist* and short story	NOVEL
writer who has been **(16)** .... regarded as one of the greatest	INCREASE
English writers. During his lifetime Conrad was admired for the **(17)**	RICH
of his prose and his renderings of dangerous life at sea and in exotic places. Conrad's	
fascination with the individual when faced with nature's invariable unconcern, man's	
(18) ...., and his inner battle with good and evil form the basis of the sub-	HATE
plot of many of his works. 'Heart of Darkness' is his most famous, finest and most	
(19) .... story, the title of which signifies both the heart of Africa and	MYSTERY
also the heart of evil, that is everything that is corrupt, nihilistic and malign; in essence,	
Conrad's **(20)** .... of the heart of man. This novel is central to	APPROXIMATE
Conrad's work and vision. Conrad's influence on later writers has been profound both	
because of his **(21)** .... technical innovations and because of the vision	MASTER
of **(22)** .... expressed through them. At his greatest Conrad examines	HUMAN
what happens when our innate dark forces are left **(23)** .... but are	RESTRAIN
given free rein and permitted to commune openly with **(24)** .... evil.	EXTERNAL
His gift is a dark **(25)** .... of the human condition.	INTERPRET

PART 3

Think of one word only which can be used appropriately in all three sentences.

0 • One doesn't need to be an expert to *appreciate* the beauty of classical music.
   • He seems confident that houses in this area will *appreciate* in value in the next few years.
   • I'll always *appreciate* your help and support.

26 • The .... fog caused a six mile tailback on the motorway.
   • A .... metal such as lead is used as ballast.
   • By calling him .... the teacher deeply upset Joe.

27 • Mr Jones, the primary school headmaster, had to .... his remarks to the teaching staff.
   • I was advised to .... my letter to the Editor in Chief.
   • I think we should try to .... the problem of truancy in schools.

28 • Pat has always wanted to be able to .... with the National Theatre Company.
   • When the chimney caught fire we had to .... quickly.
   • He doesn't .... appropriately for his age.

29 • In my ...., people don't make enough effort to recycle packaging material.
   • The treasures of the Pharaoh's tomb are on .... at the Bodley Museum.
   • The .... of the factory doesn't exactly add to the attraction of this property.

30 • He was proud to see his short .... in print.
   • Police found an .... of clothing in the boot of the suspect's car.
   • There is an .... in the constitution which states that human rights must be respected.

31 • The guard dogs were aware of our .... as we neared the entrance.
   • They needed a new .... if the business was to flourish.
   • The .... to the runway was obstructed with military tanks.

PART 4

Complete the second sentence so that it has a similar meaning to the first sentence, using the word given. Do not change the word given. You must use between three and eight words, including the word given.

0 Nobody spoke when the teacher asked who the culprit was.
   remained
   Everyone *remained silent when the teacher asked* who the culprit was.

32 She did everything possible to save her marriage.
   power
   She ....
   .... her marriage.

33 This room needs to be decorated, doesn't it?
   doing
   This ....
   ...., doesn't it?

34 My husband and I had a row about buying a car.
   words
   I ....
   .... about buying a car.

35 The government's plan to privatise the railways met with strong opposition from passengers.
   came
   The government's plan to privatise the railways ....
   .... from passengers.

36 The firm went bankrupt after failing to win the contract.
   liquidation
   The firm ....
   .... failing to win the contract.

37 That scene was so frightening I had to look away.
   bear
   That scene was ....
   .... it.

38 The introduction of the new currency has greatly affected the economy.
   impact
   The introduction of the new currency ....
   .... the economy.

39 She was miserable when her mother made her give away all her childhood toys.
   parted
   She was miserable ....
   .... all her childhood toys.

PART 5

For questions 40 - 44 read the following texts. For questions 40 - 43, answer with a word or short phrase. You do not need to write complete sentences. For question 44, write a summary according to the instructions given.

Music has permeated every human society in varying forms from the beginning of time, combining vocal and instrumental sounds. Whether it is a folk song or an orchestral composition, music is the same humanly engineered activity, which has been an important part of ritual and drama in all cultures throughout history.

Music helps people express their deep emotions and this is exemplified in traditional Portuguese Fado music. Fado is 'Portuguese Blues', melodious songs
line 8 —— that are accompanied by the guitar. Fado (literally meaning fate) is a word which carries a great number of connotations. Nostalgia, desire and melancholy are all "meanings" of Fado. The urge to express these emotions is highly developed among the Portuguese, who are a maritime people and are used to being apart from their families. A person's anguish of being unable to be with the one he loves, the pain of the loss of a loved one, the isolation which springs from the mariner's vastly empty surroundings, and the constant longing for the one place where one belongs, home, are common themes in these songs, striking chords deep inside the hearts of the poor and all those who suffer distress.

40 What does the writer mean by the phrase "Fado... is a word which carries a great number of connotations"(line 8)?

....

....

41 Why do the Portuguese feel a need to articulate the sentiments of Fado?

....

....

Aboriginal people believe that in the beginning of time, "the Dreaming", there were no visible landmarks, and the world was flat. As time progressed, creatures emerged from the ground and had the power to change at will from their animal to their human form. These forefathers created all the features of the landscape and they laid down the rules of conduct for their offspring, to whom they also gave the gift of song. In these melodies they recounted themes of the history of their own lives, sad songs which could heal the wounded and the sick, songs that could convince the sky to rain, ones that defended the community against flooding, or ones that could change the direction of the wind. For Australian Aboriginals, music and song is an integral part of their culture and religion.

In Aboriginal societies, as in many other musical cultures, a person known as the songman is highly regarded. The songman is a special performer who composes songs describing daily events; his repertoire is enriched by songs handed down from ancestors. He is often asked to perform for other groups and is rewarded for his services. This is a central part of Aboriginal ceremonies.

A song is sung as a series comprising many short verses, each of which tells a particular event or place associated with their ancestors. These history songs link the time long past with the present. The singer is part of this connection,
line 19 —— reliving parts of another era and yet a part of the current one. Aboriginal music is a living bond with their land, their past and their ancestors.

42 Who were the world's first inhabitants according to Aboriginal belief?

....

....

43 What word does the term "one" represent in line 19?

....

....

44 In a paragraph of between 50 and 70 words, summarise the themes which are prevalent in Portuguese Fado and Aboriginal ancestral songs.

....

....

....

....

....

....

....

....

Appendix 1

PHRASAL VERBS

act on = do whatever is advised/suggested
act up = behave awkwardly or badly
answer (sb) back = speak rudely to sb
answer back = defend oneself
answer for = be responsible for sth/pay for sth/vouch for
answer to = be under the command of sb/have the characteristics described
back down = cease to oppose
back out of = withdraw from
back up = support
be beneath sb = be demeaning
be down on = be hostile to sb
be down with = be ill (with disease)
be in for it = be about to receive punishment/trouble
be in with = be in favour with
be into = (informal) take an interest in sth
be off = (1) cease to want or be interested in sth, (2) have come loose, detached from sth, (3) stay away from work/school, (4) cancel, (5) be bad, unhealthy (usu food)
be on = be shown on television, at the cinema etc
be out = (1) be in bloom, (2) be extinguished, (3) be removed, (4) be absent (from home or work), (5) be wrong in calculation, (6) be unfashionable
be up to = (1) do, (2) depend on
bear on = be relevant to
bear with = be patient

balance against = assess in relation to
bank on = depend on
bear out = support the truth of
become of = happen to
blink at = show surprise
blow over = stop and be forgotten
blow up = explode
book up = reserve
break away = escape from captivity
break down = (1) fail to function, (2) lose control of feelings
break in = (1) interrupt, (2) enter a building by force
break into = suddenly start doing sth
break off = end sth suddenly
break out = (1) start suddenly (of violent events), (2) escape from a place
break through = (1) make a discovery, (2) become visible (3) achieve success despite obstacles or difficulties
break up = (1) end a relationship, (2) disperse
break with = give up sth
brush up = improve (by study)
build up = acquire gradually/accumulate

bring about = cause
bring in = introduce (law, idea)
bring off = succeed in (sth difficult)
bring on = cause an illness
bring out = publish/release
bring round/to = cause sb to regain consciousness
bring up = (1) stop, (2) mention a subject, (3) vomit, (4) raise a child
call at = visit briefly
call back = ask to return
call for = require
call in = consult
call off = cancel
call out = cause one to go on strike
call up = conscript
carry off = succeed in doing sth difficult
carry on = (1) continue, (2) behave wildly
carry out = fulfil or perform sth
carry over = last from another time
carry through = complete sth in spite of difficulties
catch on = become popular
catch up = reach sb who is ahead
chip in = add one's share of money
clear of = find innocent
clear off = run away
clear out = get rid of unwanted things
clear up = (of the weather) brighten up
charge to = bill sb
charge with = publicly accuse sb of committing a wrong deed

be done for = be ruined
come about = happen
come across = find sth or meet sb by chance
come by = obtain sth
come down to = be passed to sb
come forward = step forward
come in = become fashionable
come into = inherit
come on = progress
come out = (1) become known, (2) be published
come out in = develop
come over = happen; have a result or effect on sb
come round to = change one's opinion to another point of view; be persuaded
come round/to = regain consciousness
come through = continue to live after (sth bad)
come to = amount to a total
come up = grow

come up to = reach, equal sth
come up with = have an idea about a way to solve a problem
deal in = trade in sth
deal with = tackle a problem; cope with
do away with = abolish
do down = criticise
do out of = deprive of
do up = fasten (a coat etc)
do with = need/would like
do without = manage in spite of lack
drive at = imply, suggest
go off = happen

5b English in Use

cheat out of = prevent sb from having sth usu in an unfair way
check in = register as a guest at a hotel
check out = pay one's bill and leave a hotel
check up on = investigate sb's behaviour etc
cut back = reduce (outgoings)
cut down on = reduce (consumption)
cut in = interrupt sth
cut off = (1) isolate, (2) disconnect
cut out = omit
draw in = shorten (of days)
draw on = use part of a reserve
draw out = extend
draw up = come to a stop (of vehicles)
drop in = visit unexpectedly
drop off = decrease
drop out of = withdraw from
eat into = consume a part of sth
fall back = retreat
fall back on = turn to sth/sb for help when all else has failed
fall for = fall in love with sb
fall in = collapse
fall in with = agree to
fall off = decline
fall on = attack
fall out with = quarrel
fall through = fail to take place
feel for = sympathise
fit in = mix well with others
fit up/out = furnish/equip
fly at = attack (with blows or words)
fold up = collapse or fail
head off = prevent
join up = become a member of the military

6b English in Use

get about = (1) move about, (2) spread (of news, gossip etc)
get across = make understood
get ahead = succeed

get along/on = be on friendly terms with
get at = mean
get at sb = criticise, tease in an unkind way
get away with = escape punishment
get by = manage despite difficulties
get sb down = depress sb
get off = send
get off with = nearly escape punishment
get on = make progress
get on with = continue doing sth
get out of = avoid
get over = recover from
get round = persuade
get round to = find time
get through = contact by phone
get up to = be busy with sth surprising or undesirable
give (oneself) up = surrender
give away = (1) reveal, (2) give freely as a present
give in = (1) deliver, yield
give off = send out/emit
give out = (1) come to an end, (2) announce, (3) distribute
give up = (1) stop doing sth, (2) admit defeat
give oneself up = surrender
hype up = exaggerate the value of sth

7b English in Use

go down = (of remarks, proposals etc) be received in a specified way
go down with = become ill
go for = be sold
go in for = take part in
go into = describe, examine in detail
go off = make a sudden loud noise
go on = happen
go on with = continue sth esp after a pause
go round = be enough for everyone to have a share
go through = (1) examine sth closely or systematically, (2) consume
go up = be built
go with = be included in the price
hold back = (1) prevent development, (2) delay, (3) withhold
hold in = control (feelings, oneself)
hold off = (1) keep at a distance, (2) delay
hold on = wait
hold out = (1) last, (2) resist
hold out for = wait to get sth desired
hold out on = keep a secret from sb
hold over = postpone to a later date
hold up = (1) rob (a bank, vehicle) (2) delay

Appendix 1

8b English in Use

be kept in = be detained after normal hours as a punishment
keep at = continue working at
keep back = hide
keep down = repress
keep in with = continue to be friendly
keep on = continue doing sth
keep on at = continue talking in an irritating way
keep to = follow
keep up (with) = progress at the same rate
keep up with = (1) stay at an equal level with, (2) be informed about
land in = get into trouble, difficulties etc
land up = end (usu in difficulties)
lay aside = put aside
lay into = attack (with blows or words)
lay off = stop doing sth irritating
lay out = spend
let down = (1) disappoint, (2) lower sth
let in for = involve in trouble etc
let in on = allow sb to share a plan, secret, etc
let on = reveal a secret
let out = (1) make (a garment etc) looser or larger (opp: take in), (2) utter a cry
let sb off = not punish severely
let sb through = allow sb to pass an exam or a test
let up = become less in degree
let up on = treat sb less severely

9b English in Use

be made up = consist
lead on = persuade sb to believe or do sth by making false promises
look after = take care of
look ahead = think about the future
look at = read
look back = think about one's past
look down on = despise
look for = search for
look in = pay a short visit
look into = investigate/examine the facts relating to sth
look on = watch sth without taking part
look onto = have a view
look out = watch out; be careful
look out for = (1) search in order to find sth, (2) be alert in order to see/find sb
look over = examine (a place)
look to = rely on sb
look up = search for (a word) in a reference book
look up = visit esp after a long time
look up to = respect

make for = head for
make off with = steal sth and hurry away with it
make out = (1) complete sth, (2) claim to be, (3) discern, (4) understand
make over = transfer the ownership of sth
make sth into = convert
make up = (1) invent (a story), (2) end a quarrel, (3) compensate for sth, (4) put cosmetics on sb's face (5) form
make up for = compensate sb for the trouble one has caused them
rise up = rebel
rule out = exclude

10b English in Use

call off = cancel
live on sb/sth = get the money needed from
live through = experience over time
live up to = reach the standard that may be expected
live with = tolerate/accept sth and endure it
meet with = have as a reaction
miss out = forget to include
move on to = pass to another subject
narrow down = reduce
note down = record
pass over = ignore, overlook
hand over = give
phase out = gradually stop using
piece together = discover gradually
put about = spread (false) reports, rumours
put across = communicate
put aside/by = save for later use
put away = put into confinement
put back = delay
put down = write in a particular place
put down to = attribute to
put forward = suggest, propose
put in (a request) = make an official request
put in for = (1) apply for, (2) make an official request
put off = discourage
put off = postpone
put on = (1) gain weight, (2) pretend to have, (3) advance, (4) clothe oneself with, (5) present
put out = extinguish
put sb up = give accommodation to
put sth behind one = deliberately forget
put through = (1) carry sth out, (2) cause sb to undergo (an ordeal)
put through to sb = connect by telephone
put up with = tolerate

314

1b English in Use

un across = find by chance
un after = pursue
un away = leave (school, home etc)
un away with an idea = accept it without careful thinking even though it is wrong
un behind = be delayed
un down = (1) criticise, (2) gradually stop functioning, (3) run b down (with a vehicle)
un in = use a new vehicle carefully
un into = (1) meet by chance, (2) collide with
un off = produce quickly
un out of = exhaust the supply of sth
un through = (1) rehearse (2) use up
un up = accumulate (bills etc)
un up against = encounter difficulties
ee about = make arrangements for
ee off = accompany a traveller to his/her train etc
ee out = accompany sb to an exit
ee over = inspect properly
ee through = (1) not be deceived, (2) support sb through a difficult time
ee to = take care of
settle down = live a more permanent life-style
settle for = accept sth (less than expected)
settle in = become used to a new house or job
settle on = decide on
settle up = pay (a debt, a bill etc)

12b English in Use

set about = begin
set aside = save for a special purpose
set back = hinder
set sb back = cost sb a lot of money
set in = begin (of a period, usu bad)
set off = (1) start a reaction, (2) begin a journey (=set out)
set an animal on sb = cause an animal to attack sb
set out = begin a task/job with a specific intention
set up = (1) establish (a record), (2) start a business (3) erect
stand by = (1) remain loyal to sb, (2) do nothing to stop a bad situation, (3) be ready for action
stand down = resign from a position
stand for = (1) support sth, (2) mean, symbolise, (3) tolerate, (4) enter oneself for election
stand in for = replace temporarily
stand out = be conspicuous/obvious
stand up for = defend; support
stand up to = defend oneself against

13b English in Use

take aback = surprise
take after = look like a relative
take against = dislike sb
take away = remove
take back = withdraw a statement or comment
take down = (1) write down, (2) remove sth from a high place
take in = (1) deceive, (2) allow sb to stay in one's home, (3) understand, (4) make clothes smaller
take off = (1) remove (clothing), (2) leave the ground (of aeroplanes etc), (3) imitate sb in a comic way, (4) begin to succeed (of plans, ideas etc)
take on = (1) undertake sth, (2) employ staff, (3) accept sb as an opponent
take out = (1) extract, remove, (2) accompany sb to a theatre etc
take over = take control of sth esp in place of sb else
take sb for = mistake sb/sth for sb/sth else
take to = (1) find agreeable; like, (2) begin a habit, (3) escape to; hide in
take up = (1) begin a hobby, sport etc, (2) occupy space
take up with = become involved in (usu derog)

14b English in Use

talk about = (1) gossip about sb, (2) consider
talk at = speak to sb without listening to their replies
talk back = reply rudely
talk down to = speak to sb as if they were less clever than oneself
talk into = persuade sb to do sth
talk out = settle a problem by talking
talk out of = persuade sb not to do sth
talk round = persuade sb to agree to sth
tell against = spoil chances of success
tell apart = distinguish
tell off = scold/reprimand
think of = take sth into account
think out = prepare plans carefully
think over = reflect upon sth before making a decision
think up = invent or devise sth
turn away = refuse admittance to sb
turn down = (1) reject an offer, (2) reduce heat etc
turn in = go to bed
turn sb in = report to the authorities
turn into = convert, change
turn off = switch off
turn on = switch on
turn out = (1) assemble as a crowd, (2) produce, (3) prove to be
turn over = fall on one side
turn sth over (in one's mind) = think carefully about sth
turn to = go to sb for help
turn up = (1) arrive, (2) increase volume

Appendix 1

throw about/around = scatter sth

throw away = discard sth as useless

throw sth back at sb = remind sb of sth bad they did in the past

throw off = escape from, get free of

throw oneself into = begin to do sth energetically and enthusiastically

throw oneself on sb/sth = rely on sb/sth

throw sb out = force sb to leave

throw sth out = get rid of unwanted items

throw sb together = bring people into contact with each other

throw up = (1) give up (a job etc), (2) vomit

try on = check the fit (of clothes)

try out = test

wear away = become thin, damaged, weak, etc by constant use

wear off = disappear gradually (effect of sth)

wear out = use until useless (of clothes etc)

work off = (1) overcome the effects of sth (energy, stress, anger), (2) repay by working (a debt)

work on = be occupied with

work out = (1) find a solution by reasoning, (2) turn out successfully

work up = (1) develop, (2) excite, (3) advance (in business)

IDIOMS/FIXED PHRASES

1b English in Use

clear the air = remove suspicion/bad feeling
all along = from the beginning until now
all but = nearly, almost
all in = exhausted
all in all = when everything is considered
all the same = yet, however
all told = altogether, in total
be the apple of sb's eye = be very precious to sb; be sb's favourite
be up in arms = be very angry
for all = in spite of
for all I care = I don't care
for all I know = as far as I know
in the act of = while performing the act
in the air = uncertain
make allowances for = take special circumstances into consideration
make amends for = try to compensate for a past action
of all people = used to express annoyance/surprise
on account of = because of
on no account = under/in no circumstances
on the air = broadcasting (opp: off the air)
on the alert = watchful and prepared/on the lookout/ expecting sth
take sth into account = consider sth
on this/that account = for this/that reason
whet sb's appetite = make sb eager to have/experience more
up in the air = existing, but not talked about

2b English in Use

above board = honest
bark up the wrong tree = have a false idea about sth
be broke = have no/very little money
be full of beans = be very lively
be in sb's black books = out of favour
beat about/around the bush = avoid saying what one means directly
behind bars = in prison
big-headed = conceited; boastful
black and blue all over = covered with bruises
blessing in disguise = sth which appears bad at first but then turns out favourably
blue-eyed boy/golden boy = a favoured person
bolt from the blue = suddenly
brainwave = sudden clear idea/thought
break even = show neither loss nor profit
browned off = fed up; bored
butter sb up = flatter sb
by and large = generally speaking

catch sb red-handed = be caught while committing a crime
chip off the old block = sb who is very like one of his parents
cost a bomb = very expensive
deal a blow to = damage one's hopes
don't hold your breath = don't wait for sb/sth anxiously
drive a hard bargain = be a tough businessman
drop a brick = say sth tactlessly
feel in one's bones = feeling sth instinctively
get your own back = take/get revenge
have a bee in one's bonnet = have an obsession about sth
have butterflies in one's stomach = be very nervous about sth
in black and white = in writing
in the balance = uncertain
kick the bucket = die
lay bare = make public
make a clean breast of = confess
make one's blood boil = cause sb to become very angry
on the spur of the moment = without thinking about sth
out of the blue = suddenly and unexpectedly
ring a bell = remind sb of sth
see the back of = be glad to see sb leave
take the bull by the horns = deal with sth boldly and directly
wet blanket = dull person who spoils people's happiness

3b English in Use

a piece of cake = sth very easy to do
a red-letter day = a very important day
a wild-goose chase = a hopeless search
be caught red-handed = be caught while committing a crime
be on the cards = be likely to happen
be over the moon = be elated
call sb names = insult sb
chair a meeting = preside over a meeting
crocodile tears = false tears
cross one's mind = think of sth
cut sb dead = ignore sb
different as chalk and cheese = totally different
down in the dumps = depressed/miserable
down the drain = wasted; lost
get a bit hot under the collar = get angry, upset or embarrassed
get a problem off one's chest = tell sb else about your problem
go to the dogs = worsen
have the cheek = dare to do sth
keep one's chin up = not be discouraged
let sleeping dogs lie = avoid mentioning a subject which could cause trouble
lost cause = hopeless situation or case
off colour = look/be slightly unwell
on the dole = receiving unemployment benefit/social security
play one's cards right = act cleverly

show one's true colours = reveal one's real character

with flying colours = with great success

not count one's chickens before they're hatched = not assume sth before it happens

4b English in Use

be dying for sth = really want sth

be fit for = be good enough for

be worn out = be very tired

be green = be inexperienced

cook one's goose = end one's plans abruptly

fair and square = within the rules

fall head over heels = fall in love quickly

feel one's ears burning = have a feeling that sb is talking about you

gatecrasher = sb attending a party, event etc without an invitation

get off on the wrong foot = argue or disagree at the beginning of a relationship

give and take = compromise

have a frog in one's throat = inability to speak due to nervousness

have the gift of the gab = be able to talk well, persuasively

hear it through/on the grapevine = find out information indirectly

in a flash = very quickly

it's all Greek to me = sth new or foreign; not easily understood

keep a straight face = manage to look serious under difficult circumstances

keep an eye on sth = guard/protect sth

meet behind closed doors = meet secretly

one's flesh and blood = family member

plenty more fish in the sea = many more opportunities in life for love

put one's foot down = insist on sth

put one's foot in it = make a tactless comment

take it easy = not work too hard/relax

take sb for granted = not appreciate sb

5b English in Use

a bit of a dark horse = person with hidden abilities

be for the high jump = about to be reprimanded/punished

be in two minds about sth = not be able to decide what to do

be sound asleep = sleep deeply

be the perfect image of sb = look exactly like sb

before one can say Jack Robinson = extremely quickly

break the ice = ease the tension when one first meets people

eat one's heart out = feel jealous/sad about sth

flog a dead horse = waste time doing sth useless

fly off the handle = quickly become very angry

get out of hand = become out of control

get the hang of it = get in the habit of doing sth

go to one's head = make conceited

grey matter = brains; intelligence

hand in glove with sb = be in very close contact with sb

have a job to do sth = find sth difficult to do

have many irons in the fire = have lots of plans/possibilities in progress at the same time

have one's heart in one's mouth = be extremely anxious about sth

have time on one's hands = have free time

hold one's horses = wait, be patient

ill at ease = embarrassed; uncomfortable

keep sth under one's hat = keep sth secret

keep up with the Joneses = compete with others in status/material goods

lend sb a hand = give help to sb

like the back of one's hand = be very familiar with sth

lose heart = become discouraged

make head nor tail of = understand sth

off the cuff = without preparation

stew in one's own juice = suffer the consequences of one's own actions

straight from the horse's mouth = from the most direct source

have sb's hands full = be very busy with sth

sth comes in handy = be very useful/practical

strike gold = come across sth useful

take sth to heart = take personally/be influenced by

take to one's heels = run away

the ins and outs = the details of an activity

the tip of the iceberg = small evident part of a much larger, concealed situation

6b English in Use

at large = free, not caught

be in the know = be well-informed

bring to one's knees = destroy, humble

bury one's head in the sand = avoid or ignore reality/responsibility

come to a head = reach a critical point

drop sb a line = send sb a letter

fine kettle of fish = confused state of affairs

get rid of sth = give sth unwanted away

go to any lengths = do anything necessary to get sth you want

have kittens = be nervous/anxious about sth

keep one's fingers crossed = hope that sth will turn out well

keep oneself to oneself = live quietly, privately

make a killing = have a sudden, great success/profit

make light of = treat sth as unimportant

make/earn a/one's living = earn money

on the level = honest/sincere

pull one's leg = tease or trick sb

shed light upon = give new/further information

sleep like a log = be sound asleep
the life and soul of sth = the most lively and amusing person present somewhere
the lion's share = the biggest part/portion
turn over a new leaf = make a new start
with a view to doing sth = with the intention or hope of doing sth

7b English in Use

a night owl = person who enjoys staying up late
be second to none = be the best
cross one's mind = occur to one, have a sudden idea, recall sth
cry over spilt milk = grieve over sth that can't be put right
every nook and cranny = everywhere
feel/be down in the mouth = feel discouraged/depressed
get a move on = hurry up
get on one's nerves = irritate/annoy sb
have an early night = go to bed early
hit the nail on the head = say exactly the right thing
in a nutshell = briefly; in a few words
lose one's nerve = lose courage
make a name for oneself = become famous/respected for sth
make hay while the sun shines = take advantage of favourable circumstances
make money hand over fist = make a lot of money quickly and easily
make one's getaway = escape
moon around = look miserable
null and void = invalid; not legally binding
once in a blue moon = very rarely
put sb's name forward = nominate sb
put words into one's mouth = pretend that sb has said sth that they haven't actually said
slip one's mind = forget about sth
work a miracle = make sth almost impossible happen
give the green light to sth = give permission to proceed with sth

8b English in Use

a bitter pill to swallow = a difficult fact to accept
against all odds = despite the difficulties
be out of practice = lacking practice
come to the point = reach the main point in a discussion
fall into place = become clear
get the sack = be dismissed from one's job
get the wrong end of the stick = misunderstand completely what has been said
golden opportunity = the best chance to gain sth
grease sb's palm = bribe sb
grow out of sth = become too big for sth
have no option but = must; have no choice
in public = in the presence of other people
in the offing = likely to happen

off the point = irrelevant
once and for all = for the last time
out-and-out = complete, total
out in the open = (of secrets) revealed, known
out of print = (of books) not available anymore
out of the frying pan into the fire = from a situation to a worse/similar one
part and parcel of = basic part of
past one's prime = growing old/not at one's best
pop the question = make a proposal of marriage
short and sweet = brief but pleasant (usu ironic)
status symbol = property/possession that shows sb's high social rank wealth etc
take things to pieces = dismantle things
throw a party = have/hold a party
white elephant = useless/unwanted possession

9b English in Use

an unknown quantity = person or thing that one has no experience of
as a last resort = when all else has failed
at close quarters = from a short distance
be in a quandary = be confused; undecided
beg the question = makes people want to ask a particular question
call it quits = give up/stop
cut sb to the quick = deeply hurt sb's feelings
hit the roof = get very angry
in a rut = be stuck in a monotonous routine
in the long run = after a long period of time
it stands to reason = it is logical
keep sth quiet = keep sth secret
know the ropes = know all the details of sth
off the record = unofficial(ly)
on the quiet = secretly
open to debate = not decided/settled
out of the question = impossible
put down roots = settle down
work to rule = adhere strictly to the rules as a form of protest
rack sb's brains = think very hard about sth

10b English in Use

a long shot = a wild guess/a risk
a memory like a sieve = a poor memory
be all at sea = be in a state of confusion
be in sb's shoes = be in sb's position
be in the same boat = be in the same (usu bad) situation
be the spitting image of sb = look exactly like sb
be/get soaked to the skin = be/get very wet
be/have a close shave = barely avoid an accident/a bad situation

behind the scenes = in secret
come out of one's shell = gain personal confidence
does it show? = is it obvious?
give sb the slip = escape from sb
go for a song = be sold very cheaply
go without saying = be a foregone conclusion
hit the sack = go to bed
live out of a suitcase = travel often/not have a permanent home
make quite a scene = become angry in a dramatic way
on a shoe string = on a very small budget
pull a few strings = use influential contacts in order to obtain an advantage
pull one's socks up = make a greater effort
sleep on it = think about sth
smell a rat = suspect that sth is wrong
spill the beans = reveal a secret/the facts
stand in sb's way = prevent sb from doing sth
take ... with a pinch of salt = not believe sth completely
the last straw = the last and worst episode in a chain of bad experiences
thick-skinned = insensitive

11b English in Use

(by) trial and error = learning from one's mistakes
be ahead of one's time = have modern ideas
be (as) thick (as a brick) = be stupid
be tickled pink = be really pleased
come to a standstill = not progress/stop
come to terms with = accept a difficult situation
for the time being = temporarily
in a tick = shortly, soon
in the nick of time = just in time
kill time = pass time while waiting for sb/sth
lay the table = prepare/set the table for a meal
not be one's cup of tea = not suit one's taste
on second thoughts = having changed one's mind
out of turn = not in the correct order/time
paint the town red = have a great time
play truant = stay away from school without permission
put two and two together = arrive at the truth by looking at facts
red tape = unnecessary bureaucracy
take one's time = not to hurry
through thick and thin = whatever happens
touch and go = with uncertain result

12b English in Use

be all very well = appear satisfactory but in fact not be
be on the up and up = improve steadily
be up and about = have recovered from an illness

drive (sb) up the wall = make sb angry/annoy sb
frosty welcome = unfriendly reception
get out of bed on the wrong side = be in a bad mood
get wind of = receive information about sth indirectly
give vent to = express sth freely
give way to = give in/yield
not hold water = not seem reasonable or in accordance with the facts
make a flying visit = make a quick trip
make waves = cause trouble
no/little wonder = not surprising
quick/slow on the uptake = quick/slow to understand
set in one's ways = fixed in one's habits/routines
speak volumes = be strong evidence of sb's feelings, merits etc
under the weather = depressed/unwell
up and coming = likely to be successful
ups and downs = good things alternating with bad ones
wet behind the ears = inexperienced

13b English in Use

an old wives' tale = false belief (usually about health)
be born yesterday = be easily deceived/naive
beat sb black and blue = hit sb repeatedly until bruised
go back on one's word = not fulfil a promise (opp: keep one's word)
have a yellow streak = be a coward
not have it both ways = refuse to make a decision between two pleasant things (usu in expression "You can't have it both ways!")
in the red = owe money to a bank (opp: in the black)
see red = suddenly become very angry
green belt = the area on the outskirts of a town adjoining the country
pitch black = very dark
black tie = formal clothing
green with envy = very jealous
green (matter/issue) = concerned with ecology
have words with sb = have an argument
have/keep one's wits about one = be alert and able to deal with difficulties
in deep water = in trouble/difficulty
make sb's day = make sb very happy
see/look at sth through rose-coloured spectacles = see sth from an unrealistically positive point of view
the black sheep of the family = a disgraced family member
the pot calling the kettle black = accusing sb of a fault one has oneself
the year dot = a long time ago
until one is blue in the face = as hard/long as one possibly can (usu without success)
red herring = sth which distracts you from sth important

4b English in Use

(fight) like cat and dog = (disagree) violently

(like) a bull in a china shop = behave in a clumsy/awkward way

(make) a dog's dinner (of sth) = (make) a mess (of sth)

bear with a sore head = irritated/in a bad mood

different kettle of fish = a totally different situation etc from the one just mentioned

dog's life = a difficult, hard life

fish out of water = sb who feels uncomfortable/in unfamiliar surroundings

red rag to a bull = action, comment etc liable to provoke sb

sitting duck = an easy target

as busy as a bee/a busy bee = (sb) very busy

as the crow flies = in a direct line/by a direct route

be in the doghouse = be out of favour, in trouble

dog eat dog = ruthless competition, rivalry

dog-eared = (of books) with the corners bent and turned down through use

donkey work = boring, monotonous work

donkey's years = a long time

kill two birds with one stone = achieve two things with one action

let the cat out of the bag = reveal a secret

like water off a duck's back = having no effect

make a fool of oneself = make oneself look stupid/embarrassed/ridiculous

make a mountain out of a molehill = cause a fuss about a trivial matter

no room to swing a cat = no room at all

play cat and mouse with sb = keep sb in a state of uncertain expectation treating them alternatively cruelly and kindly

put the cat among the pigeons = cause trouble/controversy

rain cats and dogs = rain heavily

swim like a fish = swim very well

talk the hind legs off a donkey = talk for a long time, uninterrupted

the rat race = the competitive nature of modern urban life

until the cows come home = for a long time

mutton dressed as lamb = dress in a style younger than/inappropriate to your age

sour grapes = say unpleasant comments because of jealousy

sweet tooth = enjoy eating sweet things

get nowhere fast = make no/little progress

pay sb's way = contribute your share of a bill/budget

white-collar job = office/clerical work

fly on the wall = see/hear sth in a situation which does not involve you

Achilles heel = weakest point of sb's character

wash sb's hands of sb = refuse to be involved with sb

15b English in Use

a pain in the neck = annoying person/thing

be all fingers and thumbs = be awkward, clumsy

get cold feet = lose courage to do sth

give sb the cold shoulder = ignore/shun sb

have a cheek/nerve = act/speak boldly or impudently

have a sharp tongue = tend to say unkind or hurtful things

have an eye for = be a good judge of sth

look down one's nose at sth/sb = feel/act superior to sb

lose one's head = lose self-control

put one's heart and soul into sth = be devoted to sth

tongue in cheek = not serious, ironic

tooth and nail = fiercely

turn a blind eye to sth = ignore

not lose any sleep over sth = not worry about sth

jack of all trades = sb who is able to do a variety of jobs

a storm in a teacup = a lot of fuss about sth that is not important

bring sth home to sb = make sb understand how important/serious sth is

bite off more than sb can chew = try to do sth which is too difficult

in clover = living a luxurious/comfortable life

face the music = be criticised/punished for sth you have done

Appendix 3

WORDS OFTEN CONFUSED

1b English in Use

- **evade** = to avoid doing sth one is supposed to do or to avoid answering a question, often by deception
  shirk = to avoid work because of laziness
  duck = to avoid an object by a quick downwards movement
  dodge = to avoid an object by a quick sideways movement
- **sway** = to influence others' opinions so they turn from a given course
  Don't try to sway me. I'm determined to take the job.
  influence = to cause sb to think/act in a particular way
  impress = to produce a lasting, positive effect
  affect = to produce a reaction usu negative
  The nuclear leak has affected all the farmers' crops.
- **real** = true as opposed to false
  genuine = (object) what it seems to be, (person) sincere and honest
  natural = not man-made
  authentic = with known and proved origins
  valid = sth which can be used and will be accepted by people in authority (a **valid** document, ticket)
- **wealthy** = having a lot of material possessions and money
  affluent = wealthy and able to spend a lot of money
  well-off = (informal) fairly wealthy
  rich = (of food) full of ingredients which may be difficult to digest
  extravagant = (object) sth that costs more money than you can afford or sth which is beyond what is reasonable (*an extravagant lifestyle, gift*)
  lavish = (object) sth that is very elaborate and impressive and a lot of money has been spent on it (*lavish party, costumes*)
- **merchandise** = (formal) things for sale
  ware = manufactured goods of a particular type (**silverware**)
  commodity = sth which is sold for profit, an article of trade
  stock = the total amount of goods a shop has available to sell

2b English in Use

- **cure** = (tr) to successfully treat, to restore to health
  remedy = (tr) to put right, usu of situations
  heal = (tr/intr) to cure; to get better, improve
  treat = (tr) to give medical attention to
- **imitate** = to behave in exactly the same way as sb else
  copy = to produce sth that looks like the original thing
  emulate = (formal) to imitate sb because you admire them
  fake = to make sth seem genuine although actually false

- **slim** = (complimentary) not fat (NB **slim chance**: slig possibility)
  lean = (complimentary) healthily thin, without fat (also meat)
  skinny = (uncomplimentary) very thin
  slender = (complimentary) attractively thin, esp of wom
- **moulder** = to decay slowly
  rot = (intr/tr) to (cause to) decay because of bacteria e esp of vegetation
  waste = (intr/tr) to grow weak and small; to use badly
  decompose = (intr/tr) to (cause to) go bad, esp of fles
- **snarl** = to make an angry noise while showing the teet esp of dogs etc
  howl = to cry, esp of dogs; to cry with pain
  bleat = to cry, esp of sheep, goats etc
  twitter = to make a sound like a bird
- **reference** = (in the expression **in/with reference to**) used to indicate what sth relates to/in connection with
  affinity = relationship, similarity or connection
  relation = (object) connection; (person) a member one's family
  connection = relationship between two things, people groups
- **sliver** = a small thin piece or amount of sth
  chip = a small piece of sth
  crumb = small part of a larger object, esp bread, ca etc
  cube = square-shaped piece of sth (wood, sugar, mea
- **chop** = to cut sth into pieces with strong downwar movements of a knife or an axe
  shred = to cut into thin strips
  mince = to cut with a machine into small pieces (meat)
  grate = to shred small pieces off sth (cheese, carrots) b rubbing against a rough surface
- **fade** = to become less clear (with time)
  vanish = to disappear suddenly
  disappear = to be lost, to no longer be seen
  pale = to become lighter in colour
- **toss** = to throw into the air, esp of coins, pancakes etc
  throw = to launch through the air, esp using the hand an arm
  cast = to throw, let fall (stones, shadow)
  fling = to throw sth using a lot of force

3b English in Use

- **practise** = to do an action repeatedly or do exercise regularly in order to gain skill (a musical instrument)
  learn = to obtain knowledge or a skill through studying or training
  teach = to give knowledge of a particular subject to someone
  Mrs Jones teaches French at a secondary school.

coach = to train/teach esp for a specific purpose, examination or sport

instruct = to give knowledge or information to sb in a methodical manner

present (information) = to give it to people in a formal way

familiarise (yourself with sth) = to learn about sth and start to understand it

show (sb how to do sth) = to do sth yourself so that they can watch you and learn how to do it

• **entrust** = put sth/sb in the care of sb else

confide = to tell sb sth in secret

consign = to hand over/give up or send sth esp in trade

resign = to give up a job

• **punch** = to hit with a clenched fist

slap = to hit with the palm of one's hand

smack = to hit with the palm of one's hand, esp a child as a punishment

whack = to hit with a blow making a loud noise

strike = to hit; used esp for emphasis and added emotion

smash = to break sth into many pieces by hitting or dropping it

• **enhance** = to make sth better; to add to the beauty of sth
The sunshine enhanced the golden colour of her hair.

aggravate = to make sth worse

heighten = to become greater, more acute esp emotions
Tension between the police and local residents heightened last night.

intensify = to become stronger, more intense

• **profit** = to gain, esp money

gain = to obtain

earn (money, praise) = receive sth in return for work that you do; get sth because you deserve it

exploit (sb/sth) = treat sb unfairly; use sth in order to gain an advantage from it

• **commence** = (formal) to begin
The Prime Minister will commence his tour on 11 April.

instigate = to start by urging or inciting

launch = to cause sth to begin, esp an activity, campaign etc

provoke (a reaction) = to cause a reaction

• **hinder** = to delay or prevent the progress of sth
She was hindered from her work by John's incessant questioning.

block = to be in the way of sth/sb; to obstruct
The road was blocked by an overturned lorry and we couldn't pass.

bar = to obstruct esp intentionally

impede = to make sth difficult to do

obstruct = to be in the way of sb/sth

intervene (of events) = to happen suddenly in a way that stops, delays, or prevents sth from happening

• **exude (a quality or feeling)** = to show that sb has it to a great extent

exclude = to keep sb out from somewhere; to leave sb out from among the rest; decide/prove that sth is not worth considering

expunge = to get rid of sth completely because it causes problems or bad feelings
His divorce was an experience he had tried to expunge from his memory.

extricate = to free yourself or another person from a difficult, serious situation
This is the last attempt by the country to extricate itself from its economic crisis.

4b English in Use

• **goods** = things for sale

wares = (old-fashioned) things for sale usu of a travelling salesman

commodities = products exchanged in trade usu on an international basis

supplies = food equipment and other essential things that people need, especially when these are provided in large quantities

• **rear** = to look after one's young until fully-grown

bring up = to look after and educate until fully-grown

breed = to keep animals for the purpose of producing young

grow = to become or cause to become bigger

nurture (a young child, or young plant) = care for it while it is growing and developing

• **pinch** = (informal) steal an object

pilfer = steal small amounts usu from your place of work

rip off = (informal) steal from a person

swipe = steal sth very quickly while sb is not looking

acquire = (formal) to obtain for oneself; (a skill, habit etc) develop/learn
He acquired a profound knowledge of the language by careful study.

abduct = to take away (a person) unlawfully, often by force

• **gather (information, evidence)** = to collect it especially over a period of time and after a lot of hard work

collect = gather; get a large number of things because they interest you

derive = to get sth such as pleasure or benefit from a person or from an activity/situation

deduce = to reach a conclusion because of other things that you know to be true

• **inhabit** = to live in a place or region

inhabitant = person who lives (permanently) in a region or town

dwell = (formal) to live in a place
He is concerned for the fate of the tribes who dwell in the forest.

dweller = person or animal that lives in an environment
settle = to start living in a place permanently
settler = person who has come to live in a (previously uninhabited or developing) country or area
reside = to have one's home at in a place
Ruth resides with her mother in a London suburb.
resident = person who lives in a house, block of flats, area or country

6b English in Use

- **take legal aid** = to take money given by the government or another organisation to people who cannot afford to pay for a lawyer
  take legal action = an expression used to indicate that a person or company is willing to start, or has started, general legal proceedings over a matter; often used as a form of threat
  try = (usu passive) to examine in a court of law
  bring to trial = to take a criminal case to a court of law to be examined
  take sb to court = used in a similar way to "take legal action" but as a more specific and direct legal threat
  charge with = to accuse of a criminal act, esp by the police
  summon = to order officially sb to appear in court
- **restrain** = stop sb from doing what they intended or wanted to do; prevent yourself from showing an emotion
  curb = control/keep sth within limits
  Inflation needs to be curbed otherwise we are in for an economic crisis.
  check = to make sure that sth is correct or satisfactory
  inhibit = to prevent or slow down;
  Thirst inhibited the desire to eat.
  to render sb unable to express what they really feel or do what they really want
  The newcomers were too inhibited to laugh freely.
- **continually** = repeatedly, regularly, frequently
  continuously = without stopping
  She has worked with us continuously since 1990.
  perpetually = lasting for a long indefinite time usu without interruption; continually
  eternally = endlessly; often used metaphorically for emphasis *(eternally grateful)*
- **constant** = repeated many times usu in a regular manner
  incessant = extending without interruption for an indefinite period of time; often used negatively to express irritation
  steady = continuing in a regular manner
  I have a steady job and am financially secure.
  ongoing = sth which began in the past and seems unlikely to stop in the near future *(Ongoing problems)*

- **critical** = of decisive importance
  This operation is critical; without it the patient might die.
  crucial = very important usu in determining sth or resolving a problem
  essential = extremely important; necessary
  vital = extremely necessary
  significant = of importance and meaning
  grave = important, pressing and usu worrying
  I received some grave news about my brother's health and had to fly back home immediately.
  fundamental = absolutely necessary; important; essential
- **forbid** = to order sb not to do sth, not allow sth to be done
  The constitution forbids the military use of nuclear energy.
  prohibit = to forbid by law or rule
  Smoking in this area is prohibited.
  disallow = not allow or accept sth officially, because it has not been done correctly
  Our team scored again, but the whistle had gone and the goal was disallowed.
  censor = to examine officially letters or the media with the intention of removing any information regarded as secret or offensive
- **famous** = very well known
  conspicuous = easily seen; noticeable; attracting attention
  remarkable = worth speaking of; unusual
  distinguished = marked by excellent quality or deserved fame
  eminent = well-known and respected, especially for being good at one's profession
  elevated = very important or of very high rank
  The success of his latest novel has given him a certain elevated status.
  prestigious = respected and admired by people
  noteworthy = interesting; remarkable; worthy of attention

7b English in Use

- **ruin** = to damage sth so that it is useless
- **impair** = to make sth weaker or imperfect
  Loud music impairs your hearing.
- **injure** = to cause harm to a person/animal (broken limbs, wounds)
- **damage** = to destroy something in part, causing loss of value
  My carpet was damaged in a flood.
- **harm** = to have a generally bad effect on sth, not necessarily a physical effect *(harm a friendship)*
- **scan** = to look at sth quickly, usu from top to bottom, looking for particular information
- **peer at** = to look at sth closely or with difficulty, due to poor eyesight or in darkness

scrutinise = to look closely and carefully at sth
inspect = to examine sth thoroughly
glimpse = to have a passing view of sb or sth
- harass = (formal) to continually and unfairly annoy and cause trouble to sb
pester = to annoy sb with repeated requests for sth
get on at = (informal) to continually nag or tell sb to do sth
tease = (usu of children) to laugh at or make fun of in an unkind way
*He was **teased** at school for being fat.*
- chip = (tr) to break a small wedge-shaped piece off the edge of an object
smash = (tr/intr) to break violently and often deliberately into pieces
*He **smashed** his jawbone in a crash.*
snap = (tr/intr) to break suddenly esp with a sharp cracking noise
*She **snapped** the biscuit in half and we shared it.*
shatter = (tr/intr) to break (usu glass or china) into hundreds or thousands of pieces
break off = to come off or remove by force
crack = to (cause to) break without dividing into separate parts
*Don't pour hot water into the glass or it will **crack**.*

8b English in Use

- scatter = (tr/intr) to throw many things in a random manner; (with groups of people) hurriedly and randomly disperse in all directions
*The farmer **scattered** the seeds over the field.*
*Suddenly the crowd **scattered**.*
disperse = (tr/intr) to break up (a group of people or a thing) and move its component parts away in various directions (used esp with the police)
*Many arrests were made as the police attempted to **disperse** the rioters.*
strew = (tr) to drop things over a surface, esp in an untidy or careless manner
sprinkle = (tr) to drop sth in fine quantities
*She **sprinkled** sugar over the cake.*
- stagger = walk very unsteadily, for example because you are ill
reel = to move about in an unsteady way as if one is going to fall
totter = to move in an unsteady way from side to side as if about to fall
stumble = put your foot down awkwardly while you are walking or running and nearly fall over
- slide = to move smoothly but unintentionally over a surface
glide = to move smoothly and easily over a surface

slip = to slide suddenly without intention
*I **slipped** on the wet pavement and fell over.*
skid = usu with vehicles on roads to mean to slide suddenly and uncontrollably while trying to stop
- huddle = to lie close to sb/sth in a confined space, usu for protection from adverse conditions
*The children **huddled** together in the corner of the room to keep warm.*
nestle = to settle comfortably in a secure place
snuggle = (esp up) to lie in comfort close to sb/sth
*The baby **snuggled up** to its mother under the blankets.*
cuddle = to hold firmly and lovingly in one's arms
- tend = to take great care of sb/sth (a garden, a wound)
attend (to) = to be with and take care of sb/sth, usu in a professional capacity
*The patient was **attended** by several specialists.*
grow (a plant) = to put seeds or young plants in the ground and look after them as they develop
maintain = (a building, a machine) to keep it in good condition by regularly checking it and repairing it when necessary
- betray = to be disloyal; to break a moral obligation (sb's trust, confidence etc)
divulge = to give away secret information, esp personal (a secret, a source etc)
reveal = to show sth, to make sth known
*He removed the cover and **revealed** his wife's portrait.*
disclose = similar meaning to reveal but generally used with more secrecy. To show sth that was previously concealed; to make sth known
- shove = to move (sth) forward with a strong, usu careless, motion
tote = to carry
pile (things) = to form a pile gradually
*He **piled** the boxes one on top of the other.*
thrust (sth or sb) = push sth or sb quickly with a lot of force
heave = push, pull or lift sth using a lot of effort
- stem from = to have as origin
*Her interest in flowers **stems from** her childhood in the country.*
beget = to cause sth to happen or be created
*Economic tensions **beget** political ones.*
generate = to cause sth to begin and develop
*The scientist's talk **generated** further discussion of the issue.*
commence = (formal) to begin
*The academic year **commences** at the beginning of October.*
- chat = to talk to each other in an informal and friendly way
chatter = to talk quickly and continuously, usu about unimportant things

prattle = to talk a great deal without saying anything important

babble = to talk in a confused or excited way

gossip = to talk about other people's private affairs

9b English in Use

- border = dividing line between two countries
  boundary = dividing line between two private areas (between two farmers' fields, between two gardens)
  verge = point just before sth begins (the verge of war)
  brim = point at which sth is full (brim of a bowl)
  rim = edge of sth circular
  The rim of my spectacles is gold.
  (out of) bounds = (of) an area where you are not allowed to go
- susceptible = (to sth) likely to be affected by sth (negative)
  He's susceptible to fits of anger.
  liable = (to do sth) likely to do sth specific
  He's liable to be late tomorrow.
  prone = (to sth, often unexpected) likely to suffer from (prone to accidents)
  apt = (to do sth) likely to do sth, behave in some way (apt to be careless)
  sensitive (to sth) = likely to show understanding and awareness of other people's needs, problems or feelings
- shore = land right on the edge of the sea
  A boat comes into shore.
  bank = land on the edge of a river
  coast = area next to the sea
  beach = seashore area with sand or stones usu where people go to sunbathe
- seize = to take sth quickly, often with violence (seize the bank's takings)
  grab = take sth quickly, often with violence or for a selfish reason (children grab sweets)
  grasp = hold sth firmly (to grasp a child by the hand)
  clutch = hold sth tightly usu against one's body
  She clutched her bag nervously.
  take = to reach out for sth and hold it

10b English in Use

- sack = (informal) to dismiss sb from their job due to their failure to carry out duties properly
  make redundant = to dismiss sb (usu large numbers) from their job(s) due to financial problems, or because one's job is no longer necessary
  resign = to give notice and leave a job
  retire = to leave a job at retirement age (usu 60 or 65 years) or due to constant illness
- trouble = difficulty, worry, anxiety, annoyance etc
  cause = sth which produces an effect; a person, thing or event that makes sth happen

problem = a situation that is unsatisfactory and causes difficulties for people

- disaster = sth which has a negative effect (harm, loss, etc)
  cataclysm = violent disaster on a larger scale (war, volcanic eruption etc)
  calamity = misfortune or disaster usu on a smaller, more personal scale than a cataclysm
  catastrophe = sudden disaster or misfortune
- sect = closely bound religious group
  breed = type of animal which is of pure race usu dogs, cats or horses (Siamese cats, Alsatian dogs)
  tribe = group of people of the same race living as a community esp in nomadic or primitive cultures
  caste = group of people linked by rank, wealth, social position, usu in India (of a high/low social caste)
- ally = sb who supports/helps another esp in war
  accomplice = sb who helps another usu in crime or wrongdoing
  acquaintance = person who one knows but who is not a close friend
  associate = sb you are closely connected with, especially at work
- fee = charge asked by a professional for a service
  stipend = income (esp of clergymen)
  salary = fixed payment for work, made at regular intervals
  wages = weekly payment for regular work

11b English in Use

- unveil = to officially uncover sth; usu a statue
  unpack = to take sth out of a box or parcel
  unwrap = to take the paper off the outside usu of a present
  reveal = to let out a secret or scandal
- put up with = to tolerate sb or sth
  I couldn't put up with the noise anymore.
  afford = to have enough money to buy sth
  withstand = to endure sth without being badly damaged or collapsing (withstand bad treatment)
  support = to have enough money to provide food, clothing etc for dependents (support a wife and children)
- confirm = to provide (usu written) evidence as to the correctness of sth
  An ID card can confirm your identity.
  guarantee = to promise something will definitely happen
  Our company guarantees to refund your money if you are not satisfied with the product.
  assure = to tell sb with confidence
  reassure = to put sb's mind at rest when they are worried about sth

- **adventurous** = (positive) enthusiastic about doing new things or exploring new places
She'd always dreamt of an adventurous life in the tropics.
reckless = (negative) liable to do dangerous things without considering the consequences (**reckless** driving, act)
impervious = not being affected or influenced by someone's actions (**impervious** to criticism, suggestions)
foolhardy = extremely risky
It is foolhardy not to wear a helmet on a motorbike.
instinctive = resulting from instinct (an **instinctive** act; **but not** an instinctive person)
- **grind** = tedious, physical work
Factory work is a grind.
NB: used in expression **"back to the grind"** = return to work after a break
labour = physical work usu used with the adjectives "physical" or "manual"
drudgery = tedious, physical work usu unrewarding and of an unskilled nature (cleaning)
toil = tiring physical work (usu used as a verb)
He toiled in the fields all day.

2b English in Use

- **control** = keep sth within limits by force (**control** children/public spending)
stunt = keep sth/sb from growing properly (a **stunted** plant, **stunted** growth)
curb = limit or control usu emotions (**curb** temper)
temper = make sth less strong or extreme (*temper your voice*)
- **remember** = keep a fact/event in one's long-term memory (**remember** your childhood/to do sth)
recollect = (no passive voice) bring sth to mind for a short period (**recollect** doing sth/sb's name/face)
reminisce = to think with fondness about past events
She was reminiscing about her wedding day.
remind = tell sb to do sth so that they don't forget
Remind me to pay you back the £10.
memorise = commit sth (usu a poem, grammar rule, etc) to memory (**memorise** facts and figures)
- **hard-up** = (informal) short of money (**hard-up** students)
wealthy = possessing a lot of money and material possessions
tight = (informal derog) not willing to spend money
comfortable = (informal) not poor but not wealthy

3b English in Use

- **strut** = (often derog) to walk in a proud way, with even steps
scamper = (esp children and animals) to run quickly, usu playfully

slither = to move in a sliding way like a snake
slink = to move secretly and quietly esp when afraid or ashamed
- **diminish** (tr/intr) = to (make sth or sb) smaller, quieter, less important etc
dwindle = (intr) to gradually become smaller in number or amount
Supplies are dwindling.
shrink = (tr/intr) to become or make smaller in size due to water or heat
Meat shrinks while being cooked.
reduce = (tr/intr) to make or become less in number, size, degree (**reduce** the volume, **reduce** the price)
- **clothed** = wearing clothes
She was warmly clothed.
to be clad (in) = (archaic) to be dressed in
wearing = dressed in (sth)
to be dressed = to be wearing sth usu for a particular occasion

14b English in Use

- **retract** = to take back officially a statement or announcement
The politician had to retract the statement to avoid a scandal.
extract = to take or pull sth from a place/remove sth (**extract** a tooth); to obtain sth by using industrial or chemical processes (to **extract** coal); to select some information from a larger amount or source of information (a speech, a text, archives, a selection of poems)
pull out = (of troops) to withdraw from an area; (informal) to extract (a tooth)
renounce = to officially give up a claim, rank or title; refuse to associate with or acknowledge sth/sb
- **sting** = to cause pain to sb where a sharp part of an animal or insect, usu covered with poison, is pushed into one's skin (bees **sting**, jellyfish **sting**)
bite = to wound with the teeth (a dog **bites**)
stab = to wound by striking with a knife or dagger
prick = to cause pain by piercing with a sharp point (a **pinprick**)
- **refuse** = not to agree to do sth
deny = to say that one knows nothing about sth (deny all knowledge of sth)
reject = to turn down an offer, invitation
revoke = cancel or withdraw sth (**revoke** a license, a law, a document)

- **accomplish** = to do sth successfully (**accomplish** an aim)
  attain = to reach a particular level, usu with difficulty (**attain** a mark of 100%)
  gain = to obtain (**gain** power/weight)
  reach = to come to a particular point (**reach** London)
  manage = to succeed in doing usu sth difficult or demanding
- **decline** = (formal) refuse usu an invitation or offer (to **decline** an invitation to a banquet)
  renounce = to officially give up a claim, rank or title; refuse to associate with or acknowledge sth/sb
  He renounced his former business partners.
  deny = to say that sth is not true
  reject = to refuse sb's application or invitation
- **take (sb) aback** = (informal, usu passive) to surprise or mildly shock sb
  I was taken aback by his behaviour.
  astound = (usu passive) surprise or shock sb usu in a negative way, so they are unable to think
  She was astounded by the news of the crash.
  amaze = surprise sb (usu in a positive way)
  He was amazed by her intelligence.
  surprise = to create a feeling caused by sth unexpected
  (be) flabbergasted = (to be) extremely surprised by sth

- **grumble** = to find fault continually and in an ineffective bad-tempered way over trivial things (old men **grumbling** about youth today); sound of thunder or a hungry stomach
  pester = to annoy sb esp with repeated requests for sth
  A colleague has been pestering her for money.
  whine = (usu of children) to complain in an annoying way and in a high-pitched voice
  complain = to find fault, to make one's grievances known officially or unofficially
  object = express your dislike or disapproval of sth
  nag = to keep asking sb to do sth they have not done yet or do not want to do
  She never stops nagging him about staying out late.
  criticise = express one's disapproval of sb/sth and indicate what's wrong with them
  His employer criticised him for not being punctual.
- **scam** = an illegal trick usu aiming at getting money from people or avoiding paying tax (an insurance **scam**)
  snare = a trap intended usu to catch an animal (a rabbit **snare**)
  gimmick = unusual thing used in advertising to attract publicity (sales **gimmick**)
  plot = a plan to do sth secretly (**plot** against the enemy)

WORD FORMATION

Concrete noun	Abstract noun	Verb	Adjective	Adverb
	access, accessibility	access	accessible, inaccessible	accessibly
acquirer	acquisition, acquisitiveness	acquire	acquisitive	acquisitively
activity, activist	action, activism	act, activate	active, actionable	actively
adaptor	adaptation, adaption, adaptability	adapt	adaptable, adapted, adaptive	
additive	addition	add	additional, additive	additionally
	(in)adequacy		(in)adequate	(in)adequately
adult	adulthood			
	agility		agile	agilely
agreement	(dis)agreement	(dis)agree	(dis)agreeable	agreeably
	ailment	ail	ailing	
antique, antiquary, antiquarian	antiquity		antiquarian, antiquated, antiqued	
applicant, appliance	application, applicability	apply	(in)applicable, applied	applicably
	(dis)approval	(dis)approve	(dis)approved, (dis)approving	(dis)approvingly
	approximation	approximate	approximate	approximately
architecture, architect	architecture		architectural	architecturally
arts, artwork, artist, artifact	art, artwork, artistry, artificiality		arty, artistic, artful, artless, artificial	artistically, artfully, artificially
assessor	assessment	assess	assessed	
assistant	assistance	assist	assistant, (un)assisted	
attendant, attender, attendee	attendance, attention	attend	attentive, (un)attended	attentively
	austerity		austere	austerely
authoritarian	authoritarianism	authorise	(un)authorised, authorising, authoritarian, authoritative	authoritatively
authorities, authority	authority, authorisation,			
	availability	avail (sb of)	available, unavailable	
	awareness		(un)aware	
base, basics, basis	base, baseline	base	basic, based, baseless	basically
beautician	beauty	beautify	beautiful	beautifully
behaviourist	behaviour, behaviourism	behave	behavioural	
believer	belief	believe	(un)believable	(un)believably
		belittle	little	
	boast, boastfulness	boast	boastful	boastfully
			botanical, botanic	botanically
Botany, botanicals, botanist				
building, build, builder	building	build, rebuild	built, rebuilt	
captive, captor	captivity	captivate	captivated, captive, captivating	captivatingly
caretaker, carer	care, carefulness, carelessness	care	carefree, careful, careless, (un)caring	carefully, carelessly, (un)caringly
category	categorisation	categorise	categorised, categorical	categorically

Concrete noun	Abstract noun	Verb	Adjective	Adverb
	caution, precaution	caution	cautious, cautionary, precautionary	cautiously
centre	centrality	centre	central, centred	centrally
ceremony, ceremonialist	ceremoniousness, ceremonialism		ceremonial, ceremonious	ceremonially, ceremoniously
characteristics	character, characterisation	characterise	characteristic, characterful, characterless	characteristically
	comfort, discomfort	comfort	(un)comfortable	(un)comfortably
commerce, commercial	commerce, commercialisation, commercialism	commercialise	commercial, commercialised	commercially
community	communion, communication	commune, communicate	communal, (un)communicative, communicational	communally
company, companion	company, companionship	accompany	accompanying, (un)accompanied	
	comparison, comparability	compare	(in)comparable, comparative	(in)comparably, comparatively
competitor	competition, competitiveness, (in)competence	compete	competitive, competing, (in)competent	competitively, competently
complication	complication	complicate	complicating, complicated	
	(in)comprehension, (in)comprehensibility, concept, conception	comprehend	(in)comprehensible, (in)comprehensive	(in)comprehensibly, (in)comprehensively
	conceptualisation	conceive, conceptualise	(in)conceivable, conceptual	(in)conceivably, conceptually
conformer, (non)conformist	(non)conformity, conformation, conformance, conformability	conform	(non)conforming, conformable	conformably
	consequence		consequent, (in)consequential,	consequently, (in)consequentially
	consideration	consider	(in)considerate, considerable	(in)considerately, considerably
consumer	consumption	consume	consumed, consumable	
	(dis)continuance, (dis)continuation, (dis)continuity	(dis)continue	continual, (dis)continuous	continually, (dis)continuously
conventioneer	convention		(un)conventional	(un)conventionally
	conviction	convince	(un)convincing, convinced	(un)convincingly
costing(s)	cost	cost	costly	
	courage	encourage, discourage	courageous, encouraged, encouraging, discouraged, discouraging	courageously, encouragingly
creation, creator, creature, creationist	creation, creativity, creationism	create	creative	creatively

330

Concrete noun	Abstract noun	Verb	Adjective	Adverb
culturist	culture cure	culture cure	cultural, cultured cured, curative, (in)curable	culturally (in)curably, curatively
customer, customs	custom	customise, accustom	customary, (un)accustomed	customarily
damage, damages	damage	damage	damaging, (un)damaged, damageable	damagingly
	danger	endanger	dangerous, endangered	dangerously
	death	die	dead, deadly	
decoration, decorator	decor, decoration	decorate	decorative	decoratively
defender, defendant	defence, defensiveness	defend	defensive, defenceless	defensively
	definition	define	defined, (in)definable, (in)definite, definitive	definitely, indefinitely
delicacy	delicacy		delicate	delicately
denier	denial	deny	undeniable	undeniably
departure, (the) departed	departure	depart	departed	
dependant	(in)dependence, (in)dependency, dependability	depend	(in)dependent, (un)dependable	(in)dependently, (un)dependably
depth	depth	deepen	deep	deeply
destroyer	destruction, destructiveness, (in)destructibility	destroy	destructive, (in)destructible	destructively
developer	development	develop	developing, (un)developed, developable, developmental	developmentally
digit			digital	digitally
	diligence		diligent	diligently
diner, dinner		dine	dining	
discoverer	discovery	discover	discovered	
	discrimination	(in)discriminate	(un)discriminating, discriminatory, discriminative	discriminately, (un)discriminatingly, discriminatively
dispenser	dispensation, (in)dispensability	dispense	(in)dispensable	
	diversity, diversiveness, diversification	diversify	diverse	diversely
document, documentary	documentation	document	documentary	
dominion, dominator	dominance, domination	dominate	dominant, dominating	dominantly
drama, dramatics, dramatist	drama, dramatisation	dramatise	dramatic, dramatised	dramatically
economist, economics	economy	economise	economic, (un)economical	(un)economically

331

Concrete noun	Abstract noun	Verb	Adjective	Adverb
educator	education	educate	(un)educated, educational, educative, educationable	educationally
effects	affectation, effect, effectiveness	affect, effect	effective, affected, effectual	effectively
enlarger	enlargement	enlarge	large, enlarged, enlarging	largely
environmentalist	environment, environmentalism		environmental	environmentally
equaliser, equation, equator	equality	equal, equalise, equate	(un)equal, (un)equalled	(un)equally
equipment		equip	equipped	
excess	excess, excessiveness	exceed	excessive, exceeding	excessively
	exception	except	exceptional, exceptionable	exceptionally
	exclusion, exclusiveness, exclusivity	exclude	exclusive, exclusionary	exclusively
exhibition, exhibit, exhibitor, exhibitionist	exhibition, exhibitionism	exhibit	exhibitive, exhibitionistic	
	expectation, expectancy	expect	(un)expected, expectant	expectantly, unexpectedly
expenditure, expense, expender	expenditure, expense, expensiveness	expend	(in)expensive, expendable,	(in)expensively
experiment, experimenter, experimentalist	experimentation, experimentalism	experiment	experimental	experimentally
	experience	experience	(in)experienced, experiential	experientially
exploiter	exploitation	exploit	exploitable, exploitative	
exploration, explorer	exploration	explore	exploratory	
explosive	explosion	explode	explosive	explosively
exposition, exposure, exposé	exposition, exposure	expose	exposed	
extension, extender	extent, extension	extend	extensive, extended, extensible	extensively
externalist	externalisation, externals, externalism	externalise	external	externally
face		face	facial	
fact, factor			factual	factually
favourite	favour, favouritism	favour	favoured, (un)favourable, favourite	(un)favourably,
form, formula, format	formation, formulation, formalism	form, formulate	formative, (in)formal, formless	formatively, (in)formally
former			former	formerly
	freedom	free	free	free, freely
frequency	frequency	frequent	(in)frequent	(in)frequently
	generosity		generous	generously
globe	globalisation	globalise	global	globally

Concrete noun	Abstract noun	Verb	Adjective	Adverb
undergoer	going	go, undergo	going	
graces	grace, disgrace	grace, disgrace	(dis)graceful, gracious, graceless	(dis)gracefully, gracelessly, graciously
grade, gradation, gradient, gradualist	grade, gradualism	grade	grading, graded, gradual	gradually
	(in)gratitude, gratification	gratify	(un)grateful	(un)gratefully
	grudge	grudge	grudging	grudgingly
	harm	harm	harmful, harmless, unharmed	harmfully, harmlessly
hater	hate, hatred, hatefulness	hate	hating, hated, hateful, hateable	hatefully
height	height	heighten	high, heightened	high, highly
hindrance	hindrance	hinder	hindered	
historian	history		historical, historic	historically
	horror	horrify	horrific, horrifying, horrified	horrifically, horrifyingly
human, humanity, humanist, humanitarian, humanities, humankind	humanity, humanism	humanise	human, (in)humane, humanistic,	humanly, humanely, humanistically
	humility, humiliation	humble, humiliate	humble, humbled, humbling, humiliating	humbly
humourist	humour	humour	humorous, humourless	humorously
identity(card)	identity, identification	identify	identifying, (un)identified, identifiable, identical	identically
	immunity, immunisation	immunise	immune	immunising, immunised
improver	improvement, improvability	improve	improved	
increaser	increase	increase	increasing, increased, increasable	increasingly
inhabitant, habitat, habitation	(in)habitation, (in)habitability	inhabit	(un)inhabited, habitable	
inhaler, inhalant	inhalation	inhale	inhalant	
installation, installer	installation	install		
instructor	instruction	instruct	instructive, instructional	instructively
	intensity, intensification	intensify	intensive, intense	intensively, intensely
	intention, intent	intend	(un)intentional, intended	(un)intentionally
interpreter	interpretation, interpretability, interpretableness	interpret	interpretive, interpretable	interpetably
introduction	introduction	introduce	introductory	
invader	invasion	invade	invasive	
inventor, inventory	invention, inventiveness	invent	(un)inventive, inventional, inventionless	inventively
	knowledge, knowingness	know	(un)known, knowing, knowledgeable	knowingly, knowledgeably
land, landmark, landscape, landlord	landing	land	landless	

Concrete noun	Abstract noun	Verb	Adjective	Adverb
law, lawyer, lawmaker, lawsuit, lawbreaker legalisation	law legalisation, legality	legalise	(un)lawful, lawless, (il)legal, legalistic	(un)lawfully, lawlessly (il)legally
like			like, alike	alike
limit	limitation	limit	limiting, (un)limited, limitless	
locality, local, locale, location	locality, location, localisation, localism	locate, localise	local, located	locally
longitude, length	elongation, length	elongate, lengthen, prolong	long, elongate, lengthy	
loyalist	loyalty, loyalism		loyal	loyally
mark, marker	marking, remark	mark, remark	marked, remarkable	markedly, remarkably
master, mastermind, masterpiece, masterclass, masterwork, masterstroke	masterliness, mastery, masterfulness	master, mastermind	masterly, masterful	masterfully
memory, memento, memorandum (memo), memorial, memoir(s), memorabilia	memory	memorise, memo	memorable	memorably
milestone, mile	milestone, mileage			
mimic	mime, mimicry minority	mime, mimic	mimetic minor	
moment	momentum		momentary, momentous	momentarily, momentously
month			monthly	
monument	monument		monumental	monumentally
moralist	morality, morals, moral, morale	moralise	(im)moral, moralistic, amoral	(im)morally
mystic	mystery, mysteriousness, mysticism, mystification, mystique	mystify	mysterious mystical, mystifying	mysteriously, mystically
navigator	navigation	navigate	navigational	
neighbour, neighbourhood	neighbourliness		neighbouring, neighbourly	
	neutrality, neutralisation	neutralise	neutral	neutrally
noble	nobility	ennoble	noble, ennobled	nobly
norm	norm, (ab)normality, normalisation	normalise	(ab)normal, normalising	normally
note, notables	noteworthiness	note	notable, noteworthy	notably
novel, novelist, novella	novelty		novel, novelistic	novelly
number		number	numbered, numerical, numberless, (in)numerous, (in)numerable	numerically
object, objector	objection, objectivity, objectiveness, objectionability	object	objective, objectionable	objectively, objectionably

Concrete noun	Abstract noun	Verb	Adjective	Adverb
	obligation	oblige	obligatory, obliged, obliging	obligingly
observer, observatory	observation, observance	observe	observant, observable, observational	
occupant	occupation, occupancy, preoccupation	occupy	occupational, occupied, preoccupied	occupationally
	occurrence	occur		
offender	offence, offensiveness	offend	offensive, offending	offensively
origin(s), originator	origin, originality	originate	original	originally
			ordinary, extraordinary	ordinarily, extraordinarily
owner	ownership	own		
participant	participation	participate	participatory, participative	
	peace, peacefulness		peaceful	peacefully
	peculiarity		peculiar	peculiarly
percent, percentage				percent
	perception, perceptiveness	perceive	perceptive, perceptual, perceptible	perceptively, perceptually, perceptibly
perfectionist	perfection, imperfection, perfectionism	perfect	perfect, imperfect	perfectly, imperfectly
period, periodical	period		periodical, periodic	periodically
person, personality, personnel, personage impersonator	personality, persona, personification, impersonation	personalise, personify, impersonate	personal, impersonal	personally, impersonally
place	(re)placement, (dis)placement	(re)place, (dis)place	replaceable, irreplaceable	
planet			planetary	
populace, population	popularity, popularism, popularisation, unpopularity depopulation	popularise, populate	popular, unpopular populated, populous, overpopulated	popularly
portrait, portraitist	portrayal	portray		
precedent	precedence	precede	preceded, preceding, (un)precedented	(un)precedentedly
	pregnancy	impregnate	pregnant, impregnated	
pretender	pretence, pretension, pretentiousness	pretend	(un)pretentious	(un)pretentiously
prime, primer	primacy, primitiveness	prime	primary, primal, prime, primitive	primarily
proceedings, proceeds	procedure	proceed	procedural	
production, product, producer	productivity	produce, reproduce	productive, reproductive,	productively
professional	profession, professionalism	professionalise	(un)professional, professionalised	(un)professionally
	propriety, impropriety		proper, improper	properly, improperly
	prosperity	prosper	prosperous	prosperously
provider	provision	provide	provident	providently

335

Concrete noun	Abstract noun	Verb	Adjective	Adverb
provocateur	provocation	provoke	provocative	provocatively
psychologist	psyche, psychology		psychological	psychologically
publication, publisher, publicist	publicity	publicise	public, publishing, published	publicly
punisher	punishment	punish	punishing, punishable	
pursuer	pursuit, pursuance	pursue	pursuant	
question, questionnaire	question, questioning	question	(un)questionable, questioning, questioned	(un)questionably
assurance	sureness, (re)assurance	ensure, (re)assure	sure, reassuring	surely, reassuringly
receipt, receiver, reception, receptionist, receptors	receivership, reception, receptiveness, receptivity	receive	received, receptive	receptively
	recreation	recreate	recreational	
reference	reference	refer	referring	
reflector	reflection, reflectance, reflectivity, reflectiveness	reflect	reflecting, reflected, reflective	reflectively
	refusal	refuse		
relations, relatives	relation, relationship, relativity, relativism	relate	relative, related	relatively
	reliance, (un)reliability	rely	reliant, (un)reliable	(un)reliably
	relief	relieve	relieved	
	renewal	renew	new, renewed	newly
reproduction	reproduction	reproduce	reproducible, reproductive	
requirement(s)	requirement	require	required	
resistant, resistor	resistance, resistivity	resist	(ir)resistible, resistant	(ir)resistibly
restrainer	restraint	restrain	(un)restrained, restrainable	(un)restrainedly
riches	riches, richness		rich	richly
ridicule	ridicule	ridicule	ridiculous	ridiculously
runner, forerunner		run	running, runny	
safe	safety	save	safe	safely
scene, scenery	scenery		scenic	scenically
school	schooling	school	schooled	
science, scientist	science, scientism		scientific, scientistic, sciential	scientifically
sculptor, sculpture	sculpture	sculpt	sculptural, sculptured	
(re)searcher	(re)search	(re)search	(re)searching, (re)searchable	searchingly
sensor	sense, sensation, sensitivity, sensibility, sensationalism	sense	sensitive, sensible, sensory, senseless, sensational, sensual, sensuous	sensitively, sensibly, senselessly, sensationally, sensually, sensuously
sentimentalist	sentiment, sentimentality	sentimentalise	sentimental, sentimentalising, sentimentalised	sentimentally
settlement, settler	settlement	settle	(un)settled	
	shame	shame	shameful, shameless	shamefully, shamelessly

Concrete noun	Abstract noun	Verb	Adjective	Adverb
ize	sizeableness		sizeable	sizably
	significance	signify	(in)significant	(in)significantly
pecialty, specialist	specialisations,	specialise	special, specialised	specially, especially
pecification(s),	specialism	specify	(non)specific,	specifically
pecifics	specification		specifying, specified	
			spiritual, spirited,	spiritlessly
pirit	spirituality		spiritless	
	spontaneity,		spontaneous	spontaneously
	spontaneousness			
tatistics			statistical	statistically
ymbol	symbolism	symbolise	symbolic	symbolically
ubscriber, subscription	subscription	subscribe	subscribed	
ubstance	substance	substantiate	(in)substantial,	substantially
	substantiation		substantive	
uccessor	success	succeed	(un)successful	(un)successfully
	(in)sufficiency	suffice	(in)sufficient	(in)sufficiently
uperior	superiority		superior	superiorly
upposer	supposition,	suppose, presuppose	supposed,	supposedly,
	presupposition		suppositional	suppositionally
upremacist, supremo	supremacy		supreme	supremely
	susceptibility		susceptible	
echnologist	technology		technological	technologically
ermination, terminal	termination	terminate	interminable, terminal	interminably,
				terminally
errorist	terror	terrify, terrorise	terrifying, terrified	terrifyingly
	threat	threaten	threatening,	threateningly
			threatened	
ime, timer	time, timing	time	timely, timeless	
radition	tradition		traditional	traditionally
reat	treatment	treat	treatable	
ype		typify	typical	typically
ser	use, usefulness,	use	(un)used, useful,	usefully, uselessly,
	uselessness, usualness		useless, (un)usual	(un)usually
eil, veiling	unveiling	veil, unveil	(un)veiled	
irus			viral	
olunteer, voluntarist	volunteering,	volunteer	(in)voluntary,	(in)voluntarily
	voluntar(y)ism		voluntaristic	
	welcome	welcome	(un)welcome,	
			(un)welcoming	
will	(un)willingness, will	will	(un)willing, willful	(un)willingly

337

Appendix 5

Group 1 - A

abashed by/at sth (adj)
abide by (v)
abscond (with sth) from somewhere (v)
absent from (adj)
absorbed in (adj) (+ noun/gerund)
absorption by (n) (= action of being absorbed by)
absorption in sth (n) (= fascination for)
abstinence from sth (n)
abstain from sth (v)
(in) abstraction (of sth) from sth (n)
abuse of (n)
acceptable to sb (adj)
access to sth/a place (n)
accompanied by sb (adj)
accord with (v)
according to (prep)
account for (v)
accuse sb of sth (v)
accustomed to sth (adj) (+gerund)
acquaint sb with sth (v)
acquainted with sb (adj)
acquit sb of sth (v)
act for (v) (= on sb's behalf)
act of (n) (= do as advised)
act on (v) (= as a result of sth)
addicted to sth (adj)
addiction to (n)
adequate for (adj)
adhere to (v)
adjacent to (adj)
adjust to (v)
admission of (n) (= confession)
admission to/into (n) (= permission to enter a place, join a group, club etc)
admit to (v)
advantage over sb (n) (= better position than sb)
advise sb against sth (v) (= advise sb not to do sth)

advise sb of sth (v) (= inform sb about sth)
advise sb on sth (v) (= give suggestions)
affectionate towards (adj)
affinity with sb/sth (n)
afraid of + noun (adj) (spiders, the dark etc)
afraid to + verb (adj) (look, swim etc)
age of (n)
agree on sth (v) (= to reach a decision with others)
agree to (v) (= agree to do sth or allow sb else to do sth)
agree with sb about sth (v)
agree with sth (v) (= to approve of sth)
agreeable to sb/sth (adj)
ahead of (adj)
aim (sth) at (v)
allergic to sth (adj)
allusion to (n)
amazed at/by (adj)
amenable to (adj)
amount of sth (n)
amount to (v)
amused at/by (adj)
angry at sb (+ gerund) (adj)
angry with sb about sth (adj)
animosity towards (n)
annexe to (n)
annoyed at/about sth (adj)
annoyed with sb (adj)
answer to (n)
antipathetic to (adj)
anxious about/for sth (adj)
anxious for sb (adj)
apologise to sb for sth (v)
apparent in/from sth (adj)
apparent to sb (adj) (= clear, obvious)
appeal to sb (v)
apply to sb for sth (v)

appreciative of (adj)
apprehensive of/about (adj)
approve of (v)
aptitude for (n)
argue about sth (v) (= to disagree about sth)
argue for/against sth (v) (= give reasons why/why not sth should be, happen etc)
argue with sb (v)
arrest sb for sth (v)
arrive at (v) (a fixed address, a small place, conclusion)
arrive in (v) (a large area, country)
ashamed of (adj)
ask (sb) about (v) = (ask for information about sth)
ask (sb) for (v) (= say that you would like sth)
assault on (n)
assigned to (adj)
associate (sth/sb) with (v)
assure sb of (v)
astonished at/by (adj)
attached to (adj)
attempt on (sb's life) (n)
attend to sth/sb (v)
attendance at (n)
attitude to/towards (n)
auxiliary to (adj)
averse to (adj)
aversion to (n)
avoidance of (n)
aware of (adj)
awkward at/with (adj) (at dancing etc/with one's hands etc)

Group 2 - B

back out of (v)
bad at sth (adj)
bad to sb (adj)
bags of (n) (+ noun)
ban on sth (n)
barter for (v)
base sth on (v)

bash in/up (v)
basis for/of (n)
bear with sb (v)
bearer of (n)
(make a) beeline for (n)
beg (sb) for (v)
begin by (+ gerund) (v)

begin with (+noun) (v)
belief in (n)
believe in (v)
belong to sb (v)
benefit from (v)
benefit of (n)
bet (sth) on (v)

beware of (v)
bit of (n)
blame sb for sth (v) (but: **put the blame on)**
boast of/about sth (v)
book into (v)

Group 3 - C

campaign for (n)
capable of (adj)
care for sb/sth (v) (= like, look after)
(take) care of sb/sth (n)
care about sth (v) (= be concerned about)
(in) care of sb (n)
careful about (adj) (= take care when doing sth)
careful of (adj) (= avoid danger to oneself)
be careful of the dog
careful with (adj) (take care not to do harm to an object)
careless about/of (adj)
centre of (n)
certain of (adj)
challenge sb to sth (v)
change in/to (v) (= become sth else)
change sth for sth (v) (replace with)
changeable towards (adj)
characteristic of (adj)
charge at (v) (= rush towards)
charge sb with (v) (= accuse of)
cheque for (money) (n)
choice between (two things) (n)
choice in (a matter) (n)

bored with/by (adj)
borrow sth from sb (v)
bother about/with (v)
bottom of (n)
breach of (n)
break into/out of (v)

choice of (n) (a number of things)
clever at (+ gerund) (adj)
clever with (adj) (hands, tools etc)
close to (adj)
coax sb into (v)
coincide with (v)
collaborate with sb on sth/in (v) (+ gerund)
collide with (v)
comment on (v)
communicate with (v)
compare with/to (v)
complain to sb about/of sth/sb (v)
compliment on (v)
comply with (v)
concentrate on (v)
concern about (n)
confidence in (n)
confident of (adj)
confine to (v)
confusion about (n)
congratulate sb on sth (v)
connected to (adj)
connection between (n)
conscious of (adj)
consent to (v)
consist of (v)

brilliant at (adj)
bump into (v)
burst into (v)
busy with (adj)

consistent with (adj)
consult sb on/about sth (v)
consumption of (n)
content with (adj)
contrary to (adj)
contrast with/to (v)
contribute to (v)
control of/over (n)
convert to/into (v)
convince of (v)
cope with (v)
correction of (n)
correspond with (v)
count on sb for sth (v)
cover in/with (v)
crash into (v)
craving for (n)
crazy about (adj)
crime against (n)
crowded with (adj)
cruel to (adj)
cruelty to (adj)
cry about (sth which has happened (v)
cry for (sth you want) (v)
cure of (v)
curious about (adj)

Group 4 - D

dabble in/at sth (v)
damage to (n)
damaging to (adj)
danger of (n)
(make a) dash for (n)
date from (v)
deaf in (adj) (one ear)
deaf to (adj) (sb's arguments)
deal in (v) (= have a business involving particular things)
deal with (v) (manage sth)
dear to (adj)
death by (n)
decide about (a plan etc) (v)
decide on (v) (an object)
He couldn't decide on which car to buy

decline in (n)
decline to (v)
decrease by (v) (a certain amount)
decrease in (v) (size, number)
decrease in (n)
dedicate to (v)
deep in sth (adj)
(in) default of (n)
defer sth (to sth) (v)
deficiency of/in (n)
deficient in (adj)
delay in (n)
delight (sb) with/in sth (v) (= entertain/amuse sb with)
delight in (v) (take pleasure in)
delighted with (adj)

demand for (n)
demand sth from (v)
depart from (v)
depend on/upon (v)
deposit in (v) (the bank)
deposit on (v) (the ground)
deputise for sb (v)
derive from (v)
descended from (adj)
deserted by (adj)
desire for (n)
despair of (v)
destined for (adj)
destructive to (adj)
determined about (adj)
detrimental to sth (adj)

deviation from (n)
devoid of (adj) (+ noun)
devotion to (n)
die from (v) (a wound)
die of (v) (illness, hunger etc)
differ from sth (v) (= be unlike)
differ with/from sb on/about sth (v)
(= have a different opinion)
difference between (n) (two or more
things/people)
difference of (n) (amount, opinion)
different from (adj)
difficulty in (n) (+ gerund)
difficulty with (n) (+ noun)
diffident about (adj)
diligence in (n)
direct (sth) at/towards (v)
disadvantage in (n) (situation)
disadvantage of (n) (+ gerund or noun
- weakness, poverty etc)
disagree with sb on/about sth (v)
disappointed with/by/in (adj)

disapprove of (v)
disbelieve in (v)
discharge from (v)
discourage from (v)
discrimination against (n)
discrimination in favour of (n)
discussion about (n)
disgruntled at/about (adj)
disgusted at/by/with oneself/sb/sth
(adj)
dislike for sb/sth (n)
dismiss sb from (v)
displeased with sb/sth (adj)
dispose of sth/sb (v)
disqualify sb from sth (v)
disregard for/of sb/sth (n)
dissatisfied with/at sb/sth (adj)
distaste for sb/sth (n)
distinguish between (v)
distracted by (adj) (a disturbance)
distracted from (adj) (what one is doing)
dither about sth/doing sth (v)

divide sth among (v) (more than 2
people/things)
divide sth between (v) (2 people/
things)
divide sth by (v) (another number)
divide 4 by 2
divide sth into (v) (parts)
divide the cake into 6 parts
divisible by (adj)
do sth about sth (v)
doubtful about/of (adj)
dream about (v)
dream of (v) (= imagine)
drive into/from/to/at/in/with/
against/in/about/for etc (v)
due for (adj) (= deserving sth)
due to (adj) (= because of)
due to bad weather
dust (sth) off (v)
dwell in/at (v) (= live in/at a place)
dwell upon/on (v) (= think about, usu
sth unpleasant)

Group 5 - E

(at the) expense of (n)
eager for (adj)
economise on (v)
efficient at/in (adj)
eject (sb/sth) from (v)
elated at/by (adj)
eligible for (adj)
elope with sb (v)
emanate from sth/sb (v)
embark on/upon (v)
embroil (sb) in sth (v)
emerge from (v)
emphasis on (v)
empty sth out of/into/onto sth (v)
encounter with sb/sth (n)
encourage sb in sth (v)
end sth with sth (v)
engaged in (adj) (= busy with)
engaged to sb (adj) (= promised to
marry sb)
engagement to (n)
engrossed in sth (adj)
enlist (sb) as/in/for sth (v)

entice sb away from sth (v)
entitle (sb) to (v)
entranced by/with (adj)
entry into/to sth (n)
entwine (sb/sth) with/in/round sth (v)
envious of sb/sth (adj)
envy of sb - at/of sth (n)
equal to sb/sth (adj)
equivalent to sth (adj)
escape from sth (v)
essential to/for (adj)
establish oneself as sth (v) (= take
position/office)
establish oneself in (v) (place)
evacuation of (n) (+ noun)
evocative of sth (adj)
excellent at (adj) (cooking etc)
excellent with (adj) (a sword etc)
exception to (n) (+ noun)
excited about/by (adj)
exclaim at/about (v)
exclude (sb/sth) from (a place or
activity) (v)

exclusion of sb from sth (n)
excuse for (n)
excuse sb for sth (v) (= forgive sb for
sth)
excuse sb from sth (v) (= free sb from a
duty, requirement, punishment)
exempt from sth (adj)
expel sb/sth from (a place) (v)
experienced in (adj) (activity)
experienced with (adj) (tools, weapons)
experiment on (v) (animals etc)
experiment with (v) (methods etc)
expert in/at/on (adj) (activity)
expert with (adj) (tool, weapon etc)
explain sth to sb (v)
exposed to (adj)
expressive of (adj) (one's mood)
expressive with (adj) (one's hands,
voice etc)
exult at/in sth (v)

Group 6 - F

fabric of (sth) (n)
faced with (adj)
failure in (n)

faith in sb/sth (n)
faithful to sb/sth (adj)
fall from (n) (a height)

fall in (n) (prices, popularity)
famed from sth (adj)
familiar to sb (adj)

famous for (adj) (one's actions)
famous in (adj) (a country etc)
fatal to/for sb/sth (adj)
fatten (sth/sb) up (v)
favourable for/to sb/sth (adj)
fear of (+ noun) (n)
feature at (v) (the cinema)
feature in (v) (a magazine)
feature on (v) (TV)
fetch sth for sb (v)
feud with sb over sth (v)
fiddle with sth (v)
fiddle around/about (v)
fidelity to sb/sth (n)
fidget about/around (v)
fight with sb about sth/against sth (v)
filled with (adj) (+ noun)
film of (n)

fine sb for sth/doing sth (v)
finish (sth) off (v)
finish by (v) (+ gerund)
finish with (v) (+ noun)
firm (sth) up (v)
fish for sth (v)
fit for/to (adj)
fit in/into (v) (be comfortable with a particular group of people etc)
fit into (v) (= go into the right place)
fixation on/with sb/sth (n)
flair for sth (v)
flake off/away from (v)
flee from sb/sth (v)
flirt with sb (v)
flock of (n)
flow from/out of/into (v)
flow of (n)

fond of (adj)
forget about (v)
forgive sb for sth (v)
fortunate in (adj) (+ gerund)
fraternise with sb (v)
fraught with (v) (problem, risks)
free sb from sth (v)
freedom from (n) (chains, problems)
freedom of (n) (speech, action)
freshen (sth) up (v)
fret about sth (v)
friendly to sth (adj) (= not harmful to sth)
friendly with (sb) (adj)
frightened of/by sth + gerund (adj)
frown at sb/sth (v)
frown with (v) (anger, confusion etc)
full of (adj)
furious with sb about sth (adj)

Group 7 - G

(be a) genius at (n) (subject)
(be a) genius with (n) (tools etc)
(have a) genius for sth/doing sth (n)
gain by/from (+ gerund) (v)
gap between (n) (2 things)
gape at sb/sth (v)
gargle with sth (v)
garnish with sth (v)
gash in/on sth (n)
gather round sb/sth (v)
gaze at/upon (v)
generosity to/towards (n)
generous with sth (adj)
gibe at/about sb/sth (v)

giggle at (v)
glance at (v)
glare at (v)
glee at sth (n)
glisten with sth (v)
glitter with sth (v)
gloat about/over (v)
glower at sb/sth (v)
good at sth (adj)
good for sb (adj) (= good influence on sb)
good to sb (adj) (= kind to sb)
gracious to sb (adj) (= kind to sb)
graduate from (v) (university)

graduate in (v) (subject)
grapple with sb/sth (v)
grateful to sb for sth (adj)
grief at/over (n)
grievance against/with (n)
grieve at/over sth (v)
grudge against sb (n)
grumble to/at sb about/over sth (v)
guaranteed against (adj)
guaranteed for (adj) (breakage etc)
guess at (v)
guilty of (adj)

Group 8 - H

(be in the) habit of (n)
haggle with sb about/over sth (v)
hand on/over (v)
handy for sth/doing sth (adj)
hanker after/for sth (v)
happen to/upon (v) (= come across by chance)
happy about (adj) (situation)
happy in (adj) (a new house etc)
happy with sth/sb (adj)
harmful to (adj)

harmonise with (v)
hazard to (n)
Ice is a hazard to motorists
heap sth up (v)
hear about/of sth (v) (= receive information about)
hear from sb (v) (= receive a letter, a telephone call from sb)
heat sth up (v)
heir to sth (n)
hesitate about/over (v) (doing sth)

hesitate at (v) (the door etc)
hinder sb/sth from sth/doing sth (v)
hiss at sb/sth (v)
honest about sth (adj)
hope for sth (v)
hopeless at (adj) (maths etc)
hopeless with (adj) (a gun etc)
huddle up to sb/sth (v)
hunch up (v)

Group 9 - I

identical with/to sb/sth (adj)
ignorant of (adj)
(have an) impact on sb/sth (n)

impatient for sth (adj) (= eager for sth to happen)
impatient with sb (adj) (= intolerant of)

impolite to (adj)
impressed by/with (adj)
impression of sth/doing sth (n)

Appendix 5

improvement in (n) (condition, situation health)

incapable of sth/doing sth (adj)

include sb/sth in sth (v)

increase in (n) (size, number, level)

increase sth by (v) (amount, percentage)

indebted to sb for sth (adj)

independent of/from (adj)

indifferent to sth/sb (adj)

indignant at/about/over sth (adj)

indulge in sth (v)

Group 10 - J

jam sth/sb in/between sth (v)

jam-packed with sth (adj) (informal)

jealous of (adj)

jest with sb about sth (v)

jinx on sb/sth (n)

join in sb/sth (n)

join sth onto sth (v) (= attach one thing

Group 11 - K

keen on sb/sth (adj)

key sth into sth (v)

key to (n) (+ noun)

Group 12 - L

label (sth) as (v)

lace (sth) up (v)

lack of (n)

laden with sth (adj)

lag behind sb/sth (v)

lap (sth) up (v)

lather (sth) up (v)

laugh about (v) (situation)

laugh at sb/sth (v)

laze around/about (v)

lean on/towards/against/over (v)

leave for (v)

lecture on (v) (= give a lecture)

Group 13 - M

(in the) mood for sth (n)

mad at/with sb (adj)

make of sth (n)

malevolent to/towards (adj)

married to (adj)

marvel at/about (v)

mastery of sth (n)

mean to sb/with sth (adj)

meddle in sth (v)

mediate between (v)

---

inferior to sb/sth (adj)

injurious to sb/sth (adj)

innocent of (adj)

inoculate sb against sth (v)

inseparable from (adj)

insist on (v)

inspired by (adj)

insure sth/sb against (v)

intent on sth/doing sth (adj)

intention on sth/doing sth (adj)

intention of (n)

interest in (n)

to another)

join up (v) (= become a member of esp army/attach sth to sth else)

join up with sb/sth (v) (= become partners with)

joke with sb about sth (v)

jostle against sb/for sth (v)

kind to sb (adj)

knock at/on (v)

know of/about (v)

lecture sb for/about sth (v) (= scold/ warn sb)

legislate for/against (v)

lend (sth) to sb (v)

liable for (adj)

lie to sb about sth (v)

limit (sb/sth) to (v)

line (sth) with sth (v)

listen for (v) (= listen carefully to hear the telephone, doorbell etc)

listen to (v) (radio, music etc)

live at (v) (an address)

live on (v) (a big street)

mention to (v)

militate against sth (v)

mingle with sth (v)

misinform sb about (v)

mistake sb/sth for sb/sth (v)

mistaken about sb/sth (adj) (= wrong in opinion)

mistaken for (adj) (= believed to be sb/sth else)

mistrust of (n)

---

interested in/about (adj)

interfere with (v)

invest sth in (v)

investment in (n)

invitation to (n)

invite sb to sth (v)

involve sb in (v)

involved in/with sth (adj)

irrelevant to sth (adj)

irritated by/with sb, by/at sth (adj)

isolate sb from sb/sth (v)

judge sb/sth by/from sth (v)

judgement about (n) (action, crime etc)

judgement of (n) (court, judge etc)

judgement on sb (n) (punishment for sb)

juggle with sth (v)

justification for (n) (+ noun or gerund)

knowledge of/about (n)

live in (v) (a small street)

live for (v) (a particular time, person, thing)

live with (v) (person, emotion, memory etc)

long for sth/to do sth (v)

look about/around (v)

look at (v) (= view)

loyal to (adj)

lukewarm about sb/sth (adj) (= not eager)

mock at sb/sth (v)

moon around/about/over (v) (+ noun)

motion to/towards sb (v)

mould sth into sth (v)

mourn for/over sb/sth (v)

muddle (sth/sb) up (v)

mutiny against sb/sth (v)

Group 14 - N

nag at (v)
name sth/sb after/for sb (v) (= give a name to sth/sb)
name sb for/as sth (v) (= nominate sb for a position)
naturalise sb/sth in (v)
necessary for/to (adj)
necessity for/to (n)
need for (n)
negligent of (adj) (one's duties, responsibilities)

negotiate (sth) with sb (v)
nervous of (adj) (+ noun/gerund)
new to (adj) (an area, one's experience)
news of (n)
next to (adj)
nibble at sth (v)
nice to (adj)
niggle about/over (v)
nod to/at sb (v)
nominate sb as (v) (president)

nominate sb for (v) (a position)
noted for (adj)
(take) notice of (n)
notify sb of sth/sth to sb (v)
notorious as (adj) (criminal etc)
notorious for (adj) (crime etc)

Group 15 - O

obedient to sb/sth (adj)
object to sb/sth/doing sth (v)
objection to/about sth (n)
obliged to sb for sth (adj)
oblivious of/to sth (adj)
obsession with/about sb/sth (n)
obtain sth for sb (v)
obvious to sb (adj)
occur to sb (v)
offense against (n) (= breaking of a rule or law)
offense to (n) (= insult)

ogle at sb (v)
omen of sth (n)
onslaught on sb (n)
ooze out of/with (v)
operate on (v) (person)
operate with (v) (tools, instruments)
opinion of/about (n)
opposed to sth (adj)
opposite to sb/sth (adj)
optimistic about (adj)
originate sth in/from sb (v)
oust sb from sth (v)

outlay on sth (n)
outlet for sth (n)
outlook for (n) (= forecast, prediction)
weather outlook for the weekend
outlook on (n) (= opinion of)
outlook on life
outlook onto/over (n) (fields, towns etc)
outskirts of (n)
overburden sb with sth (v)
owing to (prep)

Group 16 - P

pale with (v)
part with (v)
pass by (v) (= go past)
Pass by sb's house
Christmas passed by quietly
pass on (v) (= to go on from one thing to another)
Let's pass on to the next question
patient with (adj)
pay by (v) (cheque)
pay for (v) (shopping)
pay in (v) (cash)
peck at sth (v)
peculiar to (adj)
peek at sth (v)
peeved about sth (adj)
pelt sb/sth with (v)
pernicious to sb/sth (adj)
persist in sth/doing sth (v)
pile (sth) up (v)
pity for sb/sth (n)
plague (sb/sth) with (v)
Plague me with a lot more questions
plan for (n)

plead with sb to do sth (v)
pleased with/about (adj)
pleasure in/of (n)
pledge sth to (v) (an organisation activity)
point at/to (v)
ponder on/over sth (v)
popular with (adj)
portent of sth (n)
pose for sb/sth (v)
possessive with/about (adj)
possibility of sth/doing sth (n)
postscript to sth (n)
(im)polite to (adj)
potential as (n) (+ noun)
potential for (n) (+ noun)
praise sb for sth (v)
pray to (v)
pray to sb for sth (v)
preach to sb about/against sth (v)
precaution against sth (n)
preconception about sb/sth (n)
predisposition to/towards sth (n)
prefer sth/sb to sth/sb (v)

prejudicial to/against/towards sth (adj)
prelude to sth (n)
prepare (sb/sth) for/to (v)
prepared by (adj) (+ gerund)
(be) prepared for (adj) (= ready for sth to happen)
prepared with/from (adj) (ingredients, components)
present at (adj) (event, ceremony, place)
present for (adj) (event)
Present for the parade
present in (adj) (place, court)
present sb with sth (v)
prevail against (v) (= to work against)
prevail in/among (v) (= to exist in/ among people, places etc)
prevail over (v) (= to be more powerful over)
prevail upon (v) (= persuade sb to do sth)
prevent sb/sth from doing sth (v)
previous to sb (adj)
pride in sb/sth (n)

Appendix 5

pride oneself on sth/doing sth (v)
proclivity to/towards (n)
Sudden violent rages
proficient at/in sth (adj)
prohibit sb from doing sth (v)
prone to sth (adj) (illness, infection)

proof against (n) (= which denies claim/secure against)
proof of (n) (what has been claimed)
propensity for/to/towards sth (n)
protect sb/sth against/from (v)
protection against (n)

protest about/against/at (v)
proud of (adj)
provide (sth) for sb (v)
pull at/on sth (v)
punish sb for sth (v)
puzzled about/by (adj)

Group 17 - Q

qualify (sb) as/for (v) (have/give required abilities, qualifications etc)
qualify (sb) for (v) (have/give right)
quality of (n)

quarrel with sb about/over sth (v)
quest for sth (n) (truth, happiness)
queue up (for) (v)
quick as (adj) (= comparison)

quick at (adj) (+ gerund or noun)
quiet sb/sth down (v)
quote (sth) from sb/sth (v)

Group 18 - R

race against sb/sth (n)
radiate from (v) (= originate from)
radiate with (v) (happiness etc)
rage at/against sb/sth (v)
raid on sth (n)
rally round (v)
rant at sb about sth (v)
rave at/against (v) (= act opposite to sb/sth)
reach for sth (v)
react against (v) (= act opposite to sb/sth)
react to (v) (= take action as a result of sth)
readjust to (v) (a new situation)
ready for (adj)
reason for (n)
reason with sb (v)
rebel against sth/sb (v)
receipt for (n) (proof of having paid for sth)
receipt of (n) (sth being received)
receive from (v)
recipe for (n)
recipient of sth (n) (of awards)
recite sth to sb/from sth (v)
reckless of/about sth (adj)
recoil from sb/sth at sth (v)
recommend sb/sth to sb/for sth (v)
recovery of sb/sth from sth (n)
recruit sb to sth/as sth (n)
redolent of/with sth (adj)
reduction in (n) (size etc)

reduction of (n) (amount by which sth is reduced)
refer to (v)
reference to sb/sth (n)
refrain from sth/doing sth (v)
refuge from sb/sth (n)
regard to/for (n)
regardless of (prep)
reign over (v)
rejoice at/over/in sth (v)
relapse into (v) (unconsciousness/crime)
related to (adj)
relationship between/with (n)
relative of (n)
release from (n)/(v)
relief from (n)
relish for/in (n)
rely on/upon (v)
remark on/upon/at (v)
remedy for (n)
remind of (v)
reminiscent of (adj)
remorse for sth/doing sth (n)
remote from (adj)
remove from (v)
reply to (v)
reply to/from (n)
report on/to (n)
repulsion for (n)
reputation as (n) (+ noun)
reputation for/of (n) (+ gerund)
request for sth (n)

research into/on sth (n)
resignation from (n)
resort to (v)
respected for (adj)
respite from sth (n)
respond to (v) (question, stimulus etc)
respond with (v) (= reply by doing sth
Respond with a smile
responsibility of/for (n)
responsible for (adj)
result in (v)
result of/from/in (n)
resulting from (adj) (= arising from)
resulting in (adj) (= leading to)
reticent about sth (adj)
retire from (v) (one's job)
retire to (v) (a place)
reverence for sb/sth (n)
reverse of (n)
revert to sth (v)
revolt against (v)
revolve around (v)
rhyme with (v)
rich in (adj) (humour, vitamins)
rid of (adj)
rise in/of/out (n)
risk of (n)
rival for (n) (sb's affections etc)
rival in (n) (a competition etc)
roar at (v) (object)
roar with (v) (pain, laughter)
room for (n) (creativity, correction)
rude to/towards sb (adj)

Group 19 - S

sad about (adj)
safe from sth/sb (adj)
safeguard (sb/sth) against/from sth/sb (v)

sated with sth (adj)
satisfied with (adj)
save sb/sth from (v)
scared of (adj)

schooled in sth (adj)
scorn for sth/sb (n)
scowl at sb/sth (v)
search for (v)

344

secret from sb (adj)
secret from (n)
sensible about (adj)
sensitive to (adj) (sb's needs)
sentence sb to sth (v)
separate from (adj)
separate sb/sth from (v)
sequel to sth (n)
serious about sth (adj)
set of (n)
sever sth from sth (v)
share (sth) with sb (v)
share in sth (v)
shelter (sb/sth) from sth (v)
shiver with sth (v)
shocked at/by (adj)
short of (adj)
(have a) shot at sth (n) (have a)
shout at sb (v) (from anger)
shout for sb (v) (indirectly)
shout to sb (v) (to attract attention)
shriek (v) (obscenities, a warning)
shriek with (v) (fear, etc)
shy of sth/doing sth (adj)
sick about/over (adj) (situation)
sick with (adj) (emotion)
Sick with fear
sidle up/over to sb/somewhere (v)
sigh with sth (v)
similar to sb/sth - in sth (adj)
skillful at/in (adj) (job)
skillful/skilled with/in (adj) (tool,
weapon, etc)
skilled at/in (adj) (job)
slow at (adj)
smile at sb (v)
smitten with/by sb/sth (adj)
sneer about (v) (situation)
sneer at sb/sth (v)
snipe at sb/sth (v)
snoop about/around (v)
snuggle up to sb/sth (v)
solace sb with sth (v)

Group 20 - T

talent for (n)
talk to sb about sth (v)
tamper with sth (v)
taste in (n) (clothes, etc)
taste of (n) (food, etc)
taunt sb with sth (v)
team up with sb (v)
team sb/sth with sb/sth (v)

solicitous for/about (adj)
soluble in (adj)
sorry about sth (adj)
sorry for sb (adj)
spatter sth on/over (v)
Spatter paint on the wall
spatter sth with (v)
Spatter the wall with paint
speak to sb about sb/sth (v)
specialist in (n)
spend (money) on (v)
spend (time) on sth (v)
spend (time) in/at (v) (place)
split sth into (v) (pieces)
split sth up (v) (= break sth up)
sprig of sth (n) (usu plant)
spy on sb/sth (v)
squabble with sb about/over sth (v)
squint at/through (v)
squirt (sth) out of/into/around etc from
sth (v)
stack (sth) up (v)
stamp about/around (v)
stare at (v)
stash (sth) away (v) (informal)
steal (sth) from (v)
stimulus to/for sth (n)
stock of (n)
story about/of (n)
straighten (sth) up/out (v)
strain of (n) (= quality)
There is a strain of unkindness in him.
strain on (n) (= exertion on sth)
*Buying that car will be a strain on our
resources.*
streak of sth (n)
stricken with/by sth (adj)
strip (sth) off/down (v)
strive for/after/towards (v)
struggle for sb/sth (v) (= fight for)
Struggle for breath.
struggle with sb/sth (v) (= fight with)
strum on sth (v)

terrified at sth (adj)
thank sb for sth (v)
thankful for sth (adj)
think about/of sth (v)
thirsty for sth (adj) (rain, success)
thoughtless of sb (adj)
threaten sb with sth (v)
throw sth at sb (v)

sub for sb (v)
subject to sth (ad) (alteration, approval)
submit (sth) to sb (v)
subsist on sth (v)
substitute for (n)
subversive of (adj)
succeed in sth (v)
succeed sb to sth (v) (the throne, a post)
successful in/at (adj)
successor to (n)
succumb to sth (v) (an illness, an attack)
suffer from/with (v)
sufficient for (adj)
sufficient for/to (adj)
suitable for (adj)
suited for/to (adj)
supplicate for sth (v)
support for (n)
*The fans showed their support for the
team.*
support of (n)
*Money was collected in support of
Greenpeace.*
support sb in (v) (a plan, decision etc)
support sth with (v) (money)
sure of (adj)
surge in (n) (rise in)
surge of (n) (people, the sea, etc)
surprised at/by (adj)
surrender (sb/sth) to sb (v)
surrogate for sb/sth (n)
suspect sb/sth of sth/doing sth (v)
suspicious of/about (adj)
swill (sth) out/down (adj)
swipe (out) at sth (v)
swoop down on sb/sth (v)
sympathetic to/towards/with sb (adj)
sympathise with sb about/for sth (v)
sympathy for/towards sb/sth (n)
sympathy with (n) (sb's ideas =
agreement with them)

throw sth to sb (v)
tinge sth with sth (v)
tingle with sth (v)
tinker at/with sth (v)
tired of (adj)
tolerant of (adj) (different opinions,
particular conditions)
trade in sth for sth (v)

traitor to sb/sth (n)
transition from sth to sth (n)
translate sth from sth into sth (v)
treatment for (n) (shock, lung cancer)
tribute to sth/sb (n)
trip (sb) up/over (v)
trip over sth (v)

Group 21 - U

unaware of sth (adj)
unconcerned with sth/sb (adj)
uneasy about sth (adj)
unequal in (adj) (size, etc)
unequal to (adj) (in comparison with sth else)
unfaithful to sb/sth (adj)
unfit for sth (adj)
uninterested in sb/sth (adj)

Group 22 - V

valid for (adj) (use)
valid in (adj) (a place)
valued at/for (adj) (a price/a purpose)
variation in/of sth (n)
vary in (v)
vault over sth (v)
vexed at/with sb/sth (adj)

Group 23 - W

wage sth against/on sth/sb (v)
wail about/over sth (v)
wait for (v)
wallow around/about in sth (v)
warn sb of/about sth (v)
warrant for sth (n)
wary of sb/sth (adj)
weak at/in (adj) (at the knees, in the

Group 24 - Y

yearn for sb/sth (v)
yearning for (n)

triumph over sth (v)
(make) trouble for sb (n)
(have/be in) trouble with/for (n)
He was in trouble with the police for stealing a car.
trust in (n)
tuck sth into sth (v)

unjust to sb (adj)
unmindful of sb/sth (adj)
unqualified as/for sth (adj)
unreasonable about (adj)
He was unreasonable about paying his share.
unreasonable of sb (adj) (= to behave in a particular way)
unswerving in sth (adj)

view of/to (n)
visible from (adj) (somewhere)
visible to (adj) (sb)
visible with (adj) (an instrument etc)
The moon is visible to our planet with the naked eye.
visitation of/from sb/sth (n)

head)
weary of sth/doing sth (v)
whiff of (n)
whittle away at/down sth (v)
win at (v)
wince at (v) (the thought of...)
wink at sb (v)
wish for (n)

yell (out) (v) (abuse, a name, in pain)
yell at sb about/for sth

tug at/on (v)
turn (sth/sb) around/over (v)
tussle with sb (v)
tutor sb in sth (v)
type of (n)
typical of sb/sth (adj)

upset about/with sth (adj)
upwind of sth (adj)
use of sth (n)
used for/as (adj) (employed)
used to (adj) (accustomed to)
useful to sb for/as sth (adj)
This wood will be useful to me as a table.

visitor to (n)
void of sth (adj)
votary of sb/sth (n)
vote for/against (n)
vote for/against (v)
vouch for sb/sth (v)
vulnerable to sth/sb (adj)

wish for (v)
worried about (adj)
worry about (v)
worthy at (adj)
worthy of (adj) (a reward, recognition etc)
wrestle with sb (v)
write to sb about sth (v)

yen for sth (n)

PREPOSITIONS WITH WORD PHRASES

Group 25 - At

at... km per hour
at a cost
at a disadvantage
at a discount
at a distance
at a glance
at a guess
at a loss
at a moment's notice
at a profit/loss
at all costs
at all events
at an advantage
at any rate
at breakfast/lunch
at church/school
at ease
at first hand
at first sight

at hand (= close)
at heart (= in one's real nature)
(have sb/sth) at heart (= be concerned about sb/sth)
at home
at last
at least
at length
at liberty
at night (note: in the night)
at noon
at odds with
at once
at one's request (= because sb wishes it)
at peace/war
at present
at random
at risk

at sea
at speed
at the age of
at the beginning (= when sth started)
at the end (= when sth finishes)
at the expense of
at the front of (= in the most forward position/place)
at the last possible time
at the latest (= time)
at the moment (= time)
at the point of (= at that particular time)
at the present time
at the same time
at the time (= at a particular time)
at times (= sometimes)
at work

Group 26 - By

by accident
by all accounts
by all means
by appointment
by auction
by birth
by bus/train/plane/car (but: in my own car, on the 8 o'clock train)
by chance
by cheque
by day/night
by degrees
by far
by force
by hand (= using the hands)

by heart (= from memory)
by land/sea/air
by law
by luck (= luckily)
by marriage
by means of
by mistake
by name (= using the name(s) of sb/sth)
by nature
by now
by one's side
by oneself
by order of
by post/airmail
by profession

by request (= as a response to sb's wish)
by sight (= recognise sb when you see them but have never met/talked to them)
by surprise
by the dozen
by the end (= before sth finishes)
by the side of
by the time (= before reaching a certain point)
by the way (= incidentally)
by virtue of

Group 27 - For/From

for a change
for a moment (= for a short time)
for a visit/holiday
for a walk
for a while
for ages (informal)
for breakfast/lunch/dinner
for certain
for ever
for fear of (= in case sth happens)

for good (= forever)
for granted
for hire
for life
for love (= out of love, without payment or other reward)
for nothing
for once (= on one occasion)
for sale (= to be sold)
for sb's sake

for short
for the moment (= for now, for the time being)
for the sake of
for the time being
from memory
from now on
from time to time

Appendix 5

Group 28 - In

in a (good/bad) mood
in a hurry
in a mess
in a way (= to some extent)
in action
in addition (to)
in advance (of)
in agony
in agreement with
in all
in answer to
in any case (= anyway)
in arrears
in bed
in blossom
in brief
in case (+ clause)
in case of (+ noun)
in cash
in charge (of)
in code
in comfort
in common (with)
in comparison with
in compensation for
in conclusion
in confidence
in control (of)
in danger
in debt
in detail
in difficulty
in disguise
in disorder
in doubt
in exchange for
in existence
in fact

in fashion
in favour of (= supporting)
in favour with (= liked by)
in fear of (= afraid of)
in flames
in focus
in front of (= further forward than)
in future
in gear
in general
in good/bad condition
in hand (= being dealt with)
in horror of
in ink/pencil
in length/width etc
In lengths of 10 m.
in love (with)
in moderation
in mourning (for)
in name only (= not really)
in no time (= very quickly)
in one's free time
in other words
in pain
in particular
in person
in pieces
in place of
in possession of (= owning)
in practice/theory
in principle (= theoretically)
in prison/jail
in private/public
in progress
in return
in safety
in sb's interest
in sb's opinion

in season
in secret
in self-defence
in sight (of) (= within one's range of vision)
in some respects (= in certain ways, concerning some aspects)
in stock
in summer/winter
in tears
in the air
in the beginning (= originally)
in the case of (= in the event)
in the dark
in the end (= finally)
in the flesh
in the habit of
in the meantime
in the mood for (= wanting to do sth)
in the morning
in the mountains
in the name of (= on sb's behalf)
in the news
in the nude
in the right/wrong
in time (= early enough)
in time of (= during a particular time)
in touch
in town
in tune (with)
in turn
in two/half
in uniform
in use
in vain
in view of (= because of, taking into account)
in vogue

Group 29 - On

on a ...day
on a diet
on a farm
on a journey
on a trip/cruise/excursion
on a(n) afternoon/evening
on account of (= because of)
on an expedition
on an island
on approval
on average
on bail

on balance
on behalf of
on business
on condition that
on credit
on demand
on duty
on fire
on foot
on good/bad terms with
on holiday
on impulse

on leave
on loan
on no account (= under no circumstances)
on one's mind
on one's own
on order
on paper
on principle (= according to a particular belief)
on purpose
on sale (= reduced in price)

on second thoughts
on sight (= as soon as sth is seen)
on strike
on the agenda
on the air
on the contrary
on the front/back (of a book, jacket

etc)
on the increase
on the job
on the one hand
on the other hand
on the outskirts
on the phone

on the point of (= about to)
on the radio/TV
on the trail of
on the way
on the whole
on time (= at the correct time)

Group 30

Out of

out of breath
out of control (= uncontrolled)
out of danger
out of date
out of debt
out of doors
out of fashion
out of hand
out of luck

out of order
out of pity
out of place
out of practice
out of print
out of reach
out of respect for
out of season
out of sight (= beyond one's range of

vision)
out of stock
out of the ordinary
out of the question
out of town
out of use
out of work

Off

off colour
off duty

off school/work
off the record

off the road

Under

under age
under arrest
under control (= controlled)
under discussion

under one's breath
under orders
under pressure
under repair

under the impression
under the weather

With/Without

with a view to (= intending to)
with difficulty
with luck (= hopefully)
with reference to

with regard to
with the compliments of
with the exception of
without delay

without fail
without success
without warning

Round

round the corner

To

to one's astonishment
to one's surprise

to sb's face
to this day

VERBAL CONSTRUCTIONS

Verb	Infinitive	-ing form	Noun	Clause
accuse		(sb) of stealing	of theft	
admit		lying	the lie	that he lied
advise	(you) to consider carefully	considering carefully	careful consideration	that you (should) consider carefully
aim	to travel	at travelling		
apologise		for being careless	for my carelessness	
appear	to know facts (personal construction)			that he knows the facts (impersonal construction)
ask	(me) to show him the way		(me) the way	if I could show him the way
avoid		causing accidents	accidents	
begin	to write the letter	writing the letter	the letter	
believe		in being tactful	in tact	that one could be tactful
boast		of/about succeeding	about/of his success	that he had succeeded
cease	to care	caring		
complain		(to sb) about failing	about his failure	that he had failed
concentrate		on solving the problem	on the solution	
consider	(him) to be trustworthy (believe)	explaining the situation	the explanation	that his explanation is acceptable
confess		to stealing		(that) he has stolen
continue	to work	working	the work	
dare	(him) to jump			
decide	to buy a red car	(on/against) buying a red car	on/against a red car	that he will buy a red car
demand	to be promoted		promotion	that he should be promoted
deny		breaking the vase	the accusation	that he broke the vase
describe	how to make the mask	(the process of) making the mask	the mask	
dislike		watching horror films	horror films	
dream		of travelling	of a journey	that he will travel
encourage	(me) to drink	drinking		
enjoy		visiting the museum	the visit	
excuse		his being rude	his rudeness	
exclaim			at the scenery	that the scenery was beautiful
expect	to get a gift		a gift	that he will get a gift
explain			the reason for his lateness	why he was late
fancy		having a drink	a drink	
feel	(sth) move (completed action)	(sth) moving	the movement	
find	it difficult to learn a language	learning a language difficult	languages difficult	that it was difficult to learn a language
forget	to buy (fail to remember)	buying (unable to recall)	the purchase	that I bought
hate	to travel by bus	travelling by bus	buses	
hear	(him) shout	shouting	a shout	
help	(to) repair	by repairing (method) / in repairing (type of help) / with the repairing	that man	

Verb	Infinitive	-ing form	Noun	Clause
hope	to succeed		for success	that I will succeed
imagine		seeing the accident	the accident	that I had seen the accident
insist		on paying		that I should pay
intend	to play	playing		that I should play
be interested	to learn about his success (one occasion)	in studying history (generally/always)	in history	
be kept	to do my homework	for being unprepared		
know	how to get there	about getting there	the way	that I will/can get there
laugh		at/about having misunderstood	at/about the misunderstanding	
let	(him) go			
like	to sing	singing	songs	
be likely	to phone (personal construction)			that he'll phone (impersonal construction)
love	to read novels	reading novels	novels	
make	(him) agree		an agreement	
mean	to start (intend - personal construction)	starting (involve - impersonal construction)		that I'll have to start
need	to be painted	painting	some paint	
(there will) be an opportunity	(for me) to travel abroad			
have an opportunity		of going to Italy		
order	(him) to bring the meal		a meal	that I should eat healthily
pay	(him) to fix the tap (paid before fixing)	(him) for fixing the tap (paid after fixing)	for the tap	
prefer	to listen to the radio	listening to the radio to watching television	radio programmes to TV programmes	that I listen to the radio
pretend	to understand			that I understand
promise	to investigate		an investigation	that I will investigate
propose	to undertake (intend)	undertaking (suggest)	a trip	that you should undertake
recommend	(sb) to visit	visiting	a visit	that you should visit
regret	to inform	having to inform	the decision	that we must inform
remember	to ask	asking (recall)	the place	that I asked
remind	him to post		(me) of our holiday (cause to remember)	him that he (should) post
say	to study		something	that he couldn't leave
seem	to enjoy (personal construction)			that he enjoys (impersonal construction)
show	how to knit		the knitting	that she understood how to knit
speak		(to me) of/about becoming a lawyer	(to me) of/about law	
start	to read the book	reading the book	the book	
stop	to clean the car (purpose)	cleaning the car (finish)	the car	
succeed		in passing the examination	in the examination	
suggest		finding a job	a solution (an idea)	that you (should find a job)
suspect	(him) to be the robber	(him) of robbing the bank	(him of) robbery	that he is the robber
talk		(to me) of/about seeing the paintings	(to me) of/about the paintings	

Verb	Infinitive	-ing form	Noun	Clause
tell	(her) to explain the whole story		the whole story	(her) that (she) should explain the whole story
think		of/about changing	of/about the change	that he will/might change
try	to use (attempt)	using (as an experiment)	the new machine	
understand	how to behave	(your) behaving badly	(your) behaviour	why (you) behaved badly
want	to have a car	the car wants cleaning	a car	
watch	him write (complete action)	him writing (incomplete action)	the film	how/what he's writing
wonder	how to fix	about his behaving like that	at your behaviour (surprised at)	how I could fix